A Dictionary of Hiberno-English

The Irish Use of English

Compiled and edited by

TERENCE PATRICK DOLAN

GILL & MACMILLAN

Gill & Macmillan Ltd
Hume Avenue, Park West
Dublin 12
with associated companies throughout the world
www.gillmacmillan.ie
First published in paperback 1999

0 7171 2942 X

Print origination by
Carrigboy Typesetting Services, Co. Cork
Printed by ColourBooks Ltd, Dublin

This book is typeset in Times 10 pt.

The paper used in this book comes from the wood pulp of managed forests. For every tree felled, at least one tree is planted, thereby renewing natural resources.

5 7 8 6 4

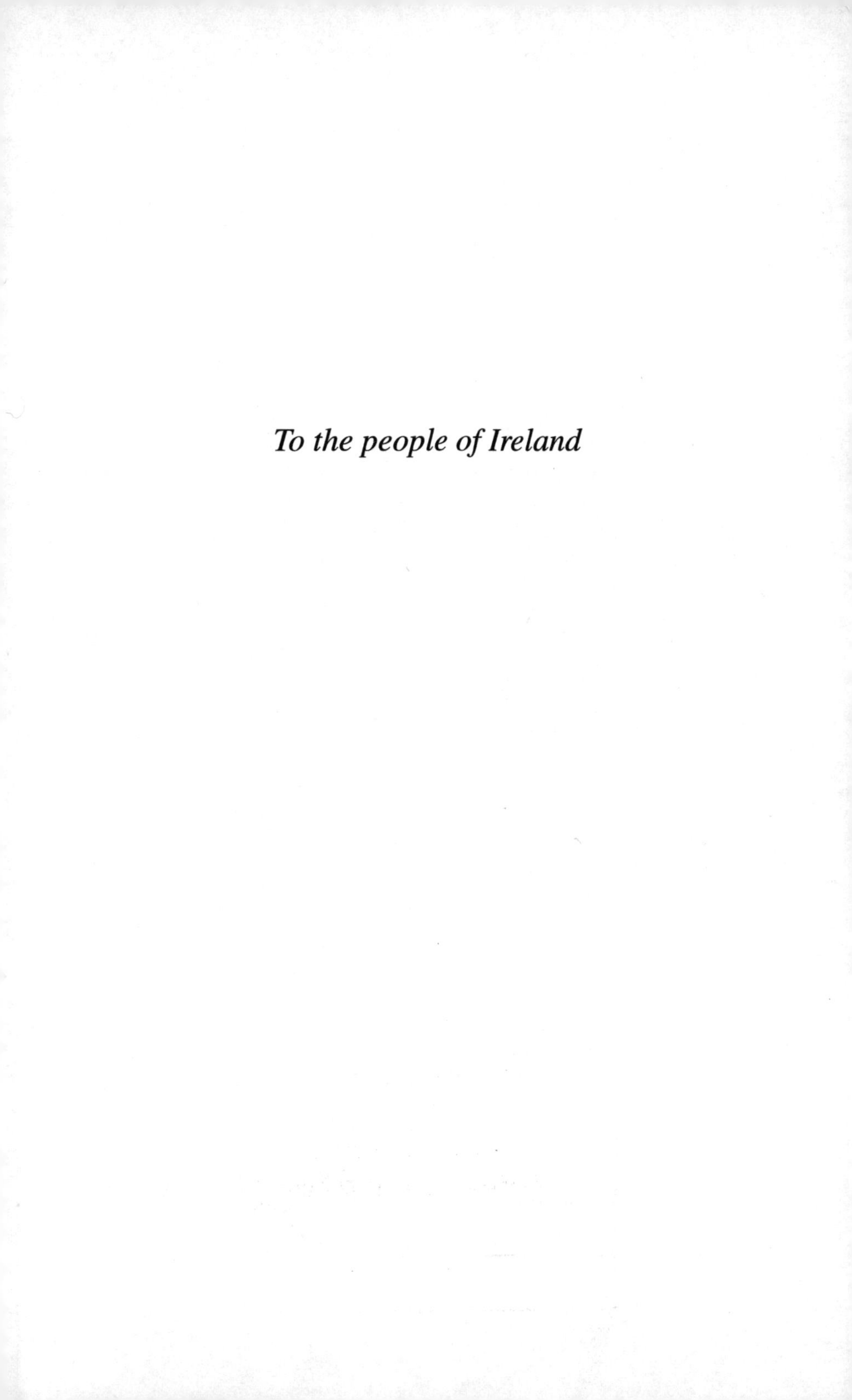

To the people of Ireland

Contents

Foreword

In the title poem to his fourth collection, *North*, which was published in 1975, Seamus Heaney summons the power of the Irish use of English. He imagines 'those fabulous raiders', the Vikings, and hears their 'ocean-deafened voices'. Then he says:

> The longship's swimming tongue
>
> was buoyant with hindsight –
> it said Thor's hammer swung
> to geography and trade,
> thick-witted couplings and revenges,
>
> the hatreds and behind-backs
> of the althing, lies and women,
> exhaustions nominated peace,
> memory incubating the spilled blood.

This is language as historical struggle, language heavy with violence, atavism, the memory of later invasions and pitched battles. By contrast with the movement and formation of language, dictionaries are irenic texts which represent peace and plenty, and a delighted unaggressive confidence in the words, phrases, usages and grammatical structures they catalogue.

Reading through Terry Dolan's magnificent dictionary, I recall the closing stanzas of 'North':

> It said, 'Lie down
> in the word-hoard, burrow
> the coil and gleam
> of your furrowed brain.
>
> Compose in darkness.
> Expect aurora borealis
> in the long foray
> but no cascade of light.

Foreword

Keep your eye clear
as the bleb of the icicle,
trust the feel of what nubbed treasure
your hands have known.'

I remember reading these lines when they were first published, twenty-three years ago, a time of enormous violence and bloodshed in the North of Ireland. I distinctly recall the effect of visual and linguistic precision in 'Keep your eye clear/as the bleb of the icicle', and I remember thinking that the word 'bleb' concentrated the many Ulster vernacular words in that plenary collection of poems. It was a word taken from the speech of the people. Later, as the political crisis in the North lengthened, I began to feel the need for a dictionary which would gather innumerable local words from all parts of Ireland together – a hospitable inclusive text which, without triumphalism, would be a national dictionary. This *Dictionary of Hiberno-English* answers that need, and here is its definition of that exact, intriguing word in 'North':

> **bleb** /blɛb/ *n., v.,* blister (JMF, Cavan); to bubble up, come out in blisters < E dial. (perhaps from the action of the lips in making a bubble or a blob). 'Quick! Run cold water on it before you get a bleb'; 'It's only a bleb – it's no harm.' Heaney, 'North' (*North,* 20): "Keep your eye clear | as the bleb of the icicle."

The movement from speech source to printed source is part of the richness of citation in this dictionary. Looking at the etymologies of many of the words it contains, we find a process of historical metamorphosis: that savoured word *scallion* began as the Old French *escalogne*, crossed the English Channel to enter English dialect, then crossed the Irish Sea to become part of Hiberno-English.

Reading through this exemplary work of scholarship, I begin to place words in the landscape. Thus a space between rocks, a cavity, a recess is a *cuas*, a pile of turf set out to dry is a *ricil*, and the hole left after the turf has been cut is a *seanpholl*. That accurate, almost philosophical, word *through-other* – 'a state of confusion, unplanned, formless, chaotic' – is a direct translation from the Irish *trína chéile*.

Foreword

To read through, as well as consult, this dictionary is to discover old friends like *scaldy* – 'an unfledged bird; an unfledged crow; the bare top of the head; a rabbit without hair'. A definite Viking word this, for it comes out of Old Norse to join the word-hoard. And how compact it is – there is no other single word I know for an unfledged bird. It's as compact as *mant* which means 'a toothless mouth; a space where teeth have fallen out'.

This dictionary is, as I say, irenic in spirit, but it also reminds us of the vitality of the language we write and speak. Beyond historical violence, beyond atrocity, beyond these bockety times, it witnesses to a creative, evolving identity we all share in.

This dictionary is both quarry and cairn, it is a living resource which connects us with the spoken language and the printed language. I admire its richness and plenitude and the long years of painstaking scholarly work that have gone into its compilation.

TOM PAULIN

Acknowledgments

The editor is indebted to Séamas Ó Catháin, Dáithí Ó hÓgáin, Rev. Ignatius Fennessy OFM, Susan Geary, Sarah McKibben, Kieran McGuire, Mary Catherine Reilly, Feargal Murphy, Gerard Fahy, Markku Filppula, Terence Odlin, Michael Montgomery, Dáithí Ó Liatháin and Micheál Holmes (of RTE) for contributions and technical assistance with the entries; to the late Tomás de Bhaldraithe for invaluable editorial advice and contributions; to the late Augustine Martin for advice and encouragement; to Vera Capková for allowing me to consult material on Hiberno-English assembled by her late husband, Petr Skrabanek; to the late Alan Bliss for advice on the teaching of Hiberno-English at UCD and to Anne Bliss for giving me material on Hiberno-English formerly in the possession of her husband; to the staff of the libraries in which the work was carried out (principally University College, Dublin, the National Library of Ireland, Trinity College, Dublin, the Bodleian Library, Oxford, the Franciscan Library, Killiney, County Dublin, the British Library, London, the University of Virginia, Charlottesville, and the Library of Congress, Washington); and to the following for many different kinds of constructive and material assistance: Sister Andrew, Morris Beja, Michael Benskin, Angela Blazy-O'Reilly, the late Harry Bourke, Dorothy Bowman, Kevin Brophy, Rose Byrne, Sandy Carlson, Andrew and Dorothy Carpenter, Leo Carruthers, Helen Clayton, Frank Columb, Patrick J. Connolly ATM, Anne Conway, Art and Emer Cosgrove, Sister Mary Cotter, Brigid Culhane, Fergus D'Arcy, Norah Davis, Rache de Almeida (ambassador of Brazil), Seamus Deane, Frank Delaney, Kevin Denny, R. W. Dent, Rev. Séamus de Vál, Judith Devlin, Morgan and Susan Dockrell, Brigid Dolan, Moira Dolan, Brian Donnelly, Thomas Dowling, Eithne Doyle, Sister Eileen, John Fanagan, A. and A. Farmar, Brian and Marie-Therèse Farrell, Breeda Fennessy, Robert FitzSimon, Thomas and the late Anna May Fleming, Jane Mary Flemming, Jack Foley, Brian Friel, Tom and Máire Garvin, Patrick Gernon, Gerard and Patricia Gillen, Manfred Görlach, Marlene Hackett, Brian and Rachel Hands, Maurice Harmon, Alan Harrison, Ted Hayes, Denis Healy, Seamus and Marie Heaney, Nancy Hopkins, Gerard and Mary Horkan, Anne Hunt, Hazel Jacob, Ellen Carol Jones, Mary Jordan, Sister Joseph, Maria Kelleher, Declan Kiberd, Benedict Kiely,

Val Kingston, Michael Laffan, William Lawlor, Joep Leerssen, John Leonard, Geert Lernout, Niall Loftus, Seán and Máirín Loftus, James McCabe, Susan McCarthy, Patrick MacDermott, the late Vincent McHugh, Stewart McKee, Rod MacManus, Gerard MacSweeny, the late Dermot Morgan, Barbara H. Moriarty, Maria Mulrooney, Christopher Murray, Margaret Murray, Munira Mutran, Mary O'Brien, Breandán Ó Buachalla, Éamon and Mary Ó Carragáin, Micheál Ó Conaill, Pat and Máire O'Connell, Joseph and Kitty O'Connor, Seán O'Connor, Ulick O'Connor, John and Sora O'Doherty, Éamonn O'Flaherty, Deirdre O'Grady, Emer O'Kelly, Colm O'Loughlin, John O'Mahony, Diarmaid Ó Muirithe, Micheál Ó Searcóid, Denis O'Sullivan, Denis B. O'Sullivan, Terence Odlin, Bridie Padian, David Pierce, Jacques Quilter, Vincent Quilter, Barry Raftery, Joan and Martin Redmond, Alan Roughley, the pupils and staff of St Columba's College, Rathfarnham, County Dublin, Fritz Senn, Ronan Sheehan, Chris Slack, Pauline Slattery, Linda Gavin Steiner, Gerard Stembridge, Ciara Steven, Betsey Taylor, David and Fiona Tipple, Michael Walsh, Peter Walsh, Alice Moore West; and to all those who have helped in various ways with the work on the dictionary, especially my students at UCD.

Any errors are the responsibility of the editor, who is also most grateful for grants from the Faculty of Arts Publications Committee of University College, Dublin, and the Arts Council.

Abbreviations and Symbols

adj.	adjective
adv.	adverb
adv.phr.	adverbial phrase
AN	Anglo-Norman
cf.	compare
colloq.	colloquial
conj.	conjunction
dial.	dialect
dimin.	diminutive
E	English
EDD	*English Dialect Dictionary* (Wright, ed.)
EModE	Early Modern English
excl.	exclamation
F	French
FDA	*Field Day Anthology of Irish Writing* (Deane, ed.)
fig.	figuratively
Gk	Greek
HE	Hiberno-English
imp.	imperative
int.	interjection
Ir	Irish
It	Italian
L	Latin
lit.	literally
LL	Late Latin
MDu	Middle Dutch
ME	Middle English
MF	Middle French
MIr	Middle Irish
ModE	Modern English
n.	noun
n.phr.	noun phrase
ODEE	*Oxford Dictionary of English Etymology* (Onions, ed.)
OE	Old English
OED	*Oxford English Dictionary* (Simpson and Weiner, eds.)
OF	Old French

OIr	Old Irish
ON	Old Norse
ONF	Old Norman French
pejor.	pejorative
phr.	phrase
pl.	plural
p.part.	past participle
prep.	preposition
pres.part.	present participle
SE	Standard English
s.v.	*sub verbo* [under the word entry]
v.	verb
v.n.	verbal noun
voc.	vocative
<	from
*	unattested form

Citations from literary sources are given in double quotation marks ("thus"); citations from non-literary sources (correspondents or oral contributors) are given in single quotation marks ('thus'). Cross-references to other entries in the dictionary are given in SMALL CAPITALS.

Pronunciation Scheme

The guide to pronunciation, given within oblique strokes /thus/, follows the system of the International Phonetic Association (IPA). This guide is intended to help those who are not familiar with Hiberno-English speech; those who are will be aware of the great differences in the pronunciation of words in different parts of the country. Regional accents are a salient feature of Hiberno-English speech, and the system adopted here cannot possibly represent such variations, nor is it intended to; but where it has been possible to identify the local pronunciation of a word, the stress and pronunciation of the relevant region are given.

Vowels

/æ/	back
/ɑː/	aren't
/eː/	able
/ɛ/	set
/iː/	evening
/oː/	corse
/ɔː/	grá
/ʌ/	lug
/uː/	lúb
/ɪ/	file
/ə/	above

Diphthongs

/ɔi/	loy
/ai/	fine
/au/	gabhlán
/iə/	fial
/uə/	cuas
/oi/	shaffoige

Consonants

/b/	black
/d/	dall
/d̪/	drisheen
/g/	garda
/h/	handsel
/l/	like
/m/	masher
/n/	náire
/p/	pairceen
/r/	relic
/s/	slag
/t/	terror
/t̪/	thivish
/v/	voteen
/ʍ/	whether
/w/	well
/z/	music
/ʃ/	Síle
/ʧ/	tinteán
/j/	yerra
/ŋ/	fallaing
/x/	tóchar
/ʒ/	breezheen
/ʤ/	jorum
/k/	cáil
/f/	figary
/ɣ/	gealgháiriteach
/θ/	thole

The primary stress in a word of two or more syllables is shown by the mark ' preceding the stressed syllable. No indication is given of secondary stress.

Introduction

I'd naw and aye
And decently relapse into the wrong
Grammar which kept us allied and at bay.
– Seamus Heaney, 'Clearances', 4, 12–14

Irish people use and speak English in a distinctive way. In vocabulary, construction, idiom and pronunciation their speech is identifiable and marked. Its characteristics reflect the political, cultural and linguistic history of the two nations, Ireland and England.

The Latin name for Ireland was Hibernia, and from that word is derived the prefix Hiberno- to describe things concerned with Ireland. Hiberno-English is the name given to the language of everyday use in Ireland, a mixture of Irish (which is enshrined in the Constitution as the 'the first official language') and English ('a second official language'). It is a macaronic dialect, a mixture of Irish and English, sometimes in the same word (e.g. 'girleen', 'maneen', etc.).

Hiberno-English has its own grammar, so obviously different in several ways from Standard English grammar that it may appear to be a 'wrong grammar', such as Seamus Heaney 'decently relapses into.'

The main intention of this dictionary is to make accessible the common word stock of Hiberno-English in both its present and past forms, oral and literary. The dictionary records words, phrases, proverbs, and sayings, as well as providing information about specific usages (e.g. 'yes' and 'no'), grammatical points of interest (e.g. 'after', 'and', 'that', 'whether'), distinctive sounds (e.g. 'th', epenthesis in 'wurrum' [worm], etc.), and Gaelicisms (e.g. '-een'). This is a wide spectrum, since it covers a fast-changing assembly of different types of speaker, with the older generation, especially those from rural areas, holding on to words and syntactical patterns that younger people, especially those from urban areas, have given up in favour of newly cast words or adaptations, which may or may not survive. To take a common example, the noun 'scanger', which refers to a rough, uncouth youth, has an obscure origin but may well be derived from the English verb 'scange', meaning to roam about, recorded in the *English Dialect Dictionary*. 'Scang' may itself be a corruption of the verb 'scavenge', to feed off or collect filthy matter; hence 'scanger' may be a corrupt, contracted form of 'scavenger'.

Introduction

Much of the vocabulary of Hiberno-English (cited as 'HE' in the dictionary) consists of words in common currency in Standard English, but an appreciable proportion of the word stock of Irish people is not standard and may be misunderstood, or not understood at all, by speakers of standard or near-standard English. It is with this Hiberno-English word stock that this dictionary concerns itself, and the categories include Irish loan-words, sometimes respelt (e.g. 'omadhawn', fool, from Irish *amadán*); words whose use has become restricted in England because they have fallen out of general use (e.g. 'to cog', to cheat in an examination); hybrid words derived from both Irish and English sources, most notably English words attached to the diminutive suffix -*een* (Irish -*ín*), as in 'priesteen', 'maneen', etc.; English words reflecting the semantic range of the Irish equivalent (e.g. 'bold', from Irish *dána*, intrepid or naughty); local words (e.g. 'glimmer-man'); colloquial vocabulary (e.g. 'scanger', 'moxie', 'naavo' – with the familiarising suffix -*o* common in Dublin speech – etc.); English words that have taken on meanings developed from an Irish context and remain restricted to that context (e.g. 'hames', in the phrase 'to make a hames of,' and 'yoke', something whose name one cannot recall, etc.). The Irish contribution to American speech is also recorded (e.g. 'slew', 'slug', etc.) or discussed (e.g. 'phoney', 'so long', etc.).

The material derives from a number of different sources, both spoken and written. The spoken sources include the replies made to letters I wrote to provincial newspapers asking readers to send me words and sayings that they use or used or heard used by their families, friends, and neighbours; contributions from listeners to the radio programme 'The Odd Word'; interviews conducted around the country; and suggestions made by my undergraduate and postgraduate students and colleagues at UCD. Literary citations are taken from relevant material dating from the Early Modern English period (approximately the sixteenth century) up to the present (Frank McCourt, Maeve Binchy, Seamus Deane, Tom Paulin, Heaney, Kavanagh, Joyce, Yeats, and others: see the list on p. 294–7). Non-literary sources provide information about relevant vocabulary (e.g. 'blaa' from Cowan and Sexton, *Ireland's Traditional Foods*, 1997).

The contributions have shown how very many Irish words in standard or disguised form are still in current use in Hiberno-English (e.g. 'magalore', merry from drink; 'a vick,' my son; 'ráiméis', silly talk). They show too that Irish people often use proverbial expressions in Irish (e.g. 'ar mhuin na muice,' well off, literally 'on the pig's back'). They also corroborate the well-known but puzzling fact that so few

Irish words have been absorbed into Standard English (such as 'galore', 'whiskey', 'slogan', 'bother', 'slew'). In this connection, analysis of the roots of words sometimes claimed to be of Irish derivation (e.g. 'kibosh', 'smashing', etc.) leads to the conclusion that their source in Irish is doubtful.

Each entry in the dictionary includes all or most of the following details: the headword; some indication of the pronunciation (according to the scheme of the International Phonetic Association); alternative forms of the headword, if there are any commonly used respellings; its part of speech or grammatical function; the meaning, or meanings, of the headword, with sources from contributors indicated (see the list on p. 297–300); the derivation, preceded by the symbol < (if the Irish form is the same as the headword it is marked '< Ir'; if from an English or other source it is marked '< OE' (Old English), etc.; a quotation or quotations illustrating the usage of the headword, from either an oral correspondent or a literary source or both (with non-literary citations in single quotation marks and literary citations in double quotation marks); a note of explanation, where useful; and a cross-reference to other relevant headwords.

Many words that are currently in use in Hiberno-English are not current in present-day Standard English and may never have been part of a countrywide word stock in British English, since they were dialectal or were words that had fallen into disuse through obsolescence. A good deal of the non-Irish vocabulary of Hiberno-English may be traced to usages and forms recorded in Joseph Wright's *English Dialect Dictionary* (six volumes, 1898–1905). In the present dictionary all the headwords that appear in Wright's dictionary are marked '< E dial.'

With regard to the roots of Irish entries, where a word or phrase has been Anglicised, the source-words or source-phrases from Irish are given in standard Irish form after the < symbol (e.g. 'maryah' < Ir *mar dhea*). Often the headword itself appears in its standard Irish form, in which case there is no need to repeat it, only to confirm its Irish derivation with '< Ir' (e.g. 'maidrín lathaí', skivvy or lap-dog, < Ir). Otherwise, for words that have become so commonplace that an Anglicised form approximating to the sounds of the Irish original has developed (e.g. 'crubeen' < Ir *crúibín*), the Anglicised form is given as the headword.

The spelling of English headwords normally follows the standard form found in other dictionaries, but for distinctively Hiberno-English versions of standard English words (e.g. 'eejit' < E 'idiot'), the headword is given in a respelt form that approximates to the way Irish people pronounce the word.

Hiberno-English is a conservative form of English, which sometimes preserves the older forms and the older pronunciations of words derived from Early Modern English, roughly from the late sixteenth and seventeenth centuries – the period in which the English settlements in Ireland became more established (see Carpenter, 1998) and in which Irish people began to emigrate to England in greater and greater numbers in search of work. This form of English, which is closely related to its immediate predecessor, Late Middle English, is the basis of modern Hiberno-English (see Bliss, 1976). Hence, the Middle English form of a headword may be provided where it illustrates the early shape of a word: for example, the preposition 'forbye', besides, which is still in fairly general use in Hiberno-English (with an entry in the *English Dialect Dictionary*), is also given its Middle English form in the entry (< E dial. < ME *forbi*).

In general, the number of words in use in Hiberno-English that are recorded in the *English Dialect Dictionary* is declining, even in that part of the country – the baronies of Forth and Bargy, County Wexford – that up until quite recently preserved words of close or approximate likeness to their Middle English ancestry (e.g. 'kiver', to cover: Middle English *kever*). As regards dialectal sub-divisions of Hiberno-English (see, for example, Traynor, 1953; Henry, 1957; Braidwood, 1969; Beecher, 1983; Macafee, 1996; Moylan, 1996), the increasing mobility of people for social and professional reasons is understandably tending to diminish or even destroy such varieties. Even so, there are still many words whose usage may be traced to a certain part of the country (e.g. 'ponger', a small vessel, and 'thole', to suffer, endure, both of which are commoner in northern parts; 'pigeon', a urinary vessel, from Cork), and this is noted where appropriate.

To give a general guide to how words are pronounced, especially for non-Irish readers, each headword is followed by an approximate rendering in phonetic symbols. Within some entries a note of explanation is added (e.g. for 'blackguard', 'crack', '-een', 'gurrier', 'hedge-school', 'smithereens', 'no', 'yes', etc.) with references for further study in relevant authorities. Various common cultural, political and religious usages that appear frequently in Irish speech and literature are also entered (e.g. 'first Friday', 'Legion of Mary', 'Society of St Vincent de Paul', 'TD', 'SC', 'Fianna Fáil', 'Fine Gael', etc.).

A BRIEF GRAMMAR OF HIBERNO-ENGLISH

Relevant entries in the dictionary will supply information about the grammar of Hiberno-English (see, for example, 'after'); but it will be useful at this stage to give a brief account of Hiberno-English grammar, because of the contentious issue of correctness that it sometimes raises and which is so well expressed by Seamus Heaney in the words quoted at the beginning of this introduction.

The prescriptive grammar-books from which Irish children are taught English grammar at school deal with Standard or British English. Obviously, the majority of the rules contained in these grammars are also suited to Hiberno-English, but in a number of significant ways Hiberno-English departs from British English, giving rise to what Heaney calls 'wrong grammar', which may, from another perspective, be seen as admissible – indeed, to an extent it may be claimed that 'wrong' English grammar is 'good' Irish grammar (but translated into English).

This claim rests on the fact that Irish grammar lies behind many so-called solecisms in Hiberno-English. There are quite a few examples, and I shall deal briefly with them here (see also Harris, 1993).

Several deviations from Standard English syntax are due to the absence of a verb 'have' in Irish. The most noted example is the construction with 'after' in place of the English 'have' in expressions such as 'I'm just after eating my dinner' (Irish: 'Tá mé tar éis mo dhinnéar a ithe'; Standard English: 'I've just eaten my dinner'), in which the 'after' represents the Irish conjunction 'tar éis' (but see O'Rahilly, *Irish Dialects, Past and Present*, 234).

Possession may be expressed in Irish by the verb 'be' (tá) and the preposition 'at' (ag); for example: 'Tá an leabhar agam,' literally 'Is the book at-me,' meaning 'I have the book.' When this construction is extended to form the statement 'I have read the book' ('Tá an leabhar léite agam'), where the participle 'léite' is separated from the verb 'tá', the separation is carried over into the Hiberno-English rendering as 'I have the book read,' rather than 'I have read the book,' as in British English (in which the sentence 'I have the book read' could be taken to imply that someone was reading the book to me).

The British English perfect and pluperfect tenses are often replaced with the past tense in Hiberno-English (see Filppula, 1996; Kallen, 1991), giving such patterns as 'Did any of you find my pen?' instead of 'Have any of you found my pen?' Substitution is also found for the English perfect and pluperfect in such non-standard usages as 'She's here this ten years' (present for perfect with 'have'), or similarly 'Where were you?' (in place of 'Where have you been?'), or 'The children are gone back to school' (in place of 'The children have gone back to school').

In Irish the verb normally stands first (verb–subject, e.g. 'Thit sé den bhalla,' he fell off the wall), whereas the basic word order of Standard

English is subject–verb ('He fell off the wall'). In Irish there are two verbs 'be': 'tá' (the substantive verb) and 'is' (the copula, a form of the verb 'be' employed to equate one part of a sentence with another). The latter is used at the head of sentences involving relative clauses, e.g. 'Is inniu atá an bhainis ann,' the wedding takes place today, literally 'Is today (on)-which-is the wedding in-it.'

The placing of the copula, 'is', at the beginning of such sentences preserves the verb–subject rule for the word order in Irish sentences; it also allows for flexibility in marking the speaker's intentions. This flexibility is evident in the way that Hiberno-English speakers adapt the copula construction: 'It is today (that) the wedding is taking place'; 'It is the wedding (that) is taking place today'; or even 'It is taking place (that) the wedding is today.' Usually in these 'cleft' sentences the relative pronoun 'that' is omitted, e.g. 'It is Kathleen (that) saw John last Christmas'; 'It was last Christmas (that) Kathleen last saw John'; 'It was John (that) Kathleen saw last Christmas.' Clauses in which the relative pronoun is omitted are known as 'contact clauses'. The omission of the relative pronoun has long been a feature of English syntax, from the Old English period (roughly the ninth to twelfth centuries onwards), in which relative pronouns were slowly developed (see Mustanoja, 1960, p. 187–208).

Irish has a habitual form of the present tense ('bíonn') as well as the substantive form ('tá'). The habitual form is concerned with the nature or 'aspect' of the action involved, whether it is instantaneous, continuing, or recurring. This gives rise in Hiberno-English to such idioms as 'I do be here every day' or (less commonly) 'I bes here every day' ('Bím anseo gach lá').

The strict rules that once governed the use of 'will' and 'shall' in Standard English have never been observed in Hiberno-English. Standard English grammar distinguished between the normal future and the emphatic future by a process of choice between 'will' and 'shall' (the normal future has 'I shall', 'you will', 'he/she/it will', 'we shall', 'you will', 'they will'; the emphatic future reverses the pattern with 'I will', 'you shall', 'he/she/it shall', 'we will', 'you shall', 'they shall'). In Hiberno-English, forms with 'will' are the norm for all pronouns and levels of emphasis, possibly because Irish has one form for the future (e.g. 'ceannóidh', I shall/will buy; 'inseoidh', I shall/will tell, etc.). The history of the confusing choice of future forms in Modern English goes back to Old English, which used the present tense to represent the future. Subsequently, in Late Old English and Early Middle English (approximately AD 1000–1250), a future tense was fabricated from the two verbs 'willan' (originally meaning 'desire, command' and later used as an auxiliary to form the future) and 'sceolan' (denoting obligation, 'shall, must, ought'). Hiberno-English speakers ignore the complications that have arisen from this background and settle for 'will': hence 'Will I wet the tea?,' 'Will we go to bed ?,' 'I'll get it for her now,' etc.

Indirect questions are normally introduced in Standard English by 'if' or 'whether'. Hiberno-English speakers avoid the use of these conjunctions, and indirect questions retain the reverse word-order of the original questions, e.g. 'I wonder what age is she,' 'Tell me is he gone out or not,' 'She asked him was he going with anyone,' 'I don't know is it that he's mad or stupid,' etc.

Irish grammar allows a greater range of uses for the conjunction 'agus' (and) than the 'and' of English. This permits non-standard usages in the formations of subordinate adverbial clauses, e.g. 'They interrupted her and she saying her prayers,' in which the 'and' could be equivalent to 'when,' 'while,' or 'although': 'when she was saying her prayers,' 'while she was saying her prayers,' 'although she was saying her prayers' (see Filppula, 1991)

Hiberno-English grammar departs from Standard English grammar in its extension of the imperative with 'let' from the first and third-person pronouns (e.g. 'Let you sit down!,' 'Let her go!,' 'Let them go!') to the second-person pronoun (e.g. 'Let you sit down'). In some parts of the country 'leave' is substituted for 'let' ('Leave you get to bed').

Expressions such as 'don't be talking' are based on Irish progressive imperatives ('ná bí ag caint' in this instance) and are non-standard within the prescriptions of Standard English grammar. The use of 'be' as an auxiliary with a progressive verbal form (e.g. 'Be starting your tea') is also non-standard.

There is no indefinite article (equivalent to Standard English 'a' or 'an') in Irish, and this absence leads to distinctive uses of the definite article in Hiberno-English, e.g. 'She came home for the Christmas'; 'His wife has the lad [cancer]'; 'He had the great colour after playing the match'; 'The mammy [my mother] is coming home today.'

The employment of singular forms of the verb with plural subjects in Hiberno-English (e.g. 'There was fifteen people there' – Irish 'Bhí cúig dhuine dhéag ann') looks like bad English grammar, but the explanation may lie in the fact that in Irish the verb, as in the example cited here with 'tá', does not change its form from singular to plural; English, of course, has to use either 'is' or 'are', as appropriate. This holds true for the whole verbal system in Irish (cf. 'cuireann sé', he puts; 'cuireann siad', they put). Speakers of Hiberno-English often retain the singular form for plural subjects, as if they were using Irish, e.g. 'The jobs around the house was too much for her'; 'The stairs is too steep for the patients.'

The distinctive marking of singular and plural forms of the second-person pronoun in Hiberno-English ('you', singular; 'yous', plural) may also be due to Irish, in which 'tá' ('you', singular) is distinguished from 'sibh' ('you', plural). Early speakers of Hiberno-English adopted analogical plural forms for the plural of 'you', based on the normal addition of *-s* employed in forming the plural of most nouns in English. Thus arose such non-standard forms as 'yous' and 'yiz', in addition to the retention of the old plural form 'ye', which in Hiberno-English does duty for both singular and plural.

It is common to find double plurals, with the sound /əz/ added to plurals in *-s*: thus 'bellows' becomes 'bellowses', 'gallows' becomes 'galluses' (to mean 'braces').

The reflexive pronoun is commonly used as an emphatic form of the nominative, e.g. 'It's myself that wrote that letter'; 'Is it yourself that's in it?' (Is it really you here?). It is also used to mean the head of the household, 'himself' or 'herself'.

The relative pronoun 'that' is often omitted, e.g. 'I know a builder will do the job for you.'

It is common for inanimate objects to be personified, usually with the feminine pronoun, e.g. 'She's a great knife, so she is.'

The pronoun 'them' is commonly used in place of 'those', e.g. 'You know all them things.'

The demonstrative 'this' is often expressed by 'that', e.g. 'That's a fine morning.'

There is a tendency to introduce a redundant personal pronoun after a common or proper noun to mark emphasis, e.g. 'Mr McGuire, he read his poems to me.'

In summary, Hiberno-English has a grammar of its own, which comprises a mixture of Standard English grammar, non-literary usage, and patterns derived from Irish grammar (see Harris, 1993).

A BRIEF HISTORY OF THE ENGLISH LANGUAGE IN IRELAND

English has been used in Ireland since the twelfth century, though not always as widely as now; nor is the picture one of uniform development (see Hogan, 1927; Bliss, 1979).

The Irish had first become exposed to English as a result of the invasion conducted by King Henry II, who had been authorised by the only English Pope, Nicholas Breakspear (who had taken the name Hadrian IV), reigning from 1154 to 1159, to unite Ireland with England, on supposedly spiritual grounds. The commanders of the invading forces spoke Norman-French, and their followers spoke English (in the form now termed Early Middle English). By the end of the twelfth century there were four languages current in Ireland: Latin, used by the senior clerics; Norman-French and English, used by the invaders, according to their class; and Irish, used by the indigenous population (see Curtis, 1919; Cahill, 1938; Bliss, 1979; Ó Murchú, 1985).

Norman-French declined within a century or so, but not before it had given words such as 'buidéal' < Norman-French *botel*, bottle, 'dinnéar' < *diner*, dinner, and 'tuáille' < *toaille*, towel, to the Irish lexicon. But English survived and took on some of the characteristics and vocabulary of Irish, as we know from such early Hiberno-English masterpieces as *The Land of Cokaygne* (dated to the early fourteenth century; see Heuser, 1965 (reprint); Henry, 1972), which – in an early foretaste of the way later users of Hiberno-English insert Irish words into English phrases and sentences – employs an Irish word, 'rossin', (< Ir *raisín*, luncheon, line 20) within an English sentence, with no sense of forcing ('The met is trie, the drink is clere, | To none, russin, and sopper' ('The food is excellent, the drink is clear | at the midday meal, luncheon, and supper').

In the fifteenth century a version of a Middle English poem, William Langland's 'Vision of Piers Plowman', was copied in Ireland, and this too displays Hiberno-English features: the verb 'sell' is spelt 'syll', thereby providing an early example of the phonemic assimilation of /ɛ/ and /ɪ/ in Hiberno-English (cf. modern Hiberno-English /tɪn/ for 'ten'); and 'followed' appears as 'folowt', thereby indicating the difference between Irish /d/ and /t/ and English /d/ and /t/ (see Heuser (reprint), 1965).

In spite of the evidence for the use of English in Ireland at the time that such writings provide, such was the power of the Irish language that by the fourteenth century even the invaders were beginning to use it. This Irish resurgence led the authorities in England to send over Lionel, Duke of Clarence, son of King Edward III, to preside over an assembly in Kilkenny, from which issued the 'Statute of Kilkenny' (written in Norman-French). This legislation was devised to deter the ruling elite from adopting Irish customs and, most importantly, from adopting Irish ('it is ordained and established that every Englishman use the English language'). It proved futile.

Irish gained strength in the fifteenth century, and English had in the main become restricted to a few towns, parts of Dublin, the area of

Fingal (north County Dublin), and the baronies of Forth and Bargy in County Wexford (see Archer; Dolan and Ó Muirithe, 1996), but in the following century the adoption of the policy of plantations reversed this trend. These began with Counties Laois and Offaly in 1549, to be followed by Munster in 1586–1592, and then Ulster in 1609 (see Foster, 1988, 59–78)

The main effect of the plantations, as far as language was concerned, was that for the first time native speakers of English were settled in what had been exclusively Irish-speaking localities. Irish people working on the estates had to learn English as best they could – not because they were enjoined to do so because of legislation but for reasons of expediency and practicality. There was another factor at work as well – that of prestige: English became associated with the image of the Big House. This factor encouraged ambitious or job-seeking Irish-speakers to learn the rudiments of the language, which might lead to preferment or employment. Their acquisition of English was a difficult process, and the form of English they developed seems to have been a striking mixture of Irish and English, in pronunciation, vocabulary, idiom, and syntax. The origins of Hiberno-English may be traced to this period (see Bliss, 1976).

From the time of the plantations, English achieved greater and greater currency in Ireland as its acceptability became more established. The foundation of Trinity College, Dublin, in 1592 and of St Patrick's College, Maynooth, in 1795 may be taken as two significant developments in this acceptability. A number of early TCD scholars have an illustrious reputation as promoters of Irish, for instance William Bedell (1571–1642), Provost of TCD (1627), who instigated the rule whereby students of Irish birth who came to study divinity had to study Irish as well, so that Irish-speaking clerics could be appointed for parish work; it was Bedell also who had the Old Testament translated into Irish. Even so, TCD had the reputation of being an exclusive repository of Englishness and English, which itself came to be regarded as the transmitter of the Protestant faith. The foundation of St Patrick's College, Maynooth, two centuries later as a seminary for Catholic priests confirmed the acceptability of English as the means of proselytising and preaching, since graduates of Maynooth spoke to their congregations in English, where appropriate.

Other events also conspired to assist the progress of English. The Penal Laws (1695–1727) encouraged the native Irish-speaking population to regard their own language and culture as symbols of failure. The Act for the Legislative Union of Ireland with Great Britain (1800) meant that would-be politicians had to learn English to speak on Irish matters at Westminster. Daniel O'Connell (1775–1847) used English as his medium of communication with the people. The year 1831 saw the introduction of a system of primary education with English as the medium of instruction, and children were given the 'bata scóir', a stick on which notches were made to indicate their use of Irish words, which was forbidden.

Worst of all, from all points of view, was the catastrophe of the Great Famine, which had a calamitous effect on the currency of Irish, since so many monoglot speakers of Irish perished. Then came the waves of emigration, which encouraged the acquisition of English as the language of advancement for use in Britain or the United States.

Since the nineteenth century English has maintained its currency in Ireland up to the present time, but it has not done so without having to succumb to many influences that are associated with the linguistic conditions of the country. In a linguistic sense it is contaminated through and through with Irish (but see Lass, 1986), and it poses many questions for its speakers about the meaning, usage, origin and context of its employment. This dictionary is aimed at answering those questions, as well as supplying information for scholars of Anglo-Irish literature who may find difficulty with words that are either not mentioned at all in other dictionaries of English or are not given their specific Hiberno-English context. It is also intended to be useful for writers who wish to capture a certain nuance of meaning that only a Hiberno-English word or saying can appropriately furnish.

This dictionary records the linguistic wealth of Hiberno-English speakers, to whom it is dedicated and from whom it is hoped will come suggestions and emendations for future research.

A Dictionary
of
Hiberno-English

A

a /ə/ *indefinite article.* The absence of an indefinite article in Irish sometimes led to confusion with the initial sound in such English words as 'enough', giving rise to formations such as 'a NOUGH'; 'I've had my 'nough now' (PR, Mayo) (cf. Ir *Tá mo dhóthain agam anois*). Healy, *Nineteen Acres*, 70: "She cried her 'nough."

a /ə/ *voc. particle* (used when speaking to somebody) < Ir. 'A mhaoineach,' my dear one; 'a Dhia,' O God; 'a chairde,' friends; 'a ghrá,' also 'agradh,' my love; 'a stór,' darling (SOM, Kerry); 'avourneen,' a term of endearment < Ir *a mhuirnín*. 'Finnegan's Wake' (song): "Arrah, Tim, avourneen, why did you die?" Joyce, *Finnegans Wake*, 468.34: "I'm dreaming of ye, azores [a stór]"; Healy, *Nineteen Acres*, 9: "Run down to the well, agradh, for a can of water." Dinneen, s.v. 'a', *interj., aspir.,* notes: 'Eng. O, though not an equivalent, represents it.'

ABCs /eːbiːsiːz/ *n.* (*colloq.*), irregular red lines on children's and women's shins caused by sitting too close to open fires (JOM, Kerry). *See* BRACKEN.

abhaile /ə'wɑljə/ *adv.,* home, homewards < Ir. 'SLÁN abhaile,' safe home. 'Tá sé níos éasca dul go dtí an baile mór ná theacht abhaile' (proverb), It's easier to go to town than to come home.

abhainnín /au'niːn/ *n.,* small river, tributary (SOM, Kerry, who adds: 'One such was the source of a natural disaster, *c.* 1903, when the Moving Bog followed its course and caused about ten deaths, the Abhainnín Chria') < Ir.

ábhairín /ɔː'vriːn/ *n.,* a small quantity, especially of liquid (SOM, Kerry) < Ir *ábhar*, amount + dimin. suffix -ÍN. 'Can I have an ábhairín of tay?'; 'Put an ábhairín of whiskey in the glass for me.'

ábhar /'ɔːvər/ *n.* 1. Appreciable quantity, fair amount (SOM, Kerry) < Ir. 'He brought a great ábhar of money home from America.' 2. Swelling, cyst (SOM, Kerry).

able /'eːbəl/ *adj.,* adequate, fit to cope with. 'He wasn't able for the job'; 'I'm not able for the stairs any more' (BC, Meath).

aboo /ə'buː/ *int.*, for ever! to victory! < Ir *abú*. Banim, *The Boyne Water*, 117: "'*Rhia Shamus Abo*!' cried the man, rising his cup . . . 'King Shamus!' repeated another, translating his friend's Irish"; Joyce, *Finnegans Wake*, 425.6–8: "Ingenious Shaun, we still so fancied, if only you would take your time so and the trouble of so doing it. Upu now!"

above /ə'bʌv/ *adv.*, loosely meaning the same as 'up' < OE *abufan*. 'We were above in Dublin at the hospital' (TF, Cavan).

abroad /ə'brɔːd/ *adv.*, outside (DOH, Limerick) < ME *on brede*. 'I left it abroad in the yard or HAGGART' (ND, Limerick).

acaointeach /ə'kiːntʃəx/ *adj.*, querulous, complaining, quarrelsome < Ir. 'He was always acaointeach FROM [from the time that, since] he was a child, God rest him!' (JF, Cavan).

ach /ɑx/ also **och** *interj.*, with a hint of sadness (SOM, Kerry) or disgust < Ir. 'Ach, don't vex me. Haven't I enough troubles as it is?' (BC, Meath).

a chara /ə'xɑrə/ *voc.*, term of endearment: my friend < Ir. 'Mhuise, a chara, come out for a walk with me and don't be moping around the house all day.' Kickham, *Knocknagow*, 57: "Billy, a chora . . . stop that!"; Joyce, *Ulysses*, 311.1–3: "And Joe asked him would he have another. 'I will,' says he, '*a chara*, to show there's no ill feeling.'" Used as the salutation in formal letters in Irish and frequently also in English; Plunkett, *Farewell Companions*, 439: "*A Chara* | I am directed by the committee to refer to your recent letter . . . " *See* MEAS.

achasán /ɑxə'sɔːn/ *n.*, insult < Ir. 'The next achasán I hear from you'll be the last' (KG, Kerry).

a chora, *see* a CHARA.

achree /ə'xriː/ *n.phr.*, term of endearment: beloved one, my dear (SOM, Kerry) < Ir *a chroí*. 'MUSHA, achree, you can tell me your troubles – you know I'll do whatever I can to help you' (KG, Kerry). Griffin, *The Collegians*, 274: "Is it going you are, achree?"

acoolsha, *see* ACUSHLA.

acushla (**machree**) /ə'kʌʃlə (mæ'xriː)/ *voc.*, term of endearment: my heart's dear one < Ir *a chuisle mo chroí* (lit. pulse of my heart). Stoker, *The Snake's Pass*, 201: "'Be the powdhers [powers], there's the masther! Git up, acushla!' – this to the younger woman"; Joyce, *Finnegans Wake*, 626.35–6: "But you're changing, acoolsha, you're changing from me."

ádh /ɔː/ *n.*, luck, good fortune (SOM, Kerry, who adds: 'in phrases like "ádh an Diabhail" (luck of the Devil), "mí-ádh", misfortune, "ámharach", lucky') < Ir. 'The ádh an Diabhail, that's what it is!' (KG, Kerry).

adhart, *see* PILIÚR.

adhastar /ˈaist̪ər/ *n.*, a halter (SOM, Kerry) < Ir. 'Give me the adhastar for the mare'; 'Put the adhastar on her: she's a biteen wild' (Kerry) (*see* -EEN).

adhmharaige /ædˈvɑːrəgə/ *n.*, luck, good fortune (KM, Kerry) < Ir *ámharaí*. 'Thanks be to God he had the adhmharaige to marry her.'

adú, *see* COIGILT.

aerach /ˈeːrəx/ *adj.*, light-hearted, carefree (SOM, Kerry, who adds: 'airy, in anglicised form') < Ir. 'What has you so aerach today?'; 'I feel very aerach with this wonderful weather.'

aeraíocht /eːˈriːəxt̪/ *n.*, garden-party with music and dancing; open-air entertainment (such as a FEIS), this latter usage probably imported under Conradh na Gaeilge (SOM, Kerry); < Ir.

afeard /əˈfiːrd/ also **afeerd**, **afreard** (PON, Dublin) *adj.*, afraid < E dial. < OE *afæred*. 'Afeard of my life,' very much afraid (LUB, Dublin). Griffin, *The Collegians*, 53: "'Don't be one bit afeerd o' me,' says the ould gentleman"; Stoker, *The Snake's Pass*, 63: "I'm afeerd yer 'an'r [your honour] has had but a poor day"; Synge, *The Playboy of the Western World*, III (*FDA*, 2, 641): "*Shawn*: I'd be afeard to be jealous of a man did slay his da."

after /ˈæːftər/, /ˈæːft̪ər/ *prep.*, used to form the HE equivalent of the SE perfect (have . . .) and pluperfect (had . . .) past tenses (see Harris, 1983, 160–1). There is no verb 'have' in Irish, and the past tenses are formed with parts of the verb 'be' with the preposition 'after' (*tar éis*). HE 'I'm after having my dinner' (Ir *Tá mé tar éis mo dhinnéar a ithe*) is the equivalent of SE 'I've just had my dinner.' It is possible to say 'I'm after having my dinner' in SE, but that could mean 'I am in pursuit of having my dinner' – the opposite of the meaning in HE. Birmingham, *The Lighter Side of Irish Life*, 170: "An Englishman who had settled in Ireland once related to me a conversation which he had with an Irish servant. 'Mary,' he said, 'will you please light the fire in my study?' 'I'm just after lighting it,' she replied. 'Then do it at once,' he said. 'Don't I tell you, sir,' she said, 'that I'm just after doing it?'" Somerville and Ross, *Some Experiences of an Irish RM*, 165: "'Twas the kitchen chimney cot fire, and faith she's afther giving Biddy Mahony the sack, on the head of it!" Joyce, *Ulysses*, 299.6: "Sure I'm after seeing him not five minutes ago"; Brown, *Down All the Days*, 45: "'Mr Brown!' the boy yelled hoarsely, 'come quick – they're after knocking down your Paddy and him with the lad on his back!'"; Doyle, *The Van*, 60: "Is she after doin' somethin' to herself?" 'After' is also found in HE in situations where SE would have 'afterwards': Stoker, *The Snake's Pass*, 25: "Go on, man dear! an' fenesh the punch after." Cf. O'Rahilly, 234: 'Although locutions of the type "he is after coming" . . . "she is after breaking the window", are so well known in Hiberno-English, the corresponding type of expression in Irish does not seem to be attested until a comparatively late period (15th cent?). To express "after" in such constructions the word originally used was *iar*, which was afterwards confused with *ar,* e.g. *tá sé (i)ar dteacht*. Later *(i)ar* in such predicates was superseded in Irish by prepositional phrases which more clearly expressed the idea of "after".'

again /ə'gɛn/ 1. *adv.,* another time (cf. Ir *arís*, again, afterwards, at some future time) < ME *agen*. 'I'll give it you again'; 'There'll be an again in it [I'll treat you next time, I'll see you again soon]' (JOD, Tipperary). 2. Also **agin** /ə'gɪn/ *adv., prep.,* against. 'They're turning again you'; 'I never seen that cow turn again anyone before' (SL, Mayo).

age /eːʤ/ *n.,* commonly used in the question 'What age are you?' (cf. Ir *Cén aois tú?*) etc., instead of the SE form 'How old are you?' Carleton, 'Denis O'Shaughnessy Going to Maynooth' (*Six Irish Tales*, 132): "'Pray what age is he?' 'Risin' four Sir'"; Kickham, *Knocknagow*, 15: "'About what age is he?' Mr. Lowe asked"; Beckett, *Waiting for Godot,* 27–8: "*Pozzo (to Vladimir):* What age are you, if it's not a rude question."

aghaidh-fidil /ai'fɪdəl/ also **i-fiddle**, **eye fiddle, high fiddle, haighfidil** *n.,* a mask made from coloured paper (SOM, Kerry), worn by boys 'out on the wren' or 'the wran' (Ir *lucht an dreoilín,* wren-boys), usually given a pronunciation approximating to 'high fiddle' < Ir *aghaidh fidil*, mask. 'Get the high fiddle on till we go out and see can we make a few bob' (Mayo); 'Your're a right i'fiddle (i.e. clown) with that on you' (RB, Waterford).

agrá /ə'grɔː/ also **agradh**, **agraw**, **a ghrá** *voc.,* 'term of endearment used by an older person to somebody of either sex' (SOM, Kerry, who adds: 'a lao [calf], term of endearment, = a ghrá') < Ir *a ghrá*. 'Come here, agra, and sit by me'; 'MUSHA agra, there's no use in complaining.' Head, *Hic et Ubique*, 113: "Fuy by St. *Patrick* agra"; Healy, *Nineteen Acres*, 9: "Run down to the well, agradh, for a can of water." *See* GRÁ; GRÁ MO CHROÍ.

agradh, *see* AGRÁ.

agrawgill /ə'grɔːgɪl/ *n.phr.,* term of endearment: my darling < Ir *a ghrá geal,* also a *ghrá ghil.* 'Agrawgill, we all have troubles – it's part of life.'

agraw machree /ə'grɔːmə'xriː/ *n.phr.,* term of endearment: O love of my heart < Ir *a ghrá mo chroí.* 'Agraw machree, you have a lovely voice' (KG, Kerry).

aguisín /ɑgə'ʃiːn/ *n.,* a little extra (JOM, Kerry), a small addition < Ir < *agus* + dimin. suffix -ÍN. 'Aguisín le huacht,' codicil to a will; 'It was the aguisín le huacht caused all the trouble.' (Note the omission of the relative pronoun THAT before the verb 'caused', a common feature of HE syntax.)

ahaygar /ə'heːgər/ *n.phr.,* term of endearment: my love < Ir *a théagair.* 'Don't be giving me that ahaygar baloney – it won't work with me' (BC, Meath).

ahint /ə'hɪnt/ *adv., prep.,* behind, at the back of < E dial. 'He lived ahint in the bog'; 'He's up in the field ahint the house sorting the spuds' (Mayo).

ahorra machree /ə'xɑrəmə'xriː/ *n.phr.,* term of endearment < Ir *a chara mo chroí.* 'Ahorra machree, tell me what part of the country do you come from?' (TJ, Sligo).

aibhleog(a) /ai'loːg(ə)/ *n.,* 'embers, coals of fire (i.e. of turf) placed on lid of oven when baking or cooking; some coals when separated from kindled ashes to form nucleus of new fire in morning' (SOM, Kerry).

aidhe /aiː/ *int.* to denote frustration, weariness: alas! my, my! (SOM, Kerry).

áiféiseach /ɔː'feːʃəx/ *adj.,* nonsensical, exaggerated to a ridiculous extent (SOM, Kerry) < Ir. 'That story is áiféiseach from start to finish – I don't believe a word of it, as you well know!'

ail /eːl/ *v.,* to be amiss with, to be afflicted < E dial. (archaic in SE) < OE *eglan,* to trouble. 'Teil v., to ail, to be amiss, "Fade teil?" What ails?' (JP, Forth and Bargy); 'What ails you? You look "black sick" today' (MC, Kildare, ex Limerick). Sheehan, *Glenanaar,* 291: "What ails you, child?"; Leonard, *Out After Dark,* 52: "'Trust him,' my mad aunt Mary said . . . 'Trust me to what?' my father said. 'What ails you?'"

aililiú /'ælɪluː/ *int.* indicating bewilderment or delight (SOM, Kerry): good heavens! amazing! < Ir. 'Aililiú, did he, BEDAD? – well, we'll all have a drink on him tonight' (BC, Meath).

áilleán /'ɔːlɔːn/ also **awlawn** *n.,* a darling, a pet; a useless person < Ir. 'She was always her mother's áilleán and now she says she doesn't want to go to England to look for work' (Galway).

ailp /ælp/ *n.,* a lump, a large piece < Ir. 'Give us an ailp of steak, will you'; 'Alping away [eating greedily] he was, when I got there' (TJ, Sligo).

ailpeen /æl'piːn/ also **alpeen** *n.,* a thick alpenstock, ashplant < Ir *ailpín.* 'Well, he gave the dog such a thrashing with the ailpeen I thought he'd kill him stone dead' (SOC, Kerry).

ailt /ælt̪/ also **alt** *n.,* a steep-sided glen, ravine; deep watercourse on mountainside; little glen < Ir. 'There's a sheep caught in one of the bushes up on the ailt – I'll have to climb up and see can I get him loose' (SL, Mayo).

aimsir /'æmʃər/ *n.,* weather; time; season < Ir. 'Is maith an scéalaí an aimsir' (proverb), Time will tell.

aingeal coimhdeachta /'æŋgəl kʌ'ʤæxtə/ *n.,* guardian angel (SOM, Kerry) < Ir.

áinleog /ɔːn'loːg/ *n.,* swallow (bird) (SOM, Kerry) < Ir. 'Watch out for the áinleogs! – it's a good sign' (KG, Kerry).

ainmhian /ænə'viən/ *n.,* lust, passion, avarice, craving, inordinate desire (SOM, Kerry) < Ir. 'He would drink the rain down, the poor man, but he can't help it; sure he has the ainmhian' (SOM, Kerry, who adds: 'a widely used word in the above contexts; also CRAOS').

ainnis /'ænəʃ/ *adj.,* miserable; untidy; disorganised; awkward; poor, ungainly (SOM, Kerry, who adds: 'no hint of corpulence, as elsewhere').

ainniseoir /ænə'ʃoːr/ *n.,* down and out, unkempt person < Ir. 'MUSHA, that poor ainniseoir isn't doing so well these days' (KG, Kerry).

airde /'ɔːrʤə/ *n.,* used in the *adv. phr.* 'in airde', high up, on top of (SOM, Kerry) < Ir. 'That girl is a bit too in airde for my liking' (KG, Kerry). 'Ainm [name] in airde' /'ænəmɪn'ɔrʤə/, reputation, being well known. 'Éirí [rising] in airde' /'airiːɪn'ɔːrʤə/, elation, exhilaration, excessive self-confidence.

aireacaí /'ærəkiː/ *n.pl.,* irritation on the backs of legs (usually after working in a bog or around cow manure); chilblains < Ir. 'They always used to have the aireacaí on the backs of their legs coming to school, and cuts on their feet too, as they carried their shoes and went barefoot' (BC, Meath).

airgead luachra /'ærəgəd̪ 'luːxrə/ *n.,* meadowsweet, the antiseptic leaves of which were used to dress wounds < Ir. 'The well field is full of airgead luachra' (TJ, Cavan).

airgead síos /'ærəgəd̪ʃiəs/ *n.phr.,* money down; ready cash < Ir. 'Airgead síos or no deal! – that's what the man said!' (BC, Meath).

airneán /ær'nɔːn/ also **arnaun** *n.,* **airneáning** *v.n.* < Ir *airneán* + E suffix *-ing,* work done late into the night; 'hint of poor organisation during daylight hours' (SOM, Kerry); visiting at night; card-playing; storytelling late at night ('no nuance of immorality') (SOM, Kerry).

'We had a great night airneánin' in Begleys' last night.' *See* BOTHÁNTAÍOCHT; CÉILÍ; COORJEEKING; RAMBLING.

airt /ært/ also **art** *n.,* point of the compass, direction. 'They came from all arts and parts [from all directions]' < Ir *aird.* Montague, 'Even English' (*Collected Poems*, 38): "Yet even English in these airts I Took a lawless turn."

airy /ˈeːri/ *adj.,* light-hearted; uncertain < E dial. < ME *eir* (cf. Ir *aerach*). 'I'm very airy about it'; 'He was very airy when I asked him about it' (KG, Kerry).

áisiúil /ˈɔːʃuːl/ *adj.,* convenient, handy < Ir. 'That's very áisiúil' (MG, Cavan).

aisling /ˈæʃləŋ/ *n.,* a vision poem < Ir. 'Sing us the SHAN VAN VOK – it's a kind of aisling' (Dublin).

aiteann /ˈæʧən/ *n.,* gorse, furze, whin < Ir. 'Aiteann caobach' /æʧənˈkeːbəx/, lumpy furze (MK, Galway). 'Aiteann Gaelach' /ˈæʧənˈgeːləx/, gorse; kind of grass that grows in tufts. 'Cut a BEART of aiteann Gaelach and put a bed under the cows' (KM, Kerry).

aithris /ˈæhrəʃ/ *n.*, narration, telling of a story < Ir. 'Well, such an aithris he put on the story – I'd have hardly recognised it at all' (KG, Kerry).

ál /ɔːl/ *n.,* a clutch of chickens, ducklings; a litter of BONHAMS; a family of children (SOM, Kerry); a brood < Ir. 'They had an ál of girls in that family' (BC, Meath); 'That was a big ál they had – bonhams and all' (ENM, Kerry). 'Deireanach [last] ar áil', youngest member of the family. 'That poor little deireanach ar áil was always a bit weak.' *See* DRÍODAR AN CHRÚISCÍN.

alanna /əˈlænə/ *voc.,* my child < Ir *a leanbh.* 'Come inside, alanna, before you get drownded' (BC, Meath). O'Casey, *Juno and the Paycock*, II, 35: "*Mrs Boyle*: An' what is it you're thinkin' of, allanna?" Joyce, *Finnegans Wake*, 377.19–20: "and the brideen Alannah is lost" (the song 'Eileen Alannah'). 'A leanbh mo chroí,' child of my heart. Kickham, *Knocknagow*, 55: "How is Norah? How is ma lanna machree?"

allaíre /ˈɑliːrə/ *n.,* being hard of hearing; partial deafness (sometimes used for simulated deafness) (SOM, Kerry) < Ir.

alp /ɑlp/ *v.,* to gulp, devour, eat greedily. 'Alping,' gulping, devouring, eating greedily (SOM, Kerry) < Ir. 'Stop alping your food, you'll get indigestion' (*see* AILP). 'Alp luachra' (lit. lizard of the rushes), 'wolfworm, in folklore, a creature which, if accidentally swallowed when drinking from a river, causes the sufferer intense thirst' (LUB, Dublin, 185).

alpeen /ælˈpiːn/ *n.,* club, heavy stick < Ir *ailpín.* 'Give me that alpeen till I see can I kill that rat' (MG, Cavan). *See* AILPEEN.

alt, *see* AILT.

altogether /'ɔːltəgɛd̪ər/ *adv.*, wholly, completely (cf. Ir *ar fad*). 'She was wild altogether,' she was completely wild. O'Casey, *The Shadow of a Gunman*, act I, 87: "*Seumas*: It's nothing when you're used to it; you're too thin-skinned altogether."

amadán /'ɑməd̪ɔːn/ also **amadaun**, **om(m)adhawn**, sometimes **'madán** (SOM, Kerry) *n.*, (male) fool; buffoon; stupid person; simpleton < Ir. 'He's a bit of an amadán'; 'Harmless he was, an old amadán after the women' (BP, Meath, heard in Roscommon); 'That amadán should never have sold the land' (KG, Kerry).

amalóg, *see* AMLÓG.

amás /ə'mɔːs/ *int.* expressing surprise: surely; take care; indeed < Ir. 'Amás, you didn't tell your father.' – 'Amás, I did, then' (SOM, Kerry).

ambaiste /əm'bɑːʃtə/ *int.* expressing incredulity: indeed! you don't say! < Ir. 'Ambaiste! but faith, then, they won't win the final' (Mayo).

ambasa /əm'bɑsə/ *int.,* by my hands! really! indeed! by dad! you don't say! 'You're having me on!' (SOM, Kerry) < Ir.

amhrán /au'rɔːn/ *n.,* song (SOM, Kerry) < Ir. 'She sang the most beautiful amhrán I ever heard in me life.'

amlóg /ɑm'loːg/ also **amalóg** *adj.,* foolish, silly, stupid woman; a thick, awkward person (ENM, Kerry). 'Amalóigín', 'an extreme version of above' (SOM, Kerry) < Ir. 'Don't spill the milk, you amalóg' (KM, Kerry).

amn't /'æmənt/ *v.* HE uses the inversion of 'I am' in negative first-person questions instead of SE 'aren't I?' Griffin, *The Collegians*, 27: "An' amn't I to know where you stop itself?"; Joyce, 'Ivy Day in the Committee Room' (*Dubliners*, 134): "Sure, amn't I never done at the drunken bowsy ever since he left school?"; Kavanagh, *Tarry Flynn*, 8: "Amn't I taking the bike, I tell you"; Brown, *Down All the Days*, 105: "'Mother of God, amn't I scourged?' panted Mother"; Leonard, *Out After Dark*, 160: "Amn't I up ladders every day of the week?"

amplush /'ɑːmpləʃ/ *n., v.,* (state of being in) a spot of bother, difficulty, uncertainty, at a loss < Ir *aimpléis* (cf. E *nonplus* < L *non plus*, not more). 'I was completely amplushed what to do'; 'At an amplush he was, I tell you, when we found him, and it was a sorry sight and no mistake' (TJ, Sligo).

amshagh /ɑːmʃə/ also **amshugh**, **amsha** *n.,* an accident, injury < Ir *aimseach* (*adj.*), accidental, unfortunate. 'It's been one amshagh after another in that family, and now this to put the KIBOSH on it' (JF, Cavan).

amú /ə'muː/ *adv.*, astray, in vain; also part of the *adv.phr.* 'dul [going] amú' < Ir (*see* DUL AMÚ).

an /ən/ *def. art.*, THE. Joyce, *Finnegans Wake*, 57.13–14: "our antheap we sensed as a Hill of Allen, the Barrow for an [= the] People."

anam, *see* M'ANAM DO DHIA IS DO MHUIRE; M'ANAM 'ON DIABHAL; D'ANAM 'ON DIABHAL.

anco martins, *see* ANDREW MARTINS.

and /ænd/ *conj*. This word has a much wider range of use in HE than in SE, because in Irish the conjunction *agus* (and) commonly functions as a subordinating adverbial conjunction (e.g. 'when', 'because', 'although', 'if') followed by a pronoun and a non-finite part of the verb or an infinitive. This feature converts to HE in such idioms as 'She came in and I dressing' (Ir . . . *agus mé ag cur mo chuid éadaigh orm*), which is ambiguous, because it can mean 'She came in when I was dressing' or 'although I was dressing' or 'because I was dressing' or 'if I was dressing,' etc. Somerville and Ross, *Some Experiences of an Irish RM*, 323: "Didn't the docther say to meself that maybe it's walking the road I'd be, and I to fall down dead!"; O'Casey, *The Plough and the Stars*, act I, 148: "*Fluther:* . . . you'd have as much chance o' movin' Fluther as a tune on a tin whistle would move a deaf man an' he dead"; Joyce, *Ulysses*, 329.7–10: ". . . old Vic, with her JORUM of mountain dew and her coachman carting her up body and bones to roll into bed and she pulling him by the whiskers and singing him old bits of songs about *Ehren on the Rhine* and come where the boose is cheaper"; Kavanagh, *Tarry Flynn*, 35: ". . . he didn't get a drop of tay and him tired working in the field all day"; Delaney, *The Sins of the Mothers*, 360: "Oh, I seen it and I coming here . . . " See Filppula (1991) and Ó Siadhail (1984).

andána /ɑn'd̪ɔːnə/ *adj.*, foolhardy, reckless, given to taking unnecessary risks < Ir. 'That fellow is only andána (i.e. only a fool, a bit simple, no good)' (KM, Kerry).

Andrew Martins /'ændruː' mɑːrtɪnz/ also **andramartins**, **anthramartins** *n.*, tricks, fooling (origin obscure, but cf. *EDD* 'merryandrew', clown, buffoon; 'Andrew', a clown, a mountebank; 'Andrewmass', the festival of St Andrew, 30 November). The *EDD*, s.v. '*Andramartin*, a silly trick, nonsense,' cites Ireland only and notes: 'Leinster. In use all over this district, Dublin included,' with citations from southern Wexford: 'Oh musha, Mick don't be goin' on with your andramartins!', McCall, 'Fenian Nights' in *Shamrock Magazine* (1894), 428. 'Don't think your andramartins can be carried out unknowst to everyone', *ib.* 453. 'He is always up to some andramartins' (LUB, Dublin); 'He is at his "Andrew Martins" again, = jig-acting, play-acting, tricks' (MC, Kildare). Joyce, *Finnegans Wake*, 393.5: "Poor Andrew Martin Cunningham!"; 467.33–4: "with his ancomartins to read the road roman."

anear /ə'niːr/ *adv., prep.,* near < E dial. 'Are we anear yet?'; 'He was anear us up in the next field but he pretended he didn't see us' (KM, Kerry).

aneen /ə'niːn/ *voc.,* term of endearment to a little girl < Ir *a iníon*, daughter (with voc. particle).

anent /ə'nɛnt/ *prep.,* opposite; concerning < E dial. < ME *anenst, anent* < OE *on efen*. 'Anent the signature, it looks very strange to me, so it does.' Stoker, *The Snake's Pass*, 17: "Tell him what ye know iv the shtories anent the hill."

Angelus /'ændʒələs/ *n.,* a prayer recited in honour of the Incarnation, taken from the first word, 'The Angel [Angelus] of the Lord declared unto Mary . . .' < L *angelus*, Gr *aggelos*, messenger. The prayer is recited at mid-day and at six o clock in the evening on the ringing of the Angelus bell; 'We had to say the Angelus at twelve o'clock every day at school'; 'The time is twelve o' clock and we pause for the Angelus.' O'Casey, *The Plough and the Stars*, stage directions for act I, 135: "On the right of the entrance to the front drawing-room is a copy of 'The Gleaners', on the opposite side a copy of 'The Angelus'" – a celebrated picture by Jean-François Millet (1814–1875) of a group of peasants saying the Angelus.

angishore /'æŋəʃoːr/ *n.,* wretched, mean person < Ir *ainniseoir*. 'A miserable looking and not whole-witted person. Generally used of women, and sympathetically. "You couldn't but pity that poor angishore"' (LUB, Dublin). *See* AINNISEOIR.

ann, *see* IN IT.

another /ə'nʌd̪ər/, in the phrase 'He's not like another,' He's odd, mad (PR, Mayo).

anró /'ɑnroː/ *n.,* hardship (MK, Galway); distress (owing to bad weather) < Ir.

anseo /ən'ʃʌ/ *adv.,* here; used to register presence at school when the teacher calls out the names of the pupils < Ir. 'Sometimes I'd call "Anseo!" for my friend when he was out MITCHING.' Paul Muldoon,

'Anseo' (*FDA*, 3, 1413): "When the master was calling the roll | At the primary school in Collegelands, | You were meant to call back *Anseo* | And raise your hand | As your name occurred. | *Anseo*, meaning, here, here and now, | All present and correct, | Was the first word of Irish I spoke."

anskeen /æn'ʃki:n/ *n.*, wild character; scheming < Ir *ainscian*. 'That fellow is a right anskeen – he's always at the centre of trouble whenever there's any' (KG, Kerry).

anthramartins, *see* ANDREW MARTINS.

anuas /ə'nuəs/ *adv., prep.*, from above < Ir. 'Braon anuas', a leak, as from a thatched roof < Ir. 'He's so mean he'd drink the braon anuas' (proverbial saying).

any more /'æni'mor/ *adv.*, not any more; 'I swear I'll do it any more.' Cf. the positive use of 'any more', as in 'He fights a lot any more' (noted by Crystal, 338).

aoileach /'iːləx/ *n.*, farm manure (SOM, Kerry, who adds: 'bod-aoileach (combination of bodach and aoileach) to indicate nonsense!, rubbish!, rather like "bullshit" in English, but with no hint of its derivation' < Ir.

ara, *see* ARRAH.

arán /ə'rɔːn/ *n.*, bread < Ir. 'The smell of the arán filled the kitchen when I walked in – it made my mouth water' (TJ, Sligo).

áras /'ɔːrəs/ also **árus** *n.* 1. Earthenware vessel used to collect cream from the dairy before churning (SOM, Kerry) < Ir. 'Make sure and bring the áras back from the CREAMERY.' 2. Abode < Ir. Áras an Uachtaráin /'ɔːrəsən 'uːəxt̪ərɔːn/ *n.* (lit. Presidential House), official residence of President of Ireland, formerly (since 1782) of Lord Lieutenant or Viceroy; 'The new ambassador presented her credentials at the Áras.'

arcán /'ɑrkɔːn/ also **arcawn** *n.*, little pig; fig. brat, little fellow, weakling (Galway) < Ir.

ard /ɔːrd̪ / *adj.*, tall, high (JF, Cavan) < Ir.

ardfheis /ɔːr'd̪ɛʃ/ *n.*, national convention of political party < Ir. 'I'll see you at the ardfheis on Friday night.'

ardnósach /ɔːrd̪'noːsəx/ *adj.*, having big notions; proud, full of airs and graces (KG, Kerry) < Ir. 'Their family were very ardnósach'; 'She was always very ardnósach because of the way she was brought up – she only had one friend in the town.'

areesh, *see* ARÍS.

arís /ə'riːʃ/ *adv.*, again, once more; encore! < Ir. 'Arís, Pat, give it another go'; 'Arís, arís, we all cried after she'd finished the song' (*see* AGAIN). Joyce,

Finnegans Wake, 104.9: "*Arishe Sir Cannon*"; 467.11: "Areesh!"

arnaun /ˈɔːrnɔːn/ *n.*, visiting at night, etc. (*see* AIRNEÁN). 'There was a big arnaun last night over at the Kennedys' (Mayo). *See* BOTHÁNTAÍOCHT; CÉILÍ; COORJEEKING; RAMBLING.

aroo /əˈruː/ also **arú**, **airiú** *int.* expressing affirmation, or indicating that something should not be taken too seriously: indeed, certainly < Ir *airú*. 'Arú, an t-amadán!', Ah, the fool! (MK, Galway); 'Aroo, bad as I like ye, it's worse without ye' (Mayo).

aroon /əˈruːn/ *int.*, term of endearment: dear, dear man, dear woman < Ir *a rún*, loved one (with *voc. particle*). 'Aroon, you haven't a clue what you're talking about.' Joyce, *Finnegans Wake*, 613.34: "While for yous, Jasminia Aruna and all your likers . . . "; O'Casey, *Juno and the Paycock*, act II, 33: "*Joxer:* Who was it led the van, Soggart [Ir SAGART, priest] Aroon? | Since the fight first began, Soggart Aroon?"

arrah /ˈærə/ also **ara**, **arra**, **arú** *int.*, now, but, really, 'phrase to indicate that a situation is not to be taken too seriously' (SOM, Kerry, who adds: 'younger people use "YERRAH"' < Ir *dhera*). 'Ara, don't bother your head with that'; 'Arú, don't be talking' (SOM, Kerry). Joyce, *Ulysses*, 303.30: "Arrah! bloody end to the paw he'd paw"; 'Finnegan's Wake' (song): "Arrah, Tim avourneen, why did you die?"; Kavanagh, *Tarry Flynn*, 34: "'Arra what?' the mother was rising in her anger, 'arra what? Is it making little of your poor father . . . ye are?'"

art, *see* AIRT.

arú, *see* ARRAH.

aruna, *see* AROON.

asachán /ɑsəˈxɔːn/ *n.*, insult, charge, reproach (SOM, Kerry, who notes: 'elsewhere achasán'); 'nuisance value, like junk mail!' (VQ, Kerry) < Ir.

asal /ˈɑsəl/ *n.*, donkey < Ir. 'He'd steal the cross off an asal's back, he's so mean!'; 'You big asal, you, go back and get it off him.'

ascaill /ˈɑskəl/ also **ascal** (SOM, Kerry) *n.*, armpit, OXTER < Ir. 'Put it under your ascaill' (KG, Kerry); 'He'd always stand outside the chapel for Mass, with the paper under his ascaill' (JMF, Cavan). *See* ASCLÁN.

Ascendancy /əˈsɛndənsi/ *n.*, the Anglo-Irish landed gentry class (E, dominant power or influence < L *ascendere (v.)*, to mount up, to climb). 'She told me that you could tell the Ascendancy from their accents, and their faces, and the company they keep' (Dublin). Cf. Welch, 23, and Foster, 167–94.

asclán /ɑskəˈlɔːn/ also **ascallán** *n.*, amount (of fodder) that can be carried under one arm (as distinct from GABHÁIL or BEART) (SOM,

Kerry) < Ir. 'An asclán of wood' (KM, Kerry). *See* ASCAILL.

aself /ə'sɛlf/ itself; even. O'Casey, *The Plough and the Stars*, act II, 175: "*Rosie*: . . . an' if I'm a prostitute aself [even if I'm a prostitute], I have me feelin's."

ask /æsk/ *n.*, newt; lizard < ME *arske, aske*, newt. 'I think I saw an ask under that stone yesterday.'

asser /'æsər/ *n.*, bedding for animals < Ir *easair*, also *asair*. 'Put some asser under the little calves or the poor things will perish' (MG, Cavan).

assogue /æ'soːg/ *n.*, stoat; weasel (KM, Kerry) < Ir *easóg*. 'An assogue would kill a rat, no problem.'

asthore /ə'st̪oːr/ *int.*, darling, my dear, my love. 'Asthoreen' (with dimin. suffix -ÍN), my dear little one < Ir *a stór*, treasure (with *voc. particle*). 'Musha asthore, there's no use crying over spilt milk' (KG, Kerry). Somerville and Ross, *The Real Charlotte*, chap. 50 (*FDA*, 2, 1055): "Owld bones is wake [weak], asthore, owld bones is wake!"

at /æt/ *prep.*, in such expressions as 'at yourself', in your usual health or good humour. 'You don't seem to be at yourself this while back' (LUB, Dublin).

at all /æ'tɔːl/ *adv.phr*. expressing assertion (cf. Ir *ar chor ar bith*); 'He didn't say one word at all at all.' Griffin, *The Collegians*, 225: "'What ails you, a'ra gal?' she asked in a softened voice; 'Arn't you betther afther the sleep at all?'"; Joyce, *Finnegans Wake*, 96.5–6: "and, ARRAH, sure there was never a marcus at all at all."

áthasach /'ɔːhəsəx/ *adj.*, delighted; joyful (SOM, Kerry); victorious < Ir. 'Home came the team, áthasach.'

a thiarcais, *see* TIARCAS.

a thiarna, *see* TIARNA.

athout /əd̪'aut/ *adv., prep., conj.*, without; unless < E dial. 'I won't go athout you come, too'; 'He was down in the well field and we might as well have been athout him for all the work he done' (TF, Cavan).

atself, *see* ITSELF.

attercop /'ætərkɑp/ also **attercap** *n.*, a peevish, bad-tempered person; a spider, hence fig. a small, insignificant person (JP, Forth and Bargy) < OE *atorcoppe* < ME *atter* (poison) + *coppe* (top, head), spider.

aumlach /'aumləx/ *adj., adv.*, awkward; clumsily (cf. Ir *amlóg*, foolish, awkward woman). 'Well, I never seen anyone doing it as aumlach as you' (BC, Meath).

avick /ə'vɪk/ also **avick o** *voc.*, my son, my boy < Ir *a mhic (ó),* son (with voc. particle and optional affectionate suffix). 'It was common to address a boy as a mhic (avic)' (POC, Cavan); 'Get up on the cross-bar, avick, and I'll bring you to Mass' (TF, Cavan). Carleton, 'Denis O'Shaughnessy Going to Maynooth' (*Six Irish Tales*, 82): "Well, I won't Dinny; I won't avick. I'll say nothin' barrin' [but only] listen"; Trollope, *The Kellys and the O'Kellys*, 272: "'Mr. Jerry, Mr. Jerry, avick,' this was addressed to the brother – 'spake a word for me'"; Joyce, *Finnegans Wake*, 406.14: "to his regret his soupay *avic* nightcap"; 621.21: "padder avilky [Ir *Peadar, a mhic*, Peadar, my son]." 'Avick macree,' son of my heart < Ir *a mhic mo chroí.*

avillish /ə'vɪlɪʃ/ *n.,* term of endearment < Ir *a mhilis.* 'I'll always be on your side, avillish' (KG, Kerry).

avoorneen /ə'vuːrniːn/ *n.,* term of endearment < Ir *a mhuirnín.* 'Don't be long away, avoorneen; you know I get worried being here all on my own.' Carleton, 'Denis O'Shaughnessy Going to Maynooth' (*Six Irish Tales*, 115): "Upon my Priesthood, it was such a goose as a priest's corpse might get upon its elbow to look at, and exclaim, *avourneen machree*, it's a thousand pities that I'm not living, to have a cut at you!"; 'Finnegan's Wake' (song): "ARRAH, Tim, avourneen, why did you die?"

aweenagh /ə'wiːnə/ *n.,* term of endearment: my darling, my dear < Ir *a mhaoineach.* 'Aweenagh, you'll be all right – don't worry your little head' (Galway). *See* A (*voc. particle*).

ax /æks/ *v.,* ask < E dial < OE *ascian.* 'Don't ax me again or I'll give you a box on the ear'; 'Axe him then [Why don't you ask him?]' (HJ, Wexford). Carleton, 'Shane Fadh's Wedding' (*Six Irish Tales*, 191): "'Ax me no questions about her, Shane,' says she"; Griffin, *The Collegians*, 33: "I took your ricommendation to the post-masther, an' axed him for the place"; Stoker, *The Snake's Pass*, 17: "'His 'an'r [his honour] was axin' me just afore the shtorm kem on as to why the Shleenanaher was called so."

aye /ai/ *adv.,* yes < E dial. (origin obscure, but possibly the first-person pronoun 'I' used to express affirmation or a variant form of 'yea', yes). 'Will you take a drink?' 'Aye, I will that!' (AF, Cavan).

B

baaree, *see* BÁIRE.

bac[1] /bɑk/ *n.,* a quirk; a want or lack < Ir. 'There's some bac in that family' (KM, Kerry).

bac[2] /bɑk/ also **back** *v.,* to hinder < Ir. 'Don't you be backing me from doing what I want to do' (BC, Meath).

bacach /ˈbɑkəx/ also **boccach** *n., adj.,* a lame person; a beggar (often lame) (SOM, Kerry); a sponging person, a mean person, 'an unwelcome guest, someone who outstays his or her welcome' (SOM, Kerry); lame, halting, dragging one's heels < Ir *bacach.* 'Be sure and don't make a bacach of yourself'; 'Bacaching as usual' (SOM, Kerry, who adds: '"Scéal /skiːəl/ bacach é" = that's an unlikely story – that's rubbish').

bacaidí, *see* BOCKETY.

bacán /ˈbɑˈkɔːn/ *n.,* an old type of door-hinge in the shape of the numeral 7, made in the local forge (SOM, Kerry) < Ir. 'He still has the bacáns on the barn doors' (KM, Kerry).

bacán bearaigh /ˈbɑkɔːn ˈbærəx/ also **backawn barragh** *n.,* a mushroom < Ir *beacán bearaigh,* toadstool. 'Don't eat those backawn barraghs – they're poison!' (Cork).

bachall /ˈbɑxəl/ *n.,* a shepherd's crook; fig. a blemish, a hooked nose, or a person with a hooked nose < Ir. 'The Bachaillins, clan who had a number of flat-nosed people in the distant past' (SOM, Kerry).

bachlóg /ˈbɑxloːg/ *n.,* a bud, a sprout (on a potato) (Mayo) < Ir.

bachram /ˈbɑxrəm/ *n.,* boisterous behaviour; fig. very heavy rain < Ir. 'There was a QUARE bachram in the pub that night' (TF, Cavan).

back /bæk/ *adv.* 'They were drinking back at Briody's when the news came through' (BC, Meath). (The Irish word *siar* means 'back' as well as 'west', hence the probably apocryphal story of the dentist asking the patient where his sore tooth was and being told, 'In the west of my mouth.')

backer /ˈbækər/ *n.* (*colloq.*), a lift on the carrier of a bicycle (Cork) < E *back* (OE *bæc*) + *-er* (OE *-ere*). 'Hop up and I'll give you a backer to Mass.' *See* CROSSER.

bacóg /ˈbɑkoːg/ *n.,* an armful, a bundle carried under one's bent arm (MK, Galway) < Ir. 'Bring a bacóg of hay over to that cow'; 'He does be up and down the road every day with his bacóg of hay for his skinny little cows.'

bad cess /bædˈsɛs/ *exclam.*, bad luck (to him, her, etc.) < E *bad* + CESS. 'Bad cess to your cheek' (LUB, Dublin). *See* SCRAN.

bad feeder /ˈbædˈfiːdər/ *n.* (*colloq.*), an animal that consumes a lot of fodder but puts on relatively little weight (GF, Galway; MG, Cavan). 'She's a bad feeder that one – I'll have to get rid of her quick.'

badhach, *see* BODACH.

badhbh /baiv/ also **bow bow** *n.,* the bogey man (said in order to frighten children); another name for the BANSHEE < Ir. 'Badhbh! badhbh! Get up that stairs quick' (Mayo).

badhbh chaointe /ˈbaivˈxiːntʃə/ *n.,* BANSHEE < Ir. 'The badhbh chaointe must be out tonight – I can hear her calling' (BC, Meath).

badóg /ˈbɑd̪oːg/ also **bodóg** *n.,* young heifer; a cow with a very low milk yield because of old age, hence term of derision < Ir *bodóg,* heifer. 'Sell that badóg to the KNACKERS!' (BC, Meath); 'Look at him with his three dried-out badógs!' (SOM, Kerry).

baicacawn /ˈbeːkəhɔːn/ *n.,* premature calf (KM, Kerry) < Ir BÉICEACHÁN. 'I don't think the baicacawn will live another night, but we'll just have to wait and see.'

bail /bɑl/ *n.,* luck; prosperity < Ir. 'The bail was always in that family' (TJ, Sligo).

baile /ˈbɑljə/ *n.,* 1. home, home place, etc.; 2. townland < Ir. 'Bun an bhaile' /bʌnəˈwɑljə/ the people living down there, implying that they are less civilised (SOM, Kerry).

baileabhair /ˈbɑluːr/ also **bailiúr** *n.,* in such phrases as 'I made a baileabhair of myself,' I made a fool of myself, 'He made a baileabhair of it,' he made a mess of it (CS, Mayo) < Ir.

báille /ˈbɔːlə/ *n.,* bailiff; fig. a loud-voiced, scolding woman < Ir. 'Nobody likes that báille when she gets on her high horse – you'd hear her in the next parish.'

bainbhín /ˈbɑnəviːn/ also **bonneen** *n.,* dimin. of BANBH < Ir.

báini, báini /ˈbɔːniːˈbɔːniː/ used to call pigs to eat < Ir *bainne! bainne!* (milk! milk!) (MK, Galway).

báinín /ˈbɔːniːn/ also **bawneen** *n.,* a kind of woollen or flannel jacket, self-tied at the base, which went out of fashion during the Second World War; now back in fashion; < Ir *báinín* (dimin. of *bán*, white). Also called 'bheist' (SOM, Kerry) < E *vest* (= waistcoat). 'I'd better bring my báinín – it'll be a cold evening' (KG, Kerry, Sligo); 'Do you think your sister would like a bawneen?' (Mayo).

bainne bó bleacht, *see* BONNYBO-BLOCK.

bainne ramhar /ˈbɑnjəˈraur/ *n.*, thick milk < Ir. 'That's great bainne ramhar – you'll have some more' (BC, Meath). *See* BONNYCLABBER.

báire /ˈbɔːrə/ also **bawra, baaree** (JP, Forth and Bargy) *n.*, a goal; a hurling match < Ir. 'That was a great báire – he'll make the county team yet.'

báire leo /ˈbɔːrəloː/ *n.phr.*, the goal is won! < Ir. 'Báire leo! – there'll be singing in the pub tonight.'

bairneach /ˈbærnəx/ *n.*, a limpet < Ir. 'Go down and scrape the bairneachs off the boat.'

bairrcin /ˈbɑːrəkiːn/ also **borrikeen** *n.*, the toe-cap on a shoe; a piece on the toe of a shoe; a toe-patch on the sole of a shoe; fig. the cover on a load of turf < Ir *barraicín*. 'It's about time you put a bairrcin on those shoes – I can see your toe sticking out.'

báite /ˈbɔːtʃə/ *adj.*, drenched, 'drowned' (SOM, Kerry) < Ir.

baitín /ˈbɑtʃiːn/ also **botteen** *n.*, a short stick < Ir. 'If you get a whack of this baitín you won't come back again so quick.'

balbh /ˈbɑləv/ *n., adj.*, a person with a speech defect; mute, dumb; with indistinct speech; an inarticulate mumbler (SOM, Kerry); 'dumb (drunk)' (SOC, Cork) < Ir.

balbhán /ˈbɑləvɔːn/ *n.*, a dumb person; a stammerer; fig. an awkward, silly person < Ir. 'The drink has made a balbhán out of him' (BC, Meath).

balcaire /ˈbɑlkərə/ *n.*, a fat, stocky person < Ir. 'Sure that balcaire can't bend down, he's so fat.'

balcais /ˈbɑlkəʃ/ *n.*, rag; garment < Ir. 'Where did you find that old balcais?'; 'Hand me the old balcais till I start cleaning the PRESS.'

balcaiseán /ˈbɑlkəʃɔːn/ *n.*, ragweed, ragwort < Ir. 'That field is full of balcaiseáns – we'll have to let the sheep at it next year.'

ballocks, *see* BOLLIX.

ball of malt, *see* MALT.

ball searc /bɑlˈʃærk/ *n.phr.*, a red or strawberry mark (small and round); a beauty spot < Ir *ball seirce*, 'love mark'. 'They say if a man has a ball searc on his body he is irresistible to women!' (KM, Kerry).

ballyrag /ˈbæliræg/ *v.*, chide, scold < E dial. (origin obscure). Trollope, *The Kellys and the O'Kellys*, 236: "But av' [if] he's nothing betther for you to do, than to send you here bally-ragging . . ."

Baluba /bəˈluːbə/ *n.* (*colloq.*), unruly or unsavoury person < a tribe of the provinces of Kasai and Katanga in the former Belgian Congo involved in a fatal attack on Irish UN troops in 1961. 'Get away out o' that, you Baluba' (Dublin). 'Balubaland,' areas of Dublin reputedly frequented by such people.

bán /bɔːn/ *n., adj.* 1. White (*see* BAWN[1]). 2. A white cow (*see* BÁNAÍ). 3. (Unploughed) grassland, lea (SOM, Kerry); an enclosed field for cows before milking; a herd of cows (*see* BAWN[2]) < Ir. 'Bring the cows up to the bawn, I'll milk them myself – it's getting very late' (Kerry).

Banagher /ˈbænəhər/ *place-name*, a town in Co. Offaly in which the novelist Anthony Trollope (1815–1882) spent some time as a Post Office surveyor but chiefly famous for its inclusion in the saying 'That beats [often pronounced /beːts/] (or bangs) Banagher,' a common reaction to something extraordinary or absurd. Banagher was once a 'pocket borough', meaning that the local lord nominated its representatives in Parliament. The town became famous for this (once-common) undemocratic way of conducting politics, so if something was really anomalous it was said to 'beat Banagher.' Trollope, *The Kellys and the O'Kellys*, 221: "Conspiracy! – av' [if] that don't bang Banagher!'"; Joyce, *Finnegans Wake*, 87.31: "bank from Banagher"; Plunkett, *Farewell Companions*, 293: "'That beats Banagher,' he said."

banaí /ˈbɑniː/ *n.*, a man who is very fond of women (Mayo) < Ir. 'I never thought he'd make a banaí – but look at him now.'

bánaí /ˈbɔːniː/ *n.* 1. Albino person or animal < Ir *bánaí*, albino < *bán*, white. 'She must have a very lonely life being a bánaí and all, and her sight not so good.' 2. The man in a white coat who administers artificial insemination (KM, Kerry). 'Go down and show the bánaí which cow has to be done.'

banbh /ˈbɑnəv/ also **bonnive** *n.*, a small pig, a sucking-pig (SOM, Kerry) < Ir. 'That sow has had more than a hundred banbhs'; 'You should have seen him chasing the banbh around the yard – I thought I'd die laughing' (BC, Meath); 'May he marry a ghost that will bear him a banbh, and may the Holy Ghost give it the scours [diarrhoea], for a cruel man is sinful.'

banger /ˈbæŋər/ *n.* (*colloq.*), 'someone on, say, a football team who is over the age limit' (KD, Dublin).

bangharda /ˈbɑnɣɔːrd̪ə/ *n.*, policewoman < Ir. The term is no longer officially used, having being dropped in favour of the general term GARDA.

banjax /ˈbændʒæks/ *v.* (*colloq.*), to ruin, destroy. Origin obscure:

Chambers English Dictionary suggests 'poss. combination of *bang* and *smash*.' 'An Irishman's Diary' (*Irish Times*, 5 October 1965, p. 9) facetiously suggested that "it is the Corkese for a public lavatory for females." Flann O'Brien, *The Third Policeman*, 85: "'Michael Gilhaney,' said the Sergeant, 'is an example of a man that is nearly banjaxed from the principle of the Atomic Theory"; Edna O'Brien, *A Pagan Place*, 97: "Emma had suggested that you hide, said your presence might banjax her position"; Plunkett, *Farewell Companions*, 375: "Nature slipped when it made beetles. Sheep too. If they fall over on their backs they're banjaxed"; Durcan, *Christmas Day*, VII, 50: "I am bejasus banjaxed."

bannacth, *see* BEANNACHT.

bannock /'bænək/ *n.*, a home-made loaf < Ir *bannach*. 'Did you make that bannock yourself?'

bánóg /'bɔːnoːg/ also **bawnogue** *n.*, a patch of green < Ir. 'They were dancing on the bawnogue until the crack of dawn.'

banshee /bæn'ʃiː/ *n.*, a female spirit whose wailing presages death in a family; a weird noise at night, said to be ghosts < Ir *bean sí*, woman of the spirit world. 'That woman looks more and more like a banshee, with the GIOBALS hanging off her' (Cork). Joyce, 'Grace' (*Dubliners*, 178): "Her faith was bounded by her kitchen but, if she was put to it, she could believe also in the Banshee and in the Holy Ghost'; Kavanagh, 'Art McCooey' (*Collected Poems*, 77): "Down the lane-way of the popular banshees"; Leonard, *Out After Dark*, 61: "Just then, there was a banshee's wail, and, dragged by her mother, Gloria came up the garden path with gobs of ice-cream trickling down her legs"; McCourt, *Angela's Ashes*, 152: "She screams at me like a banshee . . . and threatens to drag me to the priest, the bishop, the Pope himself if he lived around the corner."

bard /bærd/ *n.*, poet (lower in rank than a *file*) < Ir. 'I heard he has a bit of the bard in him.'

bardóg /bæːrd̪oːg/ *n.*, a pannier < Ir. 'Bardóg mat', *n.*, a protective covering placed over a donkey's back when carrying a creel or a basket. 'Put on the bardóg mat, otherwise she'll chafe.' *See* PARDÓG.

barelean, *see* BÉARLA.

barge /bæːrʤ/ *n., v.*, a scolding woman; to scold < E dial. 'She is always barging me' (LUB, Dublin). O'Casey, *The Plough and the Stars*, act I, 149: "*Nora*: She was bargin' out of her."

barmbrack /bærmbræk/ also **barnbrack, borreen-brack** *n.*, bread containing fruit, especially relished at Hallowe'en, when symbolic gifts (e.g. a ring to foretell marriage) are placed in the bread < Ir *bairín breac*, speckled loaf. 'What kind of a barmbrack is that? – that doesn't have a ring in it' (KG, Kerry); 'Barm bread, made from yeast, butter-milk, flour, sugar, and luke-warm water – we'd eat barm bread in winter and soda bread in summer – they'd mix cream of tartar with the flour if they had nothing else' (MOB, Mayo). Plunkett, *Farewell Companions*, 288: "Hallowe'en, as usual, saw the tea table furnished with a large barmbrack which was flanked by plates of apples and oranges, grapes and nuts."

barm bread, *see* BARMBRACK.

barrach /ˈbɑrəx/ *n.,* tow; the fibre of flax, the bad portion of flax < Ir. 'You must get rid of the barrach and leave the rest.'

barrack /ˈbærək/ *v.,* to brag, to be boastful of one's fighting powers < E dial. (*EDD,* s.v. 'barrack', cites Northern Ireland only and gives an example from Co. Antrim: 'One boy will say of another "He's only barracking", hence barracker, *sb.* a braggart; barracking, *vbl. sb.* bragging, boastfulness,' with examples from Co. Antrim, 'That fellow's a great barracker,' and notes a correspondent's remark: 'A schoolboy's term, common in Belfast and district.')

barracks /ˈbærəks/ *n.,* a GARDA station (from the use of this term by the Royal Irish Constabulary, predecessors of the Garda Síochána). 'Go down to the barracks and tell the sergeant the school's on fire!'; 'The old barracks was so damp they had to build a new station.' Roche, *A Handful of Stars,* act II, iii, 57: *"Jimmy:* . . . I want you to go up to the barracks and tell them where to find me."

barraí /ˈbɑriː/ also **borry** *n.,* an arrogant person; a bully < Ir. 'Get away, you barraí. You're great when you've drink taken but such a coward under it all!'

barrfhód /ˈbɑːroːd̪ʲ/ *n.,* top sod < Ir. 'Leave the barrfhód where it is – we'll get it the next day.'

bas[1] /bʌs/ also **bos** *n.,* palm of the hand < Ir *bos*, also *bas*. 'Bualadh bos' /buələˈbʌs/ *n.,* applause < Ir. 'Give them a great bualadh bos!' (Dublin).

bas[2] /bɑs/ *n.,* blade, lower part of hurley < Ir *bos*, also *bas*. 'He got a whack of the bas on the head and it nearly killed him' (Mayo).

bás /bɔːs/ *n.,* death; *fuair sé bás*, he died (lit. he got death) < Ir. 'She got her death on the way home from her sister's, poor thing. They say she tried to jump up on the ditch out of the way of a car and she fell into the path of another. The REMOVAL is this evening' (Cavan).

básachán /ˈbɔːsəkɔːn/ *n.,* a feeble person; a non-thriving person or animal (SOM, Kerry); fig. having the appearance of the Devil (JOM, Kerry) < Ir. 'They've all died, and to think that básachán is still alive!'

básaire /ˈbɔːsərə/ *n.*, executioner; fig. a pale-complexioned man with the look of death about him < Ir. 'He looks fairly básaire – he'll never make it through the winter.'

basóg /bɑˈsoːg/ also **boiseog** *n.*, a slap < Ir.

bastable /ˈbæstəbəl/ *n.*, an oven; a cast-iron pot used for making cakes of bread, suspended from a 'crook' over an open fire, with hot coals placed on the lid to ensure all-round heat (said to derive from Barnstaple in Devon, England, which was celebrated for its manufacture of metal pots). 'Bastable cake', a loaf baked in such an oven; 'She used make a bastable cake every day, and I've never baked one as good as her' (BC, Meath). *See* OVEN; TRÍNA CHÉILE CAKE.

bastún /bɑsˈt̪uːn/ *n.*, an uncultured person; a lout (SOM, Kerry) < Ir. '"You ignorant bastún," she said, "were you born in a shed with no doors?"' (KG, Kerry).

bata agus bóthar /bɑt̪ɑgəs ˈboːhər/ *n.phr.*, the act of being fired from a job < Ir, lit. (the) stick and (the) road. 'Johnny was given bata agus bóthar.'

bata scóir /ˈbɑt̪əˈskoːr/ *n.*, a TALLY STICK < Ir.

bawn[1] /bɔːn/ *adj.*, pet or darling, as in 'COLLEEN bawn' (darling girl), etc. < Ir *bán,* white (-headed), beautiful (MK, Galway). 'Isn't she the lovely colleen bawn – what age is she now?' (KG, Kerry). Keegan, *Songs of the Gael*, 146–7: "Oh, pray have you heard of my Bouchaleen Bawn?"

bawn[2] /bɔːn/ also **baan** *n.*, an enclosure for cattle; a yard; a paddock for cattle; the green space in front of a house < Ir *bábhún.* Hartnett, 'A Visit to Castletown House' (*FDA*, 3, 1388): "a few lit windows on a bullock bawn"; Heaney, 'Belderg' (*North*, 14): "And how I could derive | A forked root from that ground | And make *bawn* an English fort."

bawneen, *see* BÁINÍN.

bawnogue /bɔːˈnoːg/ *n.*, small paddock for calves; barn < Ir *bánóg*. 'Seán, it's about time you put the calves out in the bawnogue – they're making a mess of the byre' (ML, Mayo).

bazz /bæz/ *n.* (*colloq.*), a few days of beard growth (origin obscure); *see* BAZZER.

bazzer /ˈbæzər/ *n.* (*colloq.*), a haircut (origin obscure). 'I got a bazzer yesterday' (SB, Cork).

be /biː/ *v.*, commonly used in distinctive HE phrases with progressive verbs, such as 'Be starting your tea, otherwise it'll get cold,' also with some part of the verb 'do' indicating the nature of an action, as 'Now, he does usually be above in Greavy's, but if he's not there, well, I couldn't tell you where he'd be.' Synge, *In the Shadow of the Glen* (*FDA*, 2, 632): *"Dan:* . . . Be falling to sleep now and don't LET ON you know anything"; Joyce, *Ulysses,* 296.36: "Ah! Ow! Don't be talking!" (cf. Ir *Ná bí ag caint*, don't be talking); Joyce, *Finnegans Wake,* 24.16: "Now be aisy, good Mr Finnimore, sir"; Roche, *A Handful of Stars,* act I, i, 8: *"Jimmy:* Hey Stapler do auld Matt still be down in the boxin' club?"; Durcan, *Christmas Day,* II, 11: "Don't be talkin, Deborah"; McCourt, *Angela's Ashes,* 144: "Don't be bothering him again."

beadaí[1] /ˈbædiː/ also **baddhy** *n.,* a pet name for a goose; used to call geese < Ir. 'Baddhy, baddhy!'

beadaí[2] /ˈbædiː/ *adj.,* fastidious; pernickety about food (SOM, Kerry) < Ir. 'Eat up and don't be so beadaí!'

beads /biːdz/ *n.,* ROSARY beads < OE *gebed,* prayer. Kickham, *Knocknagow,* 599: "I have a beads blessed by himself [the Pope] for you."

beal /biːl/ *v.,* to fester, to suppurate (of a sore); to swell with pain; fig. to swell with remorse < E dial. < ME *belen*, to burn. 'Be careful of my finger – look, it's bealing. If it gets any worse I'm going down to the doctor' (TF, Cavan).

béal /beːl/ *n.,* mouth; muzzle of a gun < Ir. 'Is binn béal ina thost' (proverb), silence is golden. 'Éist do bhéal,' shut your mouth; 'I want to listen to what he's saying' (KG, Kerry). Carleton, 'Shane Fadh's Wedding' (*Six Irish Tales*, 177): "And I wouldn't have valued that so much, only that it was *Bealcam* Doherty that joined me in the ploughing that year – and I was VEXED not to take all I could out of him for he was a raal Turk himself" (in a footnote Carleton defines *Bealcam* as 'Crooked mouth').

bealach /ˈbæləx/ *n.,* a gap, a byway < Ir. 'Drive the cows out through the bealach in the top field' (MG, Cavan).

béal bocht /beːlˈbʌxt̪/ *n.phr.,* the 'poor mouth', pretending to be poor < Ir. 'You're always putting on the béal bocht – I'm fed up listening to you.' *See* POOR MOUTH.

beannacht leat /ˈbænəxt̪ˈlæt̪/ *phr.* of farewell: goodbye < Ir. 'Beannacht leat, and sure, please God, we'll see you again soon.' Banim, *The Boyne Water*, 465: "The French and Irish . . . separately wishing them 'bon soir', and 'bannacth lath', moved up the heights."

bean sí, *see* BANSHEE.

bean tí /bænˈtʃiː/ also **beantigh** *n.,* a housewife < Ir. 'Bean a' tí', the woman of the house, 'herself' (SOM, Kerry); landlady. 'Where's the beantigh?' Sheehan, *Glenanaar*, 87: ". . . he should have asked the poor, lone woman to allow him and his *bean a' tí* to be her protector." *See* LADY OF THE HOUSE.

Béarla /ˈbeːrlə/ *n.*, the English language < Ir. 'No Béarla here, MÁS É DO THOIL É.' Joyce, *Finnegans Wake*, 550.8–9: "my barelean linsteer."

bearna /ˈbæːrnə/ *n.*, a gap in a fence or ditch (SOM, Kerry); a gap in a wall (ENM, Kerry) < Ir. 'The cattle got onto the road through a bearna in the hedge' (ENM, Kerry).

bearnach /ˈbæːrnəx/ *adj.*, gapped < Ir. 'The blasted cattle won't break out again – the place is completely bearnach now' (Mayo).

beart /bært̪/ *n.*, a parcel; a quantity of rushes or fodder enclosed in a rope of two rushes (a SÚGÁN) and carried on the back (SOM, Kerry); a beart of rods, cut and tied at each end to make SCALLOPS, measured to the right length and left in the loft to be seasoned (MOB, Mayo) < Ir. 'Oifig na mbeart', parcels office in railway stations. 'Carry a beart of hay back to the heifers' (SOM, Kerry); 'The poorer people's only source of firing was the beart of sticks they would collect along the hedgerows' (SOC, Cork).

bedad /biˈdæd/ *int.*, a euphemism for 'by God.' 'Did you see the fox?' – 'Bedad, I did so' (TF, Cavan).

beddeen /ˈbɛdiːn/ *n.*, a little bed < E *bed* + dimin. suffix -EEN. 'Make a beddeen of straw for the calf while I finish the milking'; 'You'll never fit two in that bedeen' (BC, Meath).

beestings /ˈbiːstɪnz/, /ˈbeːʃtɪnz/ *n.*, the first milk drawn from a cow after calving (CS, Mayo), yellow in colour < ME *bestyng*. 'Eat the curd, drink the whey – we'd all share it and send jugs to the neighbours' (MOB, Mayo); 'When you are boiling up the beestings put a small drop of sour cream into it and that would crack it. Pour off the blithernuck [form and origin obscure] – the scum on top of the boiled beestings – or skim it off with a wooden spoon' (KM, Kerry).

beetle /ˈbiːtəl/ *n.*, *v.*, a pounder; an implement usually made of wood for pounding (e.g. for pounding potatoes in a big pot for feeding to animals), often just a wooden cudgel with a rounded end; to pound < ME *betel* < OE *bætan* to beat. 'Where's the beetle till I get the SPUDS ready for the pig' (AF, Cavan). *See* POUNDER.

Beeyankinny, corruption of BIANCONI. *See* BIAN, JAUNTING-CAR.

begannies /biˈgæniːz/ *int.* (*colloq.*), 'word used to hold the attention of the listeners in storytelling, a pause between sentences, e.g. "She was advised – begannies – to let him go away"' (Cork) (etymology obscure).

begob /bi'gɑb/, /bi'gʌb/ *int.*, corruption of 'by God'. 'Begob, I didn't expect to see you back so soon'; 'Begob, is it yourself that's IN IT? – long time no see.' Sheehan, *Glenanaar*, 161; "'THRUE for you, begobs,' said Jim"; Joyce, *Ulysses*, 300.29: "And, begob, I saw his physog do a peep in and then slidder off again."

begorra /bi'gɑrə/ *exclam.*, corruption of 'by God,' now restricted to stage Irish. 'Begorra, that's a long road you have to take on a night like this.' Trollope, *The Kellys and the O'Kellys*, 284: "'Ah, boys,' said Frank, riding up, 'if you want to see a hunt, will you keep back!' 'Begorra, we will, yer honer,' said one"; Shaw, *John Bull's Other Island*, act I (*FDA*, 2, 425): "*Tim:* An' is it the afthernoon it is already? Begorra, what I call the mornin is all the time a man fasts afther breakfast."

begrudgers /bɪ'grʌʤərz/ *n.pl.*, in the phrase 'fuck (or FECK) the begrudgers,' a common expression dismissive of people who are forever grumbling about and criticising other people's success < E prefix *be-* + *grudge* < ME *grucchen*, to grumble (cf. Gregory, *Spreading the News* (*FDA*, 2, 621): "*Tim Casey:* Why wouldn't he get a wake as well as another? Would you begrudge him that much?"). 'They say we're a nation of begrudgers, and, let me tell you, they're right: look what they said about poor old Felix when he won the money at the bingo.' Leonard, *Out After Dark*, 166: ". . . knowing that anyone who fetched him a bleak look or threw doubt on his rough-hewn goodness would be scorned as a begrudger."

béiceachán /'beːkəxɔːn/ also BAICACAWN *n.*, a bawler; fig. a premature calf < Ir. 'It's a béiceachán; I hope it'll live' (Galway).

beirtín /'bɛrtʃiːn/ also **birtín** *n.*, a small armful of straw or hay < Ir. 'I didn't even have a beirtín of hay left after the long winter – I'll have to buy a couple of bales off of Mickey' (BC, Meath).

béitín /'beːtʃiːn/ also **baiteen** *n.*, burned grass; burning weeds (for manure); burnt top-soil (KM, Kerry) < Ir.

bejabers /biː'ʤeːpərs/ *exclam.*, corruption of 'by Jesus.' 'Bejabers, is that the one you were tryin' it on with last night? She has a head like a cauliflower' (Mayo).

bellax, *see* BOLLIX.

Belleek /bə'liːk/ a brand of fine bone china made in Belleek, Co. Fermanagh (the feldspar, once found locally, is now imported from Norway) < Ir *Béal Leice*, the ford-mouth of the flagstone. 'Did you see that lovely little Belleek pig in the china-cabinet?' (KG, Kerry). Joyce, *Finnegans Wake*, 449.33–4: "leaving tealeaves for the trout and belleeks for the wary."

belt /bɛlt/ *n., v.,* blow, beating; strike, thrash < ME *belt*. 'She gave him a belt with her brolly'; 'I'll give you a belt if you're not careful' (Cavan).

Beltane /'bælt̪ənə/ *n.,* the first of May, an ancient Celtic festival, celebrated with the lighting of bonfires on hills < Ir *Bealtaine*. Lá Bealtaine, May Day. Dorgan, 'Falling South' (*The Ordinary House of Love*, 44): ". . . the melancholy | Burned out of it by the high Beltane sun."

Benediction /bɛnə'dɪkʃən/ *n.,* a short service in the Catholic Church, originating in the sixteenth century, consisting of the singing of the hymn 'Tantum Ergo' followed by a blessing given to the people by making the sign of the cross above them with the BLESSED SACRAMENT displayed in a MONSTRANCE < (O)F *bénédiction*, blessing. 'Let's go over to the hospital after Benediction.' Healy, *Nineteen Acres*, 44: "The ROSARY and Benediction on Sunday evening would come and the girls would be there."

besom /'bɪːzəm/ *n.,* a broom made from a bunch of heather (NH, Mayo) or twigs, used for sweeping the top layer of clay from a clay floor < ME *besme*. 'Look at that photo of Granny out with the besom in the STREET' (JMF, Cavan).

betimes /bi'taimz/ *adv.,* used frequently in HE to mean sometimes, at certain times, occasionally (NL, Mayo; PON, Dublin), rather than early, speedily, etc., as in SE < E dial. 'I do see him betimes in the bog cutting turf.' Durcan, *Christmas Day*, X, 62: "Betimes in the kip | I regret my life as a stoat."

better /'bɛt̪ər/ *adj.,* more < E dial. 'It's better than a week since she took ill' (JF, Cavan).

beyant /biː'jɑnt/ *adv.,* rural HE pronunciation of 'beyond' < E dial. < OE *begeondan*. 'He's over beyant in the HAGGARD.' Griffin, *The Collegians*, 233: "We have a spot o' ground beyant for the PIATEES'; McCourt, *Angela's Ashes*, 350: "If they see me they'll be running to the woman of the house, Oh, madam, madam, there's an urchin beyant that's makin' off with all the milk and bread. Beyant. Maids talk like that because they're all from the country, Mullingar heifers, says Paddy Clohessy's uncle, beef to the heels, and they wouldn't give you the steam of their piss."

bia /biə/ also **bee** *n.,* food; a call to turkeys (MK, Galway) < Ir. 'Bia! bia!'

bian /'biən/ *n.* (contraction of *Bianconi*), one of Charles Bianconi's long horse-drawn road-cars. Bianconi (1786–1875), a naturalised Italian, set up a service between Clonmel and Cahir, Co. Tipperary, in 1815; the business flourished in Munster and Connacht. 'I think there used be a bian in that old shed over there' (TJ, Sligo). Shaw, *John Bull's Other Island*, act I (*FDA*, 2, 438), stage directions: "It is a monster JAUNTING CAR . . . one of the last survivors of the public vehicles known to earlier generations as Beeyankinny cars." (Cf. Victoria Glendinning, *Trollope*, London: Hutchinson 1992, 119: "There were also Bianconis, known as Bians (pronounced Bye-anns) and named after their Italian-born owner.")

bibe /'bıbə/ *n.,* garment to keep one clean; bib; top part of apron. *See* BADHBH.

bicycle /'baisıkəl/ also **bike** *n.* (*colloq.*), a figurative and imaginative way of describing a woman of loose habits. 'She's a bicycle if ever there was one' (Wexford).

Biddy-boys /'bıdibɔiz/ also **Biddys** /'bıdiz/ *n.,* BRÍDEOGS. 'You can still see the Biddy-boys going round today' (BC, Meath).

bí do thost /biːd̪ʌ'hʌst̪/ *phr.,* be silent < Ir *bí i do thost*. 'Bí do thost! The guards are outside.'

big house /bıg'haus/ *n.phr.,* a recurring motif in Anglo-Irish literature, often symbolising the arrogance of the ASCENDANCY. Yeats, *The Unicorn from the Stars*, act III (*Collected Plays*, 367): "*Nanny:* . . . To leave the big house blazing after us, it was that crowned all!" Cf. Welch, 45–6.

bike, *see* BICYCLE.

bindings /'baindənz/ *n.,* the dealings with a solicitor in matchmaking to ensure the legal transferral of property (MOB, Mayo) < ME *binden*, to bind. 'There must have been some funny goings-on with the bindings in that marriage.'

biolar /'bılər/ *n.,* cress; water-cress (SOM, Kerry) < Ir. 'Some biolar would be nice on top of the salad' (BC, Meath).

bior /bır/ *n.,* a point; fig. pointed features < Ir. 'She's got such a bior of a chin you could shave a gooseberry on it' (JMF, Cavan).

biorach /'bırəx/ *n.,* a spiked muzzle for colts, calves, etc. < Ir. 'Put the biorach on her – she's a wild one' (Mayo).

bioránach /bır'ɔːnəx/ *adj.,* a term of contempt: prickly, difficult; 'hardy, small fellow (as of a BONHAM)' (JOM, Kerry) < Ir. 'She's a right bioránach, that one – she must have got it from the father's side' (Mayo).

birl /bɛrəl/ *v.,* to twist, spin, rotate < E dial. (probably onomatopoeiac).

birtín /bɛr'tʃiːn/ *n.,* a small quantity < Ir (dimin. of BEART). 'Keep a birtín of that bog-deal' (SOC, Kerry). See BEIRTÍN.

biscake /'bɪskeːk/ *n.,* corruption of *biscuit* < E dial. < hybrid formation of *biscuit* (OF *bescoit*) + *cake* (ON *kaka*). 'Do you have any more of those biscakes left? – the children love them' (AF, Cavan; noted by Braidwood, 34).

bithiúnach /bɪ'huːnəx/ *n.,* a thief; a rogue; 'may be used affectionately without any suggestion of wrongdoing' (SOM, Kerry) < Ir.

blaa /blæ/ also **blah, bla** *n.,* a sort of bread, bigger and lighter than a bap, made with dough shaped into small round pieces. Blaa is local to Co. Waterford, whose bakers say it was introduced by the Huguenots (Protestant refugees from France in the late seventeenth or early eighteenth century). It is thought that it is derived from the croissants they brought with them; it was called blaad and was originally made from the leftover pieces of dough before baking. 'Make me a few sandwiches with that bla, will you?' "A blaa with two *a's* is made with fresh dough | about the size of a saucer, that's the right size you know . . ." (see Cowan and Sexton, *Ireland's Traditional Foods,* 127–9).

black /blæk/ *adj., adv.,* used as an intensive: immoderate, serious, bigoted, in such expressions as 'black frost', 'black wind' (a cold east wind) (GF, Galway); also in the general sense of 'black with people' (=crowded); cf. Ir *dubh-, prefix,* great, intense, downright < *dubh (adj.),* black. 'She's black sick'; 'a black [bigoted] Protestant' (GF, Galway); 'a black Republican.' Sheehan, *Glenanaar,* 97: "Av [if] she was the blackest Prodestan' in Ireland, she have her child baptized." 'How was the chapel at the MISSION?' – 'Oh, black [crowded], thank God.'

Black and Tans /'blækən'tænz/ *n.pl.,* an irregular British force (officially known as RIC Cadets) deployed against the IRA and the civilian population from March 1920 to October 1921, so termed from the mixed colour of their uniforms and the name of a famous pack of hounds; sometimes referred to as "Auxies' (i.e. Auxiliaries) or simply as 'the Tans' < OE *blæc,* ME *tanni.* 'Granny said she'd heard tell of the Tans when they were about the place, but she never saw them herself'; 'The Tans came into the school playground and opened fire and shot the young fellow dead' (KM, Kerry); 'The Tans came in and they'd be looking for money or drink' (PR, Mayo). Leonard, *Out After Dark,* 112: "I was cast as 'Third Black and Tan', with one line: 'Which w'y did the bawstid double back?'"

blackguard /ˈblægɑːrd/ also **blaggard, blagard, bligeard** *n., v.,* ruffian, rogue, scoundrel; a cloth used for doing the dirtiest domestic chores; to behave dishonestly, to lie, to dissemble < E dial. The original usage of the word is uncertain, but its present usage in HE seems to derive from a number of synonymous or near-synonymous contexts. The unruly menials in a household (or who travelled with armies) in charge of the pots and pans etc. were called 'blackguards'. The *OED* also instances 'a guard of attendants black in person, dress or character, a street shoe-black, etc.'; it also notes a type of snuff called 'Irish Blackguard', originally an abusive name given to a shop-boy in a Dublin snuff merchant's by the owner because he made a mistake in the preparation of some snuff but which subsequently became successful and was known by the name of its creator. 'Stop your blackguarding and behave yourself.' Carleton, 'The Battle of the Factions' (*Six Irish Tales*, 203): "Who dare touch the coat of an O'Hallaghan? Where's the blackguard Connells now?"; Kickham, *Knocknagow*, 78: "D—n well the blagard knows I'm in the state of grace today"; Trollope, *The Kellys and the O'Kellys*, 235: "the blackguard nearly knocked the life out of her"; Sheehan, *Glenanaar*, 111: "'Nothin' but the usual blagardin' and ruffianism,' said Donal"; Kavanagh, *Tarry Flynn*, 23: "When she was passing Drumnay cross-roads she was set upon by a crowd of blackguards – and blackguards is no name for them – and the clothes torn off her back"; Leonard, *Out After Dark*, 27: "Are you blackguardin' me, you whoor you?"; Durcan, *Christmas Day*, III, 20: "I was a blackguard for the campari . . ."

black rabbit /ˈblækˈræbət/ *n.phr.* (*colloq.*), a person who does not go to Mass and who is visited by a priest during a MISSION in an attempt to persuade them to return to practising their religion. 'The missioner went round the parish visiting the black rabbits, and quite a few went back to church, thanks be to God!' (TJ, Sligo).

black rent /ˈblækˈrɛnt/ *n.phr.,* 'the name that came to be given to the protection money exacted, mostly by Gaelic lords, from local communities and even from the Dublin government' (*Oxford Companion to Irish History*, 48).

bladair /ˈblæd̪ər/ *n., v.,* cajolery; 'flattery, blustery talk, a gush of meaningless talk' (SOM, Kerry) < Ir *bladair* < ME *bladder, bledder* < OE *bledre*, bladder. 'He's all bladair,' he's all senseless talk. 'Bladar McHugh' – 'I do not know where McHugh came from but the phrase means "big mouth" – meaningless prattle' (SOM, Kerry). *See* BLATHER.

bladar, *see* BLADAIR.

bladhmann /'blaimən/ also **blyman** *n.,* bombast, boasting < Ir. 'If he spent more time working and less time bladhmanning he'd do a lot better for himself' (KG, Kerry).

blagard, *see* BLACKGUARD.

blain /bleːn/ *n.,* a sore, an ulcer; a disease in cattle < E dial. < OE *blegen*, pustule. 'That cow has the blain – you'd better call the vet.'

blarney /'blærni/ *n.,* sugary talk, flattery < place-name in Co. Cork. In 1602 Cormac Mac Carthaigh, who held Blarney Castle, famously duped Lord Carew, by cajoling speeches, into thinking he would get possession of it. 'Anyone would think you'd kissed the Blarney Stone, the talk that's coming out of you' (TJ, Sligo). Shaw, *John Bull's Other Island*, act I (*FDA*, 2, 432): "*Broadbent:* Very friendly of you, Larry, old man, but all blarney. I like blarney; but it's rot, all the same'"; Joyce, *Finnegans Wake,* 371.16: "grooves of blarneying" (song 'The Groves of Blarney'); 419.16: "The blarneyest blather in all Corneywall!"

blas /blɑs/ *n.* 1. Taste (SOM, Kerry); a nice taste (VQ, Kerry) < Ir. 'He always had a blas for the drink.' Joyce, *Finnegans Wake*, 235.3–4: "May thine evings e'en be blossful!" 2. Accent, pronunciation < Ir. 'She had the great Irish blas' (= she spoke perfect Irish). Egan, 'Wardsmaid in Dingle Hospital' (*Peninsula*, 82): "Hoh – ? she challenges | the question tossed in Irish by | an aged version of herself | . . . and her response comes in a swell | and the old Gaelic kingdom is there | in a *blas* never lost to schooling."

blast /blæʃt/ *n.,* a sudden attack of ill-health, a stroke, a sudden failure in a child's health; soreness of the eye; short-sightedness; blight (on potatoes) < E dial. < ME *blast,* sudden gust of wind. 'People get blasts in the eyes as they get older'; 'I got such a blast of a cold I had to stay in all week.'

bláthach /'blɔːhəx/ *n.,* buttermilk (SOM, Kerry) < Ir. 'She'd always have bláthach for us in a crock beside the dresser.'

blather /'blæd̪ər/ also **blither, blether** *n., v.,* a garrulous person who talks nonsense; to talk foolishly, incessantly < ME *bladder, bledder* < OE *bledre,* bladder (ModE *blather* is a variant of *bladder*). Yeats, *The Unicorn from the Stars,* act I (*Collected Plays,* 341): "*Thomas:* . . . you go falling into sleeps and blathering about dreams"; O'Casey, *The Plough and the Stars*, act II, 164: "*Fluther:* Will you stop your blatherin' for a minute, man"; Beckett, *Waiting for Godot,* 10: "*Estragon:* Ah stop blathering and help me off with this bloody thing"; McCourt, *Angela's Ashes,* 7: "You done enough damage with your blather, so shut your yap." *See* BLADAIR.

blather(come)skite /ˈblæd̪ər (kʌm)skait/ also **bletherum-skite, blather(um)skite** *n.,* a non-stop talker of nonsense < BLATHER (+ E *come*) + *skite* (origin obscure, but cf. *shit, v.,* to excrete). 'Well, I never heard such a blatherskite in all my born days.' Joyce, *Finnegans Wake,* 453.20–1: "Once upon a drunk and a fairly good drunk it was and the rest of your blatherumskite!" *See* SKITE[2].

bleacht /blæxt̪/ *n., adj.,* a large quantity, abundance; hospitable, generous < Ir. 'Bleacht is interchangeable with bleathach, a large quantity, esp. of money, a bleathach of produce' (SOM, Kerry, who adds: 'I would remember bleacht only in association with money).'

bléan /bleːn/ *n.,* groin (Mayo) < Ir *bléin.*

bleathach, *see* BLEACHT.

bleb /blɛb/ *n., v.,* blister (JMF, Cavan); to bubble up, come out in blisters < E dial. (perhaps from the action of the lips in making a bubble or a blob). 'Quick! Run cold water on it before you get a bleb'; 'It's only a bleb – it's no harm.' Heaney, 'North' (*North,* 20): "Keep your eye clear | as the bleb of the icicle."

Blessed Sacrament /blɛsəd ˈsækrɜmɛnt/ *n.,* the name given to the Sacrament of the Eucharist in which, under the appearances of bread and wine, the Body and Blood of Christ are substantially present; blessed < *bless v.*, to make holy (ultimately derived from OE *bletsian v.*, to bless, of which the root means blood, giving an original sense of to sprinkle and mark with blood as a sign of being hallowed) + sacrament < OF *sacrement n.*, rite. 'Don't forget to genuflect on your two knees when the Blessed Sacrament is exposed' (JF, Cavan).

bligeard /ˈblɪgərd/ *n.,* ruffian (SOM, Kerry), BLACKGUARD. 'That fella is a right bligeard' (KG, Kerry); 'He was a right bligeard, that fella, to go and steal money out of the till' (Mayo).

blirt /blʌrt/ *n.,* an outburst of tears; someone prone to bursting into tears (cf. Macafee: 'of a person, derogatory (*a*) a cry-baby; (*b*) a loud-mouth; (*c*) an untrustworthy fellow'). 'Don't be such a blirt.' Heaney, *The Midnight Verdict*, 32: "You've had your warnings, you coldrifed blirt" (*see* RIFE).

blithemeat /ˈblɑit̪miːt/ *n.,* the meal prepared for visitors on the birth of a child < E dial. (cf. *EDD*).

blob /blɑb/ *n.,* a blister, a bubble; a drop of liquid < E dial. (The *ODEE* notes: '. . . like the earlier *bluber, blober, blubber*, and the later synon. *bleb* [17th century], containing the symbolical consonant combination *bl-b*').

blobaire /ˈblʌbərə/ *n.,* a stammerer, 'a mumbler either by reason of mis-shapen or swollen lips or when a person cries and tries to speak simultaneously' (SOM, Kerry, who adds: 'blobarán, a mumbler, especially when applied to an adult') < Ir.

blobarán, *see* BLOBAIRE.

blogam, *see* BOLGAM.

blonog /ˈblʌnəg/ *n.,* grease, goose-grease (SOM, Kerry, who adds: 'rubbed into the uppers of boots to make them waterproof and pliable') < Ir *blonag.*

blossful, *see* BLAS.

blúirín /ˈbluːriːn/ *n.,* a little bit, a morsel < Ir. 'I only gave him a blúirín of cake – that won't kill him.'

bó /boː/ *n.,* cow < Ir. 'Is maith sú bó beo nó marbh' (proverb), The juice of a cow is good, dead or alive, i.e. it is always of use.

boast /boːst/ *adj.,* hollow; empty or decayed inside < E dial. (possibly < ME *borsten, v.,* to burst). 'That fruit is all boast, so it's no use for making the jam.'

boc /bʌk/ *n.,* a buck (SOM, Kerry); a playboy < Ir. 'He's a right boc, that fella' (SL, Mayo); 'The boc is just back from the States, swaggering around – he'll probably have all his money spent in a week' (KG, Kerry). *See* BOICLÉIM.

bocht /bʌkt̪/, /bʌxt̪/ *adj.,* poor < Ir. 'God be good to the old bocht man!' *See* BÉAL BOCHT.

bochtán /ˈbʌkt̪ɔːn/, /bʌxt̪ɔːn/ *n.,* a poor person; a beggar; a pathetic-looking person < Ir. 'ARRAH, that bochtán will do you no harm'; 'The bochtán deserves a home, like everyone else.'

bockety /ˈbɑkəti/ also **bacaidí** *adj.,* lame, unsteady, imperfect < Ir *bacaidí, n.,* a lame person or thing. 'It's all bockety' (said of a badly built hay or straw rick); 'He was bockety enough coming home last night' (LUB, Dublin); 'Be careful of that chair – it's got bockety legs' (SOC, Kerry); 'Watch that stool, it's a bit bacaidí' (MK, Galway). Purcell, *On Lough Derg*, 22: ". . . and further out the little businesses, upholstery workshops, bockety 'For Sale' signs on small houses." *See* BACACH.

boda bhóthair, *see* BOD AN BHÓTHAIR.

bodach /ˈbʌd̪əx/ also **badhach** *n.,* burly, robust countryman; clumsy fellow; an unintelligent person; an upstart, a churl (SOM,

Kerry, who adds: 'bodairleach, = nonsense, ill-founded statement (bodach + airleach), but with no hint of vulgarity if you tell somebody "That is bodairleach"' < Ir. 'What a bodach he is – he came all the way over here with the tractor and forgot the harvester!' It has been claimed that the American colloquial term 'buddy' (= pal) derives from 'bodach', but it is more likely to be a childish corruption of 'brother', or a corruption of 'booty'. Swift, *A Dialogue in Hybernian Stile*, 164: "A. What kind of a man is your neighbor squire Dolt? B. Why, a meer buddogh"; Joyce, *Ulysses*, 320. 20–1: "skivvies and badhachs from the county Meath."

bodachán /ˈbʌd̪əˈxɔːn/ *n.*, dimin. of BODACH (KG, Kerry) < Ir. 'He was a horrible small little bodachán of a maneen.' *See* MÍOLACH.

bodairleach, *see* BODACH.

bod an bhóthair /ˈbʌdəˈvoːhər/ also **boda bhóthair** *n.phr.*, an itinerant or travelling person; a silly person (usually a female) (SOM, Kerry) < Ir, vagrant (lit. churl of the road). 'That bod an bhóthair is here again – will you go out and tell him to clear off?' (Mayo).

bodhar /baur/ *n.*, deaf (SOM, Kerry) < Ir. 'That poor woman is bothered [deaf]. They call her Máire bodhairín' (Kerry). *See* BOTHER.

bodhrán[1] /ˈbaurɔːn/ *n.*, a deaf person (SOM, Kerry, who adds: 'I never heard it used to refer to a musical instrument'); a slow-witted, unrefined person; 'someone who wouldn't listen' (CS, Mayo) < Ir. 'He's an awful bodhrán – we'll have to get him a hearing aid from somewhere.'

bodhrán[2] /ˈbaurɔːn/ also **bowraun** *n.* 1. A shallow drum-shaped vessel, made of sheep-skin stretched over a frame, used for separating grain from chaff after flailing; a frame for carrying oats < Ir. 'After flailing, the grain is put into the bodhrán – a tall man was usually given the job: he tossed the grain away, into the wind. The chaff blew away, leaving the grain' (KM, Kerry). 2. A kind of tambourine < Ir. 'My sister tried her hand at the bowraun, but she soon tired at it' (Mayo). Montague, 'The Lure' (*Collected Poems*, 62): "the wail of tin | whistle climbs against fiddle and | the bodhrán begins." *See* BODHAR.

bodóg /ˈbʌdoːg/ *n.*, young cow; fig. a well-built young woman (MK, Galway) < Ir. 'He married a fine bodóg from Mullingar'; 'What were you doing with that bodóg last night?'

bog /bʌg/ *n.*, *adj.*, bog; soft (SOM, Kerry) < Ir. 'Vincent's drawing turf in the bog' (TF, Cavan). Heaney, 'Kinship'

(*North,* 41): "But *bog* | meaning soft, | the fall of windless rain, | pupil of amber."

bogach /ˈbʌgəx/ *n.,* 'bog-stuff before it is fashioned into sods; marshy boggy ground, a quagmire' (SOM, Kerry) < Ir.

bogach /ˈbʌgəx/ *n.,* marshy ground, in the phrase 'tóin [bottom] an bhogaigh', respelt as 'tanna bugger', 'a swallow-hole, a soft spot in the middle of a dry field, a marshy soft spot, a place into which an animal or tractor would sink. They were usually very dangerous' (RB, Waterford).

bogalore, *see* GALORE.

bogán /bʌˈgɔːn/ also **buggaun, buggeen** *n.,* an egg on which no shell has formed; fig. a 'softie', a person without much backbone (SOM, Kerry) < Ir *bogán.* 'I've never seen a buggaun, have you?' (Galway); 'Go on, you bogán, kick the ball' (Mayo).

bogtrotter /ˈbɑgtrɑtər/ *n.* (*pejor.*), a person with awkward manners, originally used of Irish people in general (because of the proliferation of bogs in rural Ireland) < Ir *bog. adj.*, soft + *trot(ter)* < ME *trotton, v.* < OF *troter, v.*; the term also draws attention to the fact that people can walk only awkwardly over the tufts in bogs, because the surface is so uneven (MK, Galway). 'Bog-trotters and YAHOOS – that's what they are, always up to no good!' McCourt, *Angela's Ashes,* 144: "That bloody ignorant bog-trotter."

bohaun /ˈbʌhɔːn/ also **bothán** *n.,* a modest dwelling; a hovel (SOM, Kerry); a little house or hut; a cabin; a stone hovel used by farmers in the summer when watching over their flocks on the mountain; a hut or small house, thatched, usually a hen-house (RB, Waterford) < Ir *bothán.* 'All they had is a little bohaun'; 'I heard someone is living in that bohaun up along the mountain.' *See* BOTHÁNTAÍOCHT.

bohereen, *see* BOREEN.

boicín /bʌˈkiːn/ *n.,* a term often used to reprimand a youth: an impish young fellow, a rake (SOM, Kerry, who adds: 'a term of disapproval – to a youth who doesn't know his place: "You are a boicín O'Meara" (whoever O'Meara was); "manly" is also used in this context, indicating being too pushy') < Ir (dimin. of BOC). 'You'd better stay quiet, you boicín!'

boicléim /ˈbʌkleːm/ *n.,* a sprightly jump; a bound; a frolic < Ir (cf. BOC). 'He was boicléiming out of his skin' (SOM, Kerry, who adds: 'literally, the leap of a buck; sometimes pocléimnigh' (the leap of a puck-goat).

boinn-leac /ˈbwɪnlæk/ *n.,* a blister, a sore on the sole of the foot; a bruise (JF, Cavan) < Ir *boinnleac.* 'I got a boinn-leac from walking on my bare feet, even though my mother said it would be good for me' (JF, Cavan).

bóithrín, *see* BOREEN.

boitíneach /bʌ'tiːnəx/ *n.,* 'a type of turf in which heather branches and roots remain intact (also may have a mud content)' (SOM, Kerry) < Ir.

boke /boːk/ *n., v.,* a belch; to vomit, retch; to get sick; to cough violently (JF, Dublin) < E dial. < ME *bolkin* < OE *bealcan*. 'They were boking all over the bus' (Dublin). 'Dry bokin', inclined to vomit but unable' (Traynor, Donegal, 29).

bolaistín /'bʌlə'ʃtiːn/ *n.,* well-built child (Galway) < Ir.

bold /boːld/ *adj.,* naughty, mischievous. In SE 'bold' is primarily associated with courageousness, but in HE the primary meaning (possibly with influence from Ir *dána, adj.,* bold, forward, audacious, daring) suggests mischievous behaviour. 'Bold boys used to make "scobs" (= faces) behind the teacher's back' (MOC, Limerick, who adds the expression 'stop scobbing at me'); 'The mother told her children not to be bold'; 'There go the Bold Fenian Men'. Leonard, *Out After Dark*, 82: "'Ah, Jasus. What beard?' 'Don't be bold. I mean, the beard you'll be wearing.'"

bolg /bʌləg/ *n.,* stomach; belly (SOM, Kerry) < Ir. 'That fella has a bolg the size of an ass' (BC, Meath).

bolgadán /'bʌləgəd̪ɔːn/ *n.,* a person with a big belly < Ir. 'That bolgadán would eat you out of house and home.'

bolgaire /'bʌləgərə/ n a stocky, fat person; a person with a prominent stomach (SOM, Kerry) < Ir. 'Yon bolgaire will never be fit enough to play on the team, although they say he can move a lot faster than you'd think' (Sligo).

bolgam /'bʌləgəm/ also **blogam** (SOM, Kerry) *n.,* a sup, a mouthful < Ir. 'Blogam of TAY' (SOM, Kerry).

bolgán béice /'bʌləgɔːn'beːkə/ *n.,* puff-ball; fig. a wind-bag < Ir. 'He turned out to be a right old bolgán béice at the meeting.'

bollaire /'bʌlərə/ *n.,* a boastful person < Ir. 'Shut up, you bollaire, we've had enough from you already.'

bollix /'bɑləks/ *n.* (*colloq.*), HE pronunciation of SE ballocks or bollocks, an expression of anger, or used perjoratively in reference to a stupid person < OE *beallucas*, testicles (the word 'ballock/bollock' did not become vulgar in SE until about the middle of the nineteenth century). 'The foreman's a right bollix.' Leonard, *Out After Dark*, 166: "Whereupon Behan unleashed the deafening roar of '*tuigim* me bollix!' and went on his way"; Joyce, *Ulysses*, 290.14: "Who's the old ballocks you were talking to?"; *Finnegans Wake*, 486.32: "Bellax, acting like a bellax"; Roche, *A Handful of Stars*, act I, i, 5: *"Stapler:* . . . Actin' the bollocks again are yeh?"

boneen /'bɑniːn/ also **bonneen** *n.*, piglet < Ir *bainbhín* (BANBH + dimin. suffix -ÍN). 'You have a nice litter of bonneens there.' Kickham, *Knocknagow*, 51: "Phil on this May evening carried a 'bonneen' under this arm."

bonham /'bɑnəm/ *n.*, a small pig, a sucking-pig < Ir BANBH. 'Are you going to keep them bonhams or sell them or what?' Healy, *Nineteen Acres*, 16: "It might be a cartload of bonhams in the fair of Charlestown."

bonnbhualadh /'bʌnvuələ/ also **boonwolla** *n.*, a blister on the side of the foot; a stone-bruise < Ir. 'Are those bonnbhualadhs you have on your feet?'

bonnive, see BANBH.

bonnloch /'bʌnləx/ *n.*, a callus, a sore on sole of foot (often caused by walking barefoot along the roads) < Ir *bonnleac*. 'She must have the bonnloch – she was lying in on the ditch when I saw her.'

bonnóg /bʌ'noːg/ also **bannock** *n.*, a scone; a cake of oat-bread < Ir. 'Make a few of those bonnógs for the tea.'

bonnyboblock /'bɑnibo'blɑk/, phonetic rendering of Ir *bainne bó bleacht,* primrose (DOS, Kerry).

bonnyclabber /'bɑniːklɑːbər/ *n.*, thick milk that could be used for churning < Ir *bainne clabair.* Dinneen, s.v. 'clabair, -air', gives 'sour thick milk; bainne clabair, id.'. The *EDD,* s.v. 'clabber[2]', gives: 'sour milk when it has grown thick and flaky.' O'Reilly's *Irish-English Dictionary,* s.v. 'clab' and 'claba', gives: '*adj.,* thick.' Kemp Malone, in *Celtica* 5 (1960), 142, suggests that bonnyclabber means 'milk of the churndash' (< Ir *clabaire*, cf. E *clapper*). Bliss (1979), 271, says this is 'probably the most frequently used Irish word in English writings of the seventeenth century.' Head, *Hic et Ubique*, 115: "Fuate shall my wife *Juane* do for de Cow dat make de buttermilk, and de bony clabber for dy child." *The Irish Hudibras*, 127: "My Banniclabber and Pottados." To make bonnyclabber, the basin of milk was skimmed at night, and then in the morning the night's milk was skimmed again, after which the cream was kept a day or two to thicken. The *EDD*, s.v. 'Bonny Clabber', cites an article in *Notes and Queries*, vol. 9 (1872), 297: "It is of a pleasant sub-acid taste, very agreeable to the palate."

boochalawn bwee /'buːhəlɔːn 'bwiː/ also **bouchaleen bwee** *n.*, ragwort < Ir *buachalán buí.* 'The river field is full of boochalawn bwee – it'll have to be cleared, so it will.'

booheeraun /'buərɔːn/ *n.*, dried cow-dung used as fuel (LUB, Dublin) < Ir *buarán*.

book /buːk/ *n.*, book, with reference to the textbook designated for a particular class at school < OE *boc* ('What book are you in?', what class are you in?), going back to the system of national schools established in 1831, when pupils were allowed to progress through school according to their knowledge of textbooks, prescribed and published by the Commissioners of National Education (GF, Galway). Synge, *The Playboy of the Western World,* act III (*FDA,* 2, 637): "*Mahon:* . . . and he a dunce never reached his second book"; O'Brien, *The Third Policeman,* 82: "'Nowadays,' said the Sergeant, 'it is nothing strange to see a class of boys at First Book'"; Kavanagh, *Tarry Flynn,* 26: "Tarry had no books except these and a couple of school readers. One was a famous Sixth Book which he had stolen from a neighbour's house some years before."

bool /buːl/ *n.,* the curved handle of a bucket, kettle, etc.; the handle of a cup or jug < E dial. 'You'll have to buy a new bucket – the bool is broken.'

booley /'buːli/ also **boley** *n., v.,* land, often quite distant from the homestead, to which cows were brought to graze and be milked during summer pasturage; enclosure; byre; the hut in which the herdsman stayed while minding the cattle; to herd cattle for such a purpose < Ir *buaile*. 'They used to go booleying in the summer'; 'I think it's time to bring the cows out to the booley this evening after the milking' (Sligo). 'Booly dogs', Irish-American slang for the police (from Peter Quinn, *Banished Children of Eve*, 1994) – connection with buaile is uncertain (BT, Dublin).

boolthaun /'buːlt̪ɔːn/ *n.,* the striking part of a flail (CS, Mayo) < Ir *buailteán.* 'He attached the boolthaun to the handle with a strip of eel-skin' (TF, Cavan). Martin, 'Some Peculiarities of Speech Heard in Breifny', 178, notes that the 'flail has the "middhilin" (E. Cavan) or "tug" (W. Cavan) or "gad" (Leitrim) – names for a very tough piece of skin (usually eel or black sally) which joins together the staff and "bowlteen" (buail, to strike).'

boon /buːn/ *n.,* a party of men, usually neighbouring farmers, helping each other out during harvests etc.; a band of workers < ME *boone*, a prayer, favour. 'In my time they still had the boon for the harvest, but you don't see it any more.' *See* MEITHEAL.

bórach /'borəx/ *adj.,* bandy-legged (SOM, Kerry), bow-legged < Ir.

bórachán /'borəxɔːn/ *n.,* bandy-legged person (SOM, Kerry) < Ir. 'That bórachán is as bandy-legged as an old terrier.'

bord /boːrd̪/ *n.,* table; board (statutory) < Ir. An Bord Pleanála /plæn'ɔːlə/, the Planning Board; 'It was passed by An Bord Pleanála, but it's a queer decision and no mistake.'

boreen /'boːriːn/ also **bohereen** *n.,* country lane; small seldom-used road, usually with grass growing up the middle < Ir BÓITHRÍN (dimin. of BÓTHAR). 'Turn left until you come to a boreen, and she lives down there.' Carleton, 'The Hedge School' (*Six Irish Tales*, 150): "About two hundred yards above this, the *boreen*, which led from the village to the main road, crosses the river, by one of those old narrow bridges"; Stoker, *The Snake's Pass,* 173: "suppose we see them down the boreen"; Stephens, *The Crock of Gold,* 172: "They swept through the goat tracks and the little boreens"; Healy, *Nineteen Acres,* 70: "between the bottom of the boreen and the cottage at the top of the hill."

borry, borrow, *see* FOLLY.

bosthoon /'bɑst̪uːn/ also **bostoon** *n.,* idle, foolish, brainless, good-for-nothing person; ignorant lout < Ir *bastún.* 'Only a bosthoon would do that!'; 'You bosthoon, you, what are you doing in my toolbox? Get out of that!' Shaw, *John Bull's Other Island,* act II (*FDA*, 2, 437): "*Keegan:* You bosthoon, you!"; Joyce, *Ulysses,* 240.4–5: "Some Tipperary bosthoon endangering the lives of the citizens"; O'Brien, *A Pagan Place,* 49: "She said what bosthoons you all were to know no Latin and no Greek."

botán /'bʌt̪ɔːn/ *n.,* a small bundle of straw < Ir. 'Put a botán of straw under the calf before you leave the byre, will you?'

bothán, *see* BOHAUN.

bothántaíocht /bʌ'hɔːnt̪iːəxt̪/ *n.,* the practice of visiting neighbouring houses to chat or play cards (SOM, Kerry, who adds: 'while the word obviously relates to BOTHÁN, there is no connotation of a poor-quality dwelling – more the opposite, since hospitality was more forthcoming in the houses of the better off') < Ir. DOH adds that it is a west Kerry usage. *See* CÉILÍ; COORJEEKING; RAMBLING.

bóthar /'boːhər/ *n.,* road (SOM, Kerry); STREET < Ir. 'I saw him just now síos an bóthar [down the road]'; 'Go n-éirí an bóthar leat,' good luck on the road, have a pleasant journey; 'Is é an bóthar mór an t-aicearra' (proverb), The main road is the shortest way.

bóthar aimhleasa /boːhər 'ævləsə/ *n.,* the road to ruin < Ir. 'He took the bóthar aimhleasa.'

bother /'bɑd̪ər/ *n., v.,* noise; state of being vexed; to vex; to trouble oneself to do something (cf. Ir *bodhaire,* deafness; hence 'bothered' in HE can mean deaf). 'Bothered. Deaf. "Are you bothered or what kind of lugs have you?"' (LUB, Dublin).

The common HE phr. 'no bother' means 'it's no trouble' (to do something) (origin obscure, but possibly *bother* might be the Irish way of pronouncing the English *n.* 'pother', choking, smoky or dusty atmosphere; flustering situation; cf. the alternative spellings in such words as *pardóg/bardóg, n.,* pannier). 'How's she cuttin' [how are you]?' – 'Not a bother on me [I'm fine].' Joyce, *Finnegans Wake,* 467.15: "Woowoolfe Woodenbeard, that went stomebathred."

bothóg /'bʌhoːg/ *n.,* shanty, hovel < Ir. 'You'll have to bulldoze that bothóg before you start reclaiming.'

bothrán /'baurɔːn/ *n.,* alternative spelling for BODHRÁN. 'There's not much to playing the bothrán. I could nearly do it myself.'

bottheen /'bɑt̪iːn/, /'bɑtʃiːn/ *n.,* a small stick, a cudgel; one who wields such a stick, a ruffian < Ir *baitín.* 'He's a right little bottheen' (BC, Meath).

bottom /'bɑtəm/ *n.,* a spool of thread, etc. < E dial. < OE *botm.* 'Get the bottom out of the box – I have to start darning again' (KG, Kerry).

botún /bʌ't̪uːn/ *n.,* a mistake (SOM, Kerry) < Ir. 'If you make another botún like the last one you'll be hearing from me, so you will.'

botúnach /bʌ't̪uːnəx/ *n.,* silly, unfortunate person < Ir *botúnach, adj.,* blundering. 'The botúnach should never have moved back to the father's place' (Mayo).

bouchal /'buəkəl/, /'buəxəl/ *n.,* boy, youth; young unmarried man < Ir *buachaill.*

bowler /'baulər/ *n.* (*colloq.*), a dog (CS, Dublin) (origin obscure).

bowling /'baulən/ *v.n.,* a game, popular in Co. Cork, played with an iron ball thrown along a road, over a course of about three miles; the lowest number of throws wins < E dial. *bowl, bowling* (a game played with a stone ball over a set course, the prize going to the player with the smallest number of throws) < F *boule* < L *bulla.* 'I was down in Cork at a bowling festival the other weekend and, do you know, it was great fun ALTOGETHER.'

bowraun *see* BODHRÁN.

bowsie /'bauzi/ *n.,* a disreputable drunkard, a lout, a quarrelsome drunkard < ME *bousen, v.,* to drink to excess. 'Bowsying around' (PON, Dublin); 'Let's not go to that pub – it's full of bowsies' (Dublin). Leonard, *Out After Dark,* 166: "Behan . . . had been an inmate . . . of both Borstal in England and Mountjoy in Dublin. Such credentials defined him as a 'character', which is usually a Dublinese synonym for a bowsie or a GURRIER"; Doyle,

The Van, 240: "'Bloody bowsies,' he said, and he threw a J-cloth onto the floor"; Durcan, 'The Marriage Contract' (*FDA,* 3, 1399): "What a noble, handsome soul she is I And what a bowsy her ex-husband was."

box /bɑks/ *v.,* in the expression 'to box the fox', to raid an orchard; origin obscure (LUB, Dublin, notes it as 'an Irish slang expression since the eighteenth century'). 'We had a character, a great man for "boxing" gardens, but he would only take certain apples' (Nolan, *The Changing Face of Dundrum,* 151).

boxty /'bɑksti/ *n.,* dish made from raw potatoes grated into a mixture of oatmeal or flour and fried in butter or baked on a griddle; potato cake (MOB, Mayo) < Ir *bacstaí.* 'My mother still makes boxty every time I go home' (Mayo). McCourt, *Angela's Ashes,* 46: "'Would you like boxty?' Malachy says, 'What's boxty?' Dad laughs. 'Pancakes, son. Pancakes made with potatoes.'"

boy /bɑi/ *voc.,* in general use of males of any age. '"ARRAH, keep the change, boy," the Corkman said' (Dublin).

boycott /'bɔikɑt/ *n., v.,* refusal to co-operate; to exclude from all social or commercial intercourse (GF, Galway) < Capt. Charles Cunningham Boycott (1832–1897), landowner and Mayo agent of Lord Erne, of Corrymore House, near Lough Mask, Co. Mayo, whose oppressed tenants and workmen as well as local business-people embarked on a celebrated policy of non-cooperation on his estate in the autumn of 1880; he left Ireland for good in 1886. 'Of course, I don't have to mention Captain Boycott, but who was he?' (AMW, Cork).

boyo /'baioː/ *n.,* affectionate term for a country fellow; a tough person < E *boy* + Ir affectionate suffix *-ó* (cf. *a mhic ó: see* AVICK). 'Go on out of that, you boyo, you haven't seen the back of me yet.' Stephens, *The Crock of Gold,* 119: "'Now, then, my young boy-o,' said the sergeant, 'none of that violence'"; O'Casey, *The Plough and the Stars,* act II, 163: *"Fluther:* . . . where th' slim thinkin' counthry boyo ud limp away from th' first faintest touch of compromization!"; Deane, *Reading in the Dark,* 113: "What's brought me here, Sergeant, is a request from His Lordship, the Bishop, that this boyo here should be brought to apologise to you."

brablach /'brɑbləx/ *n.,* rabble < Ir. 'When the brablach got going the whole place was wrecked in half an hour' (BC, Meath).

bráca /'brɔːkə/ *n.,* hut, hovel, lean-to (JOC, Kerry) < Ir. 'We had to stay in the bráca for the night because the weather was so bad.'

brácálaí /brɔːˈkɔːliː/ *n.*, awkward worker, drudge < Ir.

brack[1] /bræk/ *n.*, flaw, defect, in the phrase 'there's not a brack on it,' said of an article that is in good condition though not new < E dial. 'Brack in this sense is general in English dialects' (LUB, Dublin).

brack[2], *see* BARMBRACK; BREAC.

bracked, *see* BRACKEN.

bracken /ˈbrækən/ sometimes **brack** or **bracked** *n.*, marks on the shins caused by the heat of a fire (see Conway, 3). 'Bracked', applied to cattle, 'also to shins *breaced* from fire' (EMF, Westmeath). *See* ABCS; BRECKED.

brad(d)ach /ˈbrædəx/ *n., adj.*, thief; thieving, trespassing < Ir *bradach.* The word is normally applied to farm animals or fowl (SOM, Kerry): 'braddach cows are a damn nuisance' (Ir *an bhó bhradach,* the thieving cow). Joyce, *Finnegans Wake,* 616.31: "No brad wishy washy wathy wanted neither!"

brais /bræʃ/ *n.*, a squally shower of rain, sudden heavy shower of rain < Ir. 'Better take the coat in case there's a brais' (BC, Meath).

branar /ˈbrɑnər/ *n.*, land that is ploughed or grubbed before it is seeded (SOM, Kerry) < Ir. 'He has the land branar already.'

braoinín /ˈbreːniːn/ *n.*, a small quantity; a drop (TJ, Sligo) < Ir (dimin. of BRAON). 'I'll have a braoinín of whiskey, MÁS É DO THOIL É.'

braon /breːn/ *n.*, a drop < Ir. 'Will you give me a braon bainne [drop of milk] for the tea?' (KG, Kerry).

braon istigh /breːnəˈʃtɪg/ *adj., phr.,* fairly inebriated, 'having a good drop on board', having had a good drop taken (SOM, Kerry) < Ir. 'Braon istigh he was last night – you've never seen the like of the damage he did.'

brat /bræt/ *n.* 1. Cloak; apron (AKB, Antrim); covering; mantle, robe (SOM, Kerry) < Ir *brat.* 2. *Pejor.,* an unruly child (origin obscure, but cf. ME *bratt,* coarse mantle, rag, and Ir *brat,* mantle, apron, coarse cloth). 'You little brat – get out of here quick' (KG, Kerry).

bratóg /ˈbrɑt̪oːg/ *n.,* a rag < Ir. 'You'll get this bratóg across the face if you don't leave me alone' (Mayo).

brave /breːv/ *adj., adv.,* used as an intensive < F *brave*. 'That's brave weather,' it's a fine day. 'That's a brave lock of hay on yon tractor – I suppose he's rushing to beat the rain. There's a big spill [downpour] coming' (TF, Cavan). 'Brave and early', very early. 'He'll have to be up brave and early to be there on time.' Sheehan, *Glenanaar*, 92: "''Twas a brave ride, surely,' said the old man"; Kavanagh, 'Art McCooey' (*Collected Poems*, 77): "The sun sinks low and large behind the hills of

Cavan, | a stormy-looking sunset. 'Brave and cool.'"

breac[1] /bræk/ also **brack** *n.,* a speck of dust (SOM, Kerry); a spot, a mark, a sign of wear < Ir. 'Not a brack on it,' it's quite new (PON, Dublin).

breac[2] /bræk/ *n.,* a fish; a trout (SOM, Kerry) < Ir. 'He caught a fine breac and we had it for the breakfast the next morning' (SL, Mayo). 'Éist le glór na habhann agus gheobhaidh tú breac' (proverb), Listen to the sound of the river and you'll get a trout.

breall /bræl/ *n.,* imperfection, disfigurement, blemish (SOM, Kerry) < Ir.

breallaire /ˈbrɑːlərə/ *n.,* silly talker; careless worker (SOM, Kerry) < Ir.

brecked /brɛkt/ *adj.,* spotted < Ir *breac*. 'A nice brecked cow' (BC, Meath). *See* BRACKEN.

breezheen /briːˈʒiːn/ *n.,* a little breeze < E *breeze* + dimin. suffix -EEN. 'There's a bit of a breezheen blowing' (KG, Kerry).

brehon /ˈbrɛhən/ *n.,* a judge in early mediaeval Ireland < Ir *breitheamh*. 'Brehon laws', system of laws operating up to 17th century. Joyce, *Finnegans Wake*, 608.2–3: "as accorded to by moisturologist of the Brehons Assorceration for the advauncement of scayence."

brí /briː/ *n.,* hill < Ir. 'He's up on the brí – that's where you'll find him' (Cork).

bricín /ˈbrɪkiːn/ *n.,* a small trout; a minnow (SOM, Kerry) < Ir (dimin. of BREAC). 'The river near the house was always full of bricíns' (TF, Cavan).

brídeog /ˈbriːʤoːg/ *n.,* an image of St Brigid in the form of a doll or made of sheep's wool etc. < Ir. 'Brídeoging' *v.n.,* going in disguise from house to house on St Brigid's Day (1 February) gathering money. 'There was a brídeog in every window on the first of February' (TJ, Sligo). *See* BIDDYS, BIDDY-BOYS.

brief /briːf/ *adj.,* (of diseases) rife, prevalent < E dial. (origin obscure). 'Said only of epidemics, as in "influenza is very brief" (general in Eng. and Amer. dialects)' (LUB, Dublin).

brilleáil /ˈbrɪlɔːl/ *n.,* silly talk; tactlessness < Ir. 'Don't listen to a word of his brilleáil' (TJ, Sligo).

bring /brɪŋ/ *v.,* to take, fetch < E dial. < OE *bringan*, to bring, lead, bear, carry. 'Bring me to the films'; 'I'll bring you to the airport' (SE prefers 'take'). Kickham, *Knocknagow*, 8: "'I'll bring you to hunt the WRAN,' said Barney."

briosclán /ˈbrɪskəlɔːn/ *n.,* silverweed < Ir. 'I'll have to pull up that briosclán one of these days.'

briotach /ˈbrɪt̪əx/ *adj.,* lisping (MK, Galway) < Ir. 'Here he comes with that briotach voice of his looking for something or other.'

brobh /brʌv/ *n.,* a rush (plant) < Ir. 'Tiomsaíonn brobh beart' (proverb), Every mickle makes a muckle, Many a little makes a lot.

brocais /'brʌkəʃ/ *n.,* a person of dirty, lazy appearance < Ir. 'They say that brocais is getting married – he must have more money than he lets on.'

brock[1] /brɑk/ *n.,* a badger < Ir *broc*. 'The dogs tore the brock to bits down in the field – I felt sorry for the poor creature' (Kerry).

brock[2] /brɑk/ *n.* (*pejor.*), **brocky** *adj.,* a person with a pock-marked face; pock-marked (perhaps < Ir *broc*, badger). 'Clever Goldsmith was a brock.'

brock[3] /brɑk/ *n.*, a scrap of bread or meat; broken victuals < E dial. (*EDD* cites OE *brocca* (*dative. pl.*), fragments; *OED* gives 'brock' as a dialectal variant of 'broke' < OE *gebroc*, fragment); *v.,* 'to feed pigs with tea-bags, etc.' 'Brockman', one who feeds the pigs (Derry).

bróg /broːg/ also **brogue** *n.,* a kind of old-fashioned shoe < Ir *bróg*. 'Look at the hole in her bróg'; 'He's as ignorant as a KISH of brogues'; 'There's never an old bróg but there's the shape of a foot in it.' Joyce, *Finnegans Wake,* 14.2–4: "Kish . . . small illigant brogues'; 83.13: "kish his sprogues." *See* BROGUE.

broghais /brauʃ/ *n.,* any filthy, straggling thing; a large dirty woman < Ir. 'Look at the old broghais – God knows what all the CHILDER will turn out like.'

brogue /broːg/ *n.* 1. A stout shoe < Ir *bróg*. 2. The Irish way of speaking English < Ir *bróg,* shoe, or *barróg,* speech impediment. There is a view that Irish people used to speak English unintelligibly (as a result of linguistic contamination from Irish syntax and vocabulary), and the effect was as if they had a shoe on their tongue: cf. Breval, *The Play is the Plot,* 158: "ARRAH, is not the Brogue upon [your] Tongue." Gerard Murphy (*Éigse,* vol. 3 (1941–42), 231–9) notes that Irish literature has no phrase resembling the English 'he speaks with a brogue,' queries the connection between *bróg* and *barróg*, and draws attention to Dinneen: "barróg: . . . defective acentuation, hence the Anglo-Irish word *brogue*; barróg teangan: a lisp.' Osborn Bergin (*Éigse,* vol. 3 (1941–42), 237–9) notes the connection between OE *broc,* ON *brók* ('breeches' in ModE pl. form) and Gaelic *bráca*, hose, trousers, and states that 'bróg cannot have been originally an Irish word . . . Bróg must formerly have had a wider meaning than at present.' Sheridan, *The Brave Irishman,* 168: "*Sconce:* An Irishman! Sir, I should not suspect that; you have not the least bit of the brogue about you. *Captain:*

Brogue! No, my dear; I always wear shoes, only now and then when I have boots on." Carleton, 'The Hedge School' (*Six Irish Tales*, 163): "Kicking on the shins with the point of a brogue or shoe, bound round the edge of the sole with iron nails, until the bone was laid open, was a common punishment" (*see* HEDGE-SCHOOL); Joyce, *Finnegans Wake,* 581. 16–17: "the yet unregendered thunderslog, whose sbrogue cunneth none lordmade undersiding"; Brown, *Down All the Days,* 218: "He had a thick West of Ireland brogue."

bromach /ˈbrʌməx/ *n.,* a colt, fig. a well-built youngster (with a hint of being uncouth) (SOM, Kerry).

brón /broːn/ *n.,* sorrow < Ir. 'There's not a brón on her [a widow], i.e. she shows no signs of grief after her husband' (EMF, Westmeath).

brosna /ˈbrʌsnə/ also **brustna, brusna, bresna** *n.,* a bundle of sticks or broken branches or little pieces of wood used for kindling; small scraps of turf (SOM, Kerry) < Ir *brosna.* 'Go out along the hedges and get some brusna to light the fire.'

brothall /ˈbrʌhəl/ *n.,* hot (clammy) weather; clear, warm sunshine (SOM, Kerry) < Ir. 'A fine spell of brothall.'

brothallach /ˈbrʌhələx/ *adj.,* very warm, sultry (SOM, Kerry) < Ir. 'It's very brothallach today – I think I'll go down to the STRAND for a swim.'

Brothers, *see* CHRISTIAN BROTHERS.

broughan /ˈbrɑhən/ also **broghan, brohan, brawn** *n.,* porridge, oatmeal stirabout; gruel, 'applied only to very thin porridge contemptuously' (EMF, Westmeath) < Ir *brachán.* 'Have a bowl of broughan – it'll do you good.'

bru /bruː/ *n.* (*colloq.*), unemployment benefit, the dole (from a mispronunciation of *bureau,* as in 'welfare bureau'). 'He's on the bru again'; 'He's been on the bru for the last five years.' In Belfast the word is given the same pronunciation as Bórú in the name Brian Bórú, and a Belfast person would thus say that he or she is 'on the Brian' (see Tomelty, 70).

bruach /bruəx/ also **bruagh, broch** *n.,* fig. a ring or halo around the moon presaging unsettled weather; sign of rain coming < Ir *bruach,* border. 'There's a bruagh out tonight' (TF, Cavan).

brúitín /ˈbruːʧiːn/ *n.,* potatoes mashed with milk for young children < Ir. 'Eat up your brúitín or I'll give you a clatter' (BC, Meath).

brus /brʌs/ also **bruss, briss** *n.,* dust, turf mould (SOM, Kerry), small dry bits < Ir *brus.* 'Go out and get some brus to start a fire' (RB, Waterford); 'He made brus of it' (SOC, Cork), he beat it into small fragments, made a mess of it, botched it. 'He made brus of him, I tell you' (TJ, Sligo), he routed him, in argument or fisticuffs.

bruscar /'brʌskər/ *n.,* mould; rubbish < Ir. 'Bruscar (móna)', turf mould. 'Sweep that bruscar up from around the fire.'

buachaill /'buəkəl/, /'buəxəl/ *n.,* a boy; a young unmarried man < Ir. 'They have a fine buachaill working for them at the minute, but I think he's going to emigrate to the States, more's the pity, for them and the local team.' Sheehan, *Glenanaar*, 127: "And was that what you called a great chance, me *buachaill*?" 'Buachaill aimsire', a hired male labourer on an eleven-month system of employment (1 February to 24 December), then seven days off during Christmas, but this had to be made up by working one week during January; 'cailín aimsire', likewise (SOM, Kerry). 'Buachaill bréige', a beggar at a wedding < Ir.

buachalán buí /'buəkəlɔːn 'bwiː/, /'buəxəlɔːn'bwiː/ *n.,* ragwort (SOM, Kerry); yellow weed (VQ, Kerry) < Ir. 'I'm fed up pulling these buachaláns.'

buadán /'buəd̪ɔːn/ also **boodhawn** *n.,* the stump of a cow's horn; the bandage on a dehorned animal < Ir. 'You better put a buadán on that animal – she's losing a lot of blood' (SL, Mayo).

buaile /'buəljə/ also **booley, boolie** *n.* 1. An enclosed space outside a cowshed, including barn and dung-heap; enclosure for cattle before being housed (SOM, Kerry); a yard for cows (CS, Mayo) < Ir. 2. Fig. a bed < Ir. 'He didn't leave the buaile yet today,' he hasn't got up yet (SOM, Kerry).

buaileam sciath /'buələm'ʃkiː/ *n.,* a boaster (MK, Galway) < Ir. 'There's too much of the buaileam sciath in him for my liking.'

buailtín /'buəltʃiːn/ also **boolteen, booltheen, bowlteen** *n.* 1. Part of a flail (also *buailteán*) (EMF, Westmeath). 2. A beetle (implement for pounding potatoes etc.). 3. A yard for threshing < Ir. *See* BOOLTHAUN.

buaircín /buər'kiːn/ *n.* 1. A bung or stopper in a churn (SOM, Kerry). 2. A piece of wood put on the horns of a wicked cow (JOM, Kerry) < Ir. 'Is that a buaircín he has on that cow over there?'

bualadh /'buələ/ *n.,* beating, striking < Ir. 'When two men were using flails in the lár of sheaves they had to time their strikes on the sheaves. Each struck a 'bualadh', but not together. "Time the bualadh, and don't break my flail!"' (KM, Kerry).

bualadh bas /'buələ'bʌs/ *n.,* clapping of hands < Ir. 'A big bualadh bas for that performance' (Dublin).

buarán /ˈbuːrɔːn/ also **boorawn** *n.,* dried cow-dung (used as fuel) < Ir. 'I even remember my grandmother telling me that some children used to bring buaráns to school instead of turf' (JF, Cavan).

buckaun /ˈbʌkɔːn/ *n.,* a hinge-hook (MK, Galway; MK, Kerry) < Ir BACÁN. 'We'll never get another buckaun for this door – what do you think, Pat?'

buddogh, *see* BODACH.

buggaun, buggeen, *see* BOGÁN.

buí /bwiː/ *adj.,* yellow; tawny; jaundiced (SOM, Kerry) < Ir. 'He had a buí look about him.'

builín /ˈbɪliːn/ *n.,* a loaf < Ir. 'Quick, run down to the shop for a builín before the men come in.'

buimiléir /ˈbɪməleːr/ *n.,* a stupid man < Ir.

buinne /ˈbɪnə/ *n.,* the border of a CREEL < Ir. 'Only fill it up to the buinne – the donkey is getting old' (BC, Meath).

buinneach /ˈbɪnəx/ also **binnagh** *n.,* diarrhoea < Ir. 'He's had the buinneach ever since he came back from his holidays' (Mayo).

buinneán /ˈbɪnɔːn/ *n.,* a tender shoot, a young sapling < Ir.

búiste /ˈbuːʃʧə/ also **booshta** *n.,* a large, lazy man; an uncouth person, a boor < Ir. 'He'll not hire that búiste again' (TF, Cavan).

bull /bʌl/ *v.,* to serve a cow < E dial. < ME *bole*; used in the colloq. phr. '"Nearly" never bulled a cow,' No approximation is equal to the real thing. 'A cow is said to be bulling when she shows signs of being in heat' (MOC, Limerick).

bullán /bʌˈlɔːn/ *n.,* a bullock (SOM, Kerry) < Ir. 'Be careful when you're tying that bullán – he's very cross.'

bulling /ˈbʌlən/ *pres.part.,* angry. 'I was boolin' (HJ, Wexford); 'He was bulling (with rage) when he'd heard what they'd done' (MOC, Limerick, who writes: 'A cow is said to be bulling when she shows signs of being in heat (cf. Ir. *ar buile*, mad, furious)').

bundún /bʌnˈd̪uːn/ *n.,* bottom, rear end < Ir. 'As I plucked the goose, Gran said: "Widen the bundún with your knife and pull out the innards"' (KM, Kerry); 'Putting out one's bundún,' making a great effort (SOM, Kerry, who adds: 'no hint of vulgarity in normal usage, which was frequent and common to many speakers').

bunóc /bʌˈnoːk/ *n.,* an infant, a new-born baby (SOM, Kerry) < Ir. 'What a lovely bunóc.'

búrdún /ˈbuːrd̪uːn/ *n.,* lampoon (normally in verse form); gossip (SOM, Kerry) < Ir *burdún,* refrain (cf. E *burthen*), gossip. 'He read out the new búrdún'; 'Tell us the búrdún.'

bush /bʌʃ/ *n.,* in the phrase 'put a bush in the gap,' close the door.

but /bʌt/ *adv.,* < E. Used to express emphasis at end of statements such as 'It is, but'; 'It's a great day, but.' Paulin, *Seize the Fire,* 31: *"Prometheus:* So I'd a big head? | And who wouldn't? | I'm trapped but"; Doyle, *The Van,* 123: "Make it Guinness but, will yeh"; 216: "'What abou' the sweet but?' said Jimmy Sr. 'The ice-cream'll be water by the time they've got through their main stuff.'" Also used as a conjunction heading clauses after negative verbs: 'There isn't a student in the class but has a cough.' Sheridan, *The Brave Irishman,* 166: *"Captain:* . . . there ishn't one of these SPALPEENS that has a cabbin upon a mountain . . . but will be keeping a goon."

butt[1] /bʌt/ *n.,* a basket < E dial. (cf. *wine butt* < OF *botte?*). 'A butt of potatoes', a small bag of potatoes, or an ordinary-sized bag partly full of potatoes (GF, Galway).

butt[2] /bʌt/ *n.,* the end of anything (e.g. sheaf of corn) < E dial. (origin obscure). 'Leave me the butt of that cigarette.' Synge, *In the Shadow of the Glen* (*FDA*, 2, 634): *"Dan:* . . . or the big spiders, maybe, and they putting their webs on her, in the butt of a ditch."

butt[3] /bʌt/ *n.,* a cart; 'a sort of cart boarded at bottom and all round the sides, 15 or 18 inches deep, for potatoes, sand, etc.' (Limerick) < E. dial (*EDD* s.v. 'butt sb.[3]' gives 'a heavy two-wheeled cart made to tip'). "In Cork any kind of horse-cart or donkey-cart is called a *butt,* which is a departure from the (English) etymology. In Limerick any kind of cart except a butt is called a *car;* the word *cart* is not used at all' (PWJ, 228); 'Tackle up the donkey and butt and we'll go to the fair' (Beecher, 12)

butthoon /bʌˈt̪uːn/ *n.,* blunder < Ir *botún.* 'They made a complete butthoon of it' (KG, Kerry).

butty[1] /ˈbʌti/ *n., v.,* companion, mate (origin obscure: cf. *buddy* ?< ME *budde,* bud); to be in company with. 'They're great butties.' O'Casey, *Juno and the Paycock,* act I, 12: *"Boyle:* He's a butty o' yours, isn't he?"; Plunkett, *Farewell Companions,* 107: "There's a particular butty of mine in there." "Two men or two boys are often spoken of as 'buttying for years'" (PON, Dublin). *See* BODACH.

butty[2] /ˈbʌti/ *adj.,* difficult, awkward. 'I got it very butty to lift it up on the cart' (PON, Dublin).

C

cab /kæb/ *n.,* mouth; toothless mouth; sunken jaw (SOM, Kerry) < Ir. 'Such a cab she has on her for gossip.' 'Cab-jaw', a talkative young person.

cabach /'kɑbəx/ *adj.,* talkative; sunken-lipped < Ir. 'She's very cabach,' said of a child who listens to what older people say and repeats it elsewhere. 'Well, she's such a cabach when she has a few drinks on her – she'd talk all night' (Kildare).

cabaire /'kɑbərə/ *n.,* talkative (usually not sensible) young person, precocious person (SOM, Kerry); babbler < Ir. 'He's a great cabaire when the pints are on the table' (Mayo).

cábóg /kɔː'boːg/ *n. (pejor.),* ignorant male; 'a rustic or ignorant fellow' (VQ, Kerry); a clown (SOM, Kerry); a countryman – used as a term of derison (KM, Kerry) < Ir. 'What a cabóg he is.'

cábún /kɔː'buːn/ *n.,* a capon; fig. effeminate male (KM, Kerry) < Ir. 'That son of hers is a bit of a cábún – the way he swaggers around, it's a holy show.'

cabús /kə'buːs/ *n.,* caboose; fig. a nook on each side of an open fire in which tea etc. was left to keep dry < Ir. 'Put it in the cabús in the corner' (BC, Meath).

cac /kæk/ *n.,* excrement < Ir. 'Make sure there's no cac on your shoes before you come in – I'm just after washing the floor' (Cork). *See* MO CHAC ORT.

cacamas /'kɑkəməs/ *n.,* fit of bad temper < Ir. 'Such a cacamas out of him when he found out what happened to the car – I never seen him so angry before' (Limerick).

cadge /kædʒ/ *v.,* to beg (origin obscure). 'Toucher: someone who tries to "touch" you (i.e. cadge) for money' (KD, Dublin).

cadráil /'kɑd̪ərɔːl/ *n.,* empty chatter, gossip (HC, Cork), long-winded talk (SOC, Cork) < Ir. 'Cadrálaí', one given to foolish prattling (SOM, Kerry) < Ir. 'Cadaráiling' *v.n.,* idle gossiping, chattering, foolish prattling (VQ, Kerry) < Ir *cadráil* + E *-ing*. 'Stop your cadaráiling and come over here (TJ, Sligo).

Sheehan, *Glenanaar*, 128: "I'm thinkin' if you spind much more time in codrawlin', ye'll be lookin' for a needle in a bundle of straw, whin you search for the lambs this awful night."

caffler /'kæflər/ *n.*, a disagreeable, cheeky, quarrelsome little fellow < E dial. (cf. *cavil, v.*, to split hairs, to jest, etc. < OF *caviller*). 'That fellow is a caffler' (Beecher, Cork). 'Caffling' /'kæflən/ *v.n.*, playing practical jokes or pranks. 'If he keeps that caffling up I'll put the smile on the other side of his jaw' (BC, Meath).

cág /kɔːg/ *n.*, a jackdaw (SOM, Kerry); fig. an empty, talkative person < Ir. 'That cág would keep you talking for ages.'

caibín /'kɑbiːn/ *n.*, small mouth (MK, Galway) < Ir (dimin. of CAB). 'She'd put a big smudge of lipstick on her little caibín of a mouth' (JF, Cavan).

caid /kɑʤ/ *n.*, a hybrid game akin to rugby and GAELIC FOOTBALL (MK, Galway) < Ir *caid*, football.

caifirín /'kæfəriːn/ *n.*, small headscarf; kerchief < Ir. 'I'd better take a caifirín with me – it might rain' (KG, Kerry).

cáil /kɔːl/ *n.*, reputation < Ir. 'Má tá cáil an mhochéirí ort féadfaidh tú codladh go headra' (proverb), If you have the reputation of early rising you can sleep till midday.

caile /'kæljɛ/ *n.*, wench < Ir. 'Come over here, a chaile, and tell me what's your name' (BC, Meath).

cailey, *see* CÉILÍ.

cailín /'kɑliːn/, /kɑ'liːn/ also **colleen** *n.*, girl, maiden (SOM, Kerry) < Ir. 'She's a nice little colleen, whoever gets her' (BC, Meath); 'Gruth do Thadhg agus meadhg do na cailíní' (proverb), The best of everything for the menfolk (lit. Curds for Tadhg [typical man's name] and whey for the girls). Joyce, *Finnegans Wake*, 12.21: "like so many heegills [?Ir *buachaill*, boys + *-s*] and collines." 'Cailín óg', girl (SOM, Kerry, who adds: 'sometimes with a sinister connotation that she might know more than her prayers'). *See* COLLEEN.

cailín aimsire /kɑliːn'aimʃərə/ *n.*, hired female (seasonal) labourer (SOM, Kerry) < Ir. *See* BUACHAILL AIMSIRE.

cailleach /'kɑljəx/ also **calleach, callioch, calyagh** *n.*, a hag; a very old woman (as distinct from SEANBHEAN) (SOM, Kerry, who adds: 'a very old weathered woman') < Ir *cailleach,* nun, old woman < *caille,* veil. Michael J. Murphy, 'Return of the Boy' (*FDA*, 3, 961): "An old hag of a woman they called Sadie the Cailleach"; Healy, *Nineteen Acres,* 7: "Off the fire was the cailleach bed [footnote: bed by the kitchen fire]." Ó Dónaill s.v. 'cailleach 9', cailleach (shúgáin), recess for bed; alcove, with a long FORM in front of it.

cailleach na looha /ˈkɑljəxnə ˈluːhə/ *n.,* old woman of the ashes (CS, Mayo) < Ir *cailleach na luaithe*. 'They say there's great wisdom in that cailleach na looha.'

caillichín /ˈkɑlɪxiːn/ *n.,* precocious little girl; small old woman < Ir (dimin. of CAILLEACH).

cáim /kɔːm/ *n.,* a blemish, fault (SOM, Kerry) < Ir. 'She'd be perfect only for that cáim, the poor creature' (KG, Kerry).

caimiléireacht /kɑːməˈleːrəxt̪/ *n.,* dishonesty, crookedness, trickery (KM, Kerry) < Ir. 'There's a lot of caimiléireacht about nowadays.'

caimín /ˈkɑmiːn/ also **kimmeen** *n.,* a trick < Ir. 'That fellow's full of kimmeens. I MIND the way he took his egg, ate it, then turned it upside down and put it in your egg-cup for you to eat; the look on your face when you put the spoon into it!' (BC, Meath).

caip báis, *see* KYBOSH.

caipín /ˈkɑpiːn/ *n.,* cap < Ir. 'Has anyone seen my caipín? I won't go out without it' (Kerry).

caisearbhán /ˈkɑʃərəvɔːn/ sometimes (with metathesis) **caisreabhán** (SOM, Kerry) *n.,* dandelion; fig. a sour person < Ir. 'Turkeys and chickens love a feed of caisearbhán' (Mayo).

caisreabhán, *see* CAISEARBHÁN.

caistín /ˈkɑʃtiːn/ *n.,* a peevish person, puny person < Ir. 'That caistín of a girl is always complaining about something or other' (TJ, Sligo).

cáithnín /ˈkɔːhniːn/ *n.,* a small flake of something < Ir.

calamán /ˈkɑləmɔːn/ *n.,* a legacy (form and origin obscure). 'He's got a big calamán from America' (RB, Waterford).

call /kɔːl/ *n.,* need; claim, right (based on relationship) (SOM, Kerry) < Ir. 'You had no call to do that, = you had no right to do that' (Beecher, Cork, 14); 'There is no need for that (*níl call leis sin*)' (POC, Cavan); 'He had no call to turn my horse out of that field for I have as much call to it as he has. She said I was a STREEL, a cabin-hunter and a back-biter, but she has no call to call me out of my name, and what could be said about herself' (LUB, Dublin). Birmingham, *The Lighter Side of Irish Life*, 179: "What call had he for a dentist?"

callaire /ˈkɑlərə/ *n.,* noisy, loud talker < Ir. 'Someone tell that callaire to shut up – I can't hear myself think' (KG, Kerry).

calleach, **callioch**, *see* CAILLEACH.

cally /kæli/ *n.,* dish of mashed potatoes etc. < Ir *ceaile*, also *ceailí*. 'A plate of cally, that'll do *me*, BUT.' Healy, *Nineteen Acres*, 14: "When Grandma came with the plate of cally, Jim took it off her."

calops /'kɑləps/ *n.*, the calves of the leg < Ir *colpa*. 'What a fine pair of calops he has!' (said to a young lad in short trousers) (KM, Kerry).

calyach, *see* CAILLEACH.

cam[1] /kɑm/ *n.*, crookedness < Ir. 'Cam reilige' /kɑm'reləgə/ also 'cam an reiligín' /kɑmə 'rɛləgiːn/ *n.phr.*, a 'reel-footed' person < Ir (lit. crookedness of the graveyard). Conway, 3: 'The deformity was said to be caused by the person's mother having stumbled in a graveyard before his birth.'

cam[2] /kɑm/ *n.*, a torch, a cresset < Ir.

camán /kɑ'mɔːn/ *n.*, hurling-stick (Moylan, 56–7) < Ir. 'The camán is made from ash'; 'The clash of the camáns' (Wexford).

cam-is-díreach, *see* GOBÁN SAOR.

camóg /kəmoːg/ *n.*, a big stick (JF, Cavan); a crooked stick; a CAMOGIE stick < Ir.

camogie /kə'moːgiː/ *n.*, women's game like hurling, played with a CAMÓG < Ir *camógaíocht*. 'She took up camogie after Christmas and she's really into it now.'

canatt /kə'næt/ also **cnat, kanatt, kinatt** etc. *n.*, a mean, insignificant, unpleasant person; a sly, tricky youth; a rogue; 'a smart Alec'; a rascal (DB, Cork); a trickster (JF, Dublin) < Ir *cnat* (cf. E *gnat*). 'What a mean little kinnatt he is – I hope he burns in hell!'; 'There was always a cnat in that family'; 'The kinnatt asked me if I would give him a hand with the silage – well, DEVIL a hand he'll ever get from me.' Sheehan, *Glenanaar*, 157: "'Ye're a parcel of white-livered *kinats,*' said Lynch"; Roche, *A Handful of Stars,* act II, ii, 51: *"Paddy:* Oh when it comes to being a cannatt that fella don't need any help."

cancarach /'kɑŋkərəx/ also **cancrach** (SOM, Kerry) *adj.*, cross, cranky, bad-tempered < Ir. 'He gets very cancrach when he's tired, but otherwise he's fine.'

cancrán /kɑŋ'krɔːn/ *n.*, a cranky, bad-tempered individual (SOM, Kerry) < Ir. 'He's a right cancrán if he's not given whiskey.'

candle /'kændl/ also **canyal, cangyal** < Ir *coinneal* (PON, Dublin) *n.* Lighting votive candles is a common practice among the faithful of the Catholic Church, who set them up to burn before the BLESSED SACRAMENT, relics, shrines, or images. Candles are placed beside the corpse at a WAKE; the origin of the custom is uncertain, but there seems to have been a symbolism attached to the idea of a candle consuming itself and thereby committing a sort of sacrifice of itself. 'Have you any small change? I want to light a candle to St Anthony in thanksgiving – he's great for helping you to find something you've lost.' Heaney, 'Poor

Women in a City Church' (*Death of a Naturalist*, 42): 'The small wax candles melt to light, | Flicker in marble, reflect bright | Asterisks on brass candlesticks"; McCourt, *Angela's Ashes,* 295: "I promise the Virgin Mary the next penny I get I'll be lighting a candle"; Yeats, *The Unicorn from the Stars,* act III (*Collected Plays,* 368–9): "*Johnny:* Lay him out fair and straight upon a stone, till I will let loose the secret of my heart KEENING him! (Sets out candles on a rock, propping them up with stones.)"

cangyal, *see* CANDLE.

canon /ˈkænən/ *n.,* a priest who has been made a member of a cathedral chapter by appointment from the bishop; a 'residentiary canon' is a member of the permanent salaried staff of a cathedral responsible for the services, upkeep, administration, etc. < OE *canon* 'Hurry up! The canon is saying first Mass and he doesn't like anybody to come in late' (KG, Kerry).

cant /kænt/ *n.* 1. Auction < Ir *ceant* < OF *encant*. (The *OED* notes: 'of disputed origin . . . A disposal of property by public competition to the highest bidder; an auction. Chiefly Irish.)' 2. A dialect of English formerly spoken by the travelling people < L *cantare*, to sing, chant. (See Ó Baoill, 155–69). The two meanings and origins of 'cant' may alter the context when the word is used in situations where either meaning (or origin) would fit, e.g. 'Strong disagreement is often expressed about the priests' canting the dead . . . a sort of auction' (POC, Cavan); but Dónall Mac Amhlaigh, editor of the column in which this piece first appeared (*Ireland's Own,* 7 March 1980), suggests that the word is derived from L *cantare*, hence 'singing the dead.' Also Gammon; SHELTA.

cantlach /ˈkæntələx/ also **cantalach** *adj.,* morose, cranky (SOM, Kerry) < Ir. 'What a cantallach old hag she is!' (KM, Kerry).

canyal, *see* CANDLE.

caoch /kiːx/, /keːx/ *adj.,* partially blind; 'suffering early stages of being blind, developing cataracts' (SOM, Kerry, who adds: 'sometimes means "selective blindness"' < Ir.

caochán /ˈkiːxɔːn/, /keːˈxɔːn/ *n.,* a partially blind person; a potato without an eye and hence useless for seed purposes (SOM, Kerry); fig. a house with a single window, a tiny house < Ir. 'There used be a poor old caochán living at the bottom of the lane' (KG, Kerry).

caoineadh /ˈkiːnə/ *n.,* weeping, whimpering of a child; lament recited at a WAKE or funeral (SOM, Kerry) < Ir.

caoithiúil /ˈkiːhuːl/ *adj.*, convenient; pleasant; easy-going < Ir. 'Look at him and the caoithiúil walk of an idler on him!'

caol /kiːl/ *n.*, a narrow passage through a bog < Ir. 'Don't let the cows down the caol' (MG, Cavan).

caolach /ˈkiːləx/, /keːləx/ *n.*, a garland of elderberry (also rowan) twigs used on the churn as a charm < Ir. 'She set great store by the caolach caorthainn [caolach of rowan] when she was churning' (KM, Kerry).

caolán /ˈkiːlɔːn/ *n.*, the small intestine < Ir. 'If you were squeezing the kitten my mother would say, "Ye'll put out his caoláns"' (NH, Mayo).

caonach /ˈkiːnəx/, /keːnəx/ *n.*, moss, mould, mildew < Ir.

caor /kiːr/ *n.*, a berry (SOM, Kerry) < Ir. 'The bush is laden with caors.'

caorán /ˈkiːrɔːn/, /keːˈrɔːn/ *n.*, small pieces of turf used to kindle a fire (GF, Galway); a broken sod of turf (SOM, Kerry); a bit of turf, lighted and sent round the neighbourhood as a signal < Ir. 'Don't bring in all the big sods – throw the caoráns in too' (KM, Kerry).

capall /ˈkɑpəl/ *n.*, horse < Ir. 'Mair, a chapaill, agus gheobhair féar' (proverb), Live, horse, and you'll get grass; 'Do mhaide féin agus capall na comharsan' (proverb), Your own whip and the neighbour's horse. Griffin, *The Collegians* (1829), 82: "O Myles-na-Coppaleen [Myles of the ponies]? Poor fellow, is he in tribulation? We must have his ponies out by all means." (Cf. the character Myles-na-Goppaleen in Boucicault's *The Colleen Bawn* (1860) and the pseudonym Myles na gCopaleen (later Myles na Gopaleen) adopted by Flann O'Brien (1911–1966) for his column 'Cruiskeen Lawn' in the *Irish Times* (1940–1966).

cár /kɔːr/ *n.*, mouth open showing teeth; grin, grimace < Ir.

carbhat /ˈkɑrəvət̪/ *n.*, scarf; tie < Ir < E *cravat* < F *Cravate*, Croatian (scarf). 'He was wearing an oul carbhat and it must have been a hundred years old' (KG, Kerry).

care /keːr/ *n.*, family. 'How's the care?' (CS, Mayo). *See* CÚRAM.

carn /kɑːrn/ *n.*, heap, mound < Ir. 'Carn aoiligh', dung-heap (SOM, Kerry) < Ir.

carnaptious /kɑːrˈnæpʃəs/ also **curnoptious** etc. *adj.*, irritable, cranky < E dial. (origin obscure; Macafee gives 'Scots *carnaptious*, *curnaptious*; intensifying prefix, *car-*, *cur-* + *knap* (in the sense "to bite, to snap") + *-tious*, as in loanwords from Latin). 'A real carnaptious fellow he is if you rise him [make him angry]' (Monaghan).

caroline-hat /ˈkærəlainhæt/ *n.*, a kind of black hat fashionable from the end of the seventeenth century < E *Caroline,* relating to the time of King Charles I or II of England < L *Carolinus.* Carleton, 'The Hedge School' (*Six Irish Tales,* 146): "'And do you think, Sir,' said he, 'that I'd sind them to that dry-headed dunce, Mr Frazher, with his black coat upon him and his caroline hat, and him wouldn't taste a glass of POTEEN wanst [once] in seven years?'"; Joyce, *Finnegans Wake,* 460.9–10: "let me just your caroline for you."

carrachán /ˈkɑrəxɔːn/ *n.,* sickly, withered child; mangy creature < Ir. 'That carrachan of an ass is only fit for the KNACKER's yard' (TF, Cavan).

carrageen /ˈkɑrəgiːn/ also **carrageen moss** *n.,* type of edible seaweed found on rocks (hence the name), prepared as a blancmange-like dessert < Ir *carraigín* (dimin. of *carraig,* rock) (cf. DULSE). 'Carrageen is on the dessert menu today' (Dublin).

carraig /ˈkɑːrəg/ *n.,* rock (SOM, Kerry) < Ir.

carrow /ˈkæroː/ *n.,* wandering gambler < Ir *cearrbhach.* 'That carrow is on his rounds.'

cársán /kɔːrˈsɔːn/ *n.,* a type of wheezy cough < Ir. 'Before he became ill he had a terrible cársán' (KM, Kerry).

castóir /ˈkɑst̪oːr/ *n.,* a tool for ringing pigs < Ir. 'Get the castóir down from the shelf till we ring that pig' (AF, Cavan).

cat /kæt/ *n.,* cat < Ir. 'Is maith leis an gcat iasc ach ní maith leis a chosa a fhliuchadh' (proverb), The cat likes fish but he doesn't like getting his feet wet; 'Is ar mhaithe leis féin a dhéanann an cat crónán' (proverb), It's to suit himself that the cat purrs; 'Céard a dhéanfadh mac an chait ach luch a mharú?' (proverb), What else would the cat's son do but kill a mouse?; 'Briseann an dúchas trí shúile an chait' (proverb), You can't change (someone's) nature (lit. A cat's nature breaks out through its eyes); 'Chonaic mé cheana thú, mar a deir an cat leis an mbainne te' (proverb), I saw you before, as the cat said to the hot milk.

catach /ˈkɑt̪əx/ *adj.,* curly-haired, matted-haired (TJ, Sligo) < Ir.

catch your death, *see* DEATH.

Catechism /ˈkætəkɪzəm/ also **Catechiz** *n.,* a popular manual of Christian doctrine presented in question-and-answer form, especially the 'Maynooth Catechism', produced by the first Synod of Maynooth (1875) < mediaeval L *cathechisare* < ecclesiastical Gk *katēchizein, v.,* to sound through, to instruct orally. 'The teacher used give us an awful hammering if we didn't know our catechism off by heart, and you know, I can still remember most of it, even though it was such a long time ago' (TJ, Sligo). Sheehan, *Glenanaar,* 171: "We'll be all together, Nodlag, till death us do part, as the Catechiz says"; Joyce, 'A Painful Case' (*Dubliners,* 119): "A complete Wordsworth stood at one end of the lowest shelf and a copy of the *Maynooth Catechism,* sewn into the cloth cover of a notebook, stood at one end of the top shelf."

cathair /kɑhɜr/ *n.*, 'the City, a small cluster of houses, centre of pilgrimage in Rathmore parish; any cluster of houses (probably in line with the original Latin name); Cathair na mBacach, name of a large field in our own possession since 1940, from which about a dozen cabins had been cleared in the 1860s' (SOM, Kerry) < Ir. *See* CITY.

cathedral /kə'ti̪ːdrɜl/ *n.*, the church of a diocese which contains the permanent episcopal throne or 'cathedra' of the bishop; the mother-church of the whole diocese < Gk *kathedra*, L *cathedra*. 'We went up to Dublin to see him being ordained in the "Pro"' (JF, Cavan) (i.e. St Mary's Catholic Pro-Cathedral, designed by the amateur architect John Sweetman and opened in 1815 as an interim ('Pro') Cathedral, which has in recent times formally become the Cathedral of the Diocese of Dublin, though some Dubliners (especially the older generation) still refer to it as 'the Pro').

caubeen /'kɔːbiːn/ *n.,* an old cap or hat < Ir *cáibín.* 'Put on your old caubeen.' Carleton, 'The Hedge School' (*Six Irish Tales,* 158): "Hung about, on wooden pegs driven into the walls, are the shapeless yellow *'caubeens'* of such as can boast the luxury of a hat, or caps made of goat or hare skin"; Joyce, *Finnegans Wake,* 568.28: "That his be foison, old Caubeenhauben!"; Gogarty, *As I Was Going Down Sackville Street,* 93: ". . . the King would come over here every year and dress in a caubeen and knee-breeches an twirl a SHILLELAGH."

caulcannon, *see* COLCANNON.

caylee, *see* CÉILÍ.

céad míle fáilte /keːdmiːlə 'fɔːlʧə/ a common greeting or salute < Ir *céad míle fáilte,* a hundred thousand welcomes. 'Ireland sells its céad míle fáilte to the tourists'; 'She gave me such a céad míle fáilte – you'd think she hadn't seen me for years, instead of just last week.' Joyce, *Finnegans Wake,* 81.6: "and there are milestones in their cheadmilias." Sometimes the greeting is literally translated: Griffin, *The Collegians,* 112: "A thousand and a hundred thousand welcomes!"

ceaidé /'kæʤeː/ *n.,* a rambler; a good-for-nothing < Ir. 'That ceaidé is round here again – will you run him from the door' (Mayo).

ceailí, *see* CALLY.

ceangal /ˈkjæŋgəl/ also **coingeal** /ˈkʌŋgəl/ *n.,* a tie, a bond; a device made from the handle of a galvanised-iron bucket to stop two goats from wandering (BF, Cork) < Ir *ceangal,* also *cuingeal.* 'The goats have a ceangal on them; the one with the horns doesn't stray, but it's the other one – you'd never know where she'd get to' (AF, Cavan).

ceann /kjɑːn/, /kjaun/ *n.,* head < Ir. 'An té a bhuailtear sa cheann bíonn faitíos air' (proverb), A person who is beaten on the head knows fear.

Ceann Comhairle /kjɔːn ˈkoːrljə/, the chairperson of DÁIL ÉIREANN. 'The Ceann Comhairle is going to retire at the next election.'

ceannaigh cluasa /ˈkjæniː ˈkluəsə/ *n.phr.,* someone who buys cattle on the strength of praise he has heard of them; someone who backs horses that he hears other people backing (KM, Kerry) < Ir *ceannaigh cluasa,* buying by hearsay (lit. ear buying). 'When their horse lost, the Clareman said to his nephew, "Ah, ceannaigh cluasa!"' (KM, Kerry).

ceannbhán /ˈkjɑnəvɔːn/ also **ceannbhán bán** (SOM, Kerry) *n.,* bog-cotton (JOM, Kerry) < Ir. 'Will you just look at the ceannbán bán!'

ceap magaidh /kjæpˈmɑgə/ *n.,* an object of derision, a laughing-stock (SOM, Kerry) < Ir. 'He's become a ceap magaidh in the village.'

cearc /kjærk/ *n.,* hen (SOM, Kerry) < Ir. 'Rachaimid i bpáirt, mar adeir an sionnach leis an gcearc' (proverb), We'll be partners, as the fox said to the hen. *See* CIRCÍN.

céilí /ˈkeːliː/ also **céilidhe, cailey, caylee, kailee, kailey** *n.,* informal visit, act of visiting; an informal party for conversation, song, dance, etc.; in modern times a formally organised dance < Ir. 'Come in and make your céilí'; 'They came for a caylee'; 'Let's go to the céilí' (TF, Cavan). 'Céilidher', a person out on ceílí. 'The caileyers would come over on Sunday nights.' 'Céilí-ing', 'not going to a céilí but neighbours gathering together socially (to play cards etc.)' (VQ, Kerry). O'Brien, *At Swim-Two-Birds,* 189–90: "But after all a Ceilidhe is not the place for it, that's all. A Ceildihe is a Ceilidhe." Carleton, 'Shane Fadh's Wedding' (*Six Irish Tales,* 178): "telling the ould couple, that as he came over on his *kailee*, he had brought a drop in his pocket to sweeten his discoorse, axing [see AX] Susy Finigan, the mother, for a glass to send it round with." 'Castar na daoine ar a chéile ach ní chastar na cnoic ná na sléibhte' (proverb), People will meet again but not the hills or mountains.

céilidhe, *see* CÉILÍ.

céirseach /'keːrʃəx/ *n.*, a female blackbird; a thrush (SOM, Kerry); someone with a husky voice < Ir.

ceirtlín /'kɛrtliːn/ *n.*, a ball of thread; fig. a fat, well-built person < Ir. 'She's a fine big STRAP of a ceirtlín of a one' (BC, Meath).

céis /keːʃ/ *n.*, a store pig (four months between the piglet stage and being fully fattened) (SOM, Kerry) < Ir.

ceo /kjoː/ *n.*, fog, mist (SOM, Kerry); semen (JF, Cavan) < Ir. 'There's always a ceo in that field – there used to be a lake in it' (KG, Kerry).

ceochán /'kjoːxɔːn/ also **ciachán** /'kiəxɔːn/ *n.*, hoarseness; a person who is chronically husky (SOM, Kerry, who adds: 'if one is hoarse himself he is inclined to say he has a piachán') < Ir. 'I've a ceochán in the throat from all the smoking.'

ceofrán /'kjoːfrən/ *n.*, mist, drizzle (SOM, Kerry) < Ir. 'Ceofránach' /kjoːf'rɔːnəx/ *adj.*, misty, drizzly (MK, Galway) < Ir. 'It's a ceofránach old day. I think I'll clean out the shed.'

ceol /kjoːl/ *n.*, music < Ir. 'Tommy's great at making the old ceol with the fiddle' (BC, Meath). Sheehan, *Glenanaar,* 144: "We can have nine hours rale [real] *ceol,* before Ash Wednesday."

ceolán /'kjoːlɔːn/ *n.*, a silly, empty person, a 'ninny'; a mischievous child < Ir. 'You ceolán, will you finish your homework so we can go out and play' (Mayo).

cesh, *see* KESH.

cess /sɛs/ *n.*, in the expresson 'bad cess to you (him, etc.)', bad luck to you (him, etc.) (may be a contraction by apheresis of 'success', or a modified contraction by apheresis of 'assess', tax, rates). Stoker, *The Snake's Pass,* 88: "Bad cess to Knocknacar anyhow!"; Yeats, *The Unicorn from the Stars,* act III (*Collected Plays,* 366): "*Biddy:* . . . Or maybe that fleet of WHITEBOYS had the place ransacked before we ourselves came in. Bad cess to them that put it in my mind to gather up the FULL of my bag of horse shoes out of the forge"; Kilroy, *The Big Chapel,* 51: "His riverence [reverence] is right! Bad cess to him and his mischief."

chainey /'ʧeːni/ also **chainy, cheeny, cheney, chaineys** *n.*, china; bits of broken cups and saucers; bits of pottery used in games played by young girls (Beecher, 15) < E *china* < Persian *chīnī*, ware made from China clay. 'The ditches are full of chainies' (Dublin). Swift, *Irish Eloquence,* 76: "Your cousin desires you will buy him some cheney cups." (Bliss, in his edition of *Irish Eloquence,* 96, notes that the forms 'cheney' and 'chaney' come from the Persian adjective *chīnī,* as distinct from *China.* 'The pronunciation /tʃeːni/ was fashionable in the eighteenth century . . . Possibly Swift is here equating a fashionable pronunciation with a vulgarism.') 'Chaney-eye', artificial eye (formerly made from porcelain).

champ /ʧæmp/ *n., v.,* a dish of potatoes boiled and mashed with milk and onions and eaten with butter (origin obscure; perhaps onomatopoeic, based on the sound of chewing). 'One good plate of champ will keep you going for the whole day.' *See* PANDY.

chancer /ˈʧænsər/ *n.,* a crafty person who would try anything to get an advantage over someone < E *chance* + *-er.* 'He's a right chancer.' O'Casey, *The Plough and the Stars,* act II, 174: *"Fluther:* . . . I done as much, an' know as much about th' Labour movement as th' chancers that are blowin' about it!'"; Roche, *A Handful of Stars,* act I, i, 4: *"Tony:* . . . you're the biggest chancer I ever met."

chaney; chaney-eye, *see* CHAINEY.

chapel /ʧæpəl/ *n.,* a church. In Ireland it was customary to refer to Catholic places of worship as 'chapels' and Protestant places of worship as 'churches'. The distinction is well made in a macaronic poem by Art Mac Cumhaí (dated 1760) in which there is a dialogue between the two buildings, the 'church' speaking in English and the 'chapel' in Irish (Carpenter, *Verse in English from Eighteenth-Century Ireland,* 323–6). Kickham, *Knocknagow,* 502: "an' what do you think but I went into the chapel AFEARD uv my life that Tommy might be cast"; McCourt, *Angela's Ashes,* 68: "And she's forever on her knees ABROAD in St Joseph's chapel clackin' her ROSARY BEADS and breathing like a virgin martyr." *See* CHURCH; SCALLAN.

cheadmilias, *see* CÉAD MÍLE FÁILTE.

cheeney, cheney, *see* CHAINEY.

childer also **childher** /ˈʧɪldər/, /ˈʧɪld̪ər/ *n.pl.,* children < E dial. < ME *childre* < OE *cildru.* 'Are the childer home from school yet?' (AF, Cavan). Griffin, *The Collegians,* 65: "He was left, poor fellow, after his father dying of the *sickness* [typhus fever], with a houseful o' childer"; Stoker, *The Snake's Pass,* 19: "SURE, wasn't one of their childher tuk away iv'ry year?"; Leonard, *Out After Dark,* 77: "God, ma'am, do you want me to starve me own childer?"

Children of Mary /tʃɪldr̩ənəv 'meːri/ *n.*, name given to members of the Sodalities (= Confraternities) of the Blessed Virgin Mary, who are dedicated to fidelity to their religion and to a virtuous life through their devotion to the Mother of God; the tradition has a long history: in the twelfth century Blessed Peter de Honestis, a canon regular, founded the fraternity of the Sons and Daughters of Mary, at Ravenna, and the members wore a medal and a blue sash; the formal establishment of the Sodality of the Children of Mary, under the patronage of the Immaculate Virgin and St Agnes, took place in Rome in 1864, when they were placed under the care of the Canons Regular of the Lateran. Membership is restricted to girls and women. The Sodality of the Children of Mary Immaculate was started in 1847, inititially for young women attending institutions run by the Sisters of Charity, but after 1876 it was open to others. The badge they wear is known as the MIRACULOUS MEDAL, which consists of an oval shape bearing on one side an image of the Mother of God standing on a globe with rays of light coming from her hands, surrounded by the words 'O Mary conceived without sin! Pray for us who have recourse to thee!' It is called 'miraculous' not because it is the source of miracles for those who use it piously but because it had a miraculous origin, in that it is believed that the design was revealed by the Mother of God to Catherine Labouré, a Sister of Charity of ST VINCENT DE PAUL, who had three visions of Our Lady in 1830; the medal is worn on a blue ribbon. 'Wednesday night's when the Children of Mary meet'; 'There's a special RETREAT for the Children of Mary next week – don't forget to wear your medal!'; Healy, *Nineteen Acres*, 41: "The Children of Mary, in their virginal blue cloaks, going demurely to the altar, served all the more to remind you of the Adam-cursed animality and unworthiness of the male."

chincough /'tʃɪŋkəf/ *n.*, whooping-cough (CS, Mayo) < *kink-cough* < *kink,* gasp (through popular etymology re-formed as *chin*) + *cough* (ME *coughen*). See KINK.

chisler /'tʃɪzlər/, /'tʃɪzələr/ also **chiseller** *n.*, a hardy child, usually a boy; a child prone to stealing (KMG, Dublin) (origin obscure, but possibly a corruption of CHILDER). 'That young chisler will make a great footballer one day' (TJ, Sligo). Joyce, *Finnegans Wake,* 482.6: "But where do we get off, chiseller?"; O'Casey, *The Plough* *and the Stars,* act II, 174: *"Fluther:* An' him only a DAWNY chiselur"; Beatrice Behan, *Brendan Behan* (ed. Mikhail), 67: "He told me that at the age of six he could read aloud Robert Emmett's *Speech from the Dock.* 'That chiseller isn't reading it at all,' his relatives insisted. 'He learnt it by heart'"; Durcan, *Christmas Day,* X, 62: "When I was a chiseller we had the record at home."

Christian /ˈkrɪstʃən/ *n.,* a human being, as distinct from an animal < E dial. 'That dog has nearly as much sense as a Christian' (PWJ).

Christian Brothers /ˈkrɪstʃən ˈbrʌd̪ərz/ *n.* The Irish Christian Brothers were founded by Edmund Rice (1762–1844), who started a school for poor boys in Waterford in 1803; schools were afterwards started in other towns; in 1820 approval of the congregation was formally granted by the Pope (Pius VII, Pope 1800–1823) as 'the Institute of the Brothers of the Christian Schools of Ireland'; the name is often shortened to 'the Brothers'. 'He was educated by the Brothers – they were great for the discipline, perhaps too great, but they certainly made us learn'; Joyce, *FW*, 468.3–4: "How used you learn me, brather soboostius, in my augustan days?"; Leonard, *Out After Dark*, 55: " . . . the decent anonymity of the Christian Brothers school in Dún Laoghaire."

chuck chuck /ˈtʃʌkˈtʃʌk/ also **chook chook** *int.,* a call to hens < Ir *tiuc tiuc* (probably onomatopoeic: cf. E *chuck*). It has been suggested that this call derives from an (unattested) variant imperative of the verb 'come', **tioc*: see PWJ, 234.

chucky /ˈtʃʌki/ *n.,* a hen (*see* CHUCK CHUCK); 'also formerly used of soldiers of a regiment notorious for hen-stealing' (LUB, Dublin).

church /tʃʌrtʃ/ *n.,* a (Protestant) place of worship. O'Casey, *The Plough and the Stars,* act IV, 212: *"Corporal Stoddart:* They're puttin' 'em in a church. *Covey:* A church? *Fluther:* What sort of a church? Is it a Protestant Church? *Corporal Stoddart:* I dunnow; I suppowse so. *Fluther (dismayed):* Be God, it'll be a nice thing to be stuck all night in a Protestan' Church." *See* CHAPEL.

churching /ˈtʃʌrtʃən/ *v.n.,* a form of thanksgiving formerly made by Christian women after childbirth, involving the woman kneeling at the back of the church holding a lighted candle; she would be sprinkled with HOLY WATER by the priest, who would recite Psalm 23 and then lead her to the altar-rails, where certain prayers and responses were said, followed by a prayer for the well-being of the mother and child and a final blessing (mothers were recommended but not bound to receive it) < OE *cirice*. 'I think she's going to the chapel next week to be churched.'

ciachán, *see* CEOCHÁN.

ciall /kiəl/ *n.,* sense < Ir. 'Nuair atá an braon istigh tá an chiall amuigh' (proverb), When the drink is in, sense is out.

cianóg /'kiənoːg/ *n.,* a mite; a small coin, a farthing (a quarter of a pre-decimalisation penny, i.e. before 15 February 1971); half a farthing < Ir.

ciaróg /'kiəroːg/ *n.,* a beetle or CLOCK; a cockroach (SOM, Kerry) < Ir. 'The well is full of ciarógs'; 'That fella wouldn't give you as much as would blind a ciaróg's eye' (TF, Cavan); 'Aithníonn ciaróg ciaróg eile' (proverb), It takes one to know one (lit. One beetle recognises another).

cíb /kiːb/ *n.,* sedge (MK, Galway); the remains of grasses in turf; coarse grass < Ir. 'There was a bird singing in the cíb.'

cibeal /'kɪbəl/ *n.,* noise, clamour; wrangling, hubbub (MK, Galway) < Ir. 'They had some cibeal when the beer was drank.'

cí-cá, *see* GRUSH.

cideog /kɪ'd̪oːg/ also **kiddogue** *n.,* a covering for the head and shoulders against the rain (KM, Kerry) < Ir *cídeog*. 'Put that cideog round the baby in the GO-CAR – it looks like rain, and he's got a cold already.'

cifleog /kɪ'floːg/ *n.,* a clumsy, awkward person (KG, Kerry) < Ir. 'Look at that OMMADHAWN of a cifleog and the sight of that wall he's building – it's all askew.'

ciléar, **cíléir**, *see* KEELER.

cineálta /kɪn'ɔːlt̪ə/ *adj.,* kind, pleasant (MK, Galway) < Ir. 'Sure you wouldn't meet anyone more cineálta than him.'

cingcíseach /kɪŋ'kiːʃəx/ *adj., n.,* one born at Whitsuntide < Ir < *Cincís*, Pentecost, Whit Sunday.

cíoc /kiːk/ *int.,* peep! < Ir. 'Cíoc! Cíoc! I seen you coming' (child's saying).

cíoch /kiːx/ *n.,* breast (SOM, Kerry, who writes: 'An Dá Chíoch, the Paps') < Ir.

cíocras /'kiːkrəs/ *n.,* greed; hunger for food (MK, Galway) < Ir. 'During the Famine the cíocras was terrible in these parts.'

cíor[1] /kiːr/ *n.,* 1. Crest on a hen's head < Ir. 2. A comb (for the hair). 'Círín', a little comb for the back of the head (SOM, Kerry) < Ir.

cíor[2] /kiːr/ *n.,* 'cud' (in ruminants). 'Cogaint na círe', chewing the cud (SOM, Kerry) < Ir.

ciotach, awkward, clumsy (SOM, Kerry) < Ir. 'When someone gets into a hobble from which a little foresight would have saved him people say: "He did that very ciotach'" (*Irisleabhar na Gaedhilge,* 109).

ciotán /ˈkɪt̪ɔːn/ also **kitthawn** *n.,* the left hand; a left-handed person (MK, Galway) < Ir. 'They made him write with his right hand, even though he was a ciotán – no wonder you can't make out his writing now.'

ciotóg /ˈkɪt̪oːg/ also **citeog, kithogue** *n.,* the left hand; a left-handed person (SOM, Kerry); an awkward person < Ir. The attaching of the meaning of awkwardness to left-handedness may be due to the fact that in less enlightened days left-handed people were forced to write with their right hand, in the interests of uniformity and discipline. 'Before you shake the right hand of an enemy make sure he's not a ciotóg' (Mayo); 'You won't beat him at handball – he's a kithogue' (SL, Mayo). Healy, *Nineteen Acres,* 23: "And if you dared shuffle a chair you'd get a belt of that powerful citeog of hers"; 31: "John Mickey, who was a crack shot with the citeog"; Joyce, *Finnegans Wake,* 91.34: "upon the halfkneed castleknocker's attempting kithoguishly to lilt his holymess the paws."

ciotógach /kɪˈt̪oːgəx/ *adj.,* left-handed; awkward, clumsy (SOM, Kerry) < Ir. 'He's ciotógach, but he gets the work done.'

cipín /ˈkɪpiːn/ *n.,* a twig (SOM, Kerry) < Ir. 'I'll collect some cipíns for the fire' (JL, Mayo). 'Cipíní', small pieces of wood suitable for getting the fire started (POC, Cavan). 'Cipín solais', a match (SOM, Kerry) < Ir.

circín /kɪrˈkiːn/ *n.,* a small hen; fig. a prim little girl who is too precocious for her age (SOM, Kerry) < Ir (dimin. of CEARC). 'She's a right little circín – I don't like her at all' (KG, Kerry).

círín /kiːˈriːn/ *n.,* the lobe of the ear; the flesh of the jaw (SOM, Kerry) < Ir (dim. of *cíor,* comb).

cis[1] /kɪʃ/ *n.,* a potato or turf basket used in a field or bog and suitable for holding large quantities (SOM, Kerry) < Ir.

cis[2] /kɪʃ/ *n.,* a temporary bridge between a turf bank and the road; a causeway made from furze and sallies < Ir. 'The cis broke when we were crossing it' (TJ, Sligo). *See* CISEACH.

ciseach /kɪˈʃəx/ also **kisagh** *n.,* an improvised bridge across a stream or a ravine in a bog (SOM, Kerry); a path over the wet part of a bog made with furze and sallies; a causeway; fig. a hefty person who always seems to be getting in the way < Ir. 'The ciseach will never bear the weight of the trailer.' *See* CIS.

ciseán /'kɪʃɔːn/ *n.*, a wicker basket; a wicker frame for carts; a hamper (SOM, Kerry) < Ir. Healy, *Nineteen Acres,* 8: "The turf fire . . . had to be fed from the ciseán of sally rods", 13: "He'd take the pot of Champions [potatoes], boiling on the crook (a metal hook from which cooking pots were suspended over an open fire), and throw them into the sally rod ciseán in clouds of steam: I can still smell the suds and wet rods today." 'Ciseán éisc', a fish basket. *See* CIS.

ciseog /kɪ'ʃoːg/ *n.* 1. A flat basket-like dish made from loose-woven sallies used for straining potatoes; a shallow basket to bring in enough potatoes for a day, to strain potatoes, to hold potatoes on the table while people dined (SOM, Kerry). 2. A pair of baskets across a donkey's back, SRATHAIR FHADA (SOM, Kerry) < Ir.

ciste /kɪʃtə/ *n.*, a present of money; a hoarding of money < Ir *ciste,* treasure (cf. E *chest*). 'Children or indeed any person who had a selection of things such as nuts, apples, pennies etc. were often said to have "a right little ciste"' (POC, Cavan); 'He fell in for a ciste (= he inherited money)' (Dublin).

císte /kiːʃʧə/ *n.*, a small cake < Ir. 'She made a císte for Mary's birthday' (BC, Meath).

citeal /kɪt̪əl/, /kɪʧəl/ also **kittle** *n.*, a kettle (SOM, Kerry) < Ir. 'Is the citeal boiled till I WET the tea.'

citeog, *see* CIOTÓG.

City, the /'sɪti/ *place-name (colloq.).* 'That place in Shrone [Co. Kerry], where the ancient Irish on May Day, at the foot of the hills there, would light a fire and drive the cattle through it (it was supposed to make them healthy) is today called the "City" – folks "pay rounds" there on May Day. When folks asked the late Canon to offer Mass there he'd say "No – old pagan place"' (KM, Kerry) (cf. Ir *cathair,* stone enclosure; dwelling-place; city); *See* CATHAIR; SEANCHAÍ; TOBAR.

ciumhais /kjuːʃ/ *n.*, edge < Ir.

ciúnas /'kjuːnəs/ *n.*, silence! be quiet! (commonly used by teachers to quieten a class-room) < Ir. 'Ciúnas! or I'll get the bata [stick] out.'

clab /klɑb/ *n.*, mouth; open mouth (with wonder) < Ir. 'Dún do chlab,' shut your mouth (SOM, Kerry).

clabach /'klɑbəx/ *adj.*, garrulous (MK, Galway) < Ir. 'She's a clabach of a gossip.' *See* CLAB.

clábar /'klɔːbər/ *n.*, mud (SOM, Kerry) < Ir. 'He was covered in clábar'; 'It's hard to keep the house clean and the way he walks in with his brogues all clauber' (LUB, Dublin).

clabhstar /'klauʃt̪ər/, /'klaust̪ər/ *n.*, an ill-shapen object; something with no finesse < Ir. 'Did you ever see such a clabhstar of a hat?' (SOM, Kerry).

clabhsúr /'klausuːr/ *n.,* a celebratory feast to mark the end of harvesting, with dancing and story-telling (KM, Kerry) < Ir. 'It was great when we had the clabhsúr, but times have changed now' (Meath).

clabhta /'klaut̪ə/ *n.,* a clout, blow, box < Ir *clabhta.*

cladhaire /'klairə/ *n.,* a villain, rogue, cad (VQ, Kerry); a coward (SOM, Kerry) < Ir. 'He's a born cladhaire' (KM, Kerry). 'Sometimes with a hint of affection, referring to a rascal, a "trick of the loop"' (SOM, Kerry).

clag, *see* CLEG.

clagarnach /klɑgərnəx/ *n.,* pelting of rain; noise of heavy rain on an iron roof (SOM, Kerry) < Ir. 'Did you ever hear such clagarnach?'

claggy /'klægi/ *adj.,* sticky, glutinous; muddy < E dial. (origin obscure; cf. OE *clæg,* clay). 'That's claggy soil.' Paulin, *A New Look at the Language Question,* 13: "A glance at the prose of F. S. L. Lyons reveals a style drawn from the claggy fringes of local journalism."

claí /kliː/ *n.,* a fence (SOM, Kerry), dike, wall, barrier < Ir. 'Tá cluasa ar na claitheacha,' lower your voice: you don't want the whole world to know your business (lit. The fences have ears) (SOM, Kerry).

claibín cuinneoige /'klɑbiːn 'kɪnjoːgə/ *n.,* churn-lid < Ir. 'I'll have to get a new claibín cuinneoige made – I wonder where I'll get it done in this day and age' (BC, Meath).

claíochán /'klaixɔːn/ *n.,* partly levelled clay fence, old worn fence < Ir. 'I'll have to tell them to fix up that claíochán – their cattle are always breaking in to my field' (Mayo).

cláirín /klɔː'riːn/ *n.,* a flat board; a flat-edged implement for edging a scythe (SOM, Kerry) < Ir. 'There's a cláirín in the shed if you're looking for one.'

cláirseach /'klɔːrʃəx/ *n.,* a standing harp (Galway) < Ir.

clais /klæʃ/ *n.,* a drain, furrow, gully; a shallow drain to let water run off a surface < Ir. 'Leave the cows in the clais for tonight and we'll take them to the top field tomorrow' (KM, Kerry). 'Clais an phortaigh', *n.phr.,* a boggy ditch; a grassy piece of ground at the edge of a bog that can be grazed < Ir, ditch of the bog.

clamhsán /klau'sɔːn/ *n.,* grumbling, fault-finding, complaining (SOM, Kerry) < Ir. 'That oul one's always clamhsáning about something.'

clamhsánaí /klau'sɔːni/ *n.,* a person who complains a lot (SOM, Kerry) < Ir. 'He's a regular oul clamhsánaí.'

clamp /'klæmp/ *n.,* a heap of turf < Ir *clampa* (cf. E *clamp*).

'Make clamps of the turf up on the bank,' Carlow.

clampar /'klɑːmpər/ *n.,* undue noise (MK, Galway); a noisy quarrel, a row, dispute (SOM, Kerry, who adds: 'hence Canon Sheehan's Clampar Daly') < Ir.

clart /klɑːrt/ *n.,* a dirty woman; a cook or housewife who is unclean in her habits (origin obscure). 'She's a right clart, the way she keeps the house' (KG, Kerry). 'Clarty' *adj.,* dirty (origin obscure).

clash /klæʃ/ *n., v.,* tale-bearing, gossip; to tell tales, carry scandal (origin obscure, but perhaps an onomatopoeic formation based on the sounds of trivial talk). 'He's an awful old clash' (TJ, Sligo).

clatter /'klæt̪ər/ *n. (colloq.),* a large amount (origin obscure, but cf. *EDD:* 'a pile of loose stones or boulders,' etc.) 'He made a clatter of money' (Dublin). 'Just look at her and a clatter of children by [= with] her' (KG, Kerry).

clatty /'klæti/ *adj.,* dirty, slovenly < E dial. (cf. Du *klat,* blot, splash of dirt).

clauber, **clawber**, *see* CLÁBAR.

clay /kleː/ *n.,* loose earth < ME *clai* (cf. *ODEE:* 'stiff viscous earth'). 'He shook the clay off the spuds.' Kavanagh, 'The Great Hunger', I (*Collected Poems,* 34): "Clay is the word and clay is the flesh"; 'Bluebells for Love' (*Collected Poems,* 69): "Ah, the clay under these roots is so brown!"; *Tarry Flynn,* 39: "He gloated over his potatoes and the fine job be was making of the moulding . . . The clay was staying up nicely", 60: "Ah clay! . . . he loved that dry earth."

cleamhnas /'klaunəs/ *n.,* a relationship by marriage; a marriage arrangement, a match (SOM, Kerry) < Ir. 'Cleamhnán', a person related by marriage (CS, Mayo) < Ir. 'People related by marriage were said to be "clownies". The word for engagement or promise in marriage is *cleamhnas* (pronounced clownas)' (POC, Cavan).

cleas /klæs/ *n.,* a trick; a feat (SOM, Kerry) < Ir.

cleasaí /'klæsiː/ *n.,* trickster; playboy; acrobat (SOM, Kerry) < Ir. 'He's a fierce cleasaí, that one'; 'You couldn't be up to the tricks of that cleasaí' (TJ, Sligo).

cleas na péiste /'klæsnə'peːʃtʃə/ *n.phr.,* a kind of knot put on an animal's back to cure ills (e.g. worms) < Ir (lit. worm contrivance). 'The cord is placed on the animal's back and folks thought it cured many ills. Our local vet told me that a woman in Hollymount asked him to look at a sick calf. He came in the evening and she said, "No need to call – I made cleas na péiste on the calf's back and he's fine now." The vet told me that he made the grave mistake of laughing, and the woman gave him a sour look (PUS MUICE)' (KM, Kerry).

cleats /kliːts/ also **cleets**, **cletes** *n.pl.*, loop wheels on a tractor (Mayo) < ME *clete,* wedge < supposed OE form *cleat* (*OED* s.v. 'cleat', '1. A wedge (now applied especially to the small wedges used in securing the movable parts of a scythe and plough)'; *EDD* s.v. 'cleet-boards' sb.pl., 'mud pattens, broad flat pieces of wood fastened onto the shoes to enable a person to walk on mud without sinking').

cleave /kliːv/ also **cleeve** *n.*, a large wicker basket < Ir *cliabh.* 'Did you see the big cleave anywhere?' (MG, Cavan). 'Cleaver', a dealer in poultry (carried around in a cleave). *A Dialogue between Teigue and Dermot,* 149: "One Fellow dat you'd carry a Cleave." *See* CLIABH.

cleets, **cletes** *see* CLEATS.

cleeve, *see* CLEAVE.

cleg /klɛg/ also **clag** *n.*, a gad-fly; horse-fly < ME *clegge* < ON *kleggi*. 'It's the clegs that has the cows driven mad.' Kavanagh, 'Ante-Natal Dream' (*Collected Poems,* 129): "Thistle, ragwort, bluebottle I Cleg that maddens cattle I were crowding round me there."

cléithín /ˈkleːhiːn/ *n.*, a splint or SCOLB used in thatching < Ir. 'I think I'll go out and cut a few cléithíns today' (TF, Cavan).

cleithire /ˈkleːhərə/ *n.*, a tall, sturdy fellow < Ir. 'Do you reckon that cleithire would do a good day's work in the bog?' (Mayo).

cletes, *see* CLEATS.

cliabh /kliəv/ *n.*, a CREEL (SOM, Kerry); a basket made of rushes (often one placed on each side of a donkey for drawing turf) < Ir. *See* CLEAVE.

cliabhaire /ˈkliəvərə/ *n.*, a dealer in poultry < Ir. 'When is the cliabhaire next coming around? – I have to have a few hens ready' (Cavan).

cliabhán /kliəˈvɔːn/ *n.*, *v.*, a cradle (SOM, Kerry); to chop (sticks), to hit < Ir (dimin. of CLIABH). 'Cliabhán éin', a trap for catching birds, small animals, etc. 'You won't catch anything in that cliabhán éin the way you have it made.'

cliotar /ˈklɪt̪ər/ *n.*, noise, din, racket (but with no hint of quarrelling) (SOM, Kerry) < Ir. 'Stop that cliotar! I can't hear myself think' (KG, Kerry).

clip /klɪp/ *n.*, a colt; a sporty, forward girl < Ir. 'Nothing 'ud be too hot or too heavy for that clip' (LUB, Dublin).

clitherer /ˈklɪt̪ərər/ *n.*, a woman with too much to say (MK, Galway) < E dial. < ME *clateren, v.*, to clatter, rattle (cf. *clitter, n., v.*, clatter). 'Don't listen to that clitherer, will you!' *See* CLIOTAR.

clob /klɑb/ *n.*, a big mouth; fig. a stupid, garrulous person < Ir (*see* CLAB). 'Shut your clab or I'll give you a slap' (Limerick).

cloch /klʌx/ *n.,* a stone (SOM, Kerry) < Ir. 'He can PEG a cloch further than anyone I know.'

clochar /ˈklʌxər/ *n.,* a stony place (MK, Galway); a place with only clumps of trees and bushes and little or no grass < Ir. 'Put the cows down to the clochar.'

clochaun /ˈklʌxɔːn/ *n.,* stepping-stones across a river; a causeway < Ir *clochán,* stepping-stones. 'The clochauns had moved after the flood' (TF, Cavan).

clock /klɑk/ *n.,* black beetle < E (origin obscure); 'Don't harm the clock – it'll bring bad luck' (AF, Cavan).

clocker, *see* CLOCKING (HEN).

clocking (hen) /ˈklɑkən/ also **clacking** *pres.part., adj.,* sitting on her nest waiting for the eggs to hatch, often making clucking noises < ME *clacken.* 'Go down and see has that clocking hen laid any eggs yet' (Cavan). Griffin, *The Collegians,* 106: "'Here, Mrs. Frawley, will you have an eye to the spit a minute while I go look at them hens in the *coob* abroad? Master Kyrle might like a fresh egg for his *tay,* an' I hear them clockin'"; O'Casey, *The Plough and the Stars,* act I, 140: *"Mrs Gogan:* . . . She's like a clockin' hen if he leaves her sight for a minute"; Healy, *Nineteen Acres,* 96: "Mary Anne fussed over them like a clocking hen." 'Clocker', a hatching, broody hen (BF, Cork).

clogaidín /ˈklʌgədʒiːn/ *n.,* a small milk-bucket < Ir.

clownies, *see* CLEAMHNAS.

cluas /kluəs/ *n.,* ear (SOM, Kerry); listening < Ir. 'I'll redden your cluas if you're not careful.'

cluasán /ˈkluəsɔːn/ *n.,* someone with big ears; a blockhead, stupid person < Ir (cf. CLUAS). 'What are you doing, you big cluasán you?' (BC, Meath).

clúdóg /ˈkluːd̪əg/ *n.,* a batch of (Easter) eggs; a present of (usually Easter) eggs (MK, Galway) < Ir. 'A present of an egg or two given to a child calling at a house on Easter Sunday or Monday; a custom general sixty years ago' (LUB, Dublin [1944]). 'In Cavan we always boiled the clúdógs outside in a field on Easter Sunday.'

clúmh /kluːv/ *n.,* down; soft feathers (SOM, Kerry, who adds: 'as distinct from *cleite,* = feather') < Ir.

clutharachán /ˈklʌhərəxɔːn/ also **lucharachán** *n.,* a small child; a fairy < Ir.

cnag /knɑg/ *n.,* knock (on door), bang (SOM, Kerry) < Ir.

cnáimhseáil /knɔːvˈʃɔːl/ also **knauvshawl**, **knawvshawl**, also **cnáimhseáiling** *v.n.,* complaining, giving out (SOM, Kerry); fault-finding; grumbling

< Ir. 'Don't be cnáimhseáiling' (FD, Cork); 'Stop your knauvshawling and get on with the job.'

cnáimhseálaí /knɔːvˈʃɔːliː/ also **knawvshawley** *n.,* someone who is always finding fault; a grumbler, fault-finder (SOM, Kerry), chronic complainer < Ir; also 'cnáimhseáiler' (SOC, Cork). 'I don't know how you put up with that cnáimhseálaí of a husband of yours – I know what I'd do with him if I had him!' (BC, Meath).

cnaiste /knæʃtə/ *n.,* the side rail of a bed; the edge of a bed < Ir. 'Sit up on the cnaiste and have your breakfast.'

cnámh /knɔːv/ *n.,* bone (SOM, Kerry) < Ir. 'I found a sheep's cnámh in the bog.'

cnap /knɑp/ *n.,* a lump, a knob (SOM, Kerry, who adds: 'a cnap of butter'); fig. a stout boy; a short fat person < Ir.

cnapán /ˈknɑpɔːn/ *n.,* a hillock < Ir. 'You might get him to level that cnapán when he's finished the other jobs.'

cnat, *see* CANATT.

cníopaire /ˈkniːpərə/ *n.,* a miser, a mean person < Ir. 'What an old cníopaire he is – he'd sooner have the son labouring across the water than give him the land' (KG, Kerry).

cnoc /knʌk/ *n.,* hill, mount (SOM, Kerry) < Ir. Banim, *The Boyne Water,* 504: "It's on the highest knock, about here, though many more knocks surround us, not to be seen by raison of darkness."

cnocán /ˈknʌkɔːn/ *n.,* hillock (SOM, Kerry) < Ir (dimin. of CNOC). 'It might be bad luck to level that cnocán' (Mayo).

cnútachán /ˈknuːt̪əxɔːn/ *n.,* a gnat (MK, Galway); fig. a mean or unpleasant person < Ir. 'She's an oul cnútachán – nobody likes her.'

coach-horse, **coachman**, as in 'devil's coach-horse', 'devil's coachman', *see* DEVIL.

coarb /koːrb/ *n.,* a successor to the founder or head of a church or monastery in the Celtic church < Ir *comharba,* heir, successor. The Pope was sometimes referred to as *comharba Pheadair* (Peter's heir) (*see Oxford Companion to Irish History,* s.v. 'coarb').

cob /kɑb/ *n.,* mouth < Ir. 'He's got the cob of a fool on him.' *See* CAB.

cocán /ˈkʌkɔːn/ *n.,* top-knot of hair on a girl's head; a bun < Ir. 'She looked nice with a fine cocán' (KG, Kerry). *See* CURCAÍ.

coccagee /kʌkəˈgiː/ *n.,* cider apple; a hunting waistcoat, or the colour of this (ENM, Kerry) < Ir *cac an ghé,* goose droppings (greenish in colour).

cochall[1] /ˈkʌxəl/ *n.,* a bush of furze etc. < Ir. 'Throw a cochall of bog deal behind the fire – it'll light the room when we have an ESB strike' (KM, Kerry).

cochall[2] /ˈkʌxəl/ *n.,* an angry appearance, a frown < Ir. ‘Oh, the cochall of that one!’ (KM, Kerry).

cochallach /ˈkʌxələx/ *adj.,* angry, hot-tempered (MK, Galway) < Ir. ‘There was a cochallach on her when the cattle broke out’ (KM, Kerry).

cock /kɑk/ (up with) *v.,* to spoil, pamper < ME *cokke.* ‘I wouldn’t cock him up,’ I wouldn’t encourage his conceit’ (LUB, Dublin). Birmingham, *The Lighter Side of Irish Life,* 179–80: “A lady was enquiring for one of her under gardeners who had been suffering severely from toothache. She asked whether he had been to the dentist. ‘Dentist, is it?’ said the head gardener. ‘What CALL had he for a dentist? Cock the likes of them fellows up with a dentist!’”

cod /kɑd/ *n., v.,* hoax, joke; lie, humbug < E dial. (origin obscure). ‘Stop your codding!’ (TF, Cavan). Joyce, *Ulysses,* 298.28: “‘Are you codding?’ says I”; O’Casey, *The Shadow of a Gunman,* act I, 83: “*Seamus:* If you want to make a cod of anybody, make a cod of somebody else, an’ don’t be tryin’ to make a cod o’ me”; Kavanagh, *Tarry Flynn,* 52: “Do you think I’d start to talk philosophy to every oul’ cod I meet?”; Beckett, *Waiting for Godot,* 31: “*Pozzo:* He wants to cod me”; Roche, *A Handful of Stars,* act I, i, 4: “*Tony*: I’m not coddin’ yeh boy”; McCourt, *Angela’s Ashes,* 211: “Is it jokin’ you are? That thing about dying for the faith is all a cod.” *See* CODOLOGY.

cod-actor /ˈkɑdækt̪ər/ *n.,* someone who feigns illness (CS, Dublin); a charlatan < *cod* (origin unknown) + *actor.* ‘He can be a right cod-actor sometimes’ (TF, Cavan).

codaí /ˈkɑd̪iː/ *n.,* a big, ignorant person; a lazy, easy-going person < Ir. ‘He’s a codaí – and nothing’ll change that!’ (BC, Meath).

coddle /ˈkɑdəl/ *n.,* a kind of stew made of a variety of ingredients: meat, vegetables, etc.; a dish of bacon, butter and onions stewed or parboiled, ‘a coddle of bacon’ (PON, Dublin) < EModE *coddle, v.,* to stew (origin obscure). ‘Oh, yes, Dubliners used love have coddle on a Saturday’; Joyce, *Finnegans Wake,* 593.22–3: “to cuddle up in a coddlepot.”

codger /ˈkɑdʒər/ *n.,* old man, young child (depending on context) (origin obscure; cf. *cadger* and *catcher*). ‘He’s a mean old codger’; ‘Come on, my little codger’ (said affectionately to child) (Dublin); ‘Run away, you little codger!’ (Meath). Yeats, ‘News for the Delphic Oracle’, I (*Collected Poems,* 350): “There all the golden codgers lay, | There the silver dew"; Kavanagh, 'Who Killed James Joyce?' (*Collected Poems,* 117): "Who carried the coffin out? | Six Dublin codgers | Led into Langham Place | By W. R. Rodgers."

codladh gliúragáin /'kʌlə 'gluːrəgɔːn/ also **glúraic**, **glooracks** *n.,* numbness of hands caused by frost etc. < Ir. 'The glooracks does be at me in the cold weather, even with the gloves on me' (Louth).

codladh grifín /'kʌlə'grɪfiːn/ *n.,* pins and needles; numbness in feet or arms (SOM, Kerry) < Ir. 'When I woke this morning I had codladh grifín in my hand' (MK, Galway).

codology /kɑd'ɑləʤi/ *n.,* the practice of codding, fooling < COD + *-ology* (whimsical use of technical suffix). 'That's codology if ever there was' (Cork). Joyce, *Ulysses*, 302.26–7: "and all the codology of the business"; Leonard, *Out After Dark,* 59 ". . . she would first of all tell the ceiling that as sure as God my codology would land us all in the Union [poorhouse]."

codrawlin', *see* CADRÁIL.

cog /kɑg/ *n., v.,* crib, forbidden copying; to cheat, copy notes or homework from another < EModE (origin obscure). 'He cogged it off my slate' (LUB, Dublin); 'She had a cog in her pocket' (JMF, Cavan). Joyce, *Finnegans Wake,* 304.31: "cog it out."

cogar /'kʌgər/ also **cogher** *int., n.,* listen!; whisper! (SOM, Kerry who adds: 'Cogar mogar, intrigue, conspiracy, secret planning') < Ir. 'Ag cogarnaigh', whispering' (POC, Cavan). 'He's coghering' (Carlow) < Ir.

cogar mogar /'kʌgər'mʌgər/ *n.,* intrigue, conspiracy, secret planning; hugger-mugger (SOM, Kerry) < Ir (duplication of *cogar,* whisper). 'There was some cogar mogar going on last night – I can feel it' (KG, Kerry).

cogher, *see* COGAR.

coicín /'kʌkiːn/ *n.,* a little cock of hay < Ir (dimin. of *coca,* cock of hay). 'Make a little coicín out of what's left over.'

coigilt /'kʌgɪlʧ/ *n.,* saving, sparing (MK, Galway); covering over; fig. throwing ash over the embers of a fire; 'Banc Coigiltis', Savings Bank (MK, Galway); kindling of fire (SOM, Kerry, who notes: 'adú, kindling of fire, coigilt elsewhere') < Ir.

coileán /kʌ'lɔːn/ *n.,* a pup (SOM, Kerry); fig. a clever, sly young person < Ir. Roche, *A Handful of Stars,* act II, ii, 50: "*Paddy:* . . . Jaysus that coileain gave that poor woman an awful life so he did."

coingeal, *see* CEANGAL.

coinicéar /'kʌnəkeːr/ *n.,* a rabbit-warren; rabbit-hole < Ir. 'That field is ruined with coinicéars' (BC, Meath).

coinleach /'kʌnləx/ *n.,* a cornfield after the crop has been cut

(SOM, Kerry, who adds: 'Gealach na gcoinleach, harvest moon'); stubble < Ir. 'You'll probably see a few pheasants in the coinleach if you go up early' (Sligo).

coinnle buí /ˈkʌnləˈbwiː/ *n.*, yellow stubble, 'looking like yellow candles' (KM, Kerry) < Ir *coinnle buí,* yellow candles (but perhaps from confusion with COINLEACH). 'You'd better burn that coinnle buí before the rats nest in it' (Limerick).

coirceog /ˈkʌrkoːg/ *n.*, small heap of turf left for drying < Ir. 'He has the last of the turf in coirceogs on the side of the road' (SL, Mayo).

coireán /ˈkʌrɔːn/ *n.*, campion (rare in the west of Ireland) (MK, Galway) < Ir. 'Look at the lovely coireán beside the sea.'

coiscéim /ˈkʌʃkeːm/ *n.*, a step, footstep (SOM, Kerry) < Ir.

coiseagán /ˈkʌʃəgɔːn/ *n.*, a spancel, leg-fetter, hobble for an animal (MK, Galway) < Ir. 'There was great MEAS in Máire – she could make coiseagáns from cows' tail-hair' (KM, Kerry).

coisí /kʌˈʃiː/ *n.*, a camp-follower, a hanger-on; one who turns up at funerals, weddings etc. and cadges drinks (SOM, Kerry) < Ir (lit. a traveller by foot; foot-soldier). 'That coisí would shake hands with you with your own hand!' (SOM, Kerry).

coisín /kʌˈʃiːn/ *n.*, little foot < Ir (dimin. of *cos,* foot). 'Come here and let me see what happened to your little coisín' (KG, Kerry).

cóisireacht /ˈkoːʃərəxt̪/ *n.*, visiting a neighbour's house for a social gathering, party (Limerick) < Ir. 'We had a great night cóisireachting over the road last night' (Clare). *See* COORJEEKING.

cois teallaigh /kʌʃˈʧælɪg/ *prep. phr.*, by the fireside, around the fire < Ir.

colcannon /kɔːlˈkænən/ also **caulcannon**, **colecannon**, **kale-cannon**, etc. *n.*, a dish made of potatoes mashed with butter and milk with kale or cabbage added < Ir *cál,* kale or cabbage < ME *cale,* cabbage + *ceannann,* white-topped. 'We'll have bacon and caulcannon for the dinner' (KG, Kerry); 'Just feed the men colcannon when they come in, and put some scallions in it too.' Joyce, *Finnegans Wake,* 456.7–8: "And for kailkannonkabbis gimme Cincinnatis with Italian (but *ci vuol poco*!) ciccalick cheese"; Leonard, *Out After Dark,* 153: "On his list were the wall-eyed woman next door, who pretended to cook colcannon but was actually manufacturing poison gas."

collach /ˈkʌləx/ *n.*, a boar; fig. a crude 'jackass' of a man < Ir. 'Don't let that collach near me!' (BC, Meath).

collations /kʌ'leːʃənz/ *n.,* the two light snacks that are permitted to the faithful in addition to one full meal per day on days of fasting, when adults aged between twenty-one and fifty-nine are commanded to take only one full meal, with the collation added < L *collatio,* conference (from the reading aloud from the spiritual writers or lives of the Fathers during monastic meals; in the fourteenth century the word 'collation' became attached to the light meal taken during such readings; in the sixteenth century it was adopted for general use, meaning a light repast, but in HE it retains its earlier meaning within the practice of Catholicism). 'The priest said we could only have one meal and two collations; it'll be good for us' (JMF, Cavan).

colleen, *see* CAILÍN.

colleen bawn /'kɑliːn'bɔːn/ *n.,* a girl, young woman < Ir *cailín bán,* fair girl. Carleton, 'Shane Fadh's Wedding' (*Six Irish Tales,* 191): "with your young *colleen bawn,* that'll be your wife before the sun sets, plase the heavens'"; Joyce, *Ulysses,* 309.14–15: "and a lot of colleen bawns going about."

colley /'kɑli/ *n.,* dirt; woolly dirt under furniture < E dial. (var. form of *colly, n.,* soot; cf. *coal* < OE *col*). 'Look at the colley under the dresser – where am I going to find the time to do all the cleaning?' (Limerick).

collines, *see* COLLEEN.

collogue /kə'loːg/ *v.,* to conspire, chat confidentially (origin obscure, but cf L *colloquor, v.,* to talk together, and ModE *colleague*). 'They were having a collogue over in the corner when I came in, but when they saw me it ended quickly.' O'Casey, *Juno and the Paycock,* act I, 25: *"Juno:* D'ye mean to tell me that the pair of YOUS wasn't collogin' together here when me back was turned?"

collop[1] /'kɑləp/ *n.,* a heifer, bullock < Ir *colpach.* 'Do you think that collop is ready for the mart yet?' (Cavan).

collop[2] /'kɑləp/ *n.,* a standard measure of grazing land < Ir *colpa.*

collop[3] /'kʌləp/ *n.,* calf of leg < Ir *colpa.* 'Plaiting the collops,' walking very drunk on the street (BP, Meath, heard in Tipperary).

colly, *see* COLLEY.

colouring /'kʌlərən/ *v.n. (colloq.),* milk < E. 'Put more colouring in your tea' (KG, Kerry).

colpán /'kʌlpɔːn/ *n.,* (wooden) handle of flail, attached to the flail by a piece of leather or eelskin (TF, Cavan) < Ir.

come-all-ye /kʌ'mɔːljə/ *n. (pejor.),* a traditional ballad, especially a long-drawn-out one < *'Come all ye lads and lassies,'* etc., a common opening line of such ballads (LUB, Dublin). 'Well, he got up to sing a come-all-ye, twenty verses or more – we thought he'd never sit down!' (KG, Kerry).

comedher /kʌm'eːd̪ər/ also **comether, come hether,** *phr.,* an invitation to a romantic response < E *come hither.* 'To put the comether on,' to coax, captivate, win over (LUB, Dublin). Carleton, 'Shane Fadh's Wedding' (*Six Irish Tales,* 181): "I whispered the soft nonsense, Nancy, into poor Mary's ear, until I put my comedher on her, and she couldn't live at all without me" (in a footnote Carleton adds: *"Comedher* – come hither – alluding to the burden of an old love charm which is still used by the young of both sexes on May morning').

comhar /koːr/ *n.,* the sharing of work or equipment between neighbours; mutual assistance < Ir. 'Comharing' (also 'coring'), sharing a team of plough horses, giving each other so many days' labour (on a smaller scale than a MEITHEAL) (SOM, Kerry).

comhchliamhán /koː'kliən/ *n.,* another son-in-law in the same family (KM, Kerry) < Ir. 'Sure aren't we comhchliamháns all along, and to think I never knew till now.'

comhluadar /koː'luəd̪ər/ *n.,* convivial company; a group conversing pleasantly together (SOM, Kerry) < Ir. 'It was a nice comhluadar – even though I haven't seen them for years.'

Communion, *see* HOLY COMMUNION.

company /'kʌmpəni/, in the phr. 'keeping company', going out with a member of the opposite sex, especially used by priests questioning penitents. Healy, *Nineteen Acres,* 43: "'Anything else, my child?' 'I kept company, Father.' 'With a girl?' 'Yes, Father.' 'Well, did anything happen?' 'I kissed her Father.' 'Did she kiss you back?'"

conablach /kʌnə'blɑx/ *n.,* term of endearment: a thriving child; 'the little conablach' (SOM, Kerry, who adds: 'NB. Elsewhere [i.e. not in Sliabh Luachra] conablach = carcase, remnants') (variation of Ir CONNALBHACH).

conabras /'kʌnəbrəs/ *n.,* something like mincemeat or very small particles, as in the mild threat, 'if you don't behave I'll make conabras of you' (BP, Meath, heard in Roscommon) (perhaps a corruption of conablach, *fragments,* or CONAMAR).

conacre /'kɑneːkər/ *n.,* the practice of tenants letting small ready-ploughed patches of their land for short periods for a single crop (e.g. potatoes) and at disproportionately high rents < E *corn* + *acre.* Carleton, 'The Hedge School' (*Six Irish Tales,*

155): "Would get a good dale [deal] of Surveyin' to do in the vircinity [*sic*] of Findramore, particularly in *Con-acre time*."

conamar /'kʌnəmər/ *n.*, broken bits, fragments; fig. 'mincemeat', in such threats as 'if you don't behave I'll make conamars of you' < Ir.

condition /kən'diʃən/ *n.*, the state of being well fed. 'I wish I could get rid of this condition on me' (RC, Cavan) < E.

confession /kən'fɛʃʒn/ *n.*, the confession of sins to a priest; all mortal sins (*see* MORTALLER) committed after baptism must be confessed, together with an account of the circumstances of the sin; venial sins and mortal sins already confessed in previous visits do not have to be confessed; children are prepared for going to confession when they reach the 'Age of Reason', normally about seven years; up till recently confession was administered by a priest to a penitent in a confessional-box (a device to maintain discretion between priest and sinner which was invented by St Charles Borromeo, 1538–1584, Cardinal Archbishop of Milan, in response to scandals arising from the administration of the Sacrament of Penance in his diocese. 'Which priest is hearing confessions this evening? If it's the new man I'm not going – he goes on an on' (KG, Kerry). Joyce, *Ulysses*, 223.7–8: "He bore in mind secrets confessed"; Kavanagh, *Tarry Flynn*, 44: "Men who had forgotten what they were born for came out of the confessional, in the words of Charlie Trainor, 'ready to bull cows.' This was the effect the MISSION was having on all minds"; O'Brien, *A Pagan Place*, 41: "You went to the curate because the PARISH PRIEST was deaf and the sins had to be shouted at him"; Leonard, *Out After Dark*, 37: "When I was fourteen, Father Creedon threw me out of the confessional for not knowing the *Confiteor* [the first word of a form of general confession]"; 45: "When my turn came, the slide between the priest and penitent was slid back with such violence that my heart leaped"; Muldoon, 'Cuba' (*FDA* 3, 1413): "I could hear May from beyond the curtain [in the confessional box]. 'Bless me, Father, for I have sinned. | I told a lie once, I was disobedient once. | And, Father, a boy touched me once'"; Healy, *Nineteen Acres*, 43: ". . . one place nearer to the dark confessional box. Your heart thumped in fear as the slide on the grill opened." *See* CONFESSIONAL.

confessional /kən'fɛʃənəl/ *n.*, a cubicle inside a Catholic church in which a priest heard a penitent's CONFESSION. Kavanagh,

Tarry Flynn, 44: "Men who had forgotten what they were born for came out of the confessional, in the words of Charlie Trainor, 'ready to bull cows.' This was the effect the MISSION was having on all minds"; Leonard, *Out After Dark,* 37: "When I was fourteen, Father Creedon threw me out of the confessional for not knowing the *Confiteor* [the prayer of general confession]"; Muldoon, 'Cuba' (*FDA,* 3, 1413): "I could hear May from beyond the curtain [of the confessional]. 'Bless me, Father, for I have sinned. | I told a lie once, I was disobedient once. | And, Father, a boy touched me once"; Healy, *Nineteen Acres,* 43: ". . . one place nearer to the dark confessional box. Your heart thumped in fear as the slide on the grille opened."

Confirmation /kɑnfər'meːʃən/ *n.,* a sacrament in the Catholic church, administered by a bishop, in which a person is confirmed in their faith, usually about the age of twelve; in Ireland young people are traditionally rewarded by relatives and neighbours with gifts of money as a token of the specialness of the occasion < OF *confermer, v.*, to confirm (this verb superseded the OE verb *bisceopian*, to confirm (lit. to bishop)). 'Don't spend the confirmation money all at once' (MCR, Waterford).

connalbhach /'kʌnəlvɑx/ *n.,* term of endearment: a thriving child. 'The little connalbhach' (KM, Kerry) < Ir.

contagious /kən'teːʤəs/ *adj.,* a malapropism for 'contiguous' (near) < ME *contagious* < LL *contagiosus* (contiguous < EModE *contiguous* < LL *contiguus*). 'That house is contagious to me' (Dublin).

coob, *see* CÚB.

coolcannon, *see* COLCANNON.

coop /kuːp/ *n.,* a cage or box for poultry; fig. the lower part of a kitchen dresser where a hen and her eggs were put to hatch (BC, Meath) < E (origin obscure). 'Would you believe it, he still puts the CLOCKING hens into the coop.'

cooramagh /'kuːrəməx/ *adj.,* tender, thoughtful, careful, solicitous (KM, Kerry) < Ir *cúramach.*

coorjeeking /kuːr'ʤiːkən/ also **cuairdeeking** *pres.part.,* visiting; rambling (DOH, Limerick); going around visiting the neighbours' houses for a chat (VQ, Kerry) < Ir *cuairdíocht.* 'He does be out coorjeeking.' *See* BOTHÁNTAÍOCHT; CÉILÍ; RAMBLING.

coortin', *see* COURTING.

copaleen, *see* CAPALL.

copóg /'kʌpoːg/ *n.,* a dock-leaf (MK, Galway) < Ir. 'Neantóg a dhóigh mé, copóg a leigheas mé,' it was a nettle that stung me, a dock-leaf that cured me;

'We used always spit on a copóg and rub it onto a nettle sting.'

coracle /'kɑrəkəl/ *n.,* a small round one-person boat made of watertight hides or tarred canvas stretched over a wickerwork frame < Welsh *corwgl* (cf. Ir *curach*). 'Is that your coracle I see down there by the lake?' (JL, Mayo).

cora-grifín, *see* CURRIGRIFEEN.

corcán /'kʌrkɔːn/ *n.,* a small pot used for heating small potatoes; fig. pot belly < Ir. 'Look at the corcán on him – that's what PORTER does for you!' (BC, Meath).

corcass /'kʌrkəs/ *n.,* marshy land bordering rivers < Ir *corcach,* marsh. Griffin, *The Collegians,* 333: "'They have left the cover on the hill,' cried a gentleman who was galloping past, 'and are trying the corcass.'"

Coróin Mhuire /'kʌroːn'vɪrə/ *n.,* the Rosary (SOM, Kerry); Rosary beads < Ir. 'The smallest sign of any sickness in the house and she wants to say the Coróin Mhuire' (BC, Meath).

corp /kʌrp/ *n.,* in the phrase 'corp an Diabhail', *int.,* body of the Devil (SOM, Kerry) < Ir. Banim, *The Boyne Water,* 118: "*'Curp-an-duoul!'* cried the peasant."

Corpo /'kɔːrpo/ *n. (colloq.),* Dublin Corporation (i.e. City Council), but used for its employees. Brown, *Down All the Days,* 188: "You might know me Da. Barney Cadbury. Used to work in the Corpo. A plumber." *See* -o.

corrach /'kʌrəx/ *adj.,* rough, uneven; unstable < Ir. 'You'll never get a tractor across that bog – it's too corrach' (Galway).

corraghiob /kʌrə'gɪb/, in the phrase 'sitting on one's corraghiob,' sitting on one's heels, squatting (SOM, Kerry, who writes: 'e.g. old people smoking in a forge, squatting on their hunkers, discussing the affairs of the nation; GOGAIDE is used in the same context'). *See* GOGAIDE.

corráinín /kʌ'rɔːniːn/ *n.,* a file for a scythe (KM, Kerry) < Ir. 'Have you seen the corráinín? I can't find it anywhere.'

corránaí /kʌ'rɔːniː/ *n.,* anything of a large size (ENM, Kerry) < Ir.

corresk /'kʌrəʃk/ also **corr réisc** *n.,* a heron, a bog crane (MK, Galway) < Ir *corr réisc,* heron. 'I saw a corresh catching a fish down by the river yesterday.'

corse /koːrs/ *n.,* a corpse < E dial. < ME *cors.* 'They buried the corse this morning' (TJ, Sligo). 'Corse-house', mortuary.

cos /kʌs/ *n.,* foot < Ir. 'The MASTER used call "cos dheas, cos chlé" [right foot, left foot] when we'd be marching into school' (Cavan). Joyce, *Finnegans Wake,* 475.34–5: "within the bawl of a mascot [ass], kuss yuss, kuss cley." *See* COSNOCHTA.

cosa fuara /ˈkʌsəˈfuərə/ also **cosaí fuaraí**, **cosaí fuaraís** (SOM, Kerry) *n.pl.*, stilts (MK, Galway) < Ir (lit. cold legs). 'They had the cosa fuara out for the parade.'

cosa in airde /ˈkʌsɪnˈɑːrʤə/ *adv.phr.*, at full speed, galloping (KM, Kerry) < Ir. 'Racing down the street he was, cosa in airde.'

cosher /ˈkʌʃər/ *n.*, the practice of a chief going from house to house to be entertained by his followers; more recently going casually to a neighbour's home for a chat < Ir *cóisir*, feast, party. 'MUSHA, we only had a bit of a cosher – that was all.' Swift, *A Dialogue in Hybernian Stile*, 164: *"B:* . . . He sometimes coshers with me . . ." *See* COORJEEKING.

cosnochta /ˈkʌsnʌxt̪ə/, /kʌs ˈnʌxt̪ə/ *adj.*, barefoot (Meath) < Ir.

costnent /ˈkɑstnɛnt/ also **costinent**, **cossent** *n.*, working for wages without board and lodging, sometimes with a house and some land provided by the employer (origin obscure; perhaps < E *cost*, expense + *anent* (archaic), towards).

cot /kɑt/ a small boat; a flat-bottomed boat < E dial. 'I'll fix up the cot and we can go rowing in the lake this summer' (Galway).

country /ˈkʌnt̪ri/ *n.*, a particular district or locality < E dial. 'There's nearly no cattle in this country now' (BC, Meath). Kickham, *Knocknagow,* 495: "but I'd tear the heart out uv my body before I'd fret [frighten] the girl I'd be found uv, an' makin' her the talk uv the counthry, as he's doin'"; Trollope, *The Kellys and the O'Kellys,* 40: "the poor girl's as good as got no friends, and I wouldn't like it to be thought in the counthry, I'd taken her at a disadvantage"; Sheehan, *Glenanaar,* 265–6: "'Tell me, have you ever kem [come] across in these here counthries a fellow called Dailey . . . If iver [ever] you meet him,' continued Big Din, 'tell him there's some wan [one] on this thrack . . .' 'I will,' I said. 'But I guess that's not likely. 'Tis a big country out here.'"

county, as in 'the County Cork', *see* THE.

couple /ˈkʌpəl/ *n.*, a few (not just two). 'Give me a couple of eggs'; 'a couple of days ago.' *See* CÚPLA FOCAL.

courting /ˈkuːrtən/ *v.n.*, paying court, wooing < OF *cortoyer*. 'Yon pair's been courtin' for years' (TJ, Sligo). Sheehan, *Glenanaar,* 325: "WISHA, wasn't it quare . . . that a man who was coortin' the mother should marry the daughter?"

couterments /ˈkuːt̪ərmɛnts/ *n.pl.*, dress, belongings, things strewn about < E dial. form of *accoutrements* (by apheresis). 'Pick up your couterments and get out!' (Kildare).

cow /kau/, as in 'the cow is calling,' 'on the rant,' or 'in love,' meaning in heat (MOB, Mayo). *See* CURE.

crab /kræb/ *v.,* to anger, make cross, vex (PON, Dublin) < E dial. < OE *crabba.* 'He crabbed me with his talk' (PON, Dublin).

crabbit /ˈkræbɪt/ *p.part., adj.* 1. Shrewd, 'cute'; 'old-fashioned' (said of children, i.e. precocious) (PON, Dublin). 2. Also 'crabbed', 'crabby' (PON, Dublin), cross, bad-tempered, ill-humoured < E dial. < ME *crabbid.* 'She's a bit crabbit the day [today]'. Friel, *Translations,* act I (*FDA* 3, 1210): *"Manus:* What the hell are you so crabbed about?"

crack /kræk/ *n.,* entertaining conversation. Ir *craic* is the ModE loanword *crack* < ME *crak,* loud conversation, bragging talk; recently reintroduced into HE (usually in its Ir spelling) in the belief that it means high-spirited entertainment. 'The craic was ninety [extremely good]'; 'There does be great craic in the pub of a Saturday night when it's packed to the doors.' Spenser, *Faerie Queene,* book II, xi, 8: "vainglorious crakes [braggarts]"; Friel, *Translations,* act 3 (*FDA* 3, 1230): *"Doalty:* You never saw such crack in your life, boys"; Johnston, *Shadows on Our Skin,* 111: "I'm sorry if I muscled in on Saturday. Did I spoil your crack?"; Doyle, *The Van,* 165: "This was good crack. Sharon handed him the bag."

crá croí /krɔːˈkriː/ *n.,* chest pain < Ir. 'I have a touch of crá croí – give us a little spoonogue [Ir *spúnóg,* spoon] of brandy.'

crág /krɔːg/ *n.,* a handful < Ir. Throw a crág of meal in to the cows before you go.'

craiceáilte /ˈkrækˈɔːltʃə/ *adj.,* daft, 'cracked' (SOM, Kerry) < Ir (cf. E *cracked*).

craiceálaí /krɑˈkɔːliː/ also **creacáilí, craicawly** *n.,* a brainless, crazy person (usually female) < Ir (*see* CRAICEÁILTE). 'She was ever a craiceálaí person'; 'The craiceálaí will never be able to bring up that child by herself.'

cráin /krɔːn/ *n.,* a sow (SOM, Kerry) < Ir. 'Cráin mhuice', a surly individual; (*pejor.*) a mother < Ir *cráin mhuice,* sow. 'The cráin – she's expecting again'; 'She let a grunt out of her like a cráin.'

cráintín /ˈkrɔːntʃiːn/ *n.,* a hatching goose; an aging, wizened woman < Ir. 'Someone would want to call in to the old cráintín over the Christmas to make sure she's all right.'

cráite /ˈkrɔːt̪ə/ *p.part., adj.,* tormented with sorrow, miserable; short-tempered (SOM, Kerry), peevish (of a child when teething) < Ir. 'She's very cráite, the poor CRAYTURE' (KG, Kerry); 'MUSHA, the poor creature must be cráite living in a house like that!'

cráiteachán /'krɔːʧəkɔːn/, /'krɔːʧəxɔːn/ *n.,* a sad, tormented person < Ir. 'He's a terrible cráiteachán, the poor man.'

crane, *see* OVEN.

crannán /'krænɔːn/ *n.,* the handle of a scythe < Ir. 'Measure the crannán to the man's height.'

crannóg /'krænoːg/ *n.,* a prehistoric lake-dwelling < Ir.

craobh /kriːv/, /kreːv/ *n.,* branch < Ir. 'Craoibhín', a small branch (SOM, Kerry) < Ir (dimin. of *craobh*). 'A couple of those craoibhíns will do to block the gap for the time being.'

craobhabhar /'kriːvaur/, /'kreːvaur/ *n.,* sty (on the eye) (SOM, Kerry) < Ir. 'She has the cure for the craobhabhar: she rubs her gold ring on the eye. If that doesn't work, she puts a hot wet cloth around a wooden spoon and holds it to the sore eye' (KM, Kerry).

craos /kriːs/, /kreːs/ *n.,* gluttony; inordinate desire for food or alcohol (SOM, Kerry) < Ir. *See* AINMHIAN.

craosach /'kriːsəx/ *n., adj.,* greedy, voracious; a gluttonous person < Ir. 'I've never seen such a craosach when it comes to eating.'

crawthumper /'krɔːt̪ʌmpər/ *n.,* an ostentatiously devout person, a VOTEEN < ME *crawe,* stomach + *thumper,* one who beats. 'The crawthumper always sits up in the front seat.'

craythur /'kreːt̪ər/ also **crayture** *n.,* intoxicating liquor, especially whiskey < E dial. *creature* (using the archaic pronunciation of 'ea') < OF *créature,* a person; anything created. 'Give us a drop of the crayture, for the love of God.' Carleton, 'The Hedge School' (*Six Irish Tales,* 171): "You must bring plinty of bacon, hung beef, and fowls, bread and cabbage – not forgetting the phaties [*see* PRÁTA], and sixpence a-head for the *crathur,* boys, won't yees?"; 'Finnegan's Wake' (song): "He'd a drop o' the craythur every morn"; Joyce, *Finnegans Wake,* 4.29: "He addle liddle phifie Annie ugged the little craythur." *See* CRÉATÚR, CREATURE.

creabhar /kraur/ *n.* 1. A tick; horsefly. 2. A pikeful of hay made into a round shape during the saving process; a little cock of hay (SOM, Kerry) < Ir.

creacáilí, *see* CRAICEÁLAÍ.

creach /kræx/ *n.,* a big loss < Ir. 'Mo chreach,' alas (SOM, Kerry). 'I should have sold them a month ago – mo chreach, but sure what of it?'

creachaill /'krækəl/ *n.,* root or hulk portion of bog deal or bog oak, broken into pieces and used as fire-lighters; more recently used for carving (SOM, Kerry).

creachán /ˈkrækɔːn/ *n.,* a small potato; small pebble; fig. a puny person < Ir. 'He's only a creachán'; 'Don't be throwing creacháns at the neighbour's dog.'

creag /kræg/ *n.,* a large stone or rock (SOM, Kerry) < Ir.

creagar /krægər/ also **criogar** *n.,* a cricket (SOM, Kerry); grasshopper (TF, Cavan) < Ir. 'Will you listen to the criogars behind the fire?' (AF, Cavan).

créatúr /ˈkreːt̪uːr/ *n.,* term of endearment: a person < Ir < E or OF *creature.* 'Come here, you poor little créatúr – who did that to you?' (BC, Meath). *See* CRAYTHUR, CREATURE.

creature /ˈkriːʧər/ *n.* 1. Term of endearment: a person. 'The poor creature, she's all alone now.' 2. Whiskey < E. *See* CRAYTHUR, CRÉATÚR.

creel /kriːl/ also **kreel** *n.,* a wicker basket for transporting turf, often in pairs placed on each side of an ass's back; wickerwork side rails put on a cart for transporting sheep, pigs etc. to the fair (BF, Cork) < Ir *críol.* 'If you think this is hard work you should have had to be piling it into creels'; 'She's as honest as a creel is watertight.' Healy, *Nineteen Acres,* 35: "If you had an ass and a pair of pardógs (or creels) you got the princely sum of six and sixpence for walking behind an ass, a bouncy new pair of sally rod creels bobbing up and down as Silver did her brisk trot to Cortoon"; O'Brien, *A Pagan Place,* "The wet turf was a gift from your father to the school, a whole kreel of it sent one day in the Emma era in a burst of righteousness, because tongues were wagging." *See* PARDÓG.

creepie /ˈkriːpi/ *n.,* a small three-legged stool suitable especially for houses without a chimney, when the person sitting on it was below the smoke level < E dial. < OE *creopan v.,* to crawl, to creep. 'My father made creepies for the children' (BD, Cavan). *See* STÓILÍN.

criathar /ˈkriəhər/ *n.,* a sieve, a riddle (SOM, Kerry); a strainer for milk < Ir. 'Did you clean the criathar after you finished with it?' (MG, Cavan).

criogar, *see* CREAGAR.

crios /krɪs/ *n.,* a belt, a girdle (SOM, Kerry); the girdle worn by a friar; a multicoloured woven woollen belt originally worn by men in the Aran Islands, later a fashionable accessory < Ir *crios.* 'Sure you can get those crioses all over the country now' (BC, Meath).

criosóg /ˈkrɪsoːg/ *n.,* a rope used in place of a straddle on asses (JF, Cavan) < Ir.

crisheen, *see* CROIS.

crit /krit/ *n.,* an undersized apple; the core of an apple (RB, Waterford) < E dial. (origin obscure).

cró /kroː/ *n.,* a stall, pen, hut, stable < Ir. 'Cró na mbó', byre.

'Cró na gcearc', hen-house. 'Tie up that cow in the cró – she'll have to be tested' (SOC, Kerry). *See* TIGÍN.

crochaire /krʌkərə/ *n.,* a villain, knave (KM, Kerry) < Ir. 'If I get near that crochaire I'll knock him into the middle of next week.'

crochán /ˈkrʌxɔːn/ *n.,* the straw, bier or mattress on which a person was laid to die < Ir. 'They wouldn't let an old person die in the bed, they'd take them out in the "crochán", they called it. They used make a bed of straw beside the bed and they'd take them down and leave them beside the bed to die so they wouldn't have to take them out of the bed. They washed them in the crochán, and then burned it . . . Sometimes they'd take them out before they were dead at all. It was terrible. I suppose they had a reason for it. I never saw it done' (as explained by Annie Meagh of Coogue, Co. Mayo, in recent times). In her glossary to *The Absentee* (1895 edition), 85–6, Maria Edgeworth s.v. 'WAKE' tells much the same story: "When an Irish man or woman of the lower order dies, the straw which composed the bed, whether it has been contained in a bag to form a mattress, or simply spread upon the earthen floor, is immediately taken out of the house, and burned before the cabin door, the family at the same time setting up the death howl. The ears and eyes of the neighbours being thus alarmed, they flock to the house of the deceased, and by their vociferous sympathy excite and at the same time soothe the sorrows of the family . . . burning the straw upon which the sick man lay became a simple preservative against infection."

crock /krɑk/ *n.,* an earthenware vessel for buttermilk etc. < OE *croc.* Kavanagh, *Tarry Flynn,* 198: "She carried the two crocks to the dairy."

croí an Diabhail /kriːənˈʤaul/ *n.phr.,* the Devil's heart < Ir. 'She has the croí an Diabhail – we're all AFEARD of her' (BC, Meath).

cróilí /ˈkroːliː/ *n.,* an infirm, sickly, bedridden person (MK, Galway) < Ir *cróilí,* infirmity, state of being bedridden. 'How's the cróilí? Is he on the mend [getting better]?'

croiméal /ˈkrʌmeːl/ also **croimbéal** *n.,* a moustache (SOM, Kerry) < Ir. 'He looks a right eejit with that croiméal of his.'

cróinseach /ˈkroːnʃəx/ *n.,* a dark, swarthy woman (KM, Kerry); sometimes used as a family nickname < Ir. 'I wonder where that cróinseach came out of?'

croisín /ˈkrʌʃiːn/, /ˈkrɪʃiːn/, also **crusheen, crisheen** *n.,* a cross;

a stick with a cross-piece used in washing potatoes, gathering sea-weed etc.; 'a small piece of wood fitted onto the end of a spade handle so as to form a T' (Martin, 178) < Ir *croisín* (dimin. of *crois,* a cross). 'Get going on the spuds with that croisín!'; 'Did you ever see a crusheen being used'? (TJ, Sligo).

crompán /ˈkrʌmpɔːn/ *n.,* a knotty bit of wood (Louth) < Ir. 'We'll take that nice crompán home for the fire.'

crónán /ˈkroːnɔːn/ *n.,* humming, droning, murmuring (MK, Galway); crooning (SOM, Kerry) < Ir. 'Stop your crónán-ing and get the job done.' Joyce, *Finnegans Wake,* 41.22: "cre-moaning and cronauning."

cronauning, *see* CRÓNÁN.

crook /kruːk/, a metal hook from which cooking-pots were suspended over the fire (BC, Meath) < ME *croc*. *See* CISEÁN; CRANE; OVEN.

croppy /ˈkrɑpiː/ *n.,* a member of the United Irishmen in the insurrection of 1798, who cut their hair short, following the fashion of the French Revolution < OE *crop*. 'He had a great voice for singing, but he was at his best with 'The Croppy Boy' [popular ballad commemorating 1798] – he'd bring the tears to your eyes' (KG, Kerry).

cross[1] /krɔːs/ *n.,* in the phrase 'he'd steal the cross off a donkey's back', referring to a very mean person.

cross[2] /krɔːs/, in the phrase 'cross of four roads', a cross-roads. 'Go straight through the cross of four roads, and we'll be up on the left' (KM, Kerry).

cross[3] /krɔːs/ *adj.,* peevish by nature – a more habitual form of ill-temper than conveyed by ModE 'cross' (of mixed origins < *cross,* a gibbet, and *cross* (aphetic of *across,* in the form of a cross < ME *acros*); see *ODEE* s.v. 'across', 'cross[1,2,3]'; closer to Ir *crosta,* contrary, troublesome). 'Mind the dog – he's very cross'; 'That one in the shop's been cross as long as I've known her' (TF, Cavan).

crosser[1] /ˈkrɑsər/ *n. (colloq.),* a lift on the cross-bar of a bicycle < OE *cros (bar)* + *-er.* 'Come on, I'll give you a crosser for a bit of the way anyway' (Cork). *See* BACKER.

Crosser[2] /ˈkrɑsər/ *place-name (colloq.),* abbreviation for Crosshaven, Co. Cork.

crot, *see* cruit.

crotach /ˈkrʌt̪əx/ *n.,* a curlew (SOM, Kerry) < Ir. 'My father used love hear the crotach's call.'

cruachás /ˈkruəxɔːs/ *n.,* hardship, predicament; being in a tight spot, in a fix (SOM, Kerry) < Ir.

cruadhar /ˈkruəkər/ *n.,* stinginess; fig. a mean person < Ir. 'You won't get supper from that cruadhar!' (BC, Meath).

cruatan /ˈkruət̪ən/ *n.,* distress, hardship, difficult circumstances (SOM, Kerry) < Ir. 'There's always some cruatan or other in that family – what is it with them?' (KM, Kerry).

crúb /kruːb/ *n.,* big foot; hoof or claw (MK, Galway) < Ir. 'Get your big crúbs out of there.'

crubeen /kruːˈbiːn/ also **croobeen, crúibín** (**crúibíní** pl.) *n.,* a delicacy made from boiled pig's trotters (SOM, Kerry) < Ir *crúibín,* hoof. 'I remember when they used have crubeens after the pubs closed, but not any more' (KG, Kerry); 'Eat the crúibíns – the nicest part of the pig' (KM, Kerry).

crúcáil /ˈkruːkɔːl/ *n.,* grasping, pawing < Ir. 'Crúcálaí', a grasping person < Ir. 'You crúcálaí, you'll never reach it!'; 'What a crúcálaí you are – let me finish it' (Mayo).

crúibín, *see* CRUBEEN.

cruiskeen /kruːˈʃkiːn/ also **cruskeen** *n.,* a jug < Ir. 'Bring up a cruskeen of milk from the churn; it's on the FORM beside the dresser' (AF, Cavan). 'Crúiscín lán', 'cruiskeen lawn', a full jug (of whiskey) < Ir *crúiscín lán,* full jug. *See* DRÍODAR.

cruit[1] /krɪʧ/ *n.,* a hump < Ir. 'Get that cruit off you and walk straight if you can.' 'Cruiteach' *adj.,* hump-backed (JF, Cavan).

cruit[2] /krɪʧ/ *n.,* a harp (CS, Mayo) < Ir. 'He never knew that the cruit was the symbol of Ireland.'

cruiteachán /ˈkrɪʧəxɔːn/ *n.,* a hunchback; fig. a person bent over from arthritis (SOM, Kerry) < Ir. 'How can that poor cruiteachán even get up out of bed in the morning?' (KG, Kerry).

cruitín /ˈkrɪʧiːn/ *n.,* a little hump < Ir (dimin. of CRUIT[1]). 'He has that little cruitín since he was born' (BC, Meath).

crupper /ˈkrʌpər/ *n.,* the padded lining attached to the saddle and secured under a donkey's tail to stop the loaded CREELS or PARDÓGS from moving forward (NH, Mayo) < ME *croper* < OF *cropiere.*

crusheen, *see* CROISÍN.

cruskeen, *see* CRUISKEEN.

crústáil /ˈkruːst̪ɔːl/ *v.n.,* throwing missiles (KM, Kerry) < Ir. 'Stop crústáiling those sods at each other'; 'Tim, do you mind [remember] when we used come from school and we'd croosht Johnnie's galvanised [-iron] roof with stones?'

cruth /krʌt̪/ also **crot** (SOM, Kerry), **crooth** *n.,* shape, appearance < Ir. 'Look at the crot of him' (SOM, Kerry); 'He has the crooth o' hardship on him' (*Gaelic Churchman,* June 1923, 143).

cuach /kuex/ *n.,* cuckoo (SOM, Kerry) < Ir. 'Listen to the cuachs beside the lake!'

cuaird /kuərʤ/ *n.,* a visit; an evening visit < Ir. 'In Clare I have heard "goin' on my cuaird'" (DOH, Limerick). *See* AIRNEÁN; BOTHÁNTÁIOCHT; CÉILI; COORJEEKING; RAMBLING.

cuas /kuəs/ *n.*, a space between rocks; a cavity, a recess; a hollow (SOM, Kerry) < Ir. 'He said he hid it in the cuas next to the tree.'

cuasnóg /ˈkuəsnoːg/ *n.*, a wild bees' hive in a hedge < Ir. 'Watch out for the cuasnóg in that hedge' (Meath).

cúb /kuːb/ also **coob** *n.*, a hen-coop (SOM, Kerry) < Ir. 'Go down and fetch some eggs from the cúb.' Griffin, *The Collegians,* 106: "Here, Mrs. Frawley, will you have an eye to the spit a minute while I go look at them hens in the *coob* abroad? Master Kyrle might like a fresh egg for his *tay*, an' I hear them clockin'."

cúbóg /ˈkuːboːg/ *n.pl.*, an assortment of Easter eggs; 'a gift of eggs at Easter' (Moylan, 88) < Ir. 'The children spent the whole day yesterday asking me where the cúbóg was but I didn't say a word.'

cuddy /ˈkʌdi/ *n.*, a night's hospitality < Ir *cuid oíche* (lit. a night's share). "The 'night share' was an exaction, the overnight hospitality that a lord, with his retinue, was entitled to claim from his tenantry. It included food, lodging, and entertainment, and could be claimed either by direct billeting, or as a levy of goods to the same value; commutation for money payments became increasingly common in early modern Ireland" (MB, Tipperary).

cúilín /ˈkuːliːn/ *n.*, a little field < Ir. 'Don't plough the cúilín – it's too small' (MG, Cavan).

cuing /kɪŋ/ *n.*, a yoke; a swingle-tree; part of a plough attachment < Ir. 'What happened to the cuing? I can't find it anywhere' (Mayo).

cuirliún /ˈkɪrluːn/ *n.*, a curlew; fig. a baby < Ir. 'Look at the poor wee cuirliún in the cot!' (BC, Meath).

cuiseog /kɪˈʃoːg/ *n.*, a reed; stalk of dry grass, blade of straw (KM, Kerry) < Ir.

cúisín /ˈkuːʃiːn/ *n.*, a cushion; a small crochet square worn on the head (not as large as a shoulder-shawl) < Ir. 'Have you a cúisín for this chair, please?' (KG, Kerry).

culchie /ˈkʌltʃiː/ *n.* (*derog.*), a person from rural Ireland <? shortened form of *agricultural*, or someone from Kiltimagh (*Coillte Mach*) /kʌltʃəmɑx/, Co. Mayo (regarded as a remote place), or a form of Ir *coillteach*, a wooded place, adj., woody, sylvan (MOB, Mayo); 'I've heard it derived from "cúl an tí" (back of the house)' (KM, Kerry). Dubliners are sometimes referred to as 'culchies' (KD, Dublin); 'culchie, Dublin city person', 'culchimac, son of a Dublin person!' (Cork).

culchimac, *see* CULCHIE.

culls /kʌlz/ *n.pl.,* small lambs usually sold separately from the main flock (GF, Galway) < E dial. < EModE *cull, v.,* to select < OF *cueillir.* 'Did you sell any culls this year?'

cúlóg /'kuːloːg/ *n.,* a pillion-rider; riding pillion < Ir. 'Mary was riding cúlóg on the donkey behind John' (Limerick); 'I was riding culóg, behind him on the horse' (Cork).

cumann /'kʌmən/ *n.,* a branch of a political party < Ir *cumann,* society. 'I joined the local cumann in nineteen and forty six' (JB, Kildare: older speakers of HE often introduce 'and' between the number of the century and the year). Joyce, *Finnegans Wake,* 42.13–14: "to the balleder of which the world of cumannity singing owes a tribute"; 320.5: "cummanisht, sagd he."

cumar /'kʌmər/ *n.,* part of a bog with high banks on both sides; a ravine (SOM, Kerry) < Ir. 'We went for a cycle down to the cumar in Glenri.'

cumas /'kʌməs/ *n.,* power, means, capability < Ir. 'He has the cumas to turn the match if he put his mind to it' (Limerick).

cúnamh /'kuːnəv/ *n.,* help, assistance, in the phrase 'le cúnamh Dé,' with the help of God < Ir. 'May we all be here again at the same time next year, le cúnamh Dé' (MK, Galway); 'Such friendship is indeed worthy of celebration, and next year, le cúnamh Dé, it shall be with us' (PG, Dublin).

cúpla focal /'kuːplə'fʌkəl/ *n.phr.,* a few token words in Irish at the beginning of a speech in English < Ir *cúpla focal,* couple of words. *See* COUPLE.

cúram /'kuːrəm/ *n.,* care, responsibility; fig. family < Ir. 'How are the cúram?', how are the family? (SOM, Kerry). *See* CARE.

cúramach /'kuːrəməx/ *adj.,* careful; responsible; 'sometimes a hint of being mean about money, slow to stand a drink' (SOM, Kerry) < Ir. 'Seán cúramach', mean Seán.

curate /'kjuːrət/ *n.* 1. A priest assisting a parish priest < ME < mediaeval L *curatus.* 2. A barman, the assistant to a 'spirit-grocer'. Joyce, *Finnegans Wake,* 116.18–19: "and the curate one who brings strong waters." 3. The homely iron poker used to spare the steel implement *de luxe* (see Hayden and Hartog, 781–2).

curcaí /'kʌrkiː/ *n.,* top-knot (of hair) (Meath) < Ir. 'Let me do your hair in a curcaí for you.'

cure /kjuər/ *n.,* a local remedy for ailments, in human beings or animals, usually with one particular person in the locality regarded as having 'the cure' for a particular illness or disability (e.g. broken bones, sore throat, even skin cancer) < F *cure.* More general cures include a fox tongue or the ashes of dead wasps on an area affected by a wasp sting from a wasp. 'They reckon Paddeen Joe has the cure for most things except the drink' (TF, Sligo); 'They'd go to the holy wells for cures; if a cow was sick, they'd leave something belonging to the cow behind them' (MOB, Mayo). Kavanagh, *Tarry Flynn,* 26: "The father had the reputation of having a traditional cure for the jaundice and men and women came from far and near for the 'cure'."

curnoptious, *see* CARNAPTIOUS.

currach /kʌrəx/ *n.*, (small) boat, coracle < Ir *curach*. 'We went out in the currach yesterday and caught ten herrings' (Kerry).

Curragh, the /'kʌrə/ *place-name,* an area of level ground in Co. Kildare < Ir *corrach,* marsh.

currigrifeen /kʌrə'grɪfiːn/ also **cora-grifín** *n.*, pins and needles < Ir CODLADH GRIFÍN. 'She suffers badly from the curri-grifeen' (MK, Galway); 'I have cora-grifín in my hands from knitting – I'm not used to it' (KM, Kerry).

curse /kʌrs/ *n., v.,* swear word, foul language; to swear, use foul language < OE *curs, n.,* curse. 'Well, the cursing that came out of him!' (BC, Meath). *See* EASCAINE.

cutaidh /kʌt̪ə/ *n.,* short, worn-out stump of something, Limerick < Ir. *See* CUTTY.

cut-along /'kʌtəlɑŋ/ *n.,* HE form of 'cotillion', a country dance < E dial.

cute hoor, *see* HOOR.

cúthail /'kuːhəl/ also **cúthalach** /'kuːhəlʌx/ *adj.,* bashful, shy; backward (SOM, Kerry) < Ir. 'If you're that cúthalach you'll never get married.'

cutter /'kʌtər/ *n.,* a slate pencil < E dial. (see *EDD* s.v. 'cutter' sb.²).

cutting /'kʌtən/ *pres.part.,* in the phrase 'how's she cutting?', how are things going? how are things with you? (MOC, Limerick, who adds: 'I surmise that it originated in an enquiry by one farmer of another how the meadow was cutting in the hay-making season, but I wouldn't be sure') (cf. *EDD* s.v. 'cut' v.³).

cutty /'kʌti/ *adj., n.,* cut short, small, diminutive; a short clay tobacco pipe; a playful (short) girl < E dial. < E *cut, v.,* cut short. 'She's a fine cutty, that one – there's plenty of go in her.' Stoker, *The Snake's Pass,* 25: "'THRUE for ye!' murmured an old woman with a cutty pipe." *See* CUTAIDH.

D

dagging /ˈdægən/ *v.n.,* removing clotted locks of wool or excrement from a sheep's backside so that maggots don't lodge there and eat the flesh < E dial. (origin obscure). 'If you think I'm going dagging sheep tomorrow you can think again' (Mayo).

Dáil /d̪ɔil/ *n.,* assembly, gathering. 'Dáil Éireann', principal chamber of national parliament < Ir, assembly of Ireland. Joyce, *Finnegans Wake,* 322.16–17: "And, haikon or hurlin, who did you did at doyle today, my horsey dorksey gentryman." *See* OIREACHTAS.

dailc /dælk/ *n.,* thick-set person (or animal) < Ir. 'He's a grand dailc of a man' (KG, Kerry).

dalk /dɔːk/ also **dealg** (SOM, Kerry) *n.,* thorn < Ir *dealg*. 'I'll have to stop for a minute; I must have a dalk in my foot' (BC, Meath).

dalkey /ˈdælki/ *n.,* wire; barbed fencing-wire (MMB, Meath) < Ir *dealg* (*see* DALK).

dall /dɑl/ *adj.,* blind; dazzled (SOM, Kerry); fig. ignorant, not knowing < Ir *dall,* blind. 'I'm dall', I'm ignorant of it (ENM, Kerry). 'I saw Seán Dall [Blind Seán] on the road the other day; he's looking well' (Kerry).

dallachán /ˈdɑləxɔːn/ *n.,* a blind person; a stupid person (SOM, Kerry).

dallamullóg /ˈdɑləməloːg/ *n.,* deception, hoodwinking; bluff; self-delusion (SOM, Kerry) < Ir. *See* DALLER MALLOG.

dallapookeen /dɑləˈpuːkiːn/ *n.,* blindman's buff < Ir *dalladh púicín,* blindfold. 'She fell and cut herself when she was playing dallapookeen.'

daller mallog /ˈdɑlərˈmɑloːg/ *n.,* a disease of blindness in sheep (MJ, Mayo) < Ir DALLAMULLÓG.

dalta /ˈd̪ɑlt̪ə/ *n.,* a foster-child < Ir. 'I think the two CHILDER are daltas.'

daltheen /ˈdɑlt̪iːn/ *n.,* a spoilt child < Ir DALTA + dimin. suffix -EEN. 'That child is a proper little daltheen.'

damhán alla /ˈdaunˈɑlə/ *n.,* a spider (SOM, Kerry) < Ir.

d'anam 'on Diabhal /t̪ɑnəmən ˈdʒaul/ *int.,* a common curse:

your soul to the Devil < Ir. 'D'anam 'on Diabhal, you'll rue the day you crossed me!' (KG, Kerry). Kickham, *Knocknagow,* 26: "Thanum-on-dioul, can it be late so early?"; 'Finnegan's Wake' (song): "Thanam 'on dhoul, do ye think I'm dead?" *See* ANAM; M'ANAM 'ON DIABHAL.

dander /'d̪ɑnd̪ər/ *n., v.,* a leisurely stroll; a 'sudden notion to take a walk' (Cork); to saunter < ScotE (origin obscure). 'There she was, dandering down the road' (AH, Donegal).

daol /d̪eːl/ *n.,* a caterpillar; a long black chafer (beetle) (SOM, Kerry) < Ir. 'Look at the daol crawling under the sod of turf.'

dark[1] /dærk/ *adj.,* blind < E dial. 'She was dark blind,' she was completely blind. Kennelly, 'My Dark Fathers' (*FDA,* 3, 1361): "My dark fathers lived the intolerable day | Committed always to the night of wrong."

dark[2] /dɑrk/, with reference to bread: 'Sometimes the bread (made in an oven covered in greesh) might be unsatisfactory and the texture might be rather dark. This was said to be a dorchas. The Irish for dark is dorchas' (POC, Cavan).

DART /dært/ *n.,* for Dublin Area Rapid Transit (electric rail commuter service). 'Don't tell me you've never been on the DART!' (MCR, Waterford). Doyle, *The Van,* 92: "They got the DART straight across to Lansdowne [Road]."

dathúil /'d̪ɑhuːl/ *adj.,* beautiful, comely < Ir. 'She was looking very dathúil this morning at Mass.'

daw /d̪ɔː/ *n., adj.,* a silly, empty person; an obdurate, unreasoning person; not good at school, thick (SMC, Limerick) < Ir *dáigh, adj.* 'He's a right daw,' he's really stupid. 'He's no daw,' he's no fool.

dawny, *see* DONNY.

dea-chroí /ʤæ'xriː/ *adj.,* good-natured, good-hearted < Ir *dea-chroí* (*n.*). 'She's a little stupid, I know, but sure she's dea-chroí anyway' (KG, Kerry).

dead-house /'dɛdhaus/ *n.,* a mortuary; a house in which a corpse is laid out < E dial. 'We went to fetch him from the dead-house in the hospital in Navan' (BC, Meath). Brown, *Down All the Days,* 236: "The air in the deadhouse had been cold with a palpable dampness . . . Footsteps rang eerily on the concrete floor. Slabs jutted out from the walls, most of them filled with shrouded forms."

deadly /'dɛdli/ *adv.,* used as an intensive, both in good and bad senses < E dial (OE *deadlic*). 'How's the new car?' – 'Deadly!'

dealg, *see* DALK.

dealing /'diːlən/ *v.n.* (*colloq.*), selling cattle. 'Is he dealin' yet?' (SL, Mayo). 'There's bad dealing at the mart the day [today]; the prices are horrid bad' (TF, Cavan).

deannach /ˈʤænəx/ *n.,* dust, especially from a mill < Ir. 'You'd better clean the deannach off before you sit down to eat your dinner.'

dear /diːr/ *n.,* in the expression 'the dear knows,' God knows. In Irish there was formerly a word for God, *Fia,* similar in form and pronunciation to the word for deer, *fia.* In the Irish form of the expression (*dar Fia*), 'fia' may have been substituted for 'Fia' as a euphemism; this confusion was carried over into English, where 'deer' was then mistakenly corrected to 'dear' to make better sense. Griffin, *The Collegians,* 71: "I thought, at first, 'tis to be shaved he was coming, for, dear knows, he wanted it"; Joyce, 'A Mother' (*Dubliners,* 160): "Ah, well! We did our best, the dear knows"; Joyce, *Finnegans Wake,* 79.23–4: "the deer knowed where she'd marry!"

dearg /ˈʤærəg/ *adj. used as n.,* red, in the expression 'he gave him the dearg,' he stabbed him (a common usage in west Limerick) (GF, Galway) < Ir.

death /dɛt̪/ *n.,* in the expression 'to get (or catch) one's death', to contract a fatal illness or injury through careless behaviour. Synge, *In the Shadow of the Glen* (*FDA,* 2, 635): *"Nora:* . . . and I going out to get my death walking the roads?"; Beckett, *Waiting for Godot,* 37: *"Estragon:* . . . You'll catch your death"; Doyle, *The Van,* 45: "Let him catch his death. He deserves to die, the fuckin' EEJIT of a dog"; Bolger, *Emily's Shoes,* 165: "Sure a freezing afternoon like this you'd catch your death." *See* BÁS

death notice /ˈdɛt̪noːtɪs/ *n.,* the announcement of someone's death, together with details of the REMOVAL and the funeral, placed in a newspaper. In earlier times a card was fastened to the front door of a house in which there had been a death, inscribed with the name of the deceased. 'I didn't see his death notice in the paper; did you?' (KG, Kerry).

decade /ˈdɛkəd/, more usually /ˈdɛkət/ *n.,* in the phrase 'a decade of the ROSARY'. 'We'll say a decade of the Rosary.' Brown, *Down All the Days,* 138: "They had started on the umpteenth decade of the litany for the dead."

deck /dɛk/ *n.,* a platform made of planks erected (often at a crossroads) for dancing. 'There was fierce CRACK on the deck last night.'

deer, in the phrase 'the deer knowed,' *see* DEAR.

deifir /ˈʤɛfər/ *n.,* a hurry SOM, Kerry) < Ir. 'What deifir is on you?' (KG, Kerry).

deisigh /ˈʤɛʃɪg/ *int.,* mend your stance; get your leg out of the way (said to a cow to get her to move her right hind leg before milking) (BF, Cork) < Ir *deisigh, v.* 'Deisigh, Bessy!'

dekko /'dɛko/ *n. (colloq.),* a look < British army slang < Hindustani *dekho* (see Chambers s.v. 'dekko'). 'Take a dekko at that', (Beecher, 27, who adds: 'probably introduced to Cork by the Munster Fusiliers').

delph /dɛlf/ also **delf** *n.,* crockery, dishes < Delft, a centre for glazed earthenware in the Netherlands. 'He ran off with all my good delph.' Yeats, *The Green Helmet* (*Collected Plays,* 233): "*Conall:* Laegaire, that Helmet is mine, for what did you find in the bag | But the straw and the broken delf"; Joyce, *Finnegans Wake,* 304.25–6: "That might keep her from throwing delph"; Leonard, *Out After Dark,* 122: "and on one or two sharp days each winter one could see the white cap of Snowdon, a shard of broken delph trodden into the sea."

deoch an dorais /'ʤʌxən'd̪ʌrəʃ/ *n.,* the last drink before going home < Ir (lit. drink of the door). 'Have a deoch an dorais before you go.' 'An té a bhíonn thuas óltar deoch air; an té a bhíonn thíos buailtear cos air' (proverb), When a person is successful people drink to him; when he is down on his luck people kick him. 'Is túisce deoch ná scéal' (proverb), A drink before conversation. Sheehan, *Glenanaar,* 146: "As they said goodbye! after many a *deoch a' dorais* . . ."; Joyce, 'A Little Cloud' (*Dubliners,* 87): "Very well, then, said Ignatius Gallaher, Let us have another one as a *deoc an doruis*"; Joyce, *Finnegans Wake,* 622.29–30: "And you needn't host out with your duck and your duty."

deoir /ʤoːr/ *n.,* a drop of drink (Kerry) < Ir *deoir,* a drop. 'I won't have another deoir or I'll fall over; it's time to go home.'

deoirín /'ʤoːriːn/ *n.,* a tiny drop < Ir (dimin. of DEOIR). 'She wouldn't give me a deoirín more, and I drinking there for the past twenty years' (TF, Cavan).

deoraí /'ʤoːriː/ *n.,* a miserable-looking person, pitiable person < Ir. 'The poor deoraí has no home left to go to' (BC, Meath).

deorum, *see* JORUM.

destroy /dəs'trɔi/ *v.,* to harm, damage, discommode < OF *destruire.* 'Look – you've your trousers destroyed on the tractor' (BC, Meath). Synge, *The Playboy of the Western World,* act III (*FDA,* 2, 637): "*Mahon:* . . . for I'm destroyed travelling since Tuesday was a week"; Leonard, *Out After Dark,* 19: "It's all hours [it's very late], I'm destroyed"; McDonagh, *The Cripple of Inishmaan,* scene vi, 51: "*Bartley:* I was looking forward to the showing of the film too until me jumper became destroyed."

devil /ˈdɪvəl/ also **divil** *n.,* equivalent to a negative in such idioms as 'devil a one' (< Ir *diabhal duine*), not one, 'devil a bit' (< *diabhal é*) , not a bit < E dial. (cf. HE SORRA). The Irish versions are translations from E dial. phrases such as 'devil a many', not many. Trollope, *The Kellys and the O'Kellys,* 39: "'Talk her over, and make her tell, Barry.' 'Divil a tell, my lord, in her'"; Carleton, 'Denis O'Shaughnessy Going to Maynooth' (*Six Irish Tales,* 133): "'Devil the penny will cross my pocket for him, the unlucky thief!' replied the shrewd farmer"; Shaw, *John Bull's Other Island,* act I (*FDA,* 2, 425): "*Broadbent:* Havent you lunched? *Tim:* Divil a lunch!"; Joyce, *Finnegans Wake,* 28.4: "Dibble a hayfork's wrong with her"; Kavanagh, *Tarry Flynn,* 41: "the devil a go the Carlins ever went."

devil's needle /ˈdɪvəlzˈniːdl/ *n.,* a dragon-fly (Cavan) < Ir *snáthaid an diabhail* (cf. 'devil's coach-horse' (beetle), also 'devil's coachman'). 'You do see a lot of devil's needles coming up that part of the river in the evening.'

devil a haet /ˈdɪvələˈheːt/ *phr.,* not a bit < E dial. < *Devil ha'it,* the Devil have it (a figurative way of saying 'not a bit'). 'Devil a haet o' work I've been able to do all day!' (TF, Cavan). *See* HAET.

Devotions /dəˈvoːʃənz/ *n.,* pious acts of the faithful, usually following a well-established formula of prayers < (O)F *devotion.* 'I'll see you in the chapel, missus, after Devotions.' Leonard, *Out After Dark,* 131: "There were evening devotions, Holy Hours, Golden Hours, First Fridays and the yearly RETREAT"; Binchy, *Firefly Summer,* 492: "Us have a party! It's on our knees saying the thirty days' prayer tacked on to the rosary and ending up with a trip to devotions. That's my mother's idea of a good evening." *See* BLESSED SACRAMENT.

dhera, *see* YERRA.

dhoodeen, *see* DUDEEN.

dhrouth, *see* DROUTH.

dhudeen, *see* DUDEEN.

Dia /ʤiə/ *n.,* God < Ir. 'Is tú a deir is ní hé Dia' (proverb), God hasn't spoken yet (lit. It's you who says it and not God). 'Duine le Dia', a simpleton (SOM, Kerry).

diabhal /d̪iːl/ *n.,* devil (SOM, Kerry) < Ir. 'A chance shot will kill the diabhal.' *See* DEVIL.

Dia linn /ˈʤiːəlɪn/ *int.,* said when somebody sneezes, on hearing bad news, or as an expression of pity (SOM, Kerry) < Ir (lit. God be with us). The traditional response is 'Dia linn is Muire' (God and Mary be with us).

dícheall /ˈʤiːhəl/ *v.n.,* (making) a big effort, doing the best one can (SOM, Kerry, who adds: 'dícheallach, industrious, full of endeavour, busy') < Ir.

differ /'dɪfər/ *n.,* difference < Ir *difear* < E dial. *differ,* difference. 'I can't tell the differ between them.' Carleton, 'The Battle of the Factions' (*Six Irish Tales,* 212): "'Indeed,' replied Rose, 'for the differ of the price, I thought it better to bring it to Peggy Boyle, and be sartin [certain] of not having it spoiled'"; O'Casey, *Juno and the Paycock,* act II, 32: "*Boyle:* Now an' agen we have our differ, but we're there together all the time"; *The Plough and the Stars,* act IV, 204: "*Bessie:* If you had only seen her, you'd know to th' differ"; Healy, *Nineteen Acres,* 111: "Now he could have all the cattle and pigs he liked 'and it made no differ' to the means test man"; Leonard, *Out After Dark,* 73: "'. . . he'll only be temporary. Not like John.' 'What differ?' my mother said. 'Isn't he made for life?'"

dílis /'ʤiːləʃ/ *adj.,* genuine; loyal, dependable; dear (as in 'dear friend') (SOM, Kerry) < Ir.

dillisk /'dɪləsk/ also **duileasc, duilisc, sea-grass** /'seːgræs/ (SOM, Kerry) *n.,* burgundy-coloured edible seaweed, dulse < Ir *duileasc.* 'Is that dillisk you're chewing? Give me some of it.' Joyce, *Finnegans Wake,* 392.32–3: "and two cuts of Shackleton's brown loaf and dilisk." *See* CARRAGEEN; DULSE.

dinge /dɪnʤ/ *n., v.,* dent < E dial. < ME *dingen,* to beat, strike, bruise. 'Don't take the PONGER with the dinge in it' (AF, Cavan).

dioc /ʤʌk/ *n.,* a stoop, hunch (KM, Kerry) < Ir. 'He does be up and down the road every evening at the same time with the same dioc on him.'

dispensary /dɪs'pɛnsəri/ *n.,* a place where medicines were dispensed (now merged in 'health centres') < OF *despensour.* 'Do me a favour, will you, and pop down to the dispensary and get my pills – I've run out, but I still have the prescription.' McCourt, *Angela's Ashes,* 366: "I seen her in the Dispensary and she looks worse than my Dennis did in the bed." *See* MEDICAL HALL.

disremember /dɪsrə'mɛmbər/ *v.,* to forget < E dial. 'I disremember his name now.' *Knocknagow,* 62: "I disremember if them lines isn't in 'Lalla Rookh'"; Stoker, *The Snake's Pass,* 52: "Well, I disremember meself exactly"; O'Casey, *The Shadow of a Gunman,* act I, 95: "*Tommy:* Excuse me, Miss Powell, in the ardure ov me anger I disremembered there was a lady present."

ditch /dɪʧ/ *n.,* an earthen bank, usually with a hedgerow and sometimes also a drainage trench or stream < OE *dic* (cf. *dyke*). In SE 'ditch' normally refers to a trench, as in Beckett, *Waiting for Godot,* 9: "*Vladimir:* May one enquire where His Highness spent the night? *Estragon:* In a ditch." The *ODEE* notes both meanings, including 'long narrow embankment, OE; (dial.) embankment, dyke [16th century]'. 'Hurler on the ditch', back-seat driver (< Ir proverb *Is maith an t-iománaí an fear ar an gclaí,* the man on the ditch is a good hurler).

diúcán /'ʤuːkɔːn/ *n.,* a reed; a pipe; a drinking-straw < Ir. 'He was chewing on a diúcán as happy as Larry' (BC, Meath). *See* GEOCÁN.

divide /də'vaid/ *n.,* a portion of pig sent to each of the neighbours when the animal was killed (Mayo).

divil, *see* DEVIL.

dlaoi /dliː/ *n.,* a wisp of straw or hair; a small bundle of thatching-straw (Limerick) < Ir. 'You'll need more than a dlaoi or two to fix that hole!'

do /duː/, **do be** /'duː'biː/ *v.* In Irish the verb 'be' has a distinct form for expressing the habitualness of an action or state. HE uses an approximation of this verbal form, e.g. 'I do be here (or I be's here) every day' (Ir, *bím anseo gach lá*). Griffin, *The Collegians,* 117: "I do be often goin' in boats across to Cratloe an' them places"; Stephens, *The Crock of Gold,* 118: "I do be lonely in the night-time."

doaty, *see* DOTE.

dobhrán /'d̪aurɔːn/ *n.,* an otter; fig. a dull-witted person < Ir. 'Has that dobhrán not left the house yet? We'll be dead late' (Mayo).

dobrón /d̪ʌ'broːn/ *n.,* extreme sorrow, wretchedness < Ir. 'There was dobrón in the family for a long time after the son was killed in America' (KG, Kerry).

dock leaf /'dɑkliːf/ *n.,* the leaf of a type of wild plant used as an antidote for nettle stings < ME *dokke* + ME *leaf.* 'Are there any dock leaves? I got stung by a nettle' (AF, Cavan).

dog /dɑg/ *n.,* in the phrase 'in and out like a dog at a fair' (BD, Cavan), referring to a person who is forever hurrying in and out of the company.

dóib buí /doː'bwiː/ *n.,* yellow clay (used in grafting trees) (MOB, Mayo) < Ir. 'That dóib buí will be useful – I'll keep it, so.'

doicheall /'dʌxəl/ *n.,* lack of welcome, inhospitality; churlishness (SOM, Kerry, who adds: 'doicheallach, sullen, boorish, inhospitable) < Ir.

doirnín /dʌr'niːn/ (*pl.* **doirníní**) *n.,* one of two small grips on the handle of a scythe (KM, Kerry) < Ir. 'The doirnín broke on me, so I had to pack it in for the day.'

dóiteán /'doːʧɔːn/ *n.,* a blaze, conflagration (as of heather ablaze in a bog) (SOM, Kerry) < Ir.

dol /dʌl/ *n.,* a loop, noose (Offaly) < Ir. 'Make a dol in the rope and tie it around the calf's head.'

dollacalling /dʌlə'kɔːlən/ *v.n.,* trying to do something in a bungling way; reluctance to start work < Ir *dallacáil,* groping + E *-ing.* 'Will you stop your dollacalling and get down to work!' (Limerick).

Domhnach /d̪aunəx/ *n.*, Sunday (SOM, Kerry, who adds: 'Domhnach Cásca, Easter Sunday').

domlas /'dʌmləs/ *n.,* bile, gall; a bilious attack (SOM, Kerry) < Ir. 'He has the domlas this morning' (SOM, Kerry).

donán /'dʌnɔːn/ *n.,* a wretch, unfortunate person < Ir. 'The poor wee donán, he's always in trouble' (BC, Meath).

donas /'dʌnəs/ *n.,* misfortune; evil, badness (SOM, Kerry).

done /dʌn/ *p.part.* used for the past tense, a common feature of HE, in which the reverse also happens; both were common usages in EModE. 'I done my homework, though my pen was broke.'

donny /'dɑni/ also **dawny, dawnie** /'dɔːni/, **donsy** *adj.,* weak, in poor health, not feeling well; small, tiny < E dial. (cf. Ir *donaí, n.,* misfortune; illness). 'The donny boy got another beating after school yesterday' (JL, Mayo). Head, *Hic et Ubique,* 113: "the donny fellow"; Griffin, *The Collegians,* 147: "She has the dawniest little nose I think I ever laid my two eyes upon"; O'Casey, *The Shadow of a Gunman,* act I, 89–90: "*Minnie:* . . . a WEESHY, dawny bit of a man that was never sober."

donnybrook /'dɑnibrʌk/ *n.,* a riotous assembly, free-for-all < *Donnybrook,* a village near Dublin, now a respectable suburb, site of an uproarious weeklong fair dating from at least the thirteenth century, discontinued in the middle of the nineteenth century (FD, Dublin).

don't be, *see* BE.

doodeen, *see* DUDEEN.

doras /'d̪ʌrəs/ *n.,* a door (SOM, Kerry) < Ir. 'Dún an doras,' shut the door (KG, Kerry). 'Doras feasa fiafraí' (proverb), enquiry is the door of knowledge.

dorchas, *n.,* dark bread < Ir. 'Sometimes the bread (made in an oven covered in greesh [*see* GRÍOSACH]) might be unsatisfactory and the texture might be rather dark. This was said to be a dorchas' (POC, Cavan).

dorn /doːrn/ *n.,* a fist; a fistful of hay etc. < Ir. 'Dorn of oats', an amount held in the fist with the fingers slightly closed (SOM, Kerry) < Ir. 'Give the ass a dorn of oats' (Mayo).

dornán /'doːrnɔːn/ *n.* 1. The grip on a scythe (*see* DOIRNÍN).

'I have no dornán for the scythe. Where will I get a new one?' (BC, Meath). 2. A fistful; a small amount of flour or grain (SOM, Kerry) < Ir (dimin. of DORN).

dornóg /dʌrˈnoːg/ *n.,* a mitten worn for protection when using a bill-hook (BF, Cork) < Ir (dimin. of DORN). 'I forgot to put on the dornóg and cut myself.'

dorr /dʌr/ *n.,* anger; incitement to violence < Ir. 'Watch out! He'll have the dorr on him if you say that to him' (Mayo).

dosser /ˈdɑsər/ *n.* (*colloq.*), a lazy person, an idler (SMC, Limerick) (cf. *EDD* dos n., a sleep; a bed, lodging).

dote /doːt/ also **doaty, dotey** *n.*, 'an appetising infant or young child' (Hayden and Hartog, 781); *EDD*, s.v. 'dotey', cites Ireland only: 'a term of endearment, esp. for a child' (cf. Old Dutch *doten*, to be silly; F *radoten*, to rave, is from the same root (Chambers); ME *dotien*, *v.*, to be silly, deranged, out of one's wits). 'He's a real dote' (JR, Dublin).

dowdelling, *see* MOUTH MUSIC.

down /daun/ *adv.* In HE the phrase 'down in the room' means the room next door, not necessarily on a different level (AF, Cavan) < ME *adune*, *adown* (cf. Ir 'síos', *adv. and prep.*, down; 'thíos sa seomra', down in the room). 'Where's Janey?' – 'She's down in the room.'

drabhsóg /ˈd̪rausoːg/ *n.,* a miserable, insignificant person < Ir. 'I never heard a good word about anyone coming from that drabhsóg.'

dráchaí /ˈd̪rɔːhiː/ *adj.,* cold, wet weather < Ir. 'Another dráchaí day; will they ever end?' (Limerick).

dradaire /ˈd̪rɑd̪ərə/ *n.,* a person with prominent teeth < Ir. 'That dradaire would eat an apple through a letter-box' (saying).

draid /d̪rædʒ/ *n.,* a contemptuous grin, a leer (SOM, Kerry, who adds: 'also draidín') < Ir. 'Look at the draid on her; she must be a biteen [little bit] soft in the head' (Mayo).

dramhaíl /ˈdrɑviːl/ *n.,* trash, rubbish < Ir.

drantán /ˈdrænt̪ɔːn/ *n.,* the act of humming a tune < Ir. 'I told him to stop the drantán or he could go home; that shut him up, I can tell you.'

drass /d̪ræs/ *n.,* a turn, short time, spell < Ir *dreas.* Griffin, *The Collegians,* 132: "I always, mostly, smoke a drass before I go to bed of a night."

draw /d̪rɔː/ *v.,* take in. 'Draw the hay before it rains!' (MG, Cavan).

dreigh /d̪reː/ also **dreegh, dreech** *n., adj.,* dreariness; tedious, wearisome (cf. ME *drie,* to suffer, endure). 'It's all so dreigh, there's no doubt about it' (Louth).

dreoilín /ˈd̪roːliːn/ *n.,* a wren (SOM, Kerry); a weak, sickly person < Ir. 'He'll be no good on a silage pit – he's only a dreoilín.'

dreolán /d̪roːˈlɔːn/ *n.,* a silly person < Ir. 'That dreolán is laughing again. Would someone go over and tell her to shut up!' (KG, Kerry).

dress /d̪rɛs/ *v.,* to tidy up, set in order < OF *dresser.* 'Old people *dress* the bed; young people *make* it' (cf. Ir *leaba a chóiriú*).

dríodar /ˈd̪riːd̪ər/ *n.,* the end of a bottle, the dregs, leavings (MOB, Mayo); dregs in the shank of a pipe; sediment in the bottom of water from a well or a jug of milk (SOM, Kerry); fig. the last member of a family to be born. 'Dríodar an chrúiscín', the youngest member of a family, especially if small and well separated from the next older child (SOM, Kerry) < Ir (lit. dregs of the jug).

driseog /ˈd̪rɪʃoːg/ *n.,* a bramble; a briar < Ir. 'Pull the driseog off the sheep' (SL, Mayo).

drisheen /ˈd̪rɪʃiːn/ *n.,* a southern (especially Cork) sausage-like delicacy made from the narrow intestine of sheep, filled with blood mixed with oatmeal etc. < Ir *drisín,* intestine. 'I wouldn't eat drisheen if my life depended on it' (TJ, Sligo).

driuch /d̪rʌːk/, /d̪ruːx/ *n.,* a sickly appearance < Ir. 'Look at the driuch of him' (SOM, Kerry).

drochmheas /ˈd̪rʌxvæs/ *n.,* disrespect, lack of respect (KM, Kerry) < Ir. 'She had only drochmheas for the job I did.'

dródánaí, *see* SPANCEL.

droleen, *see* WREN.

droll /d̪roːl/ *n., adj.,* a humorous person; a tiresome or peevish person (cf. E dial. *droll* < OF *drolle*; cf. MDu *drolle*, a little chap); miserable (DOH, Limerick, who places this usage in east Limerick and notes that this meaning derives from Ir *dearóil*, 'sometimes Englished *droll* from similarity of sound'). 'He gets very droll when he has a drop taken.' Griffin, *The Collegians,* 70: "WISHA, but you're a droll man, this day"; O'Brien, *The Third Policeman,* 83–4; "'The wooden rim,' said Gilhaney slowly, 'is a death-trap in itself, it swells on a wet day and I know a man that owes his bad wet death to nothing else.' Before we had time to listen carefully to what he was AFTER saying he was half-way down the road . . . 'A droll man,' I ventured."

dromach /ˈd̪rʌməx/ *n.,* a back-band put over a horse's back during ploughing (Meath) < Ir.

dronn /d̪rʌn/ *n.,* a hump, camber < Ir. 'Mind the dronn!' (Limerick).

dropeen /ˈd̪rɑpiːn/ *n.,* a little drop < *drop* + dimin. suffix *-een*. 'It's the first dropeen that destroyed me; there's no harm at all in the last' (BC, Meath).

drouth /d̪raut̪/ also **dhrouth** *n.,* thirst < ME *droghte* (cf. ModE *drought*). 'There's such a drouth on me I could drink up the well' (JL, Mayo). Stoker, *The Snake's Pass,* 192: "The house beyant it is a public, an' shure I know I'm safe there anyhow – if me dhrouth'll only hould out!"; Synge, *The Playboy of the Western World,* act III (*FDA,* 2, 636): *"Philly:* . . . You might take your death with drouth and none to heed you."

drúcht /d̪ruːxt̪/ also **drught** *n.,* dew (SOM, Kerry) < Ir. 'Drúichtín', a slight dew < Ir. 'There's a heavy drúcht tonight' (KG, Kerry).

druchtín /ˈd̪rʌxt̪iːn/ *n.,* a small white snail; a slug (KM, Kerry) < Ir. 'The druchtíns have been at the cabbages again.'

drught, *see* DRÚCHT.

dubh /d̪ʌv/ *n.,* potato blight (hence "black '47")' (SOM, Kerry) < Ir (lit. black).

dúchán /ˈd̪uːxɔːn/ also **dubhachán** *n.,* a small round stack of turf, a CLAMP; a small rick (MK, Galway) < Ir. 'Go out and get a few sods from the dúchán.'

dúchas /ˈduːxəs/, /ˈduːkəs/ *n.,* inherited trait, looks, or features; 'nature (as distinct from nurture), innate tendency' (SOM, Kerry, who adds: 'dúchas will out') < Ir. 'He's got the dúchas of his family in his face'; 'He's got their dúchas, with his hair turning grey at such young age' (DOS, Kerry). 'Is tréine dúchas ná oiliúint' (proverb), Nature is stronger than nurture; 'Briseann an dúchas trí shúile an chait' (proverb), You can't change (someone's) nature (lit. A cat's nature breaks out through its eyes).

duck and your duty, *see* DEOCH AND DORAIS.

dúdaire /ˈduːd̪ərə/ *n.,* a clown, an idiot < Ir. 'He's an awful dúdaire' (KG, Kerry).

dudeen /ˈd̪uːdiːn/ also **dudheen, dhoodeen,** etc., **dúidín** *n.,* a short-stemmed clay pipe (SOM, Kerry), often smoked by women (in whom it often caused cancer of the lip) < Ir *dúidín* (dimin. of *dúid,* a stump, a pipe). 'It must be a short pipe or stump. Dúid is the Irish for stump' (Dónall Mac Amhlaigh, *Ireland's Own*, 7 March 1980). 'The dudeen? We used to call that sort a forty-niner' (SL, Mayo); 'The old dhoodeen gives the sweetest smoke' (SL, Mayo); 'Seventy or eighty years ago the accomplishments of an Irishman should be: To smoke his dudheen, | To drink his CRUISKEEN | To flourish his ALPEEN | To wallop a spalpeen (MacCall: Wexford)' (PWJ, 189). Sheehan, *Glenanaar,* 160: "and a well blackened dhudeen"; Beckett, *Waiting for Godot,* 35: *"Estragon:* He's a scream. He's lost his dudeen."

dúdóg /ˈd̪uːd̪oːg/ *n.*, a box on the ear < Ir. 'I'll give you a dúdóg in a minute if you don't shut up' (BC, Meath).

dúidín, *see* DUDEEN.

duileasc, *see* DILLISK.

duine le Dia, *see* DIA.

dúiric *n.*, a fat slug found in VENTERS that leaves a hole like a giant woodworm (RB, Waterford) < Ir.

dul amú /d̪ʌləˈmuː/ also **dullamoo** *v.n.*, a mistake, a misconception (SOM, Kerry); a good-for-nothing; a foolish, idiotic person < Ir (lit. going astray). 'In school, if you made a mistake the teacher would give you a poc [thump] and say, "You dul-a-moo, you'll never learn!"' (KM, Kerry); 'Whatever dul amú came over him?' (SOM, Kerry).

dulse /dʌls/ *n.*, edible seaweed < Ir *duileasc*. 'They're selling dulse in bags down in the shop now.' *See* DILLISK.

dunduckity /dʌnˈdʌkəti/ also **dunducketty** *adj.*, of a dull colour < E dial. (origin obscure). 'A contemptuous term for a nondescript colour; usu. in phr. "sky-blue scarlet turned up with dipsy gray and dunducketty mud"' (MT, Donegal). Joyce, *Ulysses,* 329.27–8: "and he . . . with his dunducketymud-coloured mug on him."

dúr /d̪uːr/ *adj.* sullen, dour, obstinate, stupid (SOM, Kerry) < Ir (cf. E *dour*).

dúramán /ˈd̪uːrəmɔːn/, a dim-witted, stupid person (SOM, Kerry) < Ir.

duskiss /ˈdʌskɪs/ *n.*, dusk < E dial. (*ODEE:* 'The form dusk is difficult to account for,' but cf. ME *dosk,* OE *dox,* dark). 'He didn't come home until duskiss.'

dúthracht /ˈd̪uːrəxt̪/ *n.*, excessive consideration, devotion < Ir. 'They've taken such dúthracht with that child he'll never come to any good.'

dúthrachtach, *adj.*, with enthusiasm, zealous, full of vigour (SOM, Kerry) < Ir.

E

e The letter 'e' is often pronounced in Hiberno-English with the same sound as 'i' /ɪ/, which may lead to confusion with such words as 'pen/pin', 'ten/tin', 'lentil/lintle', 'cemetery/symmetry', etc. It can also go in the opposite direction, with 'i' pronounced as 'e', as in 'provincial' /prəˈvɛnʃəl/ (see Crystal, 255).

éadan /ˈeːd̪ən/ *n.,* forehead (SOM, Kerry) < Ir. 'He has a big éadan; he must be intelligent.'

eagla /ˈæglə/ *n.,* fear (SOM, Kerry) < Ir. 'What eagla is on you?'

éan /eːn/ *n.,* a bird (SOM, Kerry, who adds: 'éinín, a little bird') < Ir.

earc luachra /ˈærkˈluəxrə/ *n.,* a lizard < Ir. 'Lick the earc luachra to cure a burn' (BC, Meath).

earrach /ˈærəx/ *n.,* the spring < Ir. 'An té nach gcuirfidh san earrach ní bhainfidh sé san fhómhar' (proverb), He who won't sow in the spring won't reap in the autumn.

eascaine /ˈæskənə/ *n.,* a curse; a swear-word (SOM, Kerry) < Ir. 'He let an eascaine out of him.'

eascú /æsˈkuː/ *n.,* an eel; fig. a tall thin person who has strength beyond his weight (SOM, Kerry) < Ir.

easnamh /ˈæsnəv/ *n.,* a want, a deficiency (SOM, Kerry) < Ir.

easóg /æˈsoːg/ *n.,* a weasel (SOM, Kerry) < Ir. 'I think I saw an easóg down by the river.' *See* WHITTERET.

Easter duty /iːstərˈʤuːtiː/ *n.,* the obligation on Catholics to receive HOLY COMMUNION at least once a year; in Ireland the obligation must be fulfilled between Ash Wednesday (46 days before Easter) and the octave of Sts Peter and Paul (6 July) < OE *eastre* + AN *deweté*. 'Listen, you'd better make your Easter duty before the end of the month; you heard what the priest said at first MASS last Sunday' (MF, Cavan).

eccer /ˈɛkər/ *n.* (*colloq.*), abbreviation for '(home) exercise' (homework). 'Have you your eccer done yet?' (KD, Dublin). Doyle, *The Van,* 49: "I'll check their eccers every nigh', don't worry."

eejit /ˈiːʤət/ *n.,* a silly person < E *idiot,* but less pejorative than SE 'idiot' /ˈɪdiət/. The pronunciation 'eejit' represents an approximation of the way the letters 'd' and 'i' are pronounced in Irish, in such words as 'DIA', sometimes carried over to Hiberno-English in such words as 'odious' /ˈoːdʒəs/. 'Such an eejit she married!' (KG, Kerry). Friel, *Translations,* act I (*FDA,* 3, 1211): *"Doalty:* . . . Will you shut up you aul eejit you!"; Roche, *A Handful of Stars,* act II, i, 47: *"Linda:* You needn't think you're going to make an ejit out of me at all boy"; Leonard, *Out After Dark,* 36: "Nick Keyes, oul' eejit the like of him, took you in out of God knows where"; Doyle, *The Van,* 244: "'Get out,' said Veronica. – 'Get out, go on. You bloody big eejit, yeh.'"

-een /iːn/ *suffix,* represents the Ir dimin. suffix *-ín* (which is itself of uncertain origin), as in 'dudeen' (Ir *dúidín*), 'kippeen' (Ir *cipín*); also added to personal names: cf. Yeats's character Paudeen (Ir *Páidín,* dimin. of *Pádraig*) in *The Unicorn from the Stars.* It can also be attached to English words, e.g. 'maneen' (little man), 'squireen' (small landowner with pretensions), 'careen' (little car), etc. It has a variety of connotations, ranging from mere smallness, as in 'boreen' (Ir *bóithrín*) and 'girleen' (little girl), and affection, as in *stóirín* (dim. of STÓR, darling), to disparagement, as in *anniseoirín* (wretched creature) and PRIESTEEN, as well as being used in loanwords as a loose equivalent for English suffixes such as *-ing,* as in *snaoisín* (snuff < E *sneezing*), *-on,* as in *bhaigín* (< wagon), and *-y,* as in *aintín* (< aunty). See de Bhaldraithe (1990), 85–95. 'Tom's a great little scholareen – sure Ownie's teaching him' (PR, Mayo). Kickham, *Knocknagow,* 47: "'What did you ketch, Tommy?' . . . 'a robineen'"; Joyce, *Finnegans Wake,* 39.30: "capalleens" (Ir *capaillín,* little horse, pony); 511.12: "the divileen" (little devil); Healy, *Nineteen Acres,* 128: "We used to call her 'witcheen' because she had a temper if you 'rose' her . . . She was third in our family but if you said 'witcheen' or 'cocked noseen' (she had a pert nose) . . ."; McDonagh, *The Cripple of Inishmaan,* scene ii, 17: *"Helen: I'm* not a biteen afraid of the sea."

e'er /ɛr/ *adv.,* any < E *ever.* 'Have ye e'er a bit of tobaccy on ye?' (Omurethi, Kildare).

eggler /ˈɛglər/ *n.,* a person who travels the countryside collecting and dealing in eggs < E egg + suffix *-(l)er* (< ME *-ere*). 'Does the eggler ever come around here any more?'

eidhneán /aɪˈnɔːn/ *n.,* ivy (SOM, Kerry) < Ir. 'Be careful – that eidhneán might be poisonous.'

éillín faobhair /ˈeːliːnˈfiːvər/ *n.,* a strap used for sharpening a cut-throat razor < Ir. 'Where's the éillín faobhair? I want a shave.'

éinín /ˈeːniːn/ *n.,* a little bird < Ir. 'Listen – all the éiníns are going to bed.'

eireaball /ˈɛrəbəl/ *n.,* a tail (SOM, Kerry) < Ir. 'It's hard and soft, like the cow's eireaball.'

Éireannach /ˈeːrənəx/ *adj., n.,* Irish; an Irish person < Ir. 'The teacher told each and every one of us that he should be Éireannach agus Eorpach [Irish and European]' (MC, Kildare, Mayo). Joyce, *Finnegans Wake,* 531.36–532.1: "Pass the jousters of the king, his Kovnor-Journal and eirenarch's custos himself no less."

eirenarch, *see* ÉIREANNACH.

éirí in airde /ˈeːriːɪˈnɔːrʤə/ *n.phr.* 1. Exuberant behaviour, elation, high spirits, enthusiasm. 2. Putting on airs; acting above one's station in life (SOM, Kerry), being 'all airs and graces' (VQ, Kerry) < Ir. 'Appeal to his eirí in airde and the MEAS he always had in himself' (KM, Kerry).

Éirinn /ˈeːrɪn/ *n.,* in the phrase 'bás in Éirinn' (death in Ireland), a toast to someone emigrating, hoping they will return some day, the words implying a lack of finality in the parting (SOM, Kerry, who adds: 'I have also heard this in the US') < Ir. *See* ERIN GO BRAGH.

éist *v. (imper.)*, listen < Ir (cf. *fuist,* keep quiet). 'Éist liom' /eːʃtlʌm/, listen to me. 'Éist do bhéal' /eːʃtd̪ʌˈveːl/, shut up.

ejit, *see* EEJIT.

ekker, *see* ECCER.

elder /ˈɛld̪ər/ *n.,* a cow's udder (cf. MDu *elder,* udder; the word 'udder' itself is not etymologically connected with MDu 'elder'). 'That cow's got a sore on her elder' (MOB, Mayo).

elegant /ˈɛləgənt/, /ˈɪləgənt/ (*see* E) *adj.,* good, fine, excellent. 'That's an elegant day'; 'That's an elegant child you have there.'

end /ɛnd/ *n.,* in the common phrase 'at the end of the day,' finally, when all is said and done < OE *ende.* 'At the end of the day everything worked out grand for me, thanks be to God' (KG, Kerry). *See* HEEL OF THE HUNT.

entirely /ənˈtairli/ *adv.,* a common intensive filler in HE (cf. ALTOGETHER) < ME *enterly.* 'A grand day entirely it was, to be sure.' Griffin, *The Collegians,* 33: "I'll be kilt entirely"; Trollope, *The Kellys and the O'Kellys,* 58: "Isn't the Kellys great people intirely, Mr. Barry?"; Stoker, *The Snake's Pass,* 88: "this'll be a bitther blow to her intirely!"

equal /ˈiːkwəl/ *adj.,* in the phr. 'I'm equal,' I don't care (cf. Ir *is cuma liom,* I don't care, I don't mind, lit. it is equal to me). 'It's equal to me where ye go' (MK, Galway); Griffin, *The Collegians,* 33: "It's equal to me any day, winther or summer, whether I go ten miles or twenty."

-er, *suffix,* especially common in the HE of Dublin in the coining of nicknames, frequently accompanied by the definite article. 'Aler', an alsation dog; 'the Backers', fields at the back of a housing estate; 'the Mainer', the main road in a housing estate; 'the Brunner', North Brunswick Street Christian Brothers' School; 'the Deeler', De La Salle School; 'Synger', Synge Street Christian Brothers' School; 'the Calliers', the 'California Hills' (open ground between Palmerstown, Chapelizod, and Ballyfermot); 'Croker', Croke Park (GAA stadium); 'Dalyer', Dalymount Park (soccer stadium); 'dipper', a student teacher doing the HDipEd (higher diploma in education); 'hollicrs', holidays; 'skellyer', a skeleton; 'toucher', someone who tries to 'touch' one (cadge for money) (KD, Dublin).

Erin go bragh /'eːrəngʌ'brɔː/ *int.,* up Ireland! < Ir *Éirinn go brách,* Ireland for ever. 'The shout went up "Erin go bragh!" and everyone cheered.' *See* ÉIRINN.

erra, *see* YERRAH.

errish /'ɛrɪʃ/ *n.,* a strap, a sling < Ir *eiris,* also *iris.* 'Get the errish; we'll need it to tie the creels together.'

esker /'ɛskər/ *n.,* a glacial ridge, a ridge of gravel and sand (MK, Galway) < Ir *eiscir.* 'That road follows the line of the esker right across that bit of the country, and you'll get a great view of the lake, so you will.'

esoupcans, *see* SOUPER.

evening /'iːvnɪn/ *n.*, used by HE speakers to refer to the afternoon time; 'Come to the office this evening!'; the evening period in HE is represented by 'night', as in the phrase 'Good night, President' = Good evening, President; SOM, Kerry, writes: 'tráthnóna: evening time which locally included afternoon as well as the later period'; cf. de Bhaldrathe, *English-Irish Dictionary*, s.v. 'evening': '(*Before dark*) Tráthnóna m; (*after dark*) oíche f).'

ever /'ɛvər/ *adv.,* in the HE expression 'would you ever (do something),' a sign of courtesy, not (as in SE) impatience < ME *ever.* 'Would you ever close that window?' *See* E'ER.

Exposition /ɛkspə'zɪʃən/ *n.,* the public display of the Blessed Sacrament for a period, in such a way that the faithful may satisfy their devotion by seeing the object of their prayer < L *expositio.* 'There's Exposition of the Blessed Sacrament for the FORTY HOURS starting after first MASS tomorrow morning' (JF, Cavan).

eye fiddle, *see* AGAIDH FIDIL.

F

face /feːs/ *n.,* in pejorative phrases of the pattern 'A face like that and the price of turnips!'; 'She had a face on her that would turn milk sour.'

fadálach /fɑ'd̪ɔːləx/ *adj. used as n.,* long drawn-out, boring (SOM, Kerry) < Ir. 'Such a fadálach of a sermon the priest gave – it put me half asleep.'

fadge /fædʒ/ *n.* 1. A kind of large flat loaf made with chopped-up boiled potatoes mixed with flour, cooked over a griddle. 'Oh, what I wouldn't give for some buttered fadge now!' (TJ, Sligo). 2. A bundle, a load of something (origin obscure).

fadharcán /fair'kɔːn/ *n.* 1. A knotty small man < Ir fadharcán, knot in wood. 'That *fadharcán* will see the rest of them into the grave.' 2. /'fairkɔːn/ A callus, a corn < Ir. 'I had a fadharcán on the side of my foot'; 'He has a big fadharcán on his skin' (Limerick).

fadhbán /'fɔːbɔːn/ a large floury potato < Ir. 'What a fine plate of fadhbáns you have in the middle of the table' (KM, Kerry).

fadó /fɑd̪'oː/ *adv.,* long ago – typical introduction to a story told by a SEANCHAÍ < Ir. 'Fadó fadó, there was a little leprechaun named Brogeen . . .'

faibrí /fɑi'briː/ *n.pl.,* wrinkles on the forehead; dark rings under the eyes (KM, Kerry) < Ir. 'Look at him after the night's boozing and faibrís under his eyes.'

faic /fæk/ *n.,* (with negative) nothing; not even the smallest amount (SOM, Kerry, who adds: '"faic na fríde", absolutely nothing') < Ir. 'There isn't a faic of tackling on that horse in the yard'; 'He didn't do a faic' (SOM, Kerry); 'Any news, Seán?' – 'MUSHA, faic, AVICK.'

fáideog /'fɔːdʒoːg/ *n.,* the wick of a candle; fig. the flame < Ir. 'Quinch [quench] the fáideog and go to bed' (AF, Cavan).

faikins, *see* FAIX.

failed /feːld/ *p.part.,* having declined in health. 'I saw poor old Paddy the other day and he's HORRID failed – gone down in the neck' (BP, Meath, heard in Roscommon).

faill /fæl/ *n.,* a cliff (SOM, Kerry) < Ir. 'Don't go too near that faill.'

fainic /ˈfænɪk/ *v. (imper.),* look out; mind yourself; take care (SOM, Kerry) < Ir. 'Fainic! There's a car coming the other way.'

fáinne /ˈfɔːnjə/ *n.,* a ring, circle < Ir. 'The Fáinne', a ring-shaped badge showing the wearer's preparedness to speak Irish. 'I saw him wearing the fáinne at Mass' (KG, Kerry). 'Fáinne an lae', dawn, break of day (SOM, Kerry) < Ir. *See* PHONEY.

fáinnín /fɔːˈniːn/ *n.,* a roll of cloth on top of the head on which was placed a jar or bucket to be carried (KM, Kerry, who adds: 'my gran said her mother-in-law used to draw the water from the well thus') < Ir *fáinnín* (dimin. of FÁINNE).

fairchín /ˈfærəxiːn/ *n.,* a small mallet used for closing in potato ridges after the sciolláns (portions of potatoes containing 'eyes' or seeds) were sown, usually home-made from a block of wood with a hole in the middle for the handle (Kerry) < Ir. 'You'd better close the ridges with the fairchín before it gets dark.'

faircsin /ˈfærksɪn/ *n.,* a look, appearance < Ir. 'Will you look at the faircsin of her?' (KG, Kerry).

faire /ˈfærə/ *int.,* expression of disapproval, disgust, shame, or annoyance: shame (on you) (SOM, Kerry) < Ir.

fairin', *see* FÉIRÍN.

fairy fort /ˈfeːrifoːrt/ *n.,* (usually) a smallish semi-circle of trees regarded as unlucky to dislodge, actually site of an Iron Age enclosure. 'My father and his father would often sit up by the fairy fort at the top of the lane and have a chat' (BD, Cavan). *See* RATH.

faith /feːt̪/ *int.,* in truth < E < OF *feid.* 'Faith, you did do it!' – 'Faith, I did not, then!' (Cavan). Joyce, *Ulysses,* 320.29–31: "'Tell him a tale of woe about arrears of rent and a sick wife and a squad of kids and, faith, he'll dissolve in tears on the bench"; Healy, *Nineteen Acres,* 105: "Faith 'n they gave me enough to stock Luke Colleran's chemist shop." *See* FAIX.

faix /feːks/ also **faikins** /ˈfeːkənz/ *int.,* in truth < E dial. *fay,* faith + dimin. suffix *-kin(s).* 'Faix, then, if he stole them the Guards will soon know about it' (BC, Meath). Carleton, 'Denis O'Shaughnessy Going to Maynooth' (*Six Irish Tales,* 142): "Faix, he was as stiff as they wor stout, an' wouldn't give in"; Trollope, *The Kellys and the O'Kellys,* 69: "Faix, it's a wondher he didn't murther her outright!"; Joyce, *Finnegans Wake,* 381.8–9: "well, what do you think he did, sir, but, faix, he just went heeltapping through the winespilth." *See* FAITH.

fál /fɔːl/ *n.,* a hedge, in the phr. 'ní fál go haer é,' it's not an insurmountable problem (lit. it's not a hedge up to the sky) (SOM, Kerry) < Ir.

falcaire /ˈfɑlkərə/ *n.,* a staunch, stocky person (SOM, Kerry) < Ir. 'He mightn't be fast on the ball but he's a falcaire lad, and it's what they need.'

falla /ˈfælə/ *n.,* a wall (SOM, Kerry) < Ir. 'Go left at the falla in front of the school.'

fallaing /ˈfɑləŋ/ *n.,* a mantle, a cloak (SOM, Kerry) < Ir. 'Have you any kind of a fallaing? It's lashing rain outside.'

fámaire /ˈfɔːmərə/, /ˈfæmərə/ *n.,* a big strong man, tall and well-built in proportion (SOM, Kerry), a strikingly big person < Ir. 'He was a fámaire of a man to lift that big rock' (KM, Kerry).

Famine, the /ˈfæmən/ *n.,* the Great Famine (1845–48), caused by successive failures of the potato crop, the staple diet of the majority of the population; about a million people perished and a further million emigrated within a space of about five years. 'She says her family nearly all went to America at the time of the Famine, but they still call those that are here "Yanks", after such a long time too.' Sheehan, *Glenanaar*, 209: "And they did perish . . . perished from hunger, from cold, but most of all from the famine fever"; Joyce, *Finnegans Wake,* 71.2: "behind faminebuilt walls [built to provide relief work during the Great Famine]."

famished /ˈfæmɪʃt/ *p.part.,* in the phr. 'famished with the cold,' suffering. 'Come and sit down by the fire; you must be famished with the cold' (TJ, Sligo).

famous /ˈfeːməs/ *adj.,* splendid, excellent < E dial. 'The music was ONLY famous,' the music was really good.

fánach /ˈfɔːnəx/ *adj.,* wandering; easy-going, aimless (MOB, Mayo); straying (of an animal) (SOM, Kerry) < Ir. 'That fella was always a bit fánach.'

fánadóir /ˈfɔːnədoːr/ *n.,* someone with no purpose in life (MOB, Mayo) < Ir.

fann /fɑn/ *adj.,* weak < Ir. 'I felt fann when I got the news'; 'Daddy took fann when he lifted the door' (JF, Cavan).

fanntais /ˈfɑnt̪ɪʃ/ *n.,* weakness; a collapse; a swoon (Limerick) < Ir. 'She fell in a fanntais.'

faobhar /ˈfiːvər/ *n.,* edge; keenness; determination; anger < Ir. 'There was faobhar in his eyes' (SOM, Kerry).

faoileán /ˈfiːlɔːn/ *n.,* a seagull (SOM, Kerry) < Ir. 'Look at the faoileán on the roof' (KG, Kerry).

faoiseamh /ˈfiːʃəv/ *n.,* ease, respite (from pain); easement, delivery (SOM, Kerry) < Ir. 'I've got great faoiseamh since I stood [had] th' operation up in Dublin' (BC, Meath).

faopach /'fiːpəx/ *adj.,* a predicament, a fix (KM, Kerry) < Ir. 'They're in a right faopach now, and another child on the way.'

faraor /fər'iːr/, /fər'eːr/ *int.,* alas. 'Faraor géar', alas (SOM, Kerry) < Ir. 'Faraor! – we'll have to start all over again.'

fardel, fardele /'fɑːrdəl/ *n.* (dialect of Forth and Bargy) a small bundle, pack, parcel, often used in the phr. 'pack and fardel', a burden, 'bag and baggage' (JP, Forth and Bargy) < ME *fardel* < OF *fardel.*

fardoras /'fɑrd̪ʌrəs/ *n.,* a door lintel < Ir.

farl /'færəl/ *n.,* a quarter of a potato cake < E dial. *farl* < ME **fardel* < OE *feorth-dæl,* fourth part. 'Have a soda farl'; 'Hand me down another farl – they're right tasty' (BC, Meath). O'Brien, *At Swim-Two-Birds,* 183–4: "and promised him . . . farls of wheaten-bread dipped in musk-scented liquors."

fásach /'fɔːsəx/ *n.,* a wilderness, a place overgrown with grass etc. < Ir. 'They were walking through the fásach, arm in arm' (TJ, Sligo).

fash /fæʃ/ *n., v.,* annoyance, trouble; confusion, shame (JP, Forth and Bargy); to vex, weary (of) < F *(se) fâcher.* 'Don't get fashed about the food'; 'I tell you no lie – he was that fashed he nearly hit him' (Louth). 'Don't fash your LUG,' pay no attention, never mind (Macafee).

fast /faːst/ *n.,* the act of refraining from food for religious reasons < OE *fæstan, v.* 'I broke my fast, because I didn't feel well and couldn't go to Communion.' 'Natural fast', refraining from all food, liquid or solid, from midnight for anyone going to receive HOLY COMMUNION the following morning (a regulation since abolished). 'Black fast', a fast-day on which only one meal was allowed and that not till evening, and even then, meat, eggs, butter, cheese, milk and wine were forbidden.

fathach /'fɑhəx/ *n.,* a towering, well-built person (SOM, Kerry) < Ir *fathach,* giant. 'He was a fine fathach of a man.'

FCA /ɛfsiːeː/ for Fórsa Cosanta Aitiúil [Local Defence Force]. 'When I was in the FCA I used go up to Castlebar, and they gave us a uniform and trained us in everything – it was hard but great CRAIC all the same' (JL, Mayo).

feac /fæk/ *n.,* a handle < Ir. 'He could hardly hold the feac of the spade, he was so destroyed with drink' (TF, Cavan). 'Feac láí', the handle of a spade (*see* LOY).

fead /fæd̪/ *n.,* a whistle (SOM, Kerry); a hiss < Ir. 'Give the dog a fead.'

feadaíl /fæ'd̪iːl/ *n.,* act of whistling (SOM, Kerry) < Ir.

'There he was, feadaíling along, not a care in the world' (TJ, Sligo).

feadair /ˈfæd̪ər/ *v.,* know. 'Ní fheadair, n'fheadair (mé),' I don't know < Ir.

feadán /fæˈdɔːn/ *n.,* wheezing (SOM, Kerry) < Ir. 'She won't make old bones with a feadán like that coming out of her' (KG, Kerry).

feadhain /fæn/, /fain/ *n.,* a gang (of children etc.), band, troop < Ir. 'There was a feadhain of them up at the orchard robbing apples' (BC, Meath).

feadóg /fæd̪ˈoːg/ *n.,* a tin whistle (SOM, Kerry) < Ir. 'He plays the feadóg very well.'

feaking /ˈfeːkən/ *v.part.,* looking for, searching < Ir *féachaint.* 'I was feaking all morning in the bushes but I couldn't find the keys' (Cavan).

feall /fæl/ *n.,* treachery, deceit; an evil deed < Ir. 'She let me down badly, but, as they say, filleann feall' (from the proverb *Filleann an feall ar an bhfeallaire,* the evil rebounds on the evil-doer).

feallaire /ˈfælərə/ *n.,* a traitor, deceiver (KM, Kerry) < Ir.

fear /fær/ *n.,* a man (SOM, Kerry, who adds: '"firín", little man, a "maneen"') < Ir. 'Fear tí' /færˈtiː/, 'fear an tí' /færəˈtiː/, man of the house, husband, householder. 'He's the fear an tí now since the sister died' (KG, Kerry).

féar /feːr/ *n.,* grass < Ir. 'Chloisfeadh sé an féar ag fás' (proverb), He'd hear the grass growing.

fearann /ˈfærən/ *n.,* land; plough-land; baile fearainn, townland (SOM, Kerry) < Ir. 'Will you be doing anything with the fearann this year?'

fearg /ˈfærəg/ *n.,* anger (SOM, Kerry) < Ir. 'If you saw the fearg in his face *you'd* have kept out of his way too.'

feargach /ˈfærəgəx/ *adj.,* angry (SOM, Kerry) < Ir.

féar gortach /ˈfeːrˈgʌrt̪əx/ also **forgortha** *n.,* quaking grass, 'starvation grass' (MOB, Mayo) < Ir. This refers to the strongly held folk belief that quaking grass grows on soil where a Famine victim is buried and that an unwary traveller who treads on it will suffer extreme hunger and possibly even death. A patch where 'someone neglected to leave crumbs for fairies after a picnic' (Braidwood). 'Watch out for the féar gortach up in those hills!' (KG, Kerry); 'Tháinig féar gortach orm,' I was overcome with the hunger (lit. I came upon starvation grass).

fear siúil /ˈfærˈʃuːl/ *n.,* a beggar < Ir. 'Give the fear siúil a cup of tea' (BC, Meath). *See* SHOOLER.

féasóg /feːˈsoːg/ *n.,* a whisker (SOM, Kerry) < Ir *féasóg,* a beard. 'Look at the féasógs on that fellow – wouldn't you think he'd shave!'

feast-day /ˈfiːsdeː/ *n.,* a day set apart for the commemoration of a particular belief (e.g. the Holy Trinity) or event of religious importance; a saint's day. 'She died on Mother Cyril's feast-day; I'll never forget it' (KG, Kerry).

feck[1] /fɛk/ *v.,* to steal (cf. EModE *fek* < *'fect*, by apheresis from *effect*, to accomplish a desire). 'Don't turn your back on that fella or he'll have fecked something on you, make no mistake about that!' (BC, Meath). Joyce, *Finnegans Wake*, 425.23: "Gaoy Fecks."

feck[2] /fɛk/ *int.,* euphemism for 'fuck' (*see* FUCKING). 'Feck off with yourself!' Leonard, *Out After Dark*, 53: "a shrill, complaining creature who would tell her mammy if you said 'Jasus' or 'feck'"; McDonagh, *The Cripple of Inishmaan*, scene ii, 6: "*Billy:* A fecking eej, is it?"; scene ii, 11: "*Helen:* Are you fecking coming, you fecker?"

feck[3] /fɛk/ *n.,* a game of pitch-and-toss (origin obscure). *See* ALL-A-BAA.

fecker /ˈfɛkər/ *n.* (*colloq.*), term of abuse: perhaps a euphemism for 'fucker.' Roche, *A Handful of Stars,* I, i, 6: "*Tony:* Yeah, he's a QUEER smily fecker, ain't he?"

feileastram /ˈfɛləst̪rəm/ *n.,* wild iris (SOM, Kerry) < Ir. 'Isn't it lovely to see the feileastram in bloom!'

féin /feːn/ 1. *reflexive adj., pron.*, self; 2. own (after *possessive* adj. and *n.*); 3. *adv.*, even, indeed, really < Ir. 'Is geal leis an bhfiach dubh a ghearrcach féin' (proverb), To a raven, its chick is beautiful. 'Cé a mholfadh an ghé bhréan mura molfadh sí í féin?' (proverb), Who would praise the stinking goose if she didn't praise herself? = Self-praise is no praise. McCourt, *Angela's Ashes*, 105: "they wouldn't have the likes of that in America where they're mad for the steak and all classes of poultry, flying, walking or swimming itself" (= even swimming).

feirc /fɛrk/ *n.* 1. The tilt of a hat; hence a jaunty appearance. 'Look at the feirc of him' (SOM, Kerry). 2. A pot belly, paunch < Ir.

féirín /feːˈriːn/ also **féireann** /ˈfeːrən/, **fairin'** *n.* 1. A present, a keepsake; a 'stand' (for betting) < Ir *féirín* < E *fairing*, a gift brought home from the fair. 'I must give you a féireann for the races' (SOM, Kerry). 2. An affliction; a mark left after illness (DB, Cork); something unpleasant to remember. 'He got a nice feirin out of it' (SOC, Cork); 'He's caught the féireann' (i.e. tuberculosis) (SOM, Kerry). 3. A garter (to hold knee stockings in place) (SOM, Kerry). 4. A prospective in-law of whom one disapproves. 'I hope she won't bring the feireann with her' (SOM, Kerry). Sheehan,

Glenanaar, 173: "Whenever he went to fair or market, he brought home a *fairin'* to Nodlag, sometimes a cheap brooch, or a hair comb."

feis /fɛʃ/ *n.,* a festival or competition of music etc., especially the Feis Cheoil, a national music competition < Ir. 'We're all off to the Feis next weekend.' Joyce, *Finnegans Wake*, 613.9: "Feist of Taborneccles"; Healy, *Nineteen Acres*, 101: ". . . the prim way she held her head – the Feis Ceoil [Cheoil] face you see on so many young dancers who take their dancing so seriously."

feist, *see* FEIS.

Fenian /ˈfiːnjən/ *n.,* a member of the Fenian Brotherhood, a revolutionary league founded in New York in 1858 to overthrow English rule in Ireland < Ir *Fianna* (plural of *Fiann*, mythological band of warriors). 'He's down in the pub FLUTHERED, singing 'The Bold Fenian Men [a ballad]' (Dublin).

feochadán /ˈfjoːxəd̪ɔːn/ *n.,* a thistle (KM, Kerry) < Ir. 'This field is full of feochadáns; you'll have to let the donkey loose in it.'

fiacail /ˈfiəkəl/ also **fiacal** *n.,* a tooth (SOM, Kerry) < Ir. 'You wouldn't know him with the new fiacals he got from the dentist.'

fial /fiəl/ *n.,* generous, big-hearted, hospitable (SOM, Kerry) < Ir. 'That's a fial house: you can go there any time and you'll always get something.'

Fianna Fáil /ˈfiənəˈfɔiːl/ *n.,* political party founded by Éamon de Valera in 1926 in opposition to the Anglo-Irish Treaty of 1921 and which came to power in 1932 < *Fianna Fáil*, supposed to have been the name of the legendary warrior band of Fionn mac Cumhaill < *fianna* (*pl.* of *fiann*, warrior band) + *(Inis) Fáil,* an ancient name of Ireland. The name had previously been used as the title of a short-lived weekly paper in 1914 and was also incorporated in the badge of the Irish Volunteers in 1914 in the form of the monogram *FF.*

fierce /fiːrs/ *adj., adv.,* great, abundant; (used as an intensive) very. 'It's fierce cold the night [tonight]' (SOC, Kerry). Kavanagh, *Tarry Flynn,* 33: "'Fierce great weather, Molly,' said Tarry."

figary /fɪˈgeːri/ also **figairy**, **fegary** *n.,* a fanciful mood; whimsical ideas or notions; an impulsive decision; stylish clothing < E dial. *fegary* < *vagary* < L *vagare, v.,* to wander. 'She was out and about in all her fine figaries'; 'Never mind me and my figaries – it takes me that way sometimes' (KG, Kerry).

file /ˈfɪlə/ *n.,* a maker of songs; poet-seer (ranking higher than a bard) < Ir. 'I suppose you'd call him a kind of a file.'

filloon /fiˈluːn/ *n.,* a villain (ENM, Kerry) < Ir *feileon* < E *felon* (ME *vilein*).

fine /fain/ *adj.,* in the phr. 'a fine thing', a good-looking, attractive person < OF *fin*.

Fine Gael /ˈfɪnəˈgeːl/ *n.,* a political party formed in 1933 by the amalgamation of Cumann na nGaedheal and the Centre Party under the presidency of Eoin O'Duffy (1889–1947), leader of the Army Comrades' Association ('Blueshirts') < Ir *fine Gael*, the Irish people < *fine*, kinship group, tribe + *Gael* (genitive plural), Irish people.

fiolún /fiˈluːn/ *n.,* a scrofulous ulcer; a marked infection of the bone; anthrax (ENM, Kerry) < Ir *fiolún,* necrosis, morbid infection.

fionnán /fɪnˈɔːn/ *n.,* coarse mountain grass; 'white coarse grass on cut-away bog, used for grazing cows but of little value for milk production' (SOM, Kerry) < Ir *fionnán*, purple moor-grass.

fiorin /ˈfjoːrən/ *n.,* creeping bent-grass (KM, Kerry) < Ir *feorainn.* 'That fiorin grass is all over the garden again.'

Fir Bolg /ˈfɪrˈbʌləg/ a legendary race, based on a real incursion into prehistoric Ireland < Ir *fir,* men, people + *Bolg*, tribal name (cf. L *Belgae*).

fire /fair/ *v.,* to throw. A speaker of Hiberno-English says, for example, 'Will you quit firing stones at the cattle!' instead of 'throwing'. (This usage derives from the fact that the Irish *caith* means both to throw and to shoot.) Michael J. Murphy, 'Return of the Boy' (*FDA*, 3, 961): "I used to chase the rats for him with Sadie the CAILLEACH'S bleddy [bloody] ould elastic-sided boots – fire them at the rats."

firín /fɪˈriːn/ *n.,* a little man, a 'maneen' (SOM, Kerry) < Ir (dimin. of *fear*, man). 'That little firín is as sly as a fox.'

fírinne /ˈfiːrənə/ *n.,* truth < Ir. 'Bíonn an fhírinne searbh' (proverb), The truth is bitter.

first Fridays /fʌrstˈfraideːz/ *n.phr.,* the practice of receiving HOLY COMMUNION on the first Friday of every month for nine consecutive months, based on a promise said to have been made by Christ to St Margaret-Mary (d. 1690). Plunkett, *Farewell Companions,* 35: "Then how can Granny do nine first Fridays?"

fit-up /ˈfɪtʌp/ a travelling show, with vaudeville acts (CS, Mayo, who adds: 'some of the colloquial vocabulary of Hiberno-English (possibly even such words as LATCHIKO) may have been invented by the actors in such shows, or at least given countrywide exposure') < E *fit*, to make ready + *up*.

fiú /fjuː/ *n.,* worth, as in the phr. 'mór is fiú', simulated grandeur, pomposity (SOM, Kerry) < Ir.

flah /flæː/ *n., v.,* (to engage in) sexual intercourse (cf. E dial. *flaw*, also *flah, v.,* to skin, flay; cf. also Ir *fleá* /fljɔː/, carousal, feast). 'Did you get any flah last night?' (Dublin); 'I had a great flah last night' (SB, Cork).

flahoolagh, *see* FLAITHIÚLACH.

Flaitheas /'flæhəs/ *n.,* Heaven (SOM, Kerry) < Ir. 'We'll all be in Flaitheas some day, I hope, rather than down below with Old Nick' (TJ, Sligo).

flaithiúil /flæ'huːl/ *adj.,* generous, big-hearted (MOB, Mayo), welcoming (SOM, Kerry) < Ir. 'She's the most flaithiúil woman I know.'

flaithiúlach /flæ'huːləx/ also **flahoolagh** *adj.,* generous (often used ironically) < Ir. 'You could have been a little bit more flaithiúlach and given him the loan of the bike' (BC, Meath); 'He was very flahoolagh with his chequebook, wasn't he?' Joyce, *Ulysses*, 309.16–17: "gob, flahoolagh entertainment"; *Finnegans Wake*, 498.10: "Flawhoolags F.P."

fleá /fljɔː/, /flæː/ *n.,* a feast; a festival (SOM, Kerry) < Ir. 'There'll be a great fleá up there this weekend.'

flesher /'flɛʃər/, *n.,* a butcher (Limerick) < ME *flesch*, flesh, meat + *-er*.

fligat /'flɪgət/ *n.* (*colloq.*), in the phr. 'she hasn't a fligat on her,' she hasn't a stitch of clothes on her (origin obscure, but cf. *EDD* s.v. 'flig' sb.[1], 'gaudy attire, and 'flig' adj., 'feathered, of a young bird ready to fly').

fliuch /flʌx/ *adj.,* wet, moist (SOM, Kerry) < Ir. 'It's FUAR fliuch out this morning.'

flúirse /'fluːrʃə/ *n.,* plenty < Ir. 'There was flúirse of food and drink there.' 'Flúirseach' *adj.,* abundant (KM, Kerry)

flummery /'flʌməri/ *n.,* a kind of porridge; a dish made from oats soaked in water until it turned sour, then removed from the vessel, squeezed by hand, and sieved (Ruane and McCann, Mayo) < Welsh *llymru* (*ODEE*: the 'fl' is used to represent the Welsh sound 'll').

flush /flʌʃ/ *n.,* a pool of water extending almost across a road < E dial. < *flash* (probably imitative; cf. *ODEE* s.v. 'flash' v., referring to rushing or dashing of water). Carleton, 'Shane Fadh's Wedding' (*Six Irish Tales*, 196): "But the best sport of all was when they came to the *Lazy Corner*, just at Jack Gallagher's *flush*, where the water came out a good way acrass [*sic*] the road" (in a footnote, Carleton supplies the above definition, adding, 'It is usually fed by a small mountain stream and in consequence of rising and falling rapidly, it is called "Flush"').

fluthered /'fluːt̪ərd/ *p.part.* (*colloq.*), drunk (origin obscure). 'You're fluthered!' (BC, Meath).

Roche, *Poor Beast in the Rain*, act I, i, 73: "*Georgie:* . . . if Wexford don't win that match on Sunday I'll be fluthered drunk comin' home on that bus"; cf. O'Casey's character Fluther Good in *The Plough and the Stars*. *See* STOCIOUS.

flying /ˈflaiən/ *pres.part.*, in good form < OE *fleogan*, *v.*, to fly. 'How are you, then?' – 'Flying' (TF, Cavan). Roche, *A Handful of Stars*, act I, ii, 25: "*Stapler:* How's it goin' son? *Jimmy:* Flyin'. *Stapler:* I'm flyin' so I am. *Stapler:* Yeah, you look like a fella that's flyin' alright. What are yeh doin', celebratin' or somethin'?"

fód /foːd̪/ *n.*, a sod < Ir. 'Bring a fód to school for the fire if the teacher said so; it'll keep her own backside warm if nobody else's itself' (BD, Cavan). 'Fód móna', a sod of turf (SOM, Kerry). 'Fód school', a school to which pupils brought turf for heating in winter.

fóidín mearaí /ˈfoːdiːnˈmæriː/ *n.phr.*, a 'sod of confusion' (MOB, Mayo); fig. bewilderment, confusion < Ir (lit. sod of confusion). If a traveller treads on this particular piece of ground while out walking he or she is led astray. 'Watch out for the fóidín mearaí when you're taking the path up the mountain.'

folachán /ˈfʌləxɔːn/ *n.*, a covering, a place of concealment; a hidden house under a fence (JOM, Kerry) < Ir. 'They lived in a little folachán – you'd never see it from the road.'

folly /ˈfɑli/ *v.*, to follow < E dial. < ME *folien* (cf. HE 'borry' for 'borrow' (< OE *borgian*), 'widdy' for 'widow' (< OE *widewe*), etc.). 'Folly him quick and don't lose sight of him.' Griffin, *The Collegians,* 35: "Folly on, sir – folly on"; Somerville and Ross, *The Real Charlotte,* chap. 50 (*FDA*, 2, 1053): ". . . even Michael the groom thought to himself that if he hadn't the trap to wash, he'd put the saddle on the chestnut and folly the misthress."

folt /fʌlt/ *n.*, a head of hair, especially if unkempt (SOM, Kerry) < Ir. 'Comb down that folt before you go to Mass.'

fooder /ˈfuːd̪ər/ *n.*, rush, hurry (KM, Kerry) < Ir *fuadar*. 'What fooder is on you?'; 'There was a fooder to her.'

fools, *see* STRAWBOYS.

fooster /ˈfuːst̪ər/ also **foosther**, **fústar** *n., v.*, busy, agitated behaviour (SOC, Cork); to bustle about fussily < Ir *fústar,* fussy behaviour, bustle, activity. 'Stop foostering about, will you!' (BC, Meath); 'Stop your fústaring and get on with your homework' (KG, Kerry); 'He was fústaring about the place' (SOM, Kerry, who adds: 'fústrach' *adj.,* in a rush, fidgety'). O'Casey, *The Plough and the Stars,* act I, 139: "*Mrs*

Gogan: I wondher what he is foostherin' for now?"; Durcan, *Christmas Day,* XII, 65: "I fooster for an hour or more I not knowing what I am doing." 'Foosterer', *n.,* a fussy person; a messer < Ir *fústaire* + E *-er*.

foot /fʌt/ in the phr. 'on foot of', as a result of, by reason of < OE *fot* (there is no obvious parallel in Irish). 'On foot of this, we can't go any further with this deal'; 'On foot of the charges, he had to appear in the court' (Dublin).

football /'fʌtbɔːl/ *n.,* Gaelic (Irish) football. 'He was always very good at football, and they say he played a bit of soccer too' (NL, Mayo). *See* GAELIC; SOCCER.

footer /fuːt̪ər/ also **foother** *n., v.,* fidgety, awkward behaviour; to act in a bungling manner < Ir *fútar, n.* 'She was always footering about at something' (MCR, Waterford).

footing /'fʌtən/ *v.n.,* placing three or four sods of turf on end, propped against each other, to dry out < E dial. < ME *foot*. 'Footings', *n.pl.,* small heaps of cut turf. 'I spent the whole day footing the turf and I didn't get the half of it done.' Kickham, *Knocknagow,* 495: "Nearly all the men, and most of the women, are out in the meadows . . . cutting and 'footing' turf in the bog"; Healy, *Nineteen Acres*, 29: "When you were turning turf or footing it, and you went to straighten your back to ease the pain, he was on to you."

forbye /fɑr'bai/ *prep.,* besides, in addition to; over and above < E dial. < ME *forbi*. 'She does all the house work and forbye some of the farm work as well' (AF, Cavan).

forgortha, *see* FÉAR GORTACH.

form /'fɔːrəm/, /'fʌrəm/ (with epenthetic vowel) *n.,* a long rectangular bench suitable for the school-room or for children at table < ME *forme* < L *forma*. 'She had to get rid of the two forms when the childer grew too big for them' (BC, Meath).

formad /'fʌrəməd/ *n.,* grudge, envy (SOM, Kerry) < Ir. 'He's had a formad against him for years for marrying the sister.'

fornent /fər'nɛnt/ also **forenent**, **fornenst**, **forenenst**, etc. *adv., prep.,* to, facing; in front of (Omurethi, Kildare) < E dial. < EModE *fore*, in front + *anent*, towards). 'Things will aye be some way, if they shouldnae be fornenst ither' (AKB, Antrim). 'Fornenst you', opposite to you (DOH, Limerick, who adds: 'still current'). Carleton, 'The Party Fight and Funeral' (*Six Irish Tales*, 51): "As God would have had it, the crowd didn't happen to be fornent the door, or numbers of them would have been shot, and the night was dark, too, which was in our favour"; Banim, *The Boyne*

Water, 119: "No more NOR the genteels fornent ye"; Stoker, *The Snake's Pass*, 30: "an' there foreninst him! right up the hill side he seen two min carryin' the chist [chest]"; *Finnegans Wake*, 626.21–2: "One time you'd stand fornenst me"; Leonard, *Out After Dark*, 36: ". . . isn't his poor mother better off where she is, lyin' in the wet clay of the Kill of the Grange, than to have that cur fornenst her."

fort, *see* FAIRY FORT.

for to /ˈfɔːrtə/ *prep.* used since the Early Middle English period (*c.* 1100 onwards) to express a sense of purpose; by the end of the fourteenth century it had become weakened into serving as a sign of the infinitive; during the fifteenth century 'to' supplanted 'for to' as the commonest form in this function, but 'for to' was still to be found quite frequently in EModE and is still favoured by older users of HE (see Henry, 81–104). 'I saw that man digging five feet deep for to get his wire right.' Somerville and Ross, *Some Experiences of an Irish RM*, 233: "'twas when they went up on th'excursion last month for to have their teeth pulled"; Synge, *The Playboy of the Western World* (*FDA*, 2, 637): "*Mahon:* Faith, I'm thinking I'll go walking for to view the race."

Forty Hours /ˈfɔːrtiˈaurz/ *n.*, the exposition of the Blessed Sacrament for forty hours (being the time Christ lay in the tomb), with relays of watchers kneeling and praying before the altar. 'Will you take over from me at the Forty Hours? I'll be there from three till four' (KG, Kerry).

forty-niner, *see* DUDEEN.

fostúch /fʌsˈt̪uːx/ *n.*, a grown-up youth; if applied to an adult has a pejorative connotation: an idle, lazy fellow (VQ, Kerry) < Ir. 'He was a big fostúch of a man.'

fothain /ˈfʌhən/ *n.*, shelter (SOM, Kerry) < Ir. 'He has a fothain built beside the graveyard when he's looking at the sheep in the winter.'

fothrach /ˈfʌhrəx/ *n.*, a very modest abode (said with disrespect); a ruin, a broken-down residence; a dilapidated monastery or castle (SOM, Kerry) < Ir *fothrach*, a ruin. 'What a fothrach!' (KG, Kerry).

fothram /ˈfʌhrəm/ *n.*, figwort (used for skin care) (KM, Kerry) < Ir. 'Go out and pick a few fothrams from the ditch.'

founder /ˈfaundər/ *v.*, fig. to collapse with the cold < E dial. < OF *fondrer*. 'The old lady said she was always foundered with the cold in the winter' (TJ, Sligo).

fox /fɑks/ *v.*, to act cunningly, to cheat, etc.; fig. to work in the 'black economy' (Dublin) < E dial. 'He was caught foxing by the Tax Office.' *See* BOX.

francach /ˈfrɑŋkəx/ *n.,* a rat (SOM, Kerry) < Ir. 'I saw the biggest francach I ever saw down in the potato field just now.'

fraoch /friːx/, /freːx/ *n.,* heather (found in bog) (SOM, Kerry) < Ir. 'Listen! Can you hear the sound of the wind through the fraoch?'

fraughan /ˈfrɑhən/ also **fraochán** /ˈfriːhɔːn/ *n.,* bilberry < Ir *fraochán*. 'Picking fraochans' (SOM, Kerry).

Free State /ˈfriːsteːt/ the Irish Free State (1922–1937). Plunkett, *Farewell Companions*, 94: "I once hoped for a Workers' Republic . . . it's no go now. The Free Staters don't want it." *See* SAORSTÁT ÉIREANN.

fret /frɛt/ *n., adj.,* enthusiastic; excellent < E dial. (cf. *EDD* 'to have the fret,' be excited, fume, fret) < OE *fretan, v.,* to gnaw. 'He's a fret for the football' (he's very keen on it); 'The film was a fret' (was really good) (Dublin).

friend /frɛnd/ *n.,* a relative < ME *frend*. 'Is John a friend of ours?' – 'Indeed he is: he's our cousin' (AF, Cavan).

frigging /ˈfrɪgən/ *pres.part.,* used euphemistically in place of FUCKING (origin uncertain, but. cf. E *frig*, to rub, chafe, and L *fricare*, to masturbate). 'What the frigging hell are you doing down there?' Purcell, *On Lough Derg*, 93: "And then you have to stop and stand in that frigging queue"; Roche, *A Handful of Stars*, act I, i, 9: "*Jimmy:* Wrecked him, I nearly friggin' killed him."

from /frɑm/ *conj.,* from the time when, since, after. The 'from' at the head of such HE subordinate adverbial clauses of time as 'from I was a child I liked reading' is directly based on the Ir *conj.* 'ó', from (the time when), since: 'ó tháinig mé anseo,' from (the time) I came here, etc. 'From ever I came to London I wanted to go home' (BD, Cavan).

fruit /fruːt/ *n.,* in the saying 'the fruit tastes sour when you can't reach it,' you dislike something because you cannot have it for yourself.

fuachtán /ˈfuəxt̪ɔːn/ *n.,* a chilblain (MK, Galway) < Ir. 'I'm crippled with the fuachtáns'; 'Put a cut onion on your fuachtáns and you'll get ease.'

fuadar /ˈfuəd̪ər/ *n.,* industrious activity, a great hurry, rush (SOM, Kerry) < Ir. 'I never saw such fuadar' (SOM, Kerry); 'They always put on a great fuadar when they see the boss coming' (TJ, Sligo); 'Can't you stop and chat? What fuadar is on you?' (KM, Kerry). 'Droch-fhuadar', evil intent; being up to no good < Ir.

fuairneach /ˈfuərnəx/ *n.,* a barren sheep, goat, or cow; fig. a childless woman (MK,

Galway) < Ir. 'She'll have no child, she married too late – she's an old fuairneach.'

fuairnéalach /fuər'neːləx/ *n.*, a good-for-nothing, careless person < Ir. 'That fuairnéalach Jim, he never cut the turf in time.'

fuar /fuər/ *n.*, cold (SOM, Kerry) < Ir. 'It's fuar out today.'

fuarán /fuə'rɔːn/ *n.*, a spring, a well (SOM, Kerry) < Ir. 'Take some water home from the fuarán; it'll bring good luck.'

fuath /fuə/ *n.*, great dislike; hatred; disdain (SOM, Kerry) < Ir. 'She has a fuath for him on account of the will.'

fucking /'fʌkən/ *pres.part. as adj.*, a common term of displeasure, which has lost most of its sexual connotation (origin obscure; it is not, as often claimed, from Old English, but cf. German *ficken*, to strike, have intercourse with; cf. also L *pungere,* to prick, penetrate; for the change of *p* to *f* cf. L *pater* to E *father*, etc.; James Ogier reviews the evidence for the English-German linkage in 'Sex and violence in the Indo-European languages', *Maledicta*, vol. 12 (1996), 85–90). Sometimes the word is euphemistically expressed by HE speakers as 'frigging'. 'Get out of my fucking way!'; 'Shut your fucking mouth.' Deane, *Reading in the Dark*, 98: "Fuckin' stooly. Just like your uncle"; 158: "Who's the fucker in the bedroom?"

fuílleach /'fiːləx/ also **fuíollach** *n.*, remainder, leavings, residue, (SOM, Kerry) < Ir. *See* FUÍOLLÁN.

fuinneog /fwin'joːg/ *n.*, a window (SOM, Kerry) < Ir. 'Will you just look at those fuinneogs!' (KG, Kerry).

fuíollán /'fiːlɔːn/ *n.*, a large quantity, 'lashings of' < Ir. 'They have fuíolláns of money' (SOM, Kerry). *See* FUÍLLEACH.

fuist /fwɪʃt/ *v. (imper.),* keep quiet < Ir. 'Fuist! I can't hear a word she's saying' (KG, Kerry).

fústar, *see* FOOSTER.

futa fata /'fʌt̪ə'fæt̪ə/ *n.phr.,* a confused babble; very noisy talk (e.g. at a fair); flustering (SOC, Cork) < Ir. 'When the meeting broke up there was futa fata GALORE.'

G

GAA /ʤiːeːˈeː/ for Gaelic Athletic Association. 'The GAA are making great strides with the new stand in Croke Park' (SOC, Kerry).

gab /gæb/ also **geab** /gjæb/ *n., v.,* talk, speech; idle chatter; fig. a talkative person (with the 'gift of the gab') < E dial. (origin obscure; perhaps from *gabble* (imitative)). 'Will you quit the gabbing and get on with the job!' (Cork). 'He has the gift of the geab – he must have kissed the BLARNEY Stone' (BC, Meath).

gabha /gau/ *n.,* a blacksmith < Ir. 'LOOKIT, do me a favour and bring the horse down to the gabha, there's a good boy' (MG, Cavan).

gabháil /gəˈwɔːl/ also **gwall, gawl** /gɔːl/ *n.,* an armful; the quantity carried on one outstretched arm and balanced by the other arm, as of turf, or between two outstretched arms, as of hay or straw (SOM, Kerry); < Ir. 'Throw a gabháil of hay to the donkey, will you?'; 'She put a whole gwall of turf on the fire.'

gabhairín reo /ˈgauriːnˈroː/ *n.,* a (male) snipe (SOM, Kerry) < Ir *gabhairín rua*. 'A gabhairín reo is very tasty roasted.'

gabhal-luachair /gaulˈluəxər/ *n.,* (scented flowers of) the jointed rush (KM, Kerry) < Ir. 'Gather up a few of those gabhal-luachair; they'd look nice with the other flowers.'

gabhar /gaur/ *n.,* a goat < Ir. '"Hoosh! hoosh!" said she to the gabhar' (BC, Meath).

gabhlán /ˈgaulɔːn/ *n.,* a formed piece of wood (SOM, Kerry). *See* GABHLÓG.

gabhlóg /ˈgauloːg/ also **gowlogue, gollog** /ˈgɑlɑk/ (TF, Cavan) *n.,* a forked stick; a piece of timber with a two-pronged end, useful for making a prop (MOB, Mayo); a prop for a pot etc.; a strong Y-shaped stick used to hold furze, briars etc. while they are being cut with a slasher (BF, Cork); a Y-shaped rod used for water-divining (SOM, Kerry); a catapult; the pin used to secure the movable bottom on a BARDÓG; the joining of two potato ridges;

fig. a stiff drink (Ó Muirithe, Dictionary, 74) < Ir *gabhlóg*, fork. 'The MASTER caught him with a gabhlóg, and he was PANDIED good and hard'; 'Can you find water with that gowlogue?' (TF, Cavan).

gad /gæd/ *n.*, a withe; a rope made of twisted twigs (KM, Kerry) < Ir. 'Do you think you could make a gad from those twigs?' *See* BOOLTHAUN.

gadaí /ˈgɑd̪iː/ *n.*, a thief (MOB, Mayo); a rogue, a sly person < Ir. 'Watch that gadaí, I'm telling you; he'll make off with something and you won't see sight nor sound of him again' (SL, Mayo); 'Where did such a gadaí come out of? The rest of the family is so nice and straight to your face' (BC, Meath).

gadrach /ˈgɑd̪rəx/ *n.* 1. A strong, hardy man < Ir. 2. A slow, boring person; an inactive person. 'He takes for ever to do anything, that gadrach, even if he's telling you a story – he makes a short story long, if you see what I mean' (Kerry).

Gaelic /ˈgeːlɪk/ *adj. as n.* (*colloq.*), Gaelic (Irish) football < Ir *Gaelach*, Irish. 'He'd only play Gaelic – he'd never play SOCCER' (SOC, Kerry).

Gaeltacht /ˈgeːlt̪əxt̪/ *n.*, Irish-speaking district < Ir *Gaeltacht* (lit. 'Gaeldom'). 'Seán was brought up in the Gaeltacht; that's why he got the job teaching Irish' (Mayo). Keane, *The Bodhrán Makers*, 156: "The parish in question was possessed of a sizeable Gaeltacht area"; Heaney, 'The Stations of the West' (*New Selected Poems*, 47): "On my first night in the Gaeltacht the old woman | spoke to me in English: 'You will be all right.' I sat on | a twilit bedside listening through the wall to fluent | Irish, homesick for a speech I was to extirpate."

gaff /gæf/ *n.* (*colloq.*), a house or home (origin obscure; cf. Beale: 'the most common prison word for a dwelling-place, house, or room'). 'Are yiz coming back to my gaff?' (KD, Dublin).

gaffer /ˈgæfər/ *n.*, familiar form of address to a person commanding a sense of importance < E (corruption of *grandfather*). 'Where's the gaffer?' (TJ, Sligo). Griffin, *The Collegians*, 50: "Who should he see only Dan Dawley, an' he a little gaffer the same time"; Synge, *The Playboy of the Western World*, act III (*FDA*, 2, 636): "*Philly:* . . . and she so fussy after that young gaffer."

gág /gɔːg/ *n.*, a crack, fissure; a crack in skin (KM, Kerry) < Ir. 'I could see everything that was going on through the gág in the wall.'

gáilleog /ˈgɔːloːg/ *n.*, a small drop (of drink) (Carlow) < Ir. 'Will you give me a gáilleog of whiskey for the road, MÁS É DO THOIL É?'

gairbhin /ˈgɑrəviːn/ also **scairbhín** /ˈskɑrəviːn/ *n.,* unseasonal cold and windy weather early in May (SOM, Kerry) < Ir *gairbhín* [*garbhshíon*] < *garbh*, rough + *síon*, weather; also *gairbhín* [*garbhshíon*] *na gcuach* < Ir (lit. rough weather of the cuckoos). 'It's only the gairbhin; it'll be over in a few days' (SOM, Kerry).

gairdín /ˈgaːrʤiːn/ *n.,* a garden < Ir. 'They buried Spot in the gairdín' (AF, Cavan). Healy, *Nineteen Acres*, 119: "Grandda's reaping hook . . . used to gleam after he cut rushes for thatching and haystacks in the gairdín."

gairleog /ˈgɔːrloːg/ *n.,* garlic (BC, Meath) < Ir. 'Where's the gáirleog TILL I rub a bit on your finger.'

gaisce /ˈgæʃkə/ *n.,* a deed of valour (often sarcastically); fig. a boastful person < Ir. 'What a gaisce that was!' 'Doing the gaisce', showing off (VQ, Kerry).

gaiscí /ˈgæʃkiː/ *n.,* one who performs great deeds, but normally used sarcastically < Ir *gaiscíoch*. 'If you aren't the great gaiscí!' (SOM, Kerry).

gait of going /geːtəˈgoːɪn/ *n.,* manner of going, behaviour < E *gait*, manner of walking. Kavanagh, *Tarry Flynn*, 108: "The mother . . . said: 'From now on you'll have to change your gait of going.'" 'I got a great gait of going under me,' I got a burst of enthusiasm (PJG, Dublin).

gal /gæl/ *n.,* steam; smoke (Limerick) < Ir. 'Wait till you see the gal off the kettle and then WET the tea.'

galamaisíocht /ˈgɑləməˈʃiːəxt̪/ *n.,* showing off < Ir. 'Look at her at the galamaisíocht again! I don't know how her brother puts up with her – you'd think she was somebody' (KG, Kerry).

gale-day /ˈgeːldeː/ *n.,* a day on which an instalment of rent is due < ME *gavel*, rent, tribute < OE *gafol*. 'He sold all the heifers before gale-day' (TF, Cavan).

gallagh-gunley /gæləˈgʌnliː/ *n.,* the harvest moon (KM, Kerry) < Ir *gealach na gcoinleach* (lit. moon of the stubble).

gallán /gæˈlɑːn/ *n.,* a standing-stone, pillar-stone (SOM, Kerry, who adds: 'supposed to have a connection with the "good people", hence farmers slow to remove them') < Ir.

gallery /galəri/ *n.* (*colloq.*), an entertaining, enthusiastic person <(O)F *galerie*; the use of this word in this context is difficult to explain, but it is possible that the idea of a performer or entertainer in a Minstrels' Gallery may be remotely connected; 'He's a great gallery (= he's a great sport)' (DOH, Limerick) (recorded from his parents, who come from Kilkenny); Moylan, *Kilkenny*, 134–5, s.v.

'?Gleadhair', cites '?Gallery, 1. A cheerful, noisy gathering at which there is laughing, singing and dancing . . . fun laughter and merry-making . . . a cheerful conversation . . . an amusing, entertaining person . . . 2. A fool . . . cf. Dinn[een], Ó Dón[aill], s.v gealgháire.' *See* GEALGHÁIREACH.

gallinglass, *see* GALLOGLASS.

gallivanting /gælə'væntən/ *n.*, going to lots of places; gadding about < E dial. (origin obscure, but cf. *gallant* < (O)F *galant*). 'Don't be out gallivanting all night' (BC, Meath). Yeats, 'Two Songs Written for the Tune's Sake', II (*Collected Poems*, 297): "I would that I were an old beggar | Rolling a blind pearl eye, | For he cannot see my lady | Go gallivanting by"; Joyce, *Ulysses*, 334.27–8: "Crawford gallivanting around the country at the king's expense"; Heaney, 'Traditions' (*Wintering Out*, 32): "MacMorris, gallivanting | round the Globe, WHINGED | to courtier . . ."

galloglass /'gæloglæs/ also **galloglas** *n.*, a mercenary of Scottish or Hiberno-Norse origin; a heavily armed soldier in a chief's retinue < Ir *gallóglach* < *gall*, foreigner + *óglach*, warrior. *Captain Thomas Stukeley*, 78: "gow make ready oore kerne and Gallinglasse against night"; Joyce, *Finnegans Wake*, 31.17: "two of his retinue of gallowglasses."

gallon /'gælən/ *n.*, a drinking-vessel < Ir *galún* < E *gallon*. 'The calf drank the full of the gallon of milk' (MG, Cavan). *See* GALÚN.

gallus also **gallous** /'gæləs/ *adj.*, wild, mischievous; horrid; excellent < E dial. *gallus*, gallows. 'Such a gallus lad – I don't know what'll become of him.' Synge, *The Playboy of the Western World*, act III (*FDA*, 2, 641): "*Michael:* Father Reilly's after reading it in gallous Latin"; 644: "*Pegeen:* There's a great gap between a gallous story and a dirty deed"; Joyce, *Ulysses*, 199.32–3: "'Twas murmur we did for a gallus potion would rouse a friar" (note the omission of the relative pronoun THAT before 'would').

galluses /'gæləsəs/ *n.*, braces (to hold up trousers) < *gallus* (obsolete form of *gallows*). 'He still wears the galluses to Mass of a [on] Sunday' (JMF, Cavan).

galoot also **gilloot** /gə'luːt/ *n.* (*colloq.*), an awkward, stupid man; a fool < E dial. (origin obscure; *EDD* notes '1. A soldier; 2. a man (*gen.* in contempt)'; *OED* cites American usages as source, without offering an etymology: a worthless fellow; a fool; a big, awkward creature). 'That fellow is an awful galoot' (BC, Meath); 'You big gilloot, let me do it myself' (TF, Cavan).

galore /gə'loːr/ *adv.,* enough (SOM, Kerry); plentiful, in abundance < Ir *go leor*, enough; plenty. (This is one of the few words of Irish origin that have made their way into SE usage.) 'There's snow galore outside'; 'There was singing galore till the early hours' (Cavan). Sheehan, *Glenanaar*, 90: "And there are songs and dances *galore*"; Joyce, *Finnegans Wake*, 557.3: "galorybit of the sanes in hevel." *See* MAITH GO LEOR.

galorybit, *see* GALORE.

galún /gɑ'luːn/ also **galúinín** /gɑ'luːniːn/ (SOM, Kerry) *n.,* a tin or aluminium can in which fresh milk is kept; often used to store hard sweets in a shop < Ir. *See* GALLON.

gámaí /'gɔːmiː/ *n.,* a tall, overgrown person; a foolish person < Ir. 'That gámaí is no use for a day's work in the bog' (BC, Meath).

gamal /'gɑməl/ *n.,* a stupid person (SOM, Kerry); a foolish, loutish person; a figure of fun < Ir (cf. E dial. *gomeril*). 'You'd better stop hanging round with that gamal; he'll get you into trouble, I'm telling you' (BC, Meath); 'He's always gomming about [hanging about aimlessly] around the shop, but there's no harm in him at all' (KG, Kerry).

gamalóg /'gɑməlːog/ *n.,* a silly woman or girl (SOM, Kerry); a soft, simple man < Ir. 'She must be a bit of a gamalóg: she's always giving that fellow drink.'

gambanman, *see* GOMBEEN.

game-ball /geim'bɔːl/ *adj.* (*colloq.*), expression of assent or approbation (usage mainly Dublin): good, all right, etc. (origin obscure). 'I'll see you tonight.' – 'Game-ball' (Dublin). Plunkett, *Farewell Companions*, 45: "'How's the new job going?' 'Gameball,' Paddy said."

gandal /gænd̪əl/ *n.,* a gander; a foolish, awkward or clumsy person; the walk of a clumsy person < Ir. 'Will you look at that gandal!' (SOM, Kerry), 'He was like a gandal looking into a Wellington boot' (saying).

gansey /'gænziː/ *n.*, a knitted jersey; a jersey made from the fleece of wool (MOB, Mayo) (elsewhere 'a jersey or T-shirt, esp. a coloured one; a pullover': *see* Allsopp, *Dictionary of Caribbean English Usage* (1996), s.v. 'gansey') < *Guernsey, place-name*. 'That's a nice gansey – where did you steal it!!?' (BC, Meath). Roche, *A Handful of Stars*, act I, ii, 22: "Jimmy has spied that the top of Paddy's underpants is sticking out and he has his shirt and gansy tucked down inside it"; McCourt, *Angela's Ashes*, 356: "Everything is torn, shirt, gansey, short pants, stockings."

gant /gænt/ *v.,* to yawn (cf. ME *ganien*, to yawn). 'You've been ganting all morning; you must have been on the tear (on a spree) last night' (KG, Kerry). Heaney, *The Midnight Verdict*,

25: "With her ganting gums and her mouth in a twist."

garda /ˈgɔːrd̪ʤ/ *n.*, a member of the GARDA SÍOCHÁNA < Ir *garda*, guard. *See* BANGHARDA.

Garda Síochána /ˈgɔːrd̪ə ˈʃiːxɔːnə/ *n.*, national police force < Ir *Garda Síochána* (lit. guard of the peace, influenced by original official name, Civic Guard).

garlach /ˈgɑːrləx/ *n.*, a brat, an urchin (MK, Galway); a small child < Ir. 'Come out from there, you garlach, till I get a slap at you'; 'The garlach is hiding up on top of the chest of drawers where I can't get at him.' Sheehan, *Glenanaar*, 158: ". . . he chuse to take in a little *gárlach* of a child on a Christmas night."

garron /ˈgærən/ *n.*, a gelding, nag < Ir *gearrán*. 'You won't get much for that garron' (TF, Cavan). Griffin, *The Collegians*, 150: "Whup, get up here, you old garron!"

garsún /gɑːrˈsuːn/ also **gorsoon** *n.*, a young boy < Ir. 'Get up on the cross-bar, garsún, and I'll bring you over the road' (TF, Cavan). 'Garsúinín', endearing version (SOM, Kerry) < Ir (dimin. of *garsún*). 'The blacksmith handed Tadie a hot horseshoe, saying, "Take hold of that, garsún"' (KM, Kerry, who adds: 'men referred to their penis as "the garsún"'). *See* GOSSOON.

gart /gɑːrt/ *n., adj.*, hospitality (MK, Galway); generous < Ir. 'There's great gart in that house.'

gas /gæs/ *n., adj.* (*colloq.*), fun; full of fun, amusing. It has been suggested that the widespread use of 'gas' in this sense may be connected with laughing-gas (a popular name for nitrous oxide, an anaesthetic that can induce laughter). 'He's great gas'; 'You're a gas man, and no mistake about it' (TF, Cavan); 'You're going to have great gas with me, lads' (Dublin). Joyce, *Finnegans Wake*, 577.7–8: "great gas with fun-in-the-corner"; Doyle, *The Van*, 241: "Between Tom Cruise an' YOUR MAN from Thornbirds. They were fuckin' gas"; Roche, *A Handful of Stars*, act II, iii, 65: "*Jimmy*: . . . It'd be gas wouldn't it?"; McCourt, *Angela's Ashes*, 146: "That's the way I'd like to be in the world, a gas man."

gasúr /ˈgɑsuːr/ also **gassir, gossure, gosawer** *n.*, a boy < Ir *gasúr*. 'Leave him at home; he's only a gasúr' (BC, Meath). Birmingham, *The Lighter Side of Irish Life*, 178: "'GOSSOON' . . . is simply a form of the French 'garçon', which has somehow passed into Irish speech. The true Irish word is 'gossure' . . . derived from 'gos' [*gas*], a branch, and 'ur' [*úr*], 'young' and means literally 'a young shoot"; Healy, *Nineteen Acres*, 100: 'the schoolchildren . . .

were company in their coming and their going and if they paid a call to the apple trees behind the stablings, well they were only gasúrs"; McDonagh, *The Cripple of Inishmaan*, scene i, 4: "*Kate: . . .* Billy's a good gosawer, despiting the cows."

gaum /gɔːm/ *n., v.,* a gaping person; to stare vacantly (cf. E *gome, n.,* notice, heed). 'What are you staring at, you gaum?' (Mayo). Shaw, *John Bull's Other Island*, act II (*FDA*, 2, 441): "*Cornelius:* Yah, you great gaum, you!"; O'Brien, *The Third Policeman*, 119: "*Will you sit down for Pity's sake and stop standing there like a gawm*, Joe said suddenly." *See* GOM.

gauster, *see* GOSTER.

gawp /gɔːp/ *v.,* to gape vacantly < ME *galpen*.

gazebo /gə'zeːbo/ *n.,* a tall, awkward person; a tall, angular, ungainly woman (PA, Fingall); a ramshackle house; any tall object < E dial. (origin obscure; possibly a humorous formation from *gaze* + L future verbal ending *-ebo*). 'Did you see the gazebo of a hat she was wearing? I wouldn't be seen dead in it!' (KG, Kerry).

gé /geː/ *n.,* a goose < Ir. 'Ní faide gob an ghé ná gob an ghandail' (proverb), What's sauce for the goose is sauce for the gander (lit. The beak of the goose is no longer than the beak of the gander).

geab, *see* GAB.

geabach /'gjæbəx/ *adj., n.,* loquacious (MK, Galway); fig. a gossip < Ir (cf. GAB). 'She's very geabach; keep away from her!'

geabaire /'gjæbərə/ *n.,* one given to small talk (SOM, Kerry); a fellow with too much talk (MK, Galway) < Ir (cf. GAB). 'He's a fierce geabaire.'

gead /gjæd̪/ *n.,* a blaze (white patch on horse) (KM, Kerry) < Ir. 'That foal has his mother's gead – a white blaze on the forehead'; 'She has a white gead up at the front' (KM, Kerry).

geáitse /'gɔːtʃə/ also **géaitsí** /'gɔːtʃiː/ *pl.* (SOM, Kerry) *n.,* antics, unusual gestures (SOM, Kerry); affected manner or movements; unusual gait; boldness in manner < Ir. 'Did you ever see such géaitses!'

gealach /'gæləx/ *n.,* the moon < Ir. 'Gealach na gcoinleach', harvest moon (lit. stubble moon). 'Seán na Gealaí', Jack o' lantern (SOM, Kerry) < Ir.

gealán /gæl'ɔːn/ *n.,* a sunbeam; a spark; the lighted end of a stick (KM, Kerry) < Ir.

gealgháiriteach /gæl'ɣɔːrətʃəx/ also **gealgháireach/** gæl'ɣɔːrəx/ *adj.,* pleasant, cheerful (MK, Galway) < Ir. 'I feel very gealgháiriteach this morning; it must be the weather.'

gealtaire /'gælt̪ərə/ *n.,* a long rush (plant); a splinter of bog-deal used as a torch (KM, Kerry) < Ir. 'You might try and look around for a gealtaire.'

geámaí /ˈgjɔːmiː/ *n.*, caper; accentuated gesture < Ir. 'Look at the geámaís of him' (SOM, Kerry).

geamaireacht /ˈgæmərəxt̪/ *n.*, a pantomime < Ir.

geanc /gjænk/ *n.*, a snub-nosed person (SOM, Kerry) < Ir. *See* GEANCACH.

geancach /ˈgjænkəx/ *adj.*, snub-nosed; rude, peevish (JOM, Kerry) < Ir. 'Don't talk to her; she's geancach.' *See* GEANCH.

geancánach /ˈgjænkɔːnəx/ *n.*, a kind of fairy; a LEPRECHAUN < Ir.

geansaí, *see* GANSEY.

gearán /gærˈɔːn/ *n.*, an act of complaining; a complainer < Ir. 'ARRAH, stop gearáning and do the work' (TF, Cavan).

gearrán /gæˈrɔːn/ *n.*, a castrated horse or donkey (KM, Kerry) < Ir. 'If you fall on that gate as you go over it you'll turn into a gearrán, with the sharp edges of it!'

gearrcach /ˈgjærkəx/ *n.*, a chick; a fledgling (SOM, Kerry); an infant < Ir.

gearrchaile /ˈgjærxələ/ *n.*, a little girl, a lass < Ir. 'Has the little gearrchaile made her first HOLY COMMUNION yet?' (AF, Cavan).

gearróg /ˈgæroːg/ *n.*, a short straw (in drawing lots); the short end of a ridge; a short potato drill; an uneven furrow; a stumpy, thickset girl (KM, Kerry) < Ir. 'Look at them gearrógs! Such a job he made of them!'; 'He pulled the gearróg so he had to go in and ask for the lend of the loan of the ladder.'

geasa /ˈgæsə/ *n.*, a taboo, an act of prohibition; a kind of penalty (MK, Galway); an injunction < Ir (*pl.* of *geis*). 'I put a geasa on him to return to me.'

geck /gɛk/ *n.*, *v.*, scorn, contempt; a fool; a simpleton; someone being laughed at; to scorn, deride < E dial. < EModE *gek*. 'They were gecking him all morning, so he eventually hit one of them a slap and that shut them up' (Limerick).

geek[1] /giːk/ *n.*, a squeak, slight sound < Ir *gíog*. 'There wasn't a geek out of him' (MH, Clare); 'If I hear so much as a geek while I'm out . . .' (BC, Meath).

geek[2] /giːk/ *v.*, peep < Ir *gíoc*. 'The child was geeking round the door' (MH, Clare).

geidimín /ˈgɛʤəmiːn/ *n.*, excitement; a small, annoying, flighty person, difficult to pin down (MOB, Mayo; SOM, Kerry) < Ir. 'She's a proper geidimín; you wouldn't want to take any notice of her' (SOM, Kerry).

géillín /geːˈliːn/ *n.*, a contrivance for supporting a swimmer (KM, Kerry) < Ir.

geit /gɛʧ/ *n.*, a fright (MK, Galway) < Ir. 'That knocked a fright out of [Ir bhain sé geit as] you.'

geocach /ˈgjoːkəx/ *n.*, a beggar; a cadger, a parasite (SOM, Kerry); a foolish young person < Ir. 'He's a proper geocach:

he'd shake hands with you with your own hand' (SOM, Kerry).

geocán /gjoː'kɔːn/ *n.*, a pipe, a reed; fig. a reedy, piping voice (KM, Kerry) < Ir. 'I can't listen to the geocán of her much longer.' *See* DIÚCÁN.

geois /gjoːʃ/ *n.*, a belly, a paunch; an ungainly person < Ir. 'What a geois you are! Will you never learn to be careful with the DELF?' (BC, Meath).

geonaíl /'gjoːniːl/ *n.*, a cry, a whimper (as of beagles or hounds) (MK, Galway) < Ir.

geosadán /'gjoːsəd̪ɔːn/ *n.*, ragweed; fig. a thin, weedy person < Ir. 'He's a thin little geosadán, God help him!' (KG, Kerry).

gern /girn/ also **girn** *v.*, to look savage; to snarl; to cry, whine, or whimper < E dial. (variant of *grin*). 'Some young children were said to be always gerning' (POC, Cavan).

get /gɛt/ also **git** /gɪt/ *n. (pejor.)*, a bastard < E dial. *get*, brat, bastard. 'You little get, come here till I catch hold of you!' (Mayo).

get (one's) death, *see* DEATH.

ghrá thú /'ɣrɔːhuː/ *phr.*, sham-talk (PMD, Mayo) < Ir *(mo) ghrá thú* (lit. I love you, but used ironically). *See* GRÁ.

gibiris /'gɪbərəʃ/ *n.*, nonsense < E *gibberish* (imitation of meaningless sounds). 'Stop talking gibiris and tell us the real story' (BC, Meath).

giddhom /'gjɪd̪əm/ *n.*, restlessness, friskiness (KM, Kerry) < Ir *giodam*. 'There's a great giddhom on me today.'

gilloot, *see* GALOOT.

giob /gjɪb/ *n.*, a snatch, a scrap < Ir. 'They didn't offer me a giob, and me there for over two hours' (Mayo).

giobach /'gjɪbəx/ *adj.*, untidy in dress, careless about appearance; unkempt (of hair or beard) < Ir. 'I've never seen her any other way but giobach' (JMF, Cavan).

giobal /'gjɪbəl/ *n.*, a rag; torn clothing (MOB, Mayo) < Ir. 'Old giobals', tattered clothes (SOM, Kerry).

giobalach /'gjɪbələx/ *adj.*, ragged, torn (of clothes); untidy (PMD, Mayo; SOM, Kerry). 'She was very giobalach in that oul dress' (KG, Kerry).

giob geab /'gjɪb'gjæb/ *n.*, pecking; chit-chat; 'type of conversation between wild geese' (MOB, Mayo) < Ir (cf. GEAB).

giobstaire /'gjɪbst̪ərə/ *n.*, a cheeky, saucy girl, a hussy < Ir. 'Did you hear what she said, the little giobstaire! I'll LEARN her a thing or two yet!'

giodam /'gjɪd̪əm/ *n.*, giddiness; liveliness < Ir. 'There is a giodam to his step' (KM, Kerry).

giodamán /'gjɪd̪əmɔːn/ *n.*, a giddy person < Ir. 'She's just a little giodamán,' she's a silly girl.

gíog /giːg/ *n.*, a slight sound, a peep < Ir. 'He hadn't a gíog out of him' (SOM, Kerry). *See* GEEK[1].

giolcach /ˈgjılkəx/ *n.,* a reed; reedy peat (Limerick) < Ir.

gioscaire /ˈgıskərə/ *n.,* a talkative, vigorous old man (BC, Meath) < Ir *giostaire*.

giota /ˈgıt̪ə/ *n.,* a bit or piece of something, e.g. small corner of tillage (KM, Kerry) < Ir.

girg /gırg/ *n., v.,* (to make) a creaking noise; to jar < E dial. (*EDD* cites a reference from the *Ballymena Observer* (1892): 'as boots do when unused for some time').

girn, *see* GERN.

girseach /ˈgırʃəx/ also **girse** /ˈgırʃə/ *n.,* a young girl, a lass < Ir. 'Come on, girse, and give me a hand' (AF, Cavan); 'Mary-Anne's girseach sold the geese' (KM, Kerry). Sheehan, *Glenanaar*, 149: ". . . what harrum [harm] can a poor little *girseach*, like Nodlag, be to any wan [one]?"

gistra /ˈgıst̪rə/ *n.,* a garrulous old man < Ir *giostaire*. 'Be quiet, you old gistra; I've heard enough from you' (Carlow). *See* GIOSCAIRE.

giuirléidí /guːrˈleːʤiː/ also **guirléidí** *n.,* implements; personal belongings < Ir. 'Pick up your giuirléidí and put them away' (KM, Kerry).

give out /gıvˈaut/ *v.,* to criticise, to scold (HE usage). 'It wasn't enough for him to give it to me up to my face but he had to go around giving out all sorts about me among the neighbours' (LUB, Dublin).

gizaybo, *see* GAZEBO.

gladar box /ˈglæd̪ərbɑks/ *n.phr.*, 'a dummy box for coining. To the eye of the unsuspicious victim, the "gladar box" is a mould, but the TINKER knows better' (Pádraig Mac Gréine, *Béaloideas*, vol. 4 (1934), 261).

glafaire /ˈglæfərə/ *n.,* a howler, a snarler (as of a dog); fig. a snappish person (MOB, Mayo) < Ir. 'Don't go near that glafaire; he's half mad.'

glaic /glæk/ *n.,* a grasp, clutch, half-closed hand < Ir. 'In his glaic' (SOM, Kerry).

glaise[1] /ˈglæʃə/ *n.,* greenness; rawness in the weather < Ir. 'There's a glaise in the day; I don't like it, for sure' (TJ, Sligo).

glaise[2] /ˈglæʃə/ *n.,* a stream; a boundary stream; a stream running through a bog (DOS, Kerry) < Ir. 'Stephen has dammed up the glaise again; will you clear it?' (AF, Cavan).

glám /glɔːm/ also **glaum** *n., v.,* a grab; to grab, to snatch greedily, to clasp; to handle roughly < Ir. 'She caught a glám of him' (SOM, Kerry).

glamaire /ˈglɑmərə/ *n.,* a fool, a prattler; a complainer (Limerick) < Ir. 'And that glamaire expects someone to give him a job; the way he goes on he's lucky he doesn't get a lot worse.'

glár /glɔːr/ also **glaur** *n.,* mire, soft mud; ooze, scum < Ir. 'It is still common enough to say that a person is as happy as a pig in the glár' (POC, Cavan). Montague, 'The Road's End' (*Collected Poems*, 31): "And a thick glaur floats."

glare /gleːr/ *n.,* the white of the egg (KM, Kerry) < E (origin obscure). 'I heat up the glare of an egg for her; she was too weak to eat one whole.'

glass /glæs/ *n.,* a measure of drink (the equivalent of half a pint in SE). 'A pint and a glass of stout, please'; 'He's sitting up there with his glass of stout as mean as anything' (BC, Meath).

glaur, *see* GLÁR.

gleanntán /glɑnˈt̪ɔːn/ *n.,* a glen (SOM, Kerry) < Ir. 'They called their house Gleanntán' (Dublin).

gléigeal /ˈgleːgjæl/ *adj.,* very bright (MK, Galway, who writes: 'two words meaning the same thing, = very bright: glé = bright, geal = bright') < Ir. 'I'm blinded with the sun, it's so gléigeal.'

gleo /gloː/ *n.,* a noise, a turmoil SOM, Kerry) < Ir. 'Did you ever see such gleo?.'

gleoisín /ˈgloːʃiːn/ *n.,* a babbler; a silly girl (MK, Galway) < Ir. 'Don't say a word about it while that gleoisín is around or she'll have the whole village told.'

glib /glɪb/ *n.,* a bob or fringe of hair on the forehead; a loose lock of hair; a forelock (SOM, Kerry) < Ir. 'Take that glib out of your eyes.'

glic /glɪk/ *adj.,* clever; sly < Ir. 'He's a glic one, all right'; 'An té nach bhfuil láidir ní foláir dó a bheith glic' (proverb), He who is not strong must be cunning.

gligín /glɪˈgiːn/ also **gligeen** *n.,* a little bell; fig. a prattling person; a fool; an empty-headed young person (SOM, Kerry) < Ir. 'What a gligeen you are!'

glimmer-man /ˈglimərmæn/ *n.* (*colloq.*), a Dublin Gas Company inspector during the war years who investigated contraventions of the rationing regulations (the 'glimmer' was the minimal flame that could be obtained – illegally and dangerously – from the residual gas in the system when it was turned off).

glincín /ˈglɪŋkiːn/ *n.,* a stupid, empty person; 'someone with no go in him' (MOB, Mayo) < Ir. 'That glincín! Is he ever going to learn anything?'

gliog /glɪg/, /glʌg/ *n.,* a rattle; a little bell; a dull plopping sound (MK, Galway) < Ir. 'Don't put that gliog on the cat; you'll drive it mad.'

gliogaire /ˈglɪgərə/ *n.,* a foolish prattler, one full of empty talk (KM, Kerry) < Ir. 'You can never get away from that old gliogaire; she's got all the time in the world and nothing to do but GAB.'

gliogar /ˈglʌgər/ also **glugger** *n.,* the rattling sound of a rotten egg; an addled egg; a gurgle; the slurping noise in a pipe of tobacco; fig. a foolish blabber (PMD, Mayo); a childless woman < Ir (cf. GLIOG). 'I think it's a gliogar; will we break it and see?'; 'He's a glugger, a no-good individual' (SOM, Kerry); Joyce, *Finnegans Wake*, 240.3: "poor Glugger was dazed"; Healy, *Nineteen Acres*, 53: "Mary Anne had no children of her own. In the harsh language, she was a 'glugger', the egg which never hatched out no matter how long the CLOCKING HEN sat on it." 'Ubh ghliogair', an addled egg; fig. a fearful, timid person (VQ, Kerry) < Ir.

gliomach /'glɪməx/ *adj.*, awkward; slovenly < Ir. 'Don't let him near it, he's too gliomach; he'll ruin everything' (BC, Meath).

gliondar /'glɪnd̪ər/ *n.*, delight, joyousness (SOM, Kerry) < Ir.

gliondrach /'glɪnd̪rəx/ *adj.*, joyful, glad < Ir.

gliúcach /'gluːkəx/ *adj.*, blind in one eye; (fig.) inquisitive, nosy < Ir. 'She's that gliúcach she'd AX you what had you for your dinner' (KG, Kerry).

glooracks, **glúraic**, *see* CODLADH GLIÚRAGÁIN.

glór /gloːr/ *n.*, voice; sound, noise (SOM, Kerry) < Ir. 'Éist le glór na habhann agus gheobhaidh tú breac' (proverb), Listen to the sound of the river and you'll get a trout.

glugger, *see* GLIOGAR.

glúin /gluːn/ *n.*, generation, in the phrase 'ó ghlúin go glúin,' from generation to generation (KM, Kerry) < Ir. 'There was learning there ó ghlúin go glúin.'

glúiníneach /gluː'niːnəx/ *n.*, a disease in cattle that causes the knees to swell (KM, Kerry) < Ir. "There's glúiníneach in that calf; look at the state of its knees!'

glúraic, glooracks *see* CODLADH GLIÚRAGÁIN.

gneeve /gniːv/ *n.*, the area of grass required for one cow; one-twelfth of a 'ploughland' (Limerick) < Ir *gníomh*.

gob[1] /gɑb/ *n.*, beak; mouth < Ir (cf. E dial. *gob*). 'Shut your gob,' shut your mouth. Brown, *Down All the Days,* 42: "I'll break your bloody gob O'Shea, if you don't QUIT shoving"; 'Finnegan's Wake' (song): "But Biddy gave her a belt in the gob." *See* GEAB.

gob[2] /gɑb/, shortened form of BEGOB.

gobadán /'gɑbəd̪ɔːn/ *n.*, one of the small birds that accompany the cuckoo because he was hatched out in their nest; a hanger-on, a parasite (SOM, Kerry); pejorative term for sharp-featured face < Ir.

gobaire /'gɑbərə/ *n.*, a prattler, a busybody < Ir. 'Here comes that gobaire again, so be careful what you say' (KG, Kerry).

gobán[1] /'gʌbɔːn/ *n.*, a muzzle for a calf < Ir. 'Put a gobán on that calf and wean it' (BC, Meath).

gobán[2] /'gʌbɔːn/ also **guban, gub** *n.*, 'one who pretends to have a deep knowledge of things, and has a lot to say' (EMF, Westmeath); a botch, an unskilled tradesman (SOM, Kerry); 'a captious critic, who professes knowledge he does not always possess. Gub and Guban are used ironically. Both words are contractions of the name of the master craftsman of ancient days, the famous "GOBÁN SAOR"' (PA, Fingall) < Ir *gobán*, Jack of all trades.

Gobán Saor /ˈgʌbɔːnˈseːr/ *n.,* a legendary stonemason, also credited with great wisdom (SOM, Kerry); a clever or intelligent person (VQ, Kerry), also used ironically; a Jack of all trades < Ir GOBÁN^2 + *saor*, stonemason.

go bhfóire Dia orainn /gəˈvoːrə ˈʤiːʌrɪn/ *int.,* God help us (MK, Galway) < Ir. 'Go bhfóire Dia orainn – what are you doing here?'

goblach /ˈgʌbləx/ *n.,* an amount < Ir. 'Gran used say after she made the churn, "Take a goblach of that butter and spread it on the hot bread"' (KM, Kerry).

gob-music /ˈgɑbmjuːzɪk/ *n.,* LILTING, 'MOUTH-MUSIC' < Ir *gob*, mouth + E *music*.

go brónach /gəˈbroːnəx/ *adv.,* sorrowfully (VQ, Kerry) < Ir. 'They walked back from the graveyard go brónach.'

gobshite /ˈgɑbʃait/ *n. (pejor.),* a fool; '(affectionately) an easy touch, one prone to being over-generous and over-trusting' (EH, Wicklow) < E dial. *gob*, mouth + *shite* (characteristic HE version of E *shit*). 'He's an awful gobshite.' Leonard, *Out After Dark*, 180: "'How,' Arthur Nolan said, 'can a man be so bloody insensitive?' 'Old gob-shite,' someone else said.

go-car /ˈgoːkɑːr/ *n.,* a child's push-chair < E *go* + *car*, carriage. 'She let the child fall out of the go-car and he knocked his head on the ground and he lost the use of one ear; it's a mercy that he wasn't killed stone-dead' (BC, Meath).

gog /gʌg/ *n.,* a chick; a child's term for an egg < Ir. 'Any googie for me?' (BC, Meath). *See* GOOGIE.

gogaí, *see* GOOGIE.

gogaide /ˈgʌgəʤə/ also **gogaidín** /ˈgʌgəʤiːn/ (MK, Galway) *n.,* the hunkers < Ir. 'He's down on his gogaide' (SOM, Kerry).

gogail /ˈgʌgəl/ *n.,* the cackle of hens or geese < Ir. 'The geese are gogailing; something must be disturbing them' (BC, Meath).

gogaille /ˈgʌgələ/ *n.,* dotard, a fool < Ir *gogaille*, a goose. 'The old gogaille is no harm' (TF, Cavan).

gogaireacht /ˈgʌgərəxt̪/ *v.n.,* dibbling potatoes (placing seeds in holes made with a dibble) (KM, Kerry) < Ir.

góilín /ˈgoːliːn/ *n.,* a wet spot, a small pool of water < Ir. 'Where did that góilín come from?

There must be a leak in the roof' (BC, Meath).

goirtín /ˈgʌrtʃiːn/ also **gurteen** *n.,* commonage (land with no owner and grazed by several farmers) (BF, Cork) < Ir (dimin. of *gort*, a field). 'When are you putting your sheep up on the goirtín?' (Galway).

goldar /ˈgʌld̪ər/ *n.,* a loud, angry shout; noise made indoors (KM, Kerry) < Ir. 'There was such a goldar coming from the kitchen that I turned around and went back again.'

go leor, *see* GALORE.

gollog, *see* GOWLOGUE.

gom /gɑm/ also **gam** *n.,* a silly, foolish person < Ir *gám*, variant of *gámaí*. 'He's a proper gam' (SOM, Kerry). O'Casey, *The Plough and the Stars*, act II, 173: "*Fluther:* . . . You must think Fluther's a right gom." *See* GAUM.

gombeen(-man) /ˈgɑmˈbiːn (mæn)/ *n.,* a usurer, a loan-shark < Ir *gaimbín*, usury (*fear gaimbín*, usurer); a morsel (hence *gaimbín tobac*, a bit of tobacco). 'Is it a gombeen-man he is now?' (BC, Meath). Stoker, *The Snake's Pass,* 26: "'What is a gombeen man?' I asked . . . 'A gombeen man is it? Well! I'll tell ye,' said an old shrewd-looking man . . . 'He's a man that linds you a few shillin's or a few pounds whin ye want it bad, and then niver laves ye till he has tuk all ye've got – yer land an' yer SHANTY an' yer holdin' an' yer money an' yer craps [crops]; an' he would take the blood out of yer body if he could sell it or use it any-how!'"; Joyce, *Finnegans Wake*, 344.6: "Gambanman!"; Plunkett, *Farewell Companions,* 400: "They [politicians] use them to rubberstamp everything from *gombeen* morality to book censorship."

gomerel /ˈgɑmərəl/ also **gomeral, gomeril, gommeril** *n.,* a fool, blockhead, half-wit (JF, Dublin) < E dial. (cf. Ir *gamal*). 'You great thick gomeril, didn't I tell you not to let the dog out!'

gonc /gʌŋk/ also **gunk** *n., v.,* a disappointing surprise; a 'take-in', a 'sell'; a snub; to take in, to cheat (Ulster) < Ir. 'So and so will get a quare oul gonc (gunk), when he finds out' (POC, Cavan).

googeen /guːˈgiːn/ *n.,* one who fidgets; an unsteady, giddy person (KM, Kerry) < Ir *guaigín*. 'The teacher was always dead set against googeens, whatever family they came from.'

googie /ˈguːgiː/ *n.* (*colloq.*), an egg. *See* GLIOGAR; GOG.

goosheen /ˈguːʃiːn/ *n.,* a young goose; a year-old goose < E *goose* + dimin. suffix -EEN. 'The fox came after the goosheens one night, and there wasn't much left bar [except] feathers' (TF, Cavan).

gorb /gɔːrb/ *n., adj.,* glutton; greedy < E dial. (origin obscure). 'Don't give the gorb any more until the work is done' (Mayo).

gorsoon, *see* GARSÚN.

Gorta /ˈgʌrt̪ə/ *n.,* overseas aid organisation directed towards people suffering from famine < Ir *gorta*, famine.

gortach /ˈgʌrt̪əx/ *adj., n.,* hungry (MK, Galway); hunger < Ir *gortach, adj.,* hungry. 'I have a great gortach on me; I could eat the Devil and all.' *See* FÉAR GORTACH.

gortóg /ˈgʌrt̪oːg/ *n.,* a clumsy, ungainly girl < Ir. 'I pity the man that'll marry that gortóg'; 'Wouldn't you think that gortóg would stay home and help her mother' (KG, Kerry).

gosawer, *see* GASÚR.

gossip /ˈgɑsəp/ *n.,* a godparent (a sponsor at a child's baptism who undertakes responsibility for its Christian upbringing); a friend < ME *godsib* < *God* + *sib*, relative (i.e. relative 'in God', not by blood). Michelburne, *Ireland Preserved*, 144: "*Teig:* By my Gossips hand, Gossip *Nora*"; Banim, *The Boyne Water*, 537: "'Gossip,' elevating his voice to Onagh, who still held her place in the window, 'is it time to fly my flock, yet, I wondher?'"; Joyce, *Finnegans Wake,* 316.11–12: "Good marrams and good merrymills, sayd good mothers gossip"; Plunkett, *Farewell Companions*, 227: "'It forbade intermarriage, fosterage, and gossipred' . . . 'What's gossipred?' . . . 'It might mean sponsorship . . . to go sib. If one of them stood godfather to an Irish child he'd be going sib; creating a spiritual relationship.'"

gossoon /ˈgɑsuːn/, /gɑsˈuːn/ *n.,* a boy < Ir *garsún* < E dial. *gossoon* < F *garçon* (but cf. Ir *gas*, a stem, fig. a stripling, a youth). It has been (fancifully) claimed that the French root of this word may indicate the practice of Anglo-Norman gentry calling their Irish serving-boys '*garçon*.' 'What a fine lump of a gossoon you are!' (MG, Cavan); 'Tell the gossoon to come with me; we'll find something for him to do.' Carleton, 'Denis O'Shaughnessy Going to Maynooth' (*Six Irish Tales*, 97): "An', Dinis Shaughnessy, who has a betther right to turn gintleman, nor [than] the gorsoon that studied for that?"; Griffin, *The Collegians,* 136: "Well, he called a gossoon that was going the road"; Stoker, *The Snake's Pass*, 43: "whin he was a gossoon." *See* GARSÚN.

gossure, *see* GASÚR.

goster /ˈgɑst̪ər/ also **gasther, gauster** *n., v.,* empty talk, empty chat; a gossipy person < ME *galstre, v.,* to make a noise, brag, boast (cf. *EDD* s.v. 'gauster' v. and sb.[2], 'to talk and laugh loudly and impudently; to gossip, talk idly'). O'Casey, *The*

Shadow of a Gunman, act I, 85: "*Seumas:* I've no time to be standin' here gostherin' with you – let me shut the door, Mr. Mulligan."

gouger /ˈgauʤər/ *n.* (*colloq.*), an aggressive lout, 'like GURRIER, except possibly rougher' (KD, Dublin) < E dial. < *gouge, v.*, to scratch or tear out with the nails). 'That gouger has been hanging around here a lot lately' (Dublin); 'I don't like that family; gougers all, they were, and it's still in them.'

gowk /gauk/ *n.*, cuckoo < E dial. < ME *goke*. 'Have you heard the gowk yet? It's late this year, I'm thinking' (TJ, Sligo).

gowlogue, *see* GABHLÓG.

grá /grɔː/ *n., int.*, love, liking, affection; love (to you)! < Ir. 'He has no grádh for it' (EMF, Westmeath); 'He had a great grá for her' (KG, Kerry); 'Give my grá to Maura when you're next talking to her' (BC, Meath). *See* GHRÁ THÚ; GRÁ DÉ; GRÁ GEAL; GRÁ MO CHROÍ.

grabach[1] /ˈgrɑbəx/ *adj.*, having gapped teeth < Ir.

grabach[2] /ˈgrɑbəx/ *adj., n.*, talkative, interfering; a talkative person < Ir. 'Oh, God, is that grabach ever going to shut up! I didn't come here to listen to him' (BC, Meath).

grabaire /ˈgrɑbərə/ *n.*, a talkative or precocious girl (KM, Kerry) < Ir. 'Hasn't she turned out to be a right grabaire, and you'd never think it.'

grabhar móna /ˈgraurˈmoːnə/ *n.phr.*, fragments of turf, turf-mould (MK, Galway) < Ir. 'There's nothing but grabhar móna left in the barrel; will you go out and get some more turf?'

gradam /ˈgrɑd̪əm/ *n.*, a gift; something for nothing, affection (Limerick) < Ir *gradam*, esteem.

grá Dé /grɔːˈʤeː/ *n.*, charity; act of charity < Ir. 'I don't mind doing a grá Dé for them when I think they need it' (JB, Kildare).

grafán /ˈgrɑfɔːn/ *n.*, a hoe < Ir. 'Hand me the grafán so I can cut the whins' (AF, Cavan).

grágach /ˈgrɔːgəx/ *adj.*, raucous (MK, Galway) < Ir. 'Her children were very grágach.'

grágaíl /ˈgrɔːgiːl/ *n.*, the cawing of rooks (MK, Galway) < Ir. 'It's just the grágaíl of the rooks before they go to bed.'

grá geal /ˈgrɔːgæl/ *n.phr.*, term of endearment: love < Ir (lit. bright love). 'Maggie, mo ghrá geal, put on the tea' (KG, Kerry). *See* GRÁ.

gráinneog /ˈgrɔːnjoːg/ *n.*, a hedgehog (EMF, Westmeath) < Ir. 'That's the second dead gráinneog I've seen on the road today' (TF, Cavan).

gráinseachán /ˈgrɔːnʃəxɔːn/ *n.*, young wheat boiled in milk (KM, Kerry) < Ir.

graip /greːp/ *n.*, a digging-fork, usually with four prongs < E dial. *graip*. 'Will you give me over that graip, there's a good garson' (TF, Cavan). Kavanagh,

Tarry Flynn, 74: "Mat laid down the graip"; Healy, *Nineteen Acres*, 109: "Now a graip lurched against the dairy."

gramaisc /ˈgrɑməʃk/ *n.*, a rabble, a mob; a group of children (KM, Kerry) < Ir. 'That gramaisc make a lot of noise coming from school.'

grámhar /ˈgrɔːvər/ *adj.*, affectionate; kind, tender; lovable; placid < Ir. 'She's a grámhar kind of a woman.' Sometimes used as a noun: a loving person (VQ, Kerry)

grá mo chroí /ˈgrɔːmʌˈkriː/ *n.phr.*, my darling; fig. a person who flatters; insincere praise < Ir (lit. love of my heart). 'He's full of grá mo chroí, worthless blather' (SOM, Kerry); 'He's an awful grá mo chroí!' *See* GHRÁ THÚ; GRÁ.

grand[1] /grænd/ *adj.*, fine; splendid. 'That's a grand day!'

grand[2] *prefix*, in such combinations as 'grand-aunt' /ˈgrænænt/, with the 'd' omitted from the pronunciation.

grán tonóige /ˈgrɔːnt̪ʌnˈoːgə/ *n.*, duckweed (Louth) < Ir.

grástúil /ˈgrɔːst̪uːl/ *adj.*, graceful < Ir. 'He was very grástúil when I offered him a hand with the work. He's a nice fellow.'

grawls /grɔːlz/ also **grilses** /ˈgrɪlsəz/ *n.pl.*, children (Louth) < E dial. (origin obscure). 'He stood there and all his grawls around him'; 'You know, I've lost count of all the grawls in that family.'

grawn /grɔːn/ *n.*, disgust (KM, Kerry) < Ir *gráin*. 'I felt grawn to my stomach when I heard what he did to her.'

greadadh chugat /ˈgræd̪əˈxʌgət̪/ *int.*, bad CESS to you (MK, Galway) < Ir (lit. a trouncing to you).

greas /græs/ *n.*, a turn (at something) < Ir. 'Here, you take a greas at it; I'm having a smoke'; 'If you watch them, one of them is always taking a greas breast-feeding the shovel' (i.e. leaning on it) (Mayo).

great /greːt/ *adj.*, very friendly with someone < E dial. (cf. Ir *mór le duine*, lit. great with a person). 'They're very great' (WL, Cork).

Great Famine, *see* FAMINE.

greesh, greeshy, greesach, *see* GRÍOSACH.

greet /griːt/ *n.*, *v.*, weeping; to cry, weep (AH, Donegal) < ME *greten*, to cry, weep. 'What are you greeting about now?'; 'Oh, stop greeting, for Christ's sake.'

grig /grɪg/ also **greg** /grɛg/ *v.*, to tease, tantalise; to annoy, attempt to make another jealous (DB, Cork); to tantalise by showing without sharing a thing (JP, Forth and Bargy) < Ir *griog* (cf. E dial. *greg*). 'He was grigging the son about the land' (KM, Kerry)'; 'We'd always be grigging each other as children' (Galway). O'Brien, *A Pagan Place*, 17: "Grigged too, with stories of what they would fancy for supper, trout or chicken."

grilses, *see* GRAWLS.

gríosach /ˈgrɪsəx/ also **greesach**, **greesh** /griːʃ/, **greeshy** /ˈgriːʃiː/ *n.*, the embers of a fire (SOM, Kerry); half-burnt turf; tiny coals of fire mixed with ash (EMF, Westmeath); cinders raked out and dampened in an open fire; live ashes spread on the lid of a cast-iron cooking-oven suspended over an open fire for baking bread (MOB, Mayo) < Ir *gríosach*. 'Lift the gríosach off the lid so I can turn the cake of bread.' Healy, *Nineteen Acres*, 8: "Grandma would pull out the gríosach – the coals and ash of the busy day-fires – to the front of the hearth, stand fresh sods to the back, rebuild the heart of the fire with the coals of the day."

gripe /graip/ *n.*, a trench < ME *grip*, furrow, DITCH. 'You'll need to dig a gripe there to get rid of all the water.' Kavanagh, *Tarry Flynn*, 14: "The heart was often out of her mouth that he'd turn the cart upside down in a gripe."

gríscín /griːˈskiːn/, /griːˈʃkiːn/ also **griskin, greeskeen** *n.*, pork meat taken from around the pig's heart then boiled and fried; excess lean on bacon removed when curing a pig (VQ, Kerry) < Ir *gríscín*, a chop, a small piece of meat for grilling or broiling.

grisset /ˈgrisət/ *n.*, an open lamp; 'the crucible in which the tallow in the manufacture of rush candles was melted . . . A like crucible was used in the manufacture of counterfeit coin' (Martin, 177) < ME *cresset* < OF *graisse, n.*, fat, grease.

grog /grʌg/ also **grug** *n.*, the hunkers; the haunches of a dog < Ir. 'He was sitting on his grug'; 'I was getting a pain in my grogs, so I stood up'; 'Look at the grogs on that dog: she'd run for a whole day without tiring.'

groodles /ˈgruːdlz/ *n.pl.*, bits at the bottom of a soup bowl (KM, Kerry) < Ir *grúidil*, dregs. 'I always used to love eat the groodles from the pot when I was a child.'

groop /gruːp/ *n.*, a trench or drain in a byre < E dial. < OE *grype*, sewer (cf. Du. *groep*, ditch, trench).

gruagach /ˈgruəgəx/ *n.*, a magician; a clever, tricky person < Ir. 'He's a real gruagach; mind he doesn't give you the slip' (TJ, Sligo).

gruamachán /ˈgruəməxɔːn/ *n.*, a sour face < Ir. 'Take that gruamachán off you and finish the work' (BC, Meath).

grush /grʌʃ/ *n., v.*, a scramble by children to get coins or other small gifts thrown at them; a present given to people outside a church after a wedding; 'to scatter money to be scrambled for among a crowd' (LUB, Dublin) < E dial. *grush* (variant of *crush*). 'There was a great grushing when they were going off on their honeymoon this morning' (LUB, Dublin).

guaigín /ˈguəgiːn/ *n.*, a foolish, fidgety person (KM., Kerry) < Ir. 'She can't help it, she's a bit of a guaigín'; 'Come here, you guaigín, I have some work for you to do.'

guaire /ˈguərə/ *n.*, bristle < Ir.

gual /guəl/ *n.*, coal (MK, Galway) < Ir. 'Have you any guals for the fire? It's very slow to start'; 'There's great heat in the gual.'

Guards /gɑːrdz/ *n.pl.* (*colloq.*), (members of) the GARDA SÍOCHÁNA (by partial translation and also survival of earlier official name, Civic Guard).

gub, guban, *see* GOBÁN.

guilpín /ˈgɪlpiːn/ *n.*, an unmannerly lout, uncouth person (Carlow) < Ir. 'The guilpín started to get thick so we had to pull him off and give him a warning.'

guipure /giːˈpjuːr/ *n.*, a kind of lace < E < OF *guiper, v.*, to cover with silk etc. Killanin and Duignan, 349: 'Limerick lace (guipure), made at the Good Shepherd Convent, is much sought after.'

gunk, *see* GONC.

gur /gʌr/ *n.*, in the phr. 'on the gur,' playing truant from school, MITCHING (origin uncertain). 'To be "on-gur" was to "mitch", and to mitch was to leave your home at the usual hour, and to spend the day doing anything but attending school. Fresh air and activity produced hunger and GUR CAKE was the answer' (Nolan, 33). *See* GUR-CAKE; GURRIER.

gur-cake /ˈgʌrkeːk/ *n.* (*colloq.*), a fruit slice (a once-popular confection consisting of bakery scraps mixed with mincemeat sandwiched between biscuit-like hard pastry) (origin uncertain; cf. *OED* s.v. 'gur', 'variant of *goor*, a coarse Indian sugar'; *Chambers*, s.v. 'gur, goor', 'Hindi, coarse sugar < Sanskrit *guda*'). 'The Dillon family carried on a small grocery shop, and was famous for its "Gur Cake", which was much in demand by schoolboys. To be "on-gur" was to "mitch" . . . Fresh air and activity produced hunger and gur cake was the answer' (Nolan, 33). Gur-cake is mainly associated with Dublin, and with poor children in particular, giving rise to a suggested association with GURRIER. *See* GUR.

gurrier /gʌriər/ *n.* (*colloq.*), an ill-mannered, loutish person (origin obscure, but cf. *EDD* s.v 'Gurr, *v.* and *sb.*[1]', 'to growl as a dog, n. the growl, snarl of a dog,' s.v. 'Gurr sb.[2]', 'a short, thick-set person. Hence, Gurran, sb. a very strong, thick-set person with a stubborn temper.' It is possible that the word gurrier, which is particularly attached to Dublin, may be associated with those who eat GUR-CAKE, since eating such a cake was commonly associated with children from deprived families, with the attendant proneness to irregular behaviour: *see* Cowan and Sexton, *Ireland's Traditional Foods*, 151–2: 'Over time the eating of gurcake became synonymous with poorer Dublin children, so much so that the term "gurrier" established itself in Dublin dialect, describing *one who eats gur-cake, a tough street urchin* (OED)'). 'They're all gurriers in that part of town' (JOD, Tipperary); 'Altar boy on Sunday, gurrier the rest of the week' (KD, Dublin); Kearney, *Sam's Fall*, 43: "We'd often heard their leader Cormac O'Keefe was expelled from school at the age of twelve for assaulting one of the teachers . . . We'd often hear Big Nora and Lizzie go on about them. Gurriers and GUTTIES, they called them." *See* GUR.

gurteen, *see* GOIRTÍN.

gurtóg /ˈgʌrt̪oːg/ *n.*, thick clumsy girl, ungainly < Ir. 'I pity the man that'll marry that gurtóg'; 'Wouldn't you think that gurtóg would stay home and help her mother' (KG, Kerry).

guth /gʌh/ *n.*, voice (TJ, Sligo) < Ir. 'I stayed for five hours in the bushes but I didn't hear so much as a guth.'

gutters /ˈgʌt̪ərz/ *n.pl.*, dirt, mire of the street < E dial. < OF *gutiere* < *goute*, drop. 'She had gutters all over her clothes after her fall' (TF, Cavan).

guttery /ˈgʌt̪əri/ *adj.*, muddy, mud-stained < E dial. (see GUTTERS). 'Don't bring those guttery boots into the kitchen' (BC, Meath). Kavanagh, 'The Great Hunger', IV (*Collected Poems*, 40): "The dragging step of a ploughman going home through the guttery | Headlands . . ."

gutty /gʌti/ *n.* (*colloq.*), an unpleasant person < E dial. < OE *guttas*, *n.pl.*, bowels; *EDD* s.v. 'Gutty 1' gives 'Corpulent, fat, pot-bellied; thick, gross'; s.v. 'Gutty 3', 'A fat, corpulent person'; Beecher, *A Dictionary of Cork Slang*, s.v. 'Gutty (Boy)' suggests that the derivation is 'Possibly Irish "Gotaire" – a goatish individual. Dinneen. *See* "Gutter" – a place of low breeding or vulgar behaviour. Concise Oxford Dictionary.' 'Don't behave like a gutty, for Pete's sake!' Kearney, *Sam's Fall*, 43: "GURRIERS and Gutties they called them."

gwall, *see* GABHÁIL.

H

habit /ˈhæbət/ *n.,* a shroud < ME *(h)abit*, OF *abit*. 'People had their habits bought many years before they died, and I remember Miss R. airing hers on a bush on a fine day; I remember the lovely blue ribbons' (KM, Kerry).

haet /heːt/ *n.,* in negative expressions: not a bit, etc. < E dial. *ha'it* < *Devil (a) ha'it* or *Fiend (a) ha'it*, may the Devil have it; 'haet' then took on an independent existence as a noun meaning bit, whit, atom, etc., usually in negative expressions, e.g. 'not a haet,' not a bit. 'He was around looking for money but I told him devil a haet he'd get off me' (BC, Meath). *See* DEVIL.

haggard /ˈhægərd/ also **haggart** /ˈhægərt/ *n.,* a stack-yard, a yard where hay is kept (DOH, Limerick); a kitchen-garden < ON *hey-garthr*, hay-yard. 'Six o'clock and not a cow in the haggard yet' (MG, Cavan). Cuffe, *The Siege of Ballyally Castle*, 108: "and to get into the hadgard"; Kickham, *Knocknagow*, 42: "the kitchen-garden – invariably called the 'haggart' in this part of the world"; Benedict Kiely, *A Ball of Malt and Madame Butterfly*, 183: "The wife has him tethered and SPANCELLED in the haggard"; Heaney, 'Servant Boy' (*Wintering Out*, 17: " . . . Your trail | broken from haggard to stable."

haí /haiː/ *int.* 1. Hey, hello. 2. 'Listen to me, lend me your ear' (SOM, Kerry).

haighfidil, *see* AGHAIDH FIDIL.

haitch /heːʧ/ *n.,* the name of the letter 'h' < F *hache*. The pronunciation of 'h' as 'haitch' (SE 'aitch') is a distinctive feature of Hiberno-English. 'She's got her PhD /ˈpiːheːʧˈdiː/'; 'How do you get the Spanish to use the correct haitch?' (Dublin). This pronunciation may be due to the phenomenon of hypercorrection (where a word is made more 'proper' than it actually is) or may be a survival of an earlier pronunciation of the name.

hake /heːk/ *v.,* to steal (apples) < E dial. (origin obscure, but cf. Du *haken*, to long for, to hanker).

'Instead of boxing the fox we'd sometimes say "haking"' (AC, Down).

half /hæf/ *n.,* in the phr. 'half eleven' etc., half (an hour) past eleven. 'I've been waiting here since half one; where have you been?' (Dublin).

hallion /'hæljən/ *n. (pejor.),* an aggressive, unprepossessing woman (origin obsure; cf. Macafee s.v. 'hallion', Scots, origin unknown). 'Such a hallion she turned out to be!' (TF, Cavan). Heaney, *The Midnight Verdict*, 24: "This hefty menacing dangerwoman. | Bony and huge, a terrible hallion."

hames /heːmz/ *n.pl.,* the wooden or metal pieces forming the collar on a horse, to which the traces are attached (cf. Kavanagh, *Tarry Flynn*, 62: "The harness wasn't in the best condition. The collar needed lining and the traces were tied with bits of wire in two places. He couldn't find the hames-strap"); fig. a mess, in the phrase 'to make a hames of,' to make a mess of (possibly because it is difficult to put the hames on a horse the right way up) < ME *hames*. 'You'd use bluestone [copper sulphate] to rub on the soreness made by the hames on the horse's neck' (EH, Wicklow); 'Where is he? Let me at him; he made a hames of my field' (MG, Cavan). Leonard, *Out After Dark*, 176: "Instead, I made a hames of it, mislaying a verb, marooning a noun on a foreign shore, starting a jerry-built sentence that caved in half-way through."

hanam 'on Diabhal /'hɑnəmən 'd̪iːl/ *int.,* your soul to the Devil < Ir *d'anam* [sometimes pronounced /'hɑnəm/] *'on Diabhal*. 'Hanam 'on Diabhal – you'll burn in Hell yet' (KG, Kerry).

handsel /'hænsəl/ also **hansel** *n., v.,* a present given for good luck, especially to inaugurate something new (clothes, the New Year, etc.); the first of anything sold in the day < ME *hansellen, v.* < OE *handselen, n.,* a giving into the hand of another. 'Give me hansel, sir, and I'll have luck' (Omurethi, Kildare); 'He gave him a good handsel' (EOC, Tipperary). Griffin, *The Collegians,* 278: "Garret AXED him once of a Hansel-Monday for his *hansel*, and 'tis what he gave him was that wattle, as it was standing behind the parlour doore" (a footnote explains: 'On the first Monday of the new year (called Hansel Monday) it is customary to bestow trifling gifts, which are denominated *hansels'*).

hansel, *see* HANDSEL.

hap /hæp/ *n., v.,* a dress, covering, wrap; to dress, cover (up); to comfort (Braidwood) < E dial. (origin obscure).

hash /hæʃ/ *n.,* very heavy rainfall < E dial. (*EDD* s.v. 'hash' sb.^{2} and v.^{5}). 'Hashy', wet, sleety, slushy.

hata /ˈhɑt̪ə/ *n.,* a hat (SOM, Kerry) < Ir < E *hat.*

hata cogaidh /hɑt̪əˈkʌgə/ *n.,* a (military) helmet < Ir. 'I found an old hata cogaidh in the shed; what'll I do with it?' (Mayo).

hatch /hæʧ/ *v. (colloq.),* a football term: to hang around the box or penalty area hoping for an easy goal (KD, Dublin).

have /hæv/ *v.* The absence of the verb 'have' in Irish influences the formation of tenses in HE: the 'perfect-with-have' construction, for example, is replaced by the present tense of the verb 'be', etc. (see Harris, 1993, 161). 'Eighty years I'm in this world and I've never seen the like'; 'She's dead these six months.' O'Brien, *The Third Policeman*, 89: "I am not long in this district." The English perfect is replaced by a construction closer to Irish usage. The concept of 'have' is expressed in Irish by the verb 'be' with 'at', e.g. *tá an litir aige*, he has the letter (lit. the letter is at him); and for the perfect tense the Irish construction, *tá an litir scríofa aige*, he has written the letter (lit. the letter is written at him), is represented in HE by 'he has the letter written,' which carries over the separation between the verb 'be' (*tá*) and the past participle 'written' (*scríofa*): 'He's not nice when he has drink taken.' (See Filppula, 1996, 33–55.)

haverel /ˈhævərəl/ *n.,* a talkative man; a simpleton (JF, Dublin) < E dial. < *haver, v.,* to talk foolishly (origin obscure). 'He's a bit of a haverel, but sure there's no harm in him.'

haymanger /ˈheːmæŋər/ *n.,* 'one who retails hay in small quantities' (LUB, Dublin); (form uncertain).

hazard /ˈhæzərd/ *n.,* a cab-stand < OF *hasard* (*EDD* s.v. 'hazard' sb. and v. places this usage in Ireland, Scotland, and Yorkshire). Hayden and Hartog, 781: 'A "hazard" is even the official designation of a cab-stand in Dublin, and owes its name, doubtless, to the element of luck in the prospects of obtaining a fare.'

head-the-ball /ˈhɛd̪əbɔːl/ *n.phr. (colloq.),* a crazy, happy-go-lucky sort of person. 'He's a real head-the-ball if ever there was one' (Dublin).

hear /hiːr/ *v.,* in the special sense of 'to feel, to sense.' '"Take a look at my eye, will you," he said. "I hear the pain in it"' (KM, Kerry).

heave off /hiːvˈɔːf/ *v.,* to vomit. 'If one got sick, the word used was to "heave off" – the word "vomit" wasn't used' (MC, Kildare, ex Limerick).

hedge-school /ˈhɛʤskuːl/ *n.,* a makeshift school, often under a hedge or wall, for teaching Catholics surreptitiously during the period (roughly late 17th to early 19th century) when the English made it illegal for Catholics to be educated < Ir *scoil scairte, scoil chois claí.* The scholar P. W. Joyce (1827–1914) was a pupil in such an institution (*English as We Speak It in Ireland*, 149–63), as was William Carleton (1794–1869), who describes one in his story 'The Hedge School' (*Six Irish Tales*, 156–7). Friel, *Translations*, act I (*FDA* 3, 1207) (stage directions): "The hedge-school is held in a disused barn or hay-shed or BYRE. Along the back wall are the remains of five or six stalls – wooden posts and chains – where cows were once milked and bedded."

heel of the hunt /'hiːləvd̪ə 'hʌnt/ *n.phr.,* in the phr. 'in the heel of the hunt,' finally, in the end; in conclusion. 'In the heel of the hunt, that's what happened him; he had it coming to him.'

henting /'hɛntən/, /'hɪntən/ also **hinting**, **henteen** *n.,* a furrow; the last sod of a ridge in ploughing (JP, Forth and Bargy) < ME *hent, v.,* to grasp. 'He always gets the hinting exactly right every time' (TF, Cavan).

herself /hər'sɛlf/ *reflexive pron.*, the woman of the house. 'Herself came in and got the tea' (TF, Cavan). Synge, *The Playboy of the Western World*, act III (*FDA*, 2, 636): "*Jimmy:* Did you see herself?"

high fidil, *see* AGHAIDH FIDIL.

himself /hɪm'sɛlf/ *reflexive pron.*, the man of the house. 'With himself,' by himself (cf. Ir *leis féin*) (BP, Meath, who adds: 'in Meath you may hear someone described as going for a walk with himself').

hob /hɑb/ *n.,* a surface, often whitewashed, beside the chimney or grate, used as a shelf (BF, Cork) < E dial. (origin unknown; there may be a connection with *hub*, 'the basic meaning being lump, mass' (*ODEE*); cf. 16th-century *hubbe*). 'Did you leave the tea caddy up on the hob to dry?'

hob ná hae /'hʌbnɔː'heː/ *n.phr.* (negative), a sound (Meath) < Ir. 'There wasn't a hob ná hae from the house when I was walking past.'

hois /hʌʃ/ call used in driving cattle, goats etc. < Ir. 'Shhh – can you hear him calling the cattle, *hois, hois* – I'd know that voice anywhere' (BC, Meath). *See* GABHAR; HURAIS.

hoise /hɔis/ *v.,* to raise, lift < E dial. (*ODEE*, s.v. 'hoist': 'alteration of *hoise* [16th century], perh. through taking the pt. and pp. as the stem-form').

hokey /'hoːkiː/ *n.,* in the interjection 'be [by] the hokey' /biːd̪ə'hoːkiː/ (origin obscure). 'Oh, be the hokey, that's great news about the house!' Stoker, *The Snake's Pass*, 99: "Aye, an' be the hokey, the shquire himself sez that it was a good day"; Shaw, *John Bull's Other Island*, act I (*FDA*, 2, 439): "*Cornelius*: Oh, be the hokey, the sammin's broke in two!"

Holy Communion /hoːliːkɜ ˈmjuːnjən/ *n.*, the name for the reception and consumption of the BLESSED SACRAMENT in the form of altar-bread directly into the mouth from the hand of the priest or into the left hand of the communicant and then transferred into the mouth with the right hand; the service at which children receive Holy Communion for the first time is a special event both for themselves and their parents; Holy < OE *halig*, Communion < L *communio*, (O)F *communion*. The term 'Easter Duty' refers to the obligation on Catholics to receive Holy Communion at least once a year to conform with the instruction in the section of the document headed 'Omnis utriusque sexus . . . ' (Everyone of either sex . . .) of the Fourth Lateran Council of 1215 (Canon 21); in Ireland the obligation must be fulfilled between Ash Wednesday and the Octave of Sts Peter and Paul. 'When we were young all the boys and girls dressed in white for their First Holy Communion, but it's not the same nowadays'; 'Listen, you'd better make your Easter Duty before the end of the month – you heard what the priest said at first mass last Sunday' (MF, Cavan). O'Brien, *A Pagan Place*, 16: "Before your first Holy Communion, Jewel and you practised receiving the Host."

holy day of obligation /ˈhoːliː deːɑvɑbləˈgeːʃən/ *n.* a FEAST-DAY on which Catholics are bound to attend Mass and to refrain from 'servile work' (their paid employment) unless it is essential < OE *haligdæg*. 'It's a holy day of obligation, so you shouldn't be washing the car, so you shouldn't!'

Holy Hour /ˈhoːliaur/ *n.phr.*, a devotion consisting of EXPOSITION of the Blessed Sacrament for one hour, followed by BENEDICTION; *colloq.*, the period from 2:30 to 3:30 p.m., when pubs are closed. 'We'll be going up to the Holy Hour in a few minutes.' O'Brien, *A Pagan Place*, 39: "The closets got scrubbed once a month. Girls did it in pairs, the way girls did a Holy hour in pairs."

holy show /hoːliˈʃoː/ *n.phr.*, a ridiculous sight < E dial. 'Seán, you can't go out looking like that, you look a holy show; go and put your teeth in at once!'

holy water /hoːliˈwɔːtər/ *n.*, water blessed by a priest, into which the faithful dip their fingers as they enter and leave church; up to recent times private houses often had a holy water stoup hanging on the wall beside the front door. 'Take some holy water before you go home' (KG, Kerry).

hoofling /ˈhuːflən/ *pres.part., v.n.,* crookedness of some sort in business (BP, Meath); deliberate distortion of statistics etc. (origin obscure, but cf. *EDD* s.v. 'huffle' v.^{2}, sb.^{4}, sb.^{3}, 'to rumple, to be in a tangled, confused mass'). 'Some researchers working on postgrad theses are guilty of "hoofling the figures"' (MOC, Limerick).

hooker /ˈhuːkər/ *n.*, a one-masted fishing vessel, associated particularly with Galway Bay < Du *hoeker*. 'John's away on his hooker somewhere off Galway' (Dublin). Richard Murphy, 'The Last Galway Hooker' (*FDA*, 3, 1336): "The boatwright's hammer chipped across the water | Ribbing this hooker . . . "

hooley /ˈhuːliː/ *n.*, an exuberant party (origin unknown; cf. *OED* s.v. 'hoolee, holi': 'Hindi holi. The great festival or carnival of the Hindoos, held at the approach of the vernal equinox'; Beale suggests that it is perhaps a variant of CÉILÍ).

hooligan /ˈhuːləgən/ *n.*, a (young) street rough (origin obscure; cf. Beale: from *c.* 1895, most probably from the Irish surname Ó hUallacháin, Anglicised as Houlihan or Hoolohan; *ODEE*: *c.* 1898, said to be from the name of a rowdy Irish family in London). Joyce, *Finnegans Wake*, 6.15: "all the hoolivans of the nation."

hoolivan, *see* HOOLIGAN.

hoor /huːr/ also **hure** *n.* (*colloq.*), HE version of 'whore' < OE *hore*. The pronunciation /huər/ was common in England in the sixteenth and seventeenth centuries and lasted into the nineteenth century. Hiberno-English retains this older pronunciation, while the meaning has become extended from 'prostitute' to refer to any person, male or female, who is corrupt; and it may be used affectionately as well as pejoratively, especially when qualified by the adjective 'cute'. 'You're a cute hoor, but I like you for it'; 'He's a dacent [decent] hoor, and no mistake about it, always ready to do you a good turn, however he feels'; 'That man's such a cute hoor he'd build a nest in your ear'; 'You're an awful hure for the drink' (you're over-fond of drink). Kavanagh, *Tarry Flynn*, 46: "'Isn't he the two ends of a hure?' said Eusebius"; Friel, *Translations*, act III (*FDA*, 3, 1230): "*Doalty*: . . . You hoors you! Get out of my corn, you hoors you!"; Tim Pat Coogan, *De Valera: Long Fellow, Long Shadow* (1995), 202: "Far from becoming 'reconciled to the idea,' Collins was outraged and hurt. 'The Long Whoor won't get rid of me as easily as that' was his reaction"; Gogarty, *As I*

Was Going down Sackville Street, 91: "'How are all you huers?' (It seems that in Dublin that word is bi-sexual)"; Jordan, *Night in Tunisia*, 60: "He listened to the fat boy talking about her . . . about her father who on his stretches home came back drunk and bounced rocks off the tin roof, shouting 'Hewer'. 'What does that mean,' he asked. 'Just that,' said the asthmatic boy. 'Rhymes with sure.'" Sometimes the spelling 'whore' is retained. Leonard, *Out After Dark*, 165: "He [Patrick Kavanagh] added, just as loudly, and each syllable was caked with the cow dung of Mucker, County Monaghan: 'British whoo-err!'"

hoosh /huːʃ/ *v.*, to push up, lift; to help to mount (a horse, wall, etc.) < E dial. *hoosh, n., v.*, push up. 'Give me a hoosh'; 'Hoosh me up' (LUB, Dublin); 'Well, I'll tell you, it's very sad. There she was hooshing the cattle out of the HAGGARD, and down she fell dead, Lord have mercy on her' (BC, Meath). Synge, *The Playboy of the Western World*, act III (*FDA*, 2, 638): "*Philly*: And the mountain girls hooshing him on!"

horrid /'hɑrəd/ *adj.*, used as adverbial intensive. 'He's horrid FAILED' (BP, Meath).

hot /hɑt/ *p.part.*, hit. Such forms of the past tense and past participle are common for some verbs, e.g. 'sot' ('set' or 'sit'), 'cot' (catch), 'gother' (gather). Griffin, *The Collegians*, 362: "'I'm *hot*!' returned Falvey, with a groan. 'I'm *hot*. The masther holed me with the shot.'"

hough /hɑk/ *n., v.*, the hock or ham of an animal; to hamstring, to cut the hocks of an animal; to walk awkwardly < E dial. < OE *hohsinu* (< *hoh*, heel + *sinu*, sinew), the hamstring, shortened to 'hoh', giving rise to the form 'hough' or 'hock'. 'Times were so bad then they used be out houghing the cattle, but you couldn't blem [blame] them, land was so scarce.' 'Hougher', one who maimed beasts in this way.

house /haus/ *n.*, in the phrase 'watch your house,' 'mind your house,' used by a player or spectator in a game of soccer to warn another player to watch his back.

howanever /hauən'ɛvər/ also **howandever** *adv.*, however < E dial. 'Howanever, you have to take what life throws at you.' Joyce, *Ulysses*, 309.22–3: "So howandever, as I was saying, the old dog seeing the tin was empty starts mousing around."

how are you /hau'ærjə/ *phr.* expressing ironic surprise or disbelief. 'I hope you're enjoying your holiday.' – 'Holiday how are you!' Joyce, *Finnegans Wake*, 28.31: "Anna Stacey's how are you!"

hula hul /hʌlə'hʌl/ a call to dogs that a hare has been raised and to join in the chase (SOM, Kerry) < Ir.

hubbub /'hʌbʌb/ *n.*, noisy confusion; a war-cry < Ir *ub ub, int.*, no, no. 'There was a quare hubbub when she announced she was married already' (Cavan).

huer, *see* HOOR.

huirs, *see* HURAIS.

hungry grass, *see* FÉAR GORTACH.

hunkers /'hʌŋkərz/ *n.pl.*, the hams (origin obscure). 'She squatted on her hunkers, as there was no chair'; 'We were down on our hunkers in behind the ditch, so they didn't see us.' Kavanagh, 'Spraying Potatoes' (*Collected Poems*, 78): "He hunkered down | In the shade of the orchard wall . . . "; Delaney, *The Sins of the Mothers*, 217: "Ellen dropped on her hunkers beside Thomas."

hunt /hʌnt/ *v.*, to chase away; to throw out. (Note that in Irish the past tense of the verb *seilg*, to hunt, has the same pronunciation as the past tense of *teilg*, to throw (out).) Hayden and Hartog, 780: 'The servant was impudent, and I hunted her.' Joyce, 'Eveline' (*Dubliners*, 37): "Her father used often to hunt them in out of the field with his blackthorn stick." *See* HEEL OF THE HUNT.

hurais hurais /'hʌrɪʃ'hʌrɪʃ/ also **huirs huirs** /hʌrʃhʌrʃ/, a call to pigs to come to the trough to eat their food (SOM, Kerry) < Ir. '"Hurrish, hurrish"', call to pigs' (LUB, Dublin). *See* HUIS.

hurling /'hʌrlən/ *n.*, a field game played with hurleys and a SLIOTAR. 'Hurling was never very popular in my part of the country.' Binchy, *Firefly Summer*, 311: "I saw you, dog, not half an hour ago up in the main street of this town and you had a bone the size of a hurling stick."

hurrish, *see* HUIS.

I

iarlais /ˈiːrləʃ/ *n.*, a person who remains smaller than other members of the same family; the youngest of the family (SOM, Kerry, who writes: 'if somebody is referred to as an iarlais there is a hint of delicate health and other-worldliness, as distinct from ÍOCHTAR') < Ir.

idir /ˈɪʤər/ *prep.*, in the phr. 'Dia idir sinn agus an tolc,' God between us and evil < Ir.

ignorant /ˈɪgnərənt/ *adj.*, unmannerly, crude in behaviour. 'He's from an ignorant family'; 'Don't be so ignorant and behave yourself.'

in /ɪn/ *prep.*, as in 'I am in my standing,' a literal rendering of Ir *táim i mo sheasamh*. Joyce, *Finnegans Wake*, 478.28: "Are you in your [are you a] fatherick, lonely one?" (cf. Ir *tá an fear ina bhádóir*, the man is a boatman (lit. the man is in his boatman).

-ín /iːn/, *see* -EEN.

inagh /ɪnˈjæ/ *int.*, sarcastic: is that so? < Ir *an ea*. 'I'm only forty.' – 'Forty, inagh!' Griffin, *The Collegians*, 136: "'An I seen your husband there too, ma'am.' 'My husband, inagh?' says she."

inch /ɪnʧ/ *n.*, a water-meadow, a strip of grassy land beside a river; any narrow field along the side of a river (SOM, Kerry); a small island < Ir *inse*. 'Drive the cows to the inch.' *See* INIS.

indulgence /ɪnˈdʌlʤəns/ *n.*, the remission by the Church of the temporal punishment due to those sins of which the guilt has been forgiven, usually in the sacrament of Penance (i.e. CONFESSION); the grace for an indulgence comes from what is known as the Treasury of Merits or Treasury of Satisfaction of the Church, a superabundant store of the merits of Christ, the Blessed Virgin Mary, and of the Saints, which were beyond the needs of the salvation of humanity, and which could, therefore, be used for the remission of temporal punishment due to forgiven sin; indulgences may be either plenary (an indulgence which remits the whole of the temporal punishment due for an individual's sins) or partial (indulgences which remit a part of the punishment due for sin at any given moment, expressed in human terms of time, e.g. three hundred days, seven years, etc.); there are many short indulgenced prayers, e.g. the invocation of the prayer 'Queen of the most holy Rosary, pray for us' will receive three hundred days, 'Hail, O Cross, our only hope' five hundred days, and so forth; the precise significance of these designated periods of time has never been defined; suffice it to say that the possibility of receiving indulgences is a great comfort to the faithful < L *indulgentia* (before the Reformation (16th century) the word 'pardon' (< OF *pardun*, remission) was used in place of 'indulgence'). 'You'll get an indulgence if you say those prayers after Mass.'

inis /ˈɪnəʃ/ *n.*, a water-meadow < Ir. 'I think we could put the cows in the inis next week' (Kerry). *See* INCH.

in it /ˈɪnɪt/ *adv.phr.,* there, in existence, alive, present (representing Ir *adv.* 'ann'). 'The week that's in it,' the week we are talking about at present (Ir *an tseachtain atá ann*); 'The dinner was on the table, and the priest was in it [present]'; "Mike, is it yourself that's in it?' is that you, are you here? (KG, Kerry). Banim, *The Boyne Water*, 214: "'Don't mind him,' said the Whisperer; 'it's the dead o' the night that's in it, gineral, honey'"; Somerville and Ross, *Some Experiences of an Irish RM*, 113: "An' if it's the divil himself is in it, I'll rattle him into the lake!"; Gregory, *Spreading the News* (*FDA*, 2, 623): "*Tim Casey*: Is it yourself at all that's in it?"; Joyce, *Ulysses*, 309.33–4: "and his eye all bloodshot from the drouth is in it"; Joyce, 'The Sisters' (*Dubliners*, 14: "Ah, poor James! she said. God knows we done all we could, as poor as we are – we wouldn't see him want anything while he was in it"; Stephens, *The Crock of Gold*, 71: 'WISHA, one time, – when HIMSELF was in it – I could go about the house all day long, cleaning the place"; O'Casey, *Juno and the Paycock*, act II, 42: "*Mrs. Madigan*: Well, now, it ud be hard to refuse seein' the suspicious times that's in it"; *The Plough and the Stars*, act I, 137: "*Mrs. Gogan*: . . . There's prettiness an' prettiness in it"; Brown, *Down All the Days*, 85: "You persecuted me while you was in it and took me youth away!"

inse, *see* INCH.

insense /ɪnˈsɛns/ *v.*, to make to understand, convince, show < E dial. < ME *insense*. 'It took a long time to insense him that he was wrong' (LUB, Dublin).

inside /ɪn'said/ *adv.*, at one's place of work, etc. 'There's a great rivalry inside' (Dublin).

Intermediate Certificate /ɪntər 'miːdiətsər'tɪfɪkət/ also **Inter (Cert)** /'ɪntər(sərt)/ *n.*, state examination (recently renamed Junior Certificate) taken half way through secondary school. 'How did you do in th'Inter?' (Meath). *See* LEAVING CERTIFICATE.

íochtar /'iːxt̪ər/ *n.*, the smallest and weakest bonham; a pig that, though healthy, is smaller and leaner than other members of the same litter (SOM, Kerry); a person who remains much smaller than other members of the same family (SOM, Kerry); the youngest of the family < Ir. 'Johnny is the íochtar' (SOM, Kerry). *See* IARLAIS.

iomrall /'ɪmrəl/ *n.*, confusion (as after heavy drinking or being unconscious) (SOM, Kerry) < Ir. 'Iomrall aithne', 'mistaken identity, often mentioned in Fenian days after informant passed through a mysterious fog or spell' (SOM, Kerry).

Íosa /'iːsə/ *n.*, Jesus (SOM, Kerry) < Ir. 'Íosa Críost', *int.* expressing surprise: Jesus Christ (SOM, Kerry) < Ir.

Irish /'airɪʃ/ *adj.*, relating to Ireland or its people < OE *Iras*, inhabitants of Ireland < OIr *Ériu*, Ireland. Some English dictionaries gloss this word in a pejorative way, e.g. 'Irish: . . . self-contradictory, ludicrously inconsistent (as Irish thought and speech is traditionally supposed to be).' 'That's very Irish all right.'

is /ɪz/ *v.* Verbs in Irish, including 'tá' (is, are), usually have the same form in the singular and plural. This may account for the common practice in HE of using a singular verb with a plural subject, e.g. 'Your hands is cold' (Ir *tá do lámha fuar*). Joyce, 'Ivy Day in the Committee Room' (*Dubliners*, 141): "No, but the stairs is so dark."

is ea /ɪʃ'æ/ also **sea** *adv.*, yes < Ir. The word 'yes' is rarely used in HE, because after questions speakers follow the practice of Irish in repeating the verb or some form of it: 'Is this yours?' (Ir 'An leatsa é seo?') – 'It is mine' (Ir. 'Is liom'). (Note that the E *adv.* 'yes' itself ultimately derives from two words, 'yea' and the subjunctive 'sie', = let it be.) *See* YES.

it is, it was /ɪt'ɪz/, /ɪt'wɑz/ *phr.*, HE equivalent of Ir copula verb 'is', which permits variation of emphasis in sentences such as 'It is John saw Mary yesterday,' or 'It is yesterday John saw Mary,' or 'It is Mary John saw yesterday.' Griffin, *The Collegians*, 148: "Is it to drink you say she used?"; Stephens, *The Crock of Gold*, 117: "Is it hanging him you'll be, God help us?" Frequently the copula equivalent 'it is' or 'it was' is suppressed, and its absence causes the complement to be put at the head of a sentence, giving it added emphasis. Joyce, 'Two Gallants' (*Dubliners*, 54): "Cigarettes every night she'd bring me and paying the tram out and back"; O'Casey, *The Plough and the Stars*, act III, 183: "*Mrs. Gogan*: . . . is it wounded y're, Mrs. Clitheroe, or what?"

itself /ɪt'sɛlf/ *reflexive pron.* The Irish word *féin* means both 'even/only' and 'self'; these terms were therefore perceived as synonymous by early speakers of English in Ireland, hence such sentences as 'Is there any chance of a pound itself?' (even a pound), or clauses such as 'if you're comin' after John itself' (even if you're coming after John); 'sure if I had a potato or two itself it'd do.' Griffin, *The Collegians*, 271: "An' amn't I to know where you stop itself?"; Joyce, *Ulysses*, 320.5: "GOB[2], we won't be let even do that much itself"; Kavanagh, *Tarry Flynn*, 7: "Are you going to go to Mass at all or do you mean to be home with them atself [itself]?"; McCourt, *Angela's Ashes*, 105: "They wouldn't have the likes of that in America where they're mad for the steak and all classes of poultry, flying, walking or swimming itself."

J

jackeen /'ʤækiːn/ *n.* (*pejor.*), a self-assertive Dubliner with pro-British leanings < *Jack*, familiar name for John Bull, nickname for an Englishman (from the stereotypical Englishman in *The History of John Bull*, a collection of pamphlets by John Arbuthnot, 1712) + dimin. suffix -EEN. 'I'm fed up of that jackeen calling me a CULCHIE' (Meath). 'I know how Jackeen came about – My grandfather was a jackeen, born in Dublin. At the turn of the century when Queen Victoria was visiting Dublin the children were all given small flags to wave – small Union Jacks or Jackeens' (AMW, Cork). Joyce, *Finnegans Wake*, 620.23–4: "You were pleased as Punch, recitating war exploits and pearse orations to them jackeen gapers." *See* SEÁN BUÍ; SHONEEN.

jag /ʤæg/ *n.* (*colloq.*), a 'date' (Cork) (origin uncertain; cf. E dial. *jag, v.,* to stab, prick, pierce; Beale, s.v. 'jagging, go jagging', 'to make social visits, especially in order to gossip').

Janey Mac /'ʤeːni'mæk/ *int.* (*colloq.*), one of several euphemisms for 'Jesus' (in this context usually pronounced /'ʤeːzəz/ by HE speakers); cf. 'St James's Night!; Bejapers!; Jabers!; Jeepers!; Jee-whizz!, Jeez!

janglers /'ʤæŋglərz/ *n.* (*colloq.*), in the phr. 'took the janglers,' became upset (cf. *jangle, v.,* to upset, irritate < OF *jangler*). 'She took the janglers when she got the smell of drink off him' (Mayo).

jant, *see* JAUNTING-CAR.

jar[1] /ʤær/ *n.* (*colloq.*), a hot-water bottle (made of stoneware) < F *jarre*. 'Take a jar to bed with you' (BC, Meath).

jar[2] /ʤær/ *n.* (*colloq.*), a pint of beer < F *jarre*. 'Have a jar,' have a drink. 'Jarred' (*colloq.*), drunk. 'He was half-jarred, but he still got up on the tractor and drove home, in the dark too.' Brown, *Down All the Days*, 249–50: "Can't go home without a jar be hook or be crook"; Leonard, *Out After Dark*, 13: "Then we can have a jar for old time's sake at the Queen's"; Roche, *A Handful of Stars*, act I, ii, 29: "*Swan:* He'd have a fair few jars in him too, I'd say. Drunk more than likely."

jarvey /'ʤærvi/ *n.*, a jaunting-car driver < *Jarvis*, proper name (possibly in memory of a noted 19th-century hackney-coach driver called Jarvis). 'The jarvey gave us a wonderful ride around the lakes of Killarney' (KG, Kerry). Joyce, *Ulysses*, 339. 30: "'Off with you,' says Martin to the jarvey."

jaunting-car /'ʤɑntiŋkær/ *n.*, a light, two-wheeled horse-drawn open vehicle once popular in Ireland, with a seat for the driver and side seats for the passengers, either facing each other ('inside jaunting-car') or seated back to back ('outside jaunting-car') < *jaunt, v.*, to take a short journey + *car* < ME *carre* (ultimately of Celtic derivation). 'Jant' /ʤænt/ *n.*, a lift in a car (KD, Dublin). 'Will you give me a jant?' Griffin, *The Collegians*, 328: "The house-maid and Winny sat on the coffin, and three or four followed on an outside jaunting-car"; Shaw, *John Bull's Other Island*, act I (*FDA*, 2, 438), stage directions: " . . . the car has arrived . . . It is a monster jaunting car, black and dilapidated, one of the last survivors of the public vehicles known to earliest generations as Beeyankiny cars, the Irish having laid violent tongues on the name of their projector, one Bianconi, an enterprising Italian." *See* BYAN.

jerring, *see* MITCH.

jig /ʤɪg/ *n., v.*, a lively traditional dance; to dance in a lively manner; to jerk about (origin obscure; a derivation from OF *gigue, n., giguer, v.*, leap in a lively fashion, is unlikely). The word is often used imprecisely in HE to mean something like 'to put MOUTH-MUSIC to.' 'I'll jig [lilt] it for you.' O'Casey, *The Plough and the Stars*, act II, 179: "*Rosie:* . . . Dancin' a jig in the bed"; Durcan, *Christmas Day,* III, 16: "Procuring me with his galoshes | To dance a jig on my ego . . . "

jorum /'ʤoːrəm/ also **deorum** *n.*, a large jug; a vessel for holding liquids; a good drink; a drink of whiskey or punch, usually at a WAKE (RB, Waterford) < E dial. (origin obscure, but cf. Joram in the Old Testament (2 Sam. 8:10), who 'brought with him vessels of silver, and vessels of gold, and vessels of brass'; cf. also Ir *deoir* /ʤoːr/, a drop). 'You'll have an oul' jorum before you set off' (TJ, Sligo). Joyce, *Ulysses*, 329. 7–8: "old Vic, with her jorum of mountain dew."

jouk /ʤuːk/ *v.*, to dodge, duck out of sight < E dial. Friel, *Translations,* act I (*FDA*, 3, 1213): "*Doalty:* Please, Máire. I want to jouk in the back here."

just /ʤʌst/ *adv.,* intensive: exactly, precisely, indeed. 'Are you hungry?' – 'I am, just' (Cavan) < E dial. < OF *juste*.

K

kailee, kailey, *see* CÉILÍ.

kailkannonkabbis, kalecannon, *see* COLCANNON.

kanatt, *see* CANATT.

keeler /ˈkiːlər/ also **ciléar, cíléir** /ˈkiːleːr/ *n.*, a shallow wooden tub with iron hoops, about $1\frac{1}{2}$ feet high, used to keep the day's milk in; a butter tub; a tub without handles; a feeding-trough for pigs and calves < E dial. < ME *calen*, *v.*, to make cold. 'Throw a few nuts into the keeler for the cows'; 'Look at the BONNIVES at the ciléar; they'll tip it over – watch! Didn't I tell you they'd do it!' (Mayo). Griffin, *The Collegians*, 106: "I remember Jug Flannigan . . . was in the same way losin' all her butter, an' she got it again by puttin' a taste o' the last year's butter into the churn, before churnin' along with the crame [cream], and into every keeler in the house."

keen[1] /kiːn/ *v., v.n.*, to lament, to wail shrilly over the dead; an act of lamenting; crying (of children) < Ir *caoin* /kiːn/ *v.*; *caoineadh* /kiːnə/ *v.n.* 'A dog is said to keen when it sets up a dismal whining' (Omurethi, Kildare); 'I never knew that child but he was keening' (LUB, Dublin). 'Keener', a professional mourner at a funeral or WAKE. 'Mná caointe', keening women. Griffin, *The Collegians,* 49: "'Twas all his trouble to see would he keep the woman at the wake from *keening* over the dead corpse"; Stoker, *The Snake's Pass*, 26: "There was a long pause, broken only by one of the old women, who occasionally gave a sort of half-grunt, half-sigh . . . She was a 'keener' by profession, and was evidently well fitted to, and well drilled in, her work"; Yeats, *The Unicorn from the Stars*, act III (*Collected Plays,* 368–9): "*Johnny:* . . . Lay him out fair and straight upon a stone, till I will let loose the secret of my heart keening him!"; McGuinness, *Observe the Sons of Ulster Marching towards the Somme*, part IV (*FDA*, 3, 1266): "*McIlwaine:* . . . Now they're not going to come to their senses listening to a squealing woman keening after death."

keen[2] /kiːn/ *adj.* (*colloq.*), attractive < OE *cene*. 'Mary is plain, but Jane is very keen' (KM, Kerry).

keeroge, *see* CIARÓG.

kern /kɛrn/ *n.*, light-armed foot-soldier; fig. a boor < Ir *ceithearn*. 'Ir. *ceithearn* is a collective noun, meaning "band", "troop", and was applied particularly to light-armed militia, foot-soldiers without helmet or body armour. In English guise, the word is more familiar as *kern*(*e*), which came to signify such soldiery as well as the band to which he belonged; it is uncertain whether Ir. *ceithearn* was so used . . . The kern is frequently contrasted with the GALLOGLAS in 16th century and later accounts . . . Mr Nicholls [Nicholls, *Gaelic and Gaelicised Ireland*, 85–6] considers that the kern, rather than being a particular sort of infantry, should be regarded as the ordinary freeman at arms, whose means precluded owning a horse' (MB, Tipperary, *c.* 1432). *Captain Thomas Stukeley*, 78: "gow make ready oore kerne and Gallinglasse against night."

kesh /kɛʃ/ also **cesh** *n.*, a makeshift bridge (sods or branches placed on poles etc.) across a river or bog; a bridge over a drain in a bog (CS, Mayo); a causeway < Ir. *ceis*, wattle causeway. Long Kesh, formerly the name of a prison in Northern Ireland, now called the Maze. 'A kesh may become a slough in wet weather' (PMD, Mayo); 'You'll have to fix up that kesh if you want to run a tractor over it' (KG, Kerry). Heaney, 'Nerthus' (*Wintering Out*, 49): "A seasoned, unsleeved taker of the weather, | Where kesh and LOANING finger out to heather."

kib /kɪb/ *n.*, *v.*, a thick, narrow spade used for planting potato seeds; to plant seeds with this implement < E dial. (cited for Ireland only in *EDD*). 'Kibbin(g)', a system of planting potatoes, seed by seed (cf. Ir *cipín*, little stick).

kibe /kaib/ *n.*, a chilblain, especially on the heel (origin obscure, but cf. Welsh *cibwst*, chilblains). Carleton, 'The Hedge School' (*Six Irish Tales*, 164): "'I say, Misther Kavanagh,' said the strange master, 'what angle does Dick's heel form in the second step of the treble, from the kibe on the left foot to the corner of the door FORNINST him?"

kibosh, *see* KYBOSH.

kiddogue, *see* CIDEOG.

kill[1] /kɪl/ *n.*, a monastic cell, church < Ir *cill*. 'The teacher showed us a picture of a kill at school today.'

kill[2], *see* KILT.

kilt /kilt/ *p.part.*, hurt, injured; upbraided < *killed*. The SE verb 'kill' means to put to death, whereas the HE usage is much less serious. 'I'll be kilt if I don't get home in time for the TEA' (Dublin); "'Twas the hardship kilt him.' Griffin, *The Collegians,* 74: "Oh, murther; there's the bell again; I'll be kilt entirely!"; Durcan, *Christmas Day*, IV, 29: " . . . keep out of the kitchen | Or I'll kill you . . . "

kimmeen, *see* CAIMÍN.

kinatt, *see* CANATT.

kind /kaind/ in the expression 'kind father for him,' 'kind mother for her,' you've got your nature from your father (or mother) < OE *cynd fæder,* father's nature < *cynd, n.,* birth, nature, descent + *fæder*, father (qualifying noun in genitive) (cf. Ir *is dual athar duit é*, it is the nature of the father to you). Swift, *Dialogue in Hybernian Stile,* 164: "A. And a good warrnt you have, it is kind father for you."

kink /kɪŋk/ *n., v.,* a fit of coughing or laughing; to cough, to gasp for breath; to choke with laughter < E dial. < ME *kinc*. 'He went into a kink of laughing'; 'The child had a bad kink of whooping cough' (LUB, Dublin). *See* CHINCOUGH.

kippeen /ˈkɪpiːn/ also **kippen** *n.,* a little stick < Ir. *cipín*. 'Get some kippens to light the fire.

kisagh, *see* CISEACH.

kish /kɪʃ/ *n.,* a wicker container or pannier < Ir *cis*. 'Bring in a kishful of spuds for the dinner' (BC, Meath); 'As ignorant as a kish of brogues' (LUB, Dublin). Joyce, *Finnegans Wake*, 13.36–14.1–2: "a crone that hadde a wickered Kish FOR TO hale dead turves from the bog lookit under the blay of her Kish"; 83.13: "kish his sprogues" [kish of BROGUES]. *See* PARDÓG.

kitchen /ˈkɪʧən/ *n., v.,* condiment, relish; anything eaten with potatoes, such as a "dippy" of melted bacon fat; to season; to use sparingly < E dial. (ME *kichene*). 'The meal is running short, we'll have to kitchen it (i.e., to serve out sparingly) from now on' (LUB, Dublin). Griffin, *The Collegians*, 289: "The PIATEZ are everything – the *kitshen* little or nothin'" (a footnote explains *kitshen* as 'anything eaten with potatoes'); Gregory, *The Workhouse Ward* (*FDA*, 2, 627): "*Mrs. Donohoe:* . . . a handful of periwinkles to make kitchen."

kithogue, *see* CIOTÓG.

kitthawn, *see* CIOTÁN.

kittle, *see* CITEAL.

knacker /ˈnækər/ *n.,* someone dealing in horses (for excessive profit) (SMC, Limerick); (*pejor.*) a person involved in shady deals (cf. *knack*, trick, device); (*pejor.*) a member of the travelling community; an impotent man < E dial. (origin obscure). 'That dirty little knacker has ran off with my toolbox.' Kennelly, *Blood Wedding*, 11: "*Mother:* The knife, the knife . . . The curse of God on all the knives and the devil's knacker that invented them."

knackered /ˈnækərd/ *p.part.* (*colloq.*), tired, worn out (origin obscure). 'I'm that knackered, I couldn't do another stroke.' Doyle, *The Van*, 86: "'Where're you goin'?' said Paddy. – 'Home,' said Jimmy Sr. – 'I'm knackered.'"

knauvshaul, **knawvshawl**, *see* CNÁIMHSEÁIL.

knock[1] /nɑk/ *v.*, in the phr. 'that knocked a fright out of you' (MK, Galway) (Ir *bhain sé geit asat*).

Knock[2] /nɑk/ *place-name*, a village in Co. Mayo, a place of pilgrimage since 1879 (following a supposed apparition of the Virgin Mary), now also site of an airport < Ir *An Cnoc*, the hill. 'Let's go to Knock on Sunday and make the STATIONS; it'll be good for us.' Healy, *Nineteen Acres*, 140: "Small wonder then when the new Government yielded to the Dublin knock-Knock campaign and abandoned the project, walking away from the 'soggy, boggy, foggy' airport in the middle of nowhere."

kreel *see* CREEL.

kuss, *see* COS.

kybosh /ˈkaibɑʃ/ also **kibosh** *n.*, *v.*, nonsense, affectation, usually in the construction 'put the kibosh on'; to put an end to, finish off, do for. Origin obscure: various claims have been made for its origin, including Yiddish, Anglo-Hebraic, Turkish, and Irish, with *kybosh* sometimes regarded as a re-formation of Ir *caidhp (an) bháis* or *caidhpín (an) bháis*, 'cap of death', the black cap or judgment cap worn by judges when pronouncing sentence of death (cf. Michael Hewson, *A Word-list from South West Clare*, 184). The *ODEE* gives an origin in the 19th century and adds: 'apparently associated with "bosh" [Turkish *boş*, empty, worthless], nonsense.' 'Things were bad before, but you put the kybosh on them' (MH, Clare). O'Brien, *A Pagan Place*, 170: "She said all her grand schemes were kiboshed."

L

lab /lɑb/ *n.*, a great sum of money, a nest egg; something valuable (MK, Galway) < Ir. 'I'm sure he left a nice lab after him.'

lábán /lɔːˈbɔːn/ *n.*, a rotten egg (KM, Kerry) < Ir. 'It's a lábán; throw it away. *See* GLUGGER.

lace /leːs/ *v.*, to beat severely < Ir *léas*. 'If you don't lace into them in the second half you'll lose the match' (NL, Mayo).

lách /lɔːx/ *adj.*, sociable, affable; kind-hearted, generous (KM, Kerry); tender, loving < Ir. 'He's a nice lách sort of a fellow' (KG, Kerry).

ladar /ˈlɑd̪ər/ *n.*, a ladle; fig. interference, in such expressions as 'putting your ladar into the conversation' (MOB, Mayo) < Ir. 'He's always putting in his ladar' (MH, Clare); 'Why did you have to put in your ladar?' (SOM, Kerry).

ladaránach, *see* LEADRÁNACH.

ladhar[1] /lair/ also **lyre** *n.*, the land between two converging rivers or hills; a wet part of a bog where cows could graze (KM, Kerry) < Ir *ladhar*. 'Drive the cows down to the ladhar.'

ladhar[2] /lair/ *n.*, 1. A fistful; a large open handful. 'Throw a few ladhars of meal to the hens' (SOM, Kerry). 2. A web between the fingers or toes (SOM, Kerry) < Ir.

ladhróg /ˈlairoːg/ *n.*, a short drill in the corner of a field (Limerick) < Ir.

lady of the house /ˈleːdiːɑfd̪ə ˈhaus/ *n.phr.* (cf. Ir BEAN TÍ). Synge, *In the Shadow of the Glen* (*FDA*, 2, 629): "*Tramp:* Good evening to you, lady of the house."

laí /liː/ *n.*, shafts of a car; door-post (SOM, Kerry) < Ir.

láí, *see* LOY.

laidhricín /ˈlairəkiːn/ *n.*, the little finger (MK, Kerry) < Ir. 'He's only the size of your ladhraicín.'

laincis /ˈlæŋkəʃ̪/ *n.*, a hobble for a goat; a spancel (SOM, Kerry) < Ir. 'Take the laincis off the goat; I think he'll stay quiet from now on.'

laingeal /ˈlæŋgəl/ *n.*, a spancel, side-spancel (KM, Kerry) < Ir. 'Go down to the shed and see if you can find the laingeal TILL we put it on this cow to quieten her a bit.'

láithreán /ˈlɔːhrɔːn/ *n.,* a building-site; the lay-out for a building (MK, Galway) < Ir. 'How much do you think he paid for that láithreán? You'll never guess how much!'

lambaste /læmˈbeːst/, /læm ˈbeːʃt/ *v.,* to beat (origin obscure, but cf. E *lam*, to thrash; *baste*, to cudgel). 'He got such a lambasting when they caught him!'

lámhacán /ˈlɔːvəkɔːn/ *n.,* creeping on hands and feet; act of crawling like a child < Ir. 'Look – he's going lámhacán' (on seeing a child crawl).

lamp /læmp/ *v.* (*colloq.*), to look at, stare at (origin uncertain, but cf. E *lamp*, which in its transferred sense may mean 'to light with a lamp'). 'He's always lamping the women' (SB, Cork).

lán /lɔːn/ *adj.,* full. 'Bolg lán', a full stomach (SOM, Kerry) < Ir.

lán an mhála, *See* LAUNA-VAULA.

lang /læŋ/ in the phr. 'on the lang,' missing school without permission, MITCHING (WL, Cork) (origin obscure). 'We're going on the lang tomorrow – do you want to come?' (Mayo).

langable /ˈlæŋˈeibəl/ also **languable, land-gavel** *n.,* land-tax; rent for land, with a special connotation in Irish history (EOF, Dublin) < ME *londgavel*, land tax < OE *land*, land + *gafol*, tax, tribute.

langered /ˈlæŋərd/ also **langers** *p.part.*, drunk (origin obscure, but cf. E *langern*, to languish, lie sick, and Ir *longar*, swaying motion). 'We'll all go out and get langered tomorrow night' (Mayo); 'He was langers' (MOC, Limerick).

lao, *see* AGHRÁ.

lapa /ˈlæpə/ also **lop, lapeen, laipín** /ˈlæpiːn/ *n.,* a claw, a foot; a goose's webbed foot when eaten < Ir *lapa* (*laipín*, dimin.). 'My grandmother told me she used to eat boiled lapa when she was young' (KM, Kerry).

lapadáil /ˈlæpəd̪ɔːl/ *v.n.,* wading, splashing knee-deep in water (SOM, Kerry); playing with food; awkwardness < Ir. 'Stop that lapadáiling!'

lapeen, *see* LAPA.

lár /lɔːr/ *n.,* the middle of the floor of a loft (MK, Galway) < Ir *lár*, middle. 'It's up in the lár, where I left it.'

larrup /ˈlɑrəp/ *n., v.,* a thrashing; a blow (LUB, Dublin); to beat, strike, wallop < E dial. (origin obscure, but cf. 'to leather', 'to lather'). 'I'll give you a right larruping if you do that again!'; 'She gave him a few larrups' (SOM, Kerry). *See* LEADAR.

lash /læʃ/ *v., n.* (*colloq.*)*,* to move fast; to make an attempt (cf. various senses of E dial. *lash, v.,* to work at anything with great vigour; (of water) to dash, to rush). 'I lashed home for my dinner'; 'Now lash into them in the second half and don't let them get a single score'; 'Give it a lash, Jack!'

lashings /'læʃənz/ *n.pl.*, plenty, abundance < E dial. (origin obscure). Stoker, *The Snake's Pass,* 99: "'an' ye've lashins iv money'"; O'Casey, *The Shadow of a Gunman,* act I, 89: "*Davoren (giving her the milk):* There, will you have enough? *Minnie*: Plenty, lashins, thanks"; Roche, *Poor Beast in the Rain,* i, ii, 84: "*Molly:* . . . Eileen is only after tellin' me that there was lashin's of talent."

lasóg /læ'soːg/, /lə'soːg/ also **lossogue** *n.*, a blaze of light; a sudden blaze from a turf fire (KM, Kerry); a small bundle of sticks for lighting a fire (KM, Kerry) < Ir. 'There was such a lasóg from the fire!'

latchiko /'lætʃəko/ *n. (colloq., pejor.),* an unpleasant, disagreeable person (origin obscure; it has been suggested that the 'latch' suggests children who have to let themselves in by the latch and thus become delinquent as time goes on). 'Who are you calling a latchiko? Watch yourself!'; 'Those latchiko organisations' (Down). Healy, *Nineteen Acres*, 62: "You looked a bit of a latchiko going to school in Lowpark in hand-me-down American knickerbockers." *See* FIT-UP; GURRIER.

latter /'læt̪ər/ *adj.*, last < E dial. < OE *lætra*. 'In the latter end he went to see the doctor' (BC, Meath). Yeats, *The Unicorn from the Stars,* act I (*Collected Plays,* 329–30): "*Thomas:* . . . A coach, now, is a real thing and a thing that will last for generations and be made use of to the last, and maybe turn to be a hen-roost at its latter end."

lauchy /'lɔːkiː/ also **laughy** *adj.*, pleasant < Ir. LÁCH. 'People who were nice and friendly were said to be laughy' (POC, Cavan).

launa-vaula /'lɔːnə'vɔːlə/ also **launawaula** (LUB, Dublin) *n., adj.,* a sufficiency, quite enough; inebriated; the affection shown by people when they are drunk < Ir *lán an mhála,* the full of the bag. 'I have launa-vaula here, thanks very much'; 'They were lán an mhála coming home from the village' (SOM, Kerry).

lazy-beds /'leːzibɛdz/ *n.pl.*, beds for potatoes formed from soil taken from the furrows alongside; disused potato drills (JMC, Dublin) < E. 'You can still see the lazy-beds on the mountainsides in some places'.

leaba /'læbə/ *n.,* a bed < Ir. 'He's taken to the leaba' (SOM, Kerry).

leac /læk/ *n.,* a flagstone (SOM, Kerry) < Ir. 'All that was left of the house was a few leacs near where the half-door used be.'

leaca /'lækə/ *n.,* a (reclaimed) sloping piece of land stretching up the side of a mountain (KM, Kerry) < Ir. 'Take the cows to the leaca.'

leadaí /'læd̪iː/ *n.,* a lazy, useless person, an idler (MK, Galway) < Ir. ‘Don’t marry him; he’s a leadaí if ever there was one!’

leadaí na luatha /'læd̪iːnə'luəhə/ *n.phr.,* a lazy person (or pet) always sitting by the fire, a sit-by-the-fire (MK, Galway) < Ir (lit. lazybones of the ashes). ‘That dog’s useless, an absolute leadaí na luaithe!’

leadair /'læd̪ər/ *v.,* to beat, to thrash < Ir. ‘Just leadair into them in this half; don’t let them away with anything’ (Mayo); ‘She gave him a good leadar-ing’ (SOM, Kerry). ‘Leadaráil’, ‘leadradh’, a beating, a trouncing (SOM, Kerry). *See* LARRUP.

leadhb /laib/ *n.,* a rag, strip, shred; fig. a ragged woman; a disorganised, unkempt woman, a useless person (SOM, Kerry) < Ir. ‘The children had all the clothes in leadhbs when I got back home.’

leadóg /'læd̪oːg/ *n.,* a blow to the face with the palm of the hand (MK, Galway) < Ir. ‘He hit him a leadóg that sent him flying across the floor.’

leadránach /læd̪'rɔːnəx/, /læd̪ə 'rɔːnəx/ *adj.,* tedious (MK, Galway), long-winded, boring (SOM, Kerry); talkative in a drawling way < Ir. ‘He’s very leadránach’; ‘He mightn’t have much to say but he’s fairly leadránach when he gets a few pints into him.’

leamh /læv/ *adj.,* insipid, flat (as of beer); silly. ‘That pint is very leamh’ (SOM, Kerry); ‘Your excuse is very leamh’ (SOM, Kerry) < Ir.

léan, *see* MO LÉAN.

leanbh /lænəv/ *n.,* a child (SOM, Kerry) < Ir. ‘My poor leanbh, he won’t hurt you again; I’ll see to that.’

leanbh mo chroí /'lænəvmʌ'kri/ *int.,* child of my heart < Ir. ‘Oh, leanbh mo chroí, promise me you won’t do that again.’

lear /lær/ *n.,* a big number (of people); a large quantity < Ir. ‘He brought a great lear of money home from America’ (SOM, Kerry).

learn /lɛrn/ *v.,* to teach < E dial. < ME *lernen*, to teach. ‘I’ll learn you to slack!’

léas /leːs/ *n., v.,* an ear of corn; gleaning, hand-gleaning < Ir.

leath /læh/ *n.,* 1. Half < Ir. ‘Leathphingin’, a halfpenny. 2. One of a pair < Ir. ‘Leathshúil’, one eye (SOM, Kerry) < Ir.

leathar /'læhər/ *n.,* leather (SOM, Kerry, who adds: ‘“Seán dubh Buí bríste leathair” [black John Bull with leather breeches], derisory term for landlord or anybody with English sympathies’).

leathbhuachaill /læ'vuəxəl/, /læ'vuəkəl/ *n.,* a half-wit < Ir *leath*, half + *buachaill*, boy. ‘Go on, you leathbhuachaill, and hit him a box’ (Mayo).

leathóinseach /læˈhoːnʃəx/ *n.,* a fool < Ir *leath*, half + *óinseach*, fool (woman). 'The leath-óinseach that stayed at home will never make a go of the farm' (BC, Meath).

left-footer /ˈlɛftˈfʌtər/ *n.,* a Protestant (Catholics in the North of Ireland were once said to use the right foot in digging with a spade and Protestants the left). 'They claim he was a left-footer and all' (Cavan). Plunkett, *Farewell Companions*, 172: "'Need I tell you his religion?' 'Digs with the left foot, I suppose.'"

Legion of Mary /ˈliːʤʒnɑv ˈmeːriː/ *n.*, an international organisation of voluntary workers devoted to helping the sick, the poor, the destitute, and the underprivileged; the Legion was founded in 1921 by Frank Duff (1889–1980), who was a member of the Society of ST VINCENT DE PAUL, and Matt Lalor; seven years later the Legion founded the Morning Star Hostel, Dublin, for destitute men, and also a similar hostel for women and unmarried mothers (see PENITENTS); Duff retired from the civil service in 1933 and worked full-time for the good cause until his death < L *legio*, OF *legiun*, L *Maria*, Aramaic *Maryam*. 'She goes down the quays for the Legion – I don't know how she doesn't be frightened down there at night, but God is good, and I am sure He protects her in the good work she does' (Dublin). Healy, *Nineteen Acres*, 42: "Some girls had a Legion-of-Mary way of holding a partner, keeping you at a distance." *See Oxford Companion to Irish History* s.v. 'Legion of Mary' and 'prostitution'.

leibide /ˈlɛbəʤə/ *n.,* a foolish, weak person; an awkward, clumsy person (SOM, Kerry) < Ir. 'Leibideach', awkward, clumsy. 'Ah, he's just a poor old leibide.'

leicneach /ˈlɛknjəx/ *n.,* swelling of the jaw; mumps (MK, Kerry) < Ir. 'Is it the leicneach that that child has?'

leipreachán, *see* LEPRECHAUN.

leisce /ˈlɛʃkə/ *n.,* laziness; reluctance to get on with a task < Ir. 'There's nothing wrong with that fellow but pure leisce.' 'Leisciúil', lazy. 'Leisceoir', a lazy person (SOM, Kerry) < Ir.

leite /ˈlɛʧə/ *n.,* oatmeal STIRABOUT (SOM, Kerry) < Ir. 'Put up the leite and let's get on' (TJ, Sligo).

leithscéal /lɛˈʃkeːl/ *n.,* an excuse < Ir. 'He always has some leithscéal or other; you'd get tired listening to him' (KG, Kerry).

leochaileach /ˈloːkələx/, /ˈloːxələx/ *adj.,* frail, delicate; fragile, tender (MK, Galway) < Ir. 'After the flu you were very leochaileach.'

leoga, *see* MUISE.

leor /loːr/ *adj.,* enough < Ir. 'Is leor nod don eolach' (proverb),

A hint is enough for the knowledgeable person. *See* GALORE.

lep /lɛp/ *v.,* leap < E dial. (OE *hleapan*). 'He came lepping like I don't know what you'd call it over the ditch; you'd think there was a mad bull behind him, but it was only a bullock mad with the heat' (Mayo).

leprechaun /ˈlɛprəkɔːn/ also **leipreachán** *n.,* a dwarflike sprite; an industrious fairy seen at dusk or in moonlight mending a shoe < Ir *leipreachán*. Stoker, *The Snake's Pass,* 140: "Maybe ould Joyce too 'd become a leprachaun!"; O'Brien, *The Third Policeman*, 86: "They are lively as twenty leprechauns doing a jig on top of a tombstone."

let /lɛt/ *v.,* in such phrases as 'let you sit down,' frequently used in place of the imperative for the second person command or wish. In some parts of Ireland 'let' is replaced by 'leave' ('Leave you sit here'). Kickham, *Knocknagow,* 13: "Yes, Grace, let you and Mary come with us"; Synge, *The Playboy of the Western World,* act III (*FDA*, 2, 637): "*Mahon:* . . . let you give me a supeen, for I'm destroyed travelling since Tuesday was a week"; Yeats, *The Unicorn from the Stars*, act III (*Collected Plays*, 378): "*Johnny:* . . . Let you come and face now the two hundred men you brought out"; O'Brien, *The Ante-Room*, 142: "Run down, let you – and tell them . . . that I'd like to hear some music."

let on /lɛtˈɑn/ *v.,* to pretend, disclose, reveal (cf. Ir *ligim orm*, I let on). 'I never let on I recognised him'; 'Don't let on you see him.' Yeats, *The Unicorn from the Stars,* act III (*Collected Plays,* 373): "*Biddy:* He is dead. If it was letting on he was, he would not have let that one rob him and search him the way she did"; Gregory, *The Workhouse Ward* (*FDA*, 2, 625): "*Michael Miskell:* . . . Selling them to the nuns in the convent you did, and letting on they to be your own"; Joyce, *Ulysses,* 322.1: "So Bloom lets on he heard nothing."

líbín /liːˈbiːn/ *n.,* a minnow; a very small fish; some thing or person dripping wet < Ir. 'You poor wet líbín' (SOM, Kerry).

lick-the-statues /ˈlɪkd̪əˈstætʃuːz/ *n.phr.* (*colloq.*), a gossip; a CRAWTHUMPER. 'That one's a real lick-the-statues type' (KG, Kerry).

lief /ˈliɪf/, **liefer** /ˈliːfər/ *adv.,* (more) willingly, soon(er) < E dial. < ME *lefe*. 'I'd as lief swim the Channel as take a plane after what happened last time' (JF, Cavan); 'I'd as lief have Tom as Jack' (LUB, Dublin). Synge, *The Playboy of the Western World,* act III (*FDA*, 2, 641): "*Shawn:* . . . I'd liefer live a bachelor."

life /laif/ *n.*, in the phr. 'the life of the land', a person whose lifetime is used to mark the duration of a lease (cf. Ir *saolaí*). 'S. was an old FENIAN and even went on a trip to America. This trip was undertaken to find "the life of the land". The "life" was Humphrey M., and it was the done thing at the time that the rent would not be raised by Lord M. (the landlord) whilst that man ("the life of the land") lived' (KM, Kerry).

lig do scíth, *see* SCÍTH.

like[1] /laik/ *n.*, in the phr. 'the like(s) of' (cf. Ir *leithéid*). Synge, *The Playboy of the Western World*, act III (*FDA*, 2, 640): "*Michael:* . . . a fine, stout lad, the like of you."

like[2] /laik/ *adv.*, likely. 'I had like to fall out of my STANDING when I heard tell of it' (LUB, Dublin).

like[3] /laik/ *adv.* (*colloq.*), used as a filler: as it were, etc. 'That's the story, like'; 'You know yourself, like.

lillibullero (bullen-a-la) /ˈlɪliːbə ˈleːro (bʌlənəˈlæ)/ *n.*, refrain (probably intending to represent Irish sounds) of a song ridiculing the Catholic Irish promoted by King James II: 'Lilli bullero, lilli bullero bullen a la, | Lero lero, lilli bullero, lero lero bullen a la, | Lero lero, lilli bullero, lero lero bullen a la' (see *Verse in English from Eighteenth-Century Ireland*, 37–9, and *The Oxford Companion to Irish History*, 1998, s.v. 'Lilliburl ero').

lilt /lɪlt/ *v.*, to make MOUTH-MUSIC < ME *lilte*. 'Lilting' /ˈlɪltən/ *v.n.*, making a special kind of musical sound with the mouth (cf. Ir *portaireacht bhéil*). McGuinness, *Observe the Sons of Ulster Marching towards the Somme,* part 4 (*FDA*, 3, 1269): "*McIlwaine:* How can we have music? Sing a hymn? *Anderson:* Lilt or something. Go on, lilt."

líob /liːb/ *n.*, a sodden rag, in the phr. 'Tá mé i mo líob,' I'm drenched < Ir.

liobar /ˈlɪbər/ *n.*, a hanging lip; a tattered, slovenly person; an untidy woman (MK, Galway) < Ir. 'I don't know who'd take him, with a liobar like that hanging off him' (KG, Kerry); Joyce, *Finnegans Wake*, 245.13: "Lubbernabohore" [*liobar na mbóthar,* a tramp].

liobarnach /ˈlɪbərnəx/ *adj.*, awkward (KM, Kerry) < Ir. *See* LIOBAR.

lios, *see* LISÍN.

lioscán /lɪˈskɔːn/ *n.*, gleanings (KM, Kerry) < Ir.

lisín /ˈlɪʃiːn/ *n.*, a small 'fairy fort' < Ir (dimin. of *lios*, ringfort). 'We used to play up by the lisín when we were children' (BC, Meath).

liú /luː/ *n.*, a shout, a yell < Ir. 'He let a liú out of him' (SOM, Kerry). 'Liúigh', to cry loudly.

liúdaí /ˈluːd̪iː/ *n.*, a slovenly, good-for-nothing person < Ir.

'That liúdaí will never make anything of herself.'

liúdar /'luːd̪ər/ *n.,* a whack, a blow < Ir. 'He gave him a few liúdars, and that quietened him' (SOM, Kerry).

liúdramán /'luːd̪rə'mɔːn/ *n.,* a big, lazy man (VQ, Kerry); a loafer (SOM, Kerry) < Ir. 'He's nothing but a liúdramán.' Joyce, *Ulysses*, 304. 7–8: "there was an old one there with a cracked loodheramaun of a nephew"; *Finnegans Wake*, 21.30: "and he became a luderman."

liúigh, *see* LIÚ.

loaning /'loːnən/ *n.,* a lane, a by-road < E dial. < ME *lone* + suffix *-ing*. 'I went home by the loaning so I wouldn't have to pass by the house' (Meath).

lob /lɑb/ *n.,* a lump; money, savings < E dial. (cf. East Frisian *lob(be), n.,* a hanging lump of flesh (*ODEE*)). 'No-one ever knew him to spend much, so he is bound to have a lob somewhere' (LUB, Dublin, who also notes the use of 'lob' to mean 'something worth consideration; always used negatively, "Musha, he's no great lob"').

loch /lɑx/ *n.,* a lake < Ir. 'He's down at the loch fishing.'

lochán /'lʌhɔːn/ *n.,* a small lake, a pond; a pool, a puddle (SOM, Kerry; KM, Kerry) < Ir (dimin. of LOCH). 'Don't fall into the lochán and destroy your clothes!'

lochtán /lʌk'ṱɔːn/ *n.,* a terrace; a space on a cliff where people can stand and view < Ir. 'I was standing in the lochtán, and the wind nearly carried me off' (KM, Kerry).

lock /lɑk/ *n.,* a quantity of something < E dial. *lock* < ME *loc* (cf. Ir *loca*). 'Bring in that lock of hay'; 'We had a lock of drink in Gravies last night' (Mayo); 'I'll have it for you in a lock of minutes' (Cavan). Kavanagh, *Tarry Flynn*, 34: "Go out one of yez an bring in a lock of sticks for the fire"; Healy, *Nineteen Acres*, 97: "What kind of spuds have ye in Dublin? Jim, put a lock of them Champions in a bag for them."

locked /lɑkt/ *p.part.* (*colloq.*), very drunk, overpowered with drink. 'Let's go out and get locked' (Dublin).

log /lɑg/ *n.,* a pool of water (KM, Kerry) < Ir. 'Mind you don't step into the logs or you'll ruin your shoes.'

logán /'lʌgɔːn/ *n.,* a small pit or hole < Ir. 'Watch out for the logán and don't hurt yourself.'

loigín /lɪ'giːn/ *n.,* the bones forming the cavities around the tail-end of a cow < Ir. 'He was the first one to notice that the loigíns were down in her, and he was right: she calved the next day' (KM, Kerry).

lóipín /loː'piːn/ *n.,* a dirty or torn stocking (KM, Kerry); a cloth fixed on hen's claws to hinder them from scratching the earth < Ir. 'She shouldn't be let out with those lóipíns on her; she's the talk of the town.'

lon dubh /lʌn'd̪ʌv/ *n.*, a blackbird (SOM, Kerry) < Ir.

lone /loːn/ *adj.*, lonely; single, unmarried < E (aphetic of *alone*, < OE *all*, entirely + *ana*, by oneself). 'He's a poor old lone one; I'll do what I can for him' (KG, Kerry).

loodheramaun, *see* LIÚDRAMÁN.

lookit /'lʌkət/ *int.* to draw attention: see here (cf. *look at*). 'Now lookit here, if it's a fight you want you'd better go outside' (Cavan).

lorgadán, *see* LORGÁN.

lorgán /'lʌrgɔːn/ also **lorgadán** *n.*, a LEPRECHAUN (KM, Kerry) < Ir. 'There's many people said they seen lorgáns down in that field.' Keane, *The Bodhrán Makers,* 187: "'It is lorgadáns, dad, or what?' young Johnny Hallapy asked."

losset /'lʌsət/ also **losad** *n.*, a kneading-tray, often square, with a wooden rim, for making cakes or bread (MK, Galway) < Ir *losaid*. 'Take out the losset; I want to make some soda bread.'

lossogue, *see* LASÓG.

Lourdes /luːrdz/ *n.*, a town between Pau and Tarbes in southern France where Our Lady appeared on eighteen occasions to a local girl, Bernadette Soubirous, between 11 February and 16 July 1858; it is a very popular place of pilgrimage for Irish people. Binchy, *Firefly Summer*, 336: "She wondered when would poor Mrs Ryan be able to travel to Lourdes, the fund had been generously subscribed."

louser /'lauzər/ *n. (pejor.),* an inferior, objectionable person < ME *lus*, louse. 'Get away from me, you louser. Can't you see I'm busy!' (Dublin).

loy /lɔi/ *n.*, a narrow spade, especially for digging turf < Ir *lái*. 'Yes, that's a loy' (MB, Galway). Synge, *The Playboy of the Western World,* act III (*FDA*, 2, 636): "*Philly:* . . . and the great blow he hit with the loy"; Healy, *Nineteen Acres,* 119: " . . . an old loy, one corner broken but still sound"; 122: "The loy I took and gave to a folk-museum in Bonniconlon where artefacts of a disappearing age were being treasured."

luachair ghabhair /'luəxər 'gaur/ *n.*, coarse grass, netweed < Ir. 'The meadow is full of luachair ghabhair; it won't make for good silage' (Galway).

luachra /'luəxrə/ *n.pl.*, rushes < Ir. 'A loochry spot is swampy rushy ground' (Omurethi, Kildre). *See* ALP LUACHRA.

luaithreamhán /luə'rauɔːn/ *n.*, a heap of ashes; fig. someone sitting too near the fire on a fine day < Ir. 'Get up and go out, and don't be such a luaithreamhán!'

Luas /luəs/ *n.*, name of the proposed Dublin light rail system < Ir *luas*, speed. 'There's going to be terrible upset to the traffic round the centre of Dublin when they're building the Luas' (Dublin).

luascadh /ˈluəskə/ *n.*, rocking, swinging, swaying (SOM, Kerry) < Ir.

luascán /ˈluəskɔːn/ *n.* 1. A swing, a hammock (SOM, Kerry) < Ir. 2. A frog (SOM, Kerry) < Ir.

lúb /luːb/ *n.*, a stitch; a twist, a knot, a loop; a loop of tape for a button < Ir. 'Make a lúb in the rope and we'll catch her like the cowboys' (Mayo).

lúbaire /ˈluːbərə/ *n.*, a rogue, a CHANCER; a twister, a 'sweet talker' (SOM, Kerry, who adds: 'used with a certain sense of admiration') < Ir < LÚB. 'What a lúbaire he turned out to be; he'd chance anything!' (JF, Cavan).

lúbán /luːˈbɔːn/ *n.* 1. Something twisted and its shape distorted; fig. a failure to do something right < Ir < LÚB. 'You're making a lúbán of it' (to someone trying to repair something) (KM, Kerry). 2. A LÚBAIRE. 'He's a proper lúbán; he trims his sails to suit the wind' (SOM, Kerry).

lúb ar lár /ˈluːbɛrˈlɔːr/ *n.phr.*, a mistake in a piece of work < Ir (lit. dropped stitch). 'There's many the lúb ar lár in that bit of work' (BC, Meath).

lubbernabohore, *see* LIOBAR.

luck-penny /ˈlʌkpɛni/ *n.*, 'the amount, sometimes only a bit of silver, handed back by the seller to the buyer after the bargain is concluded; this applies only to the sale of goats, pigs, sheep, horses, and cattle' (Omurethi, Kildare, 534). Sometimes the words are reversed, giving 'penny-luck'. 'When she paid the surgeon, he gave her back change and said "penny-luck"' (KG, Kerry).

lúdramán, *see* LIÚDRAMÁN.

lug /lʌg/ *n.*, an ear; the handle of a pot; the small handle for hooks on the side of a pot (MH, Clare) < E dial. (origin obscure; *Chambers* s.v. 'lug' compares Swedish *lugga, v.*, to pull by the hair). 'You'll get a clip in the lug if you do that again' (TF, Cavan); 'Are you BOTHERED, or what kind of lugs have you?' (LUB, Dublin).

lúibín /luːˈbiːn/ *n.*, a twist or turn in a road (KM, Kerry) < Ir. 'Take the cows down to the lúibín. I have the gate left open.'

lúidín /luːˈd̪iːn/ *n.*, the little finger (MH, Clare; SOM, Kerry) < Ir. 'I could beat you with my little lúidín; so keep your mouth shut.'

luíochán /liː(ə)ˈxɔːn/ *n.*, lying down (KM, Kerry) < Ir.

lumper /ˈlʌmpər/ *n.*, a large type of potato widely used before the Great Famine (CS, Mayo) (origin obscure; cf. E *lump*).

lúrapóg lárapóg /ˈluːrəpoːg ˈlɔːrəpoːg/ a children's guessing-game played indoors in winter (MOB, Mayo) < Ir. 'No playing lúrapóg lárapóg today – can't ye see it's a fine day?'

lurch /lʌrʧ/ *n.* (*colloq.*), a slow, intimate dance (KD, Dublin) (origin obscure).

lus na fola /ˈlʌsnəˈfʌlə/ *n.*, shepherd's-purse (plant), pounded with goose grease for use as a cure for running sores (KM, Kerry) < Ir.

luthargán /ˈlʌhərgɔːn/ *n.*, a leprechaun; a fool < Ir. 'Get out of me way, you luthargán. There's work to be done' (Mayo).

lynching /ˈlɪnʧən/ *v.n.*, hanging a person for a supposed offence other than in accordance with the law. Two explanations are offered, one American and one Irish. In 1686 James Lynch of Piedmont, Virginia, was appointed to conduct trials on an informal basis because the nearest law court was some distance away (hence 'Lynch law'); in 1526 James Lynch Fitz-Stephen, warden (mayor) of Galway, passed sentence of death on his own son on his being found guilty of murder. Also used figuratively: 'She'll have me lynched unless I get back from the pub before she goes to bed.'

M

mac /mɑk/ also **mack** *n.*, son; boy, child < Ir *mac*, son. In the early development of surnames (*c.* 10th century onwards), a surname was formed by prefixing *Mac* (son) to the father's name or *Ó* (grandson) to that of a grandfather or remoter ancestor (the form 'Mc' is simply an abbreviation of 'Mac'). 'They say the McGuires come from Fermanagh'; 'How is my poor mac?' (EMF, Westmeath). 'A mhic,' son < Ir (*a*, voc. particle + *mhic* (vocative), son). Joyce, *Finnegans Wake*, 101.33: "mackavicks" (*maca mhic*, sons of a son). 'Every mac máthar', everyone < Ir *gach mac máthar* (lit. every mother's son) (SOM, Kerry). *See* AVICK.

macalla /mɑk'ɑlə/ *n.*, an echo < Ir.

macha /'mɑxə/ *n.*, an enclosure or HAGGARD for holding cattle (KM, Kerry) < Ir. 'Put the calves in the macha for the time being.'

máchail /'mɔːxəl/ *n.*, a stain, blemish, defect, disfigurement < Ir. 'To put a máchail on (something), to damage' (Moylan, 171).

machree /mə'kriː/ term of endearment: my dear < Ir *mo chroí*, my heart. 'Nanny machree, I'm sorry for your trouble' (BC, Meath). Joyce, *Ulysses*, 286.18–19: "'Ben machree', said Mr Dedalus, clapping Ben's fat back shoulder-blade."

mackavicks, *see* MAC.

macoghamade, *see* OGHAM.

macushla /mək'ʌʃlə/ term of endearment: my dear, my darling < Ir *mo chuisle* (lit. my pulse). 'Patty macushla, wet the tea, will you, please?' (KG, Kerry).

mad /mæd/ *adj.*, angry < Ir *ar buile*. 'I was BLACK mad altogether when Stephen dammed our river with sods of turf' (AF, Cavan).

madra /'mɑd̪rə/ also **mada** /'mɑd̪ə/ *n.*, a dog < Ir. 'Madra rua', fox < Ir (lit. red dog). 'Coinnigh an cnámh agus leanfaidh an mada thú' (proverb), Keep the bone and the dog will follow you; 'Tá chuile mhada teann ag a dhoras féin' (proverb), Every dog is brave at his own door.

magalore, *see* MAITH GO LEOR.

maide /'mɑʤə/ *n.*, a stick; a beam. 'Maide trasna', the trunk of a tree retrieved from a bog to make a CISEACH (SOM, Kerry) < Ir.

maide briste /mɑʤə'brɪstə/ *n.*, tongs (KM, Kerry) < Ir.

maide ceangail /'mɑʤə'kæŋgəl/ *n.*, the cross-tie of the roof in old houses (KM, Kerry) < Ir.

maidrín lathaí /'mɑdriːn'lɑhiː/ *n.*, a lapdog; a menial (SOM, Kerry) < Ir (lit. little dog of the mud). 'Don't be making a maidrín lathaí of yourself.'

maig /mɑg/ *n.*, one's head inclined to one side; sulkiness (KG, Kerry) < Ir.

maighdean /'maiʤən/ *n.*, a maiden; a virgin (SOM, Kerry) < Ir. An Mhaighdean Mhuire /ʌn'waiʤən'wɪrə/, the Virgin Mary.

máilín /mɔː'liːn/ *n.*, a little bag < Ir (dimin. of MÁLA). 'Hand me the máilín and I'll give you a few pence for yourself; you're a great boy' (KG, Kerry).

máilín sáite /'mɔːliːn'sɔːʧə/ *n.*, a bag for holding potato sets while sowing (KM, Kerry) < Ir.

máinléad /mɔːn'leːd̪/ also **máilléad** /mɔː'leːd̪/ *n.*, a stupid person, a blockhead < Ir (lit. mallet). 'You stupid máinléad!' (SOM, Kerry).

maintainer /meːn'teːnər/ *n.*, one who interferes, usually with the threat of violence, to prevent the due process of law from damaging his client's interests (MB, Tipperary).

mairtíneach /mɑːr'ʧiːnəx/ *n.*, a disabled person < Ir. 'He's been a mairtíneach since birth, but he's made great headway, God be good to him' (BC, Meath).

maiste /'mɑʃtə/ *int.*, indeed (SOM, Kerry) < Ir (variant of *ambaiste*). 'Maiste, she has your heart broke, but you'd have to love her all the same' (KG, Kerry).

maistín /mɑʃ'ʧiːn/ *n.*, a ferocious-looking dog; fig. a bad-tempered, whinging child (MOB, Mayo); a rude, ill-bred person; a bully < Ir. 'I hate it when that maistín of a child comes here with his mother'; 'Such a maistín he was at school, and look at the cut of him now – you'd think butter wouldn't melt in his mouth!' (Mayo).

maith go leor /mɑgʌ'loːr/ also **mongalore, mau-galore** *n.phr.*, good enough, all right (LUB, Dublin); happy in himself or herself (MOB, Mayo); a little bit drunk, tipsy (SOM, Kerry) < Ir *maith go leor*, good enough. 'Don't mind him: he's maith go leor' (Meath). *See* GO LEOR.

make strange /meːkst̪reːnʤ/ *phr.*, to become uncomfortable or nervous or uneasy or distraught; this usage seems to be restricted to HE and based on the Irish idiom (*see* de Bhaldraithe s.v. 'strange, 3' and Ó Dónaill s.v. 'coimhthíos':

'coimhthíos a dhéanamh le duine, to "make strange" with someone; to keep aloof from, be shy in the presence of, someone. *Rinne an leanbh coimhthíos liom*, the child made strange with me, was afraid to come near me') 'That child never makes strange, even when she meets new people – her brother was the very opposite. He'd whinge away if anybody came up to the GO-CAR.' Paulin, *A New Look at the Language Question*, 17: "Many words which now appear simply gnarled, or which 'make strange' or seem opaque to most readers, would be released into the shaped flow of a new public language"; Leonard, *Out After Dark*, 68: "The reason I like Micky Farrell . . . is because he's so open and above board and doesn't make strange."

mala /'mɑlə/ *n.*, an eyebrow (KM, Kerry) < Ir.

mála /'mɔːlə/ n., a bag < Ir. 'Sure she bought that *oul* mála at an auction for a pound' (KG, Kerry). *See* LÁN AN MHÁLA.

malavogue /'mɑləvoːg/ *v.*, to beat; to chastise, punish < E dial. (cf. Ir *malabhóg*; see R. Ó Scannláin, *Éigse*, vol. 5 (1945–47), 107). 'Such a malavoguing she gave him!' (PMD, Mayo).

mallafoosther /mɑlə'fuːst̪ər/ also **mollafoosdar** (MH, Clare) *v.*, to give a beating to < F *mal*, bad + Ir FÚSTAR. 'If you don't stop that messing I'll mallafoosther the both of you!' (PMD, Mayo).

malt /mɔːlt/ *n.*, in the phr. 'ball of malt,' a glass (large measure) of whiskey (Dublin) < *ball*, perhaps rhyming slang (cf. 'a cow and calf,' a half (glass) of whiskey) + *malt*, whiskey (as made from malt). Joyce, *Finnegans Wake*, 498.18: "after plenty of his fresh stout and his good balls of malt"; O'Casey, *The Plough and the Stars*, act I, 148: "*Fluther*: . . . Have a glass o' malt, Fluther"; 'A Ball of Malt and Madame Butterfly' (short story by Benedict Kiely).

mam /mæm/ *n.*, mother < Ir *mamaí, mam*. 'Mam, is the dinner ready yet?' (Mayo).

mám /mɔːm/ also **maum** *n.*, the fill of one's hands (MOB, Mayo); the contents of two hands joined together (larger than a LADHAR) (SOM, Kerry) < Ir. 'He took a mám of meal /meːl/ from the bin' (AF, Cavan); 'a mám of water from the spring well on the way home from school' (SOM, Kerry).

mamailíneach /mɑmə'liːnəx/ *n.*, a small person with short legs; a waddler; a lazy, useless person (KM, Kerry) < Ir. 'Run after those cows, you mamailíneach, and don't let them get out the gap.'

mammy /'mæmi/ *n.*, mother < Ir *mamaí*.

man /mæn/. In combinations in which 'man' is used as a suffix (e.g. 'chairman'), speakers of HE tend to retain the full stress in their pronunciation of 'man', whereas speakers of Standard or near-Standard English reduce the vowel to /ə/.

Man Above, the /mæn'əbʌv/ *n. (euphemism)*, God < Ir *an Fear Thuas*. 'There is no one I have to look for help from, barring yer Honour and the Man Above' (Omurethi, Kildare); 'It all depends on the Man Above' (BD, Cavan); Leonard, *Out After Dark*, 49: " . . . Sure aren't we all in the hands of the Man Above?"

m'anam do Dhia is do Mhuire /mɑnəmd̪ə'jiəsd̪ə'wɪrə/ *int.*, my soul to Jesus and Mary, said by a person when tired < Ir. *See* ANAM.

m'anam 'on Diabhal /'mɑnəm ən'ʤaul/ *int.*, my soul to the Devil < Ir. '"M'anam 'on Diabhal," she said when she saw me' (KG, Kerry); 'M'anam 'on Diabhal! Wasn't he lucky not to get caught by the Guards?' (TF, Sligo). Sheridan, *The Brave Irishman*, 166: "*Captain*: Monomundioul, there ishn't one of these SPALPEENS that has a cabbin upon a mountain . . . BUT will be keeping a goon." *See* D'ANAM 'ON DIABHAL.

man-eater /'mæniːtər/ also **man-keeper** /'mænkiːpər/ *n.*, a newt; a lizard. Hogan notes: 'This is a special Anglo-Irish [i.e. HE] name, and depends on Irish folk-lore. In parts of the U.S. a kind of salamander is call a *man-eater*, which may be a borrowing from Anglo-Irish – *Man-keeper* is I think a more general Anglo-Irish word for the newt, but it is not used in Mr Ua Broin's district [south-west Co. Dublin].'

mangaire /'mɑŋgərə/ *n.*, a pedlar; a travelling salesman (with a hint of disapproval) (SOM, Kerry) < Ir. 'The mangaire sold me the glass door of an old washing-machine as a fruit bowl' (ML, Mayo).

mankeeper, *see* MAN-EATER.

manly /'mænli/ *adj.*, precocious; forward (SOM, Kerry). 'Don't be so manly when I'm talking to you! Have manners on you, just for once' (KG, Kerry). *See* BOICÍN.

mannerly /'mænərli/ *adj.*, well-mannered (TJ, Sligo) < E dial. < ME *manereliche*. 'They were mannerly children in spite of all.'

man of the house, *see* FEAR.

mant /mɑnt/ 1. *n.*, a toothless mouth; a space where teeth have fallen out (KM, Kerry) < Ir. 'The poor fella; I don't know how he manages to eat anything with that mant – he should get a set of false teeth.' 2. *n. used as v.*, to take an uneven handful out of a cake (MOB, Mayo).

mantach /'mɑnt̪əx/ *adj.*, toothless; gap-toothed; having indistinct speech (SOM, Kerry); a mouthful < Ir. 'Take a mantach out of that cake of bread' (ENM, Kerry).

mantachán /'mɑn̪təkɔːn/ *n.*, a gap-toothed person; a person who has lost some front teeth (MH, Clare); a person with indistinct speech because of missing teeth (SOM, Kerry) < Ir. 'Would you believe that mantachán is going to Rome to get married this winter?' (BC, Meath).

mantóg /mɑn't̪oːg/ *n.*, a mouth halter for horses, muzzle for lambs; person with a gap in teeth; person who speaks clumsily (KM, Kerry) < Ir. 'Can you make out a word that mantóg is saying?'

maoilín /mwiːl'iːn/ *n.*, a hornless cow < Ir. 'They reckon all the cows up that way have always been maoilíns, because it's the only way they can eat the grass in between the rocks' (KM, Kerry).

maoineach /'mwiːnəx/ *n.*, a cherished one, beloved person < Ir. 'A mhaoineach' (with *voc. particle*), dearly beloved (SOM, Kerry) < Ir.

maol /mwiːl/ also **meel** *adj.*, bald; hornless (of a cow); dehorned; a bank with no bushes on it < Ir. 'Get the vet to the maol cow'; 'A meel ditch – a bank with no bushes growing in it' (Meath). 'Maol bó', 'bó mhaol', a cow with no horns < Ir. 'Maolgharbh', sunburn on cattle – only white parts are sunburnt, and the hair falls out and the skin crusts (KM, Kerry). 'In Canada and in Ireland a hornless cow is called a mooley' (Hayden and Hartog, 783).

maolaí /mwiːliː/ a pet name for a hornless cow (SOM, Kerry) < Ir. *See* MOILEY.

marbhán /'mɑrəvɔːn/ *n.*, a dead body; fig. a listless person < Ir. 'That marbhán is more dead than alive' (SOM, Kerry).

marbhánach /mɑrə'vɔːnəx/ n., a lazy, spiritless person < Ir. 'MUSHA, it was hardly worth watching; the whole team was marbhánach' (KG, Kerry).

marbhfháisc /mɑrə'vɔːʃk/ *n.*, a strip of cloth put around the face of a dead body < Ir. 'Mrs Mac was great for laying out the corpse with the marbhfháisc' (Cork).

marcach /'mɑrkəx/ *n.*, a rider, a jockey (SOM, Kerry) < Ir.

margadh mór /'mɑrəgə'moːr/ *n.*, a market (often used of a big market before Christmas) (KM, Kerry) < Ir.

mark /mærk/ *n.*, in the expression 'God save the mark!', an expression of scorn (origin obscure; cf. Brewer s.v. 'God bless (or save) the mark': 'a kind of apology for introducing a disagreeable subject,' as in Shakespeare, *1 Henry IV*, act I, iii, where Hotspur, apologising to the king for not sending the prisoners according to command, says that the messenger was a 'popinjay', who made him mad with his unmanly ways and talked "so like a waiting-gentlewoman | Of guns, and drums, and wounds, God save the mark!" It is suggested that the 'mark' is possibly a sign of the cross and the phrase a kind of supplication). Joyce, *Finnegans Wake*, 487.26–9: "God save the monk! I won't mind this is, answering to your strict crossqueets, whereas it would be as unethical for me now to answer as it would have been nonsensical for you then not to have asked."

marla /ˈmɔːrlə/ *n.*, modelling-clay, especially as used by children in school < Ir < E *marl*. 'He loves playing with marla, day and night.'

maryah /mɑrˈjæ/, /mɑrəˈjæ/ also **mauryah, moryah** *int. (ironic)*, indeed; allegedly (added to a term or statement to question its truth or to scorn it) < Ir *mar dhea* (lit. as it were). 'She's a great cook – maryah'; 'Friend, maryeah! Some friend he was!' (KG, Kerry); 'He's asleep, mauryah' (i.e. pretending). Joyce, *Ulysses*, 331.32–3: "Beggar my neighbour is his motto. Love, Moya! He's a nice pattern of a Romeo and Juliet"; Johnston, *Shadows on Our Skin*, 121: "A singer as well as a hero.' 'Hero.' Joe's voice was bitter. 'Mauryah.'"

Mary's fern /ˈmeːriːzˈfɛrn/ *n.*, bracken (because of a legend that St Joseph used it for bedding for the Virgin Mary and the Christ-child).

más é do thoil é /mɔːʃəːd̪ə ˈhʌləː/ *phr.*, please < Ir. 'Will you help me on with my coat, más é do thoil é?' (KG, Kerry). Joyce, *Finnegans Wake*, 37.25: 'Irish saliva [Ir *seile*, saliva], *mawshe dho hole*."

masher /ˈmæʃər/ *n.*, an attractive man (origin obscure, but cf. Beecher, 64, who suggests a derivation from Ir *maise*, beauty; *maiseach*, beautiful). 'I think Jack Hanlon was then working on a painting that he called *The Masher*' (MCR, Waterford).

masla /ˈmɑslə/ *n.*, an insult, hurt (SOM, Kerry) < Ir.

masmas /ˈmɑsməs/ *n.*, nausea (from eating too much); morning sickness < Ir. 'The masmas is at me again' (BC, Meath).

masmasach /mɑsməˈsəx/ *adj.*, disgusting, nauseating (with reference to food) (SOM, Kerry) < Ir.

Mass /mæs/ *n.*, the Catholic service of the Eucharistic sacrifice < OE *mæsse* < L *missa*. Kilroy, *The Big Chapel*, 178: "He said Mass in hail and rain and sunshine without as much as a glance at the open sky above his head"; Durcan, *Christmas Day*, II, 10: "I should do this more often – | Not go to Mass. |

It is difficult not to go to Mass. | Mass is the only chance | One has to be in company." Sometimes a Mass is popularly referred to according to its duration: Joyce, 'The Boarding House' (*Dubliners*, 69: "She would have lots of time to have the matter out with Mr Doran and then catch short twelve at Marlborough Street" (i.e. the PRO-CATHEDRAL). 'First Mass' /ˈfʌrstmæs/, the first Mass said by a priest on a given day, or the first Mass a priest says after his ordination. 'I do go to first Mass, and then the day is free' (BC, Meath).

massive /ˈmæsəv/ *adj.* (*colloq.*), outstanding, beautiful, imposing < E < F *masse* (but cf. SB, Cork, who suggests a derivation from OIr *mas*, excellence of appearance or external quality; fine, handsome). 'Mary, your dress is massive' (i.e. lovely); 'He's ONLY massive' (Dublin).

Mass rock /ˈmæsrɑk/ *n.*, a large rock on which open-air Mass was said in a secluded location during the time of the Penal Laws (1690s onwards). 'They've got a Mass rock in the Folk Park. Have you been up to see it?' (AH, Donegal).

master /ˈmæst̪ər/ *n.*, the usual title for a male teacher in a national school. 'There goes Master McKeown – a great teacher; all the children love him' (AF, Cavan). Heaney, 'Station Island' V (*Station Island*, 72): "'Master,' those elders whispered, 'I wonder, master . . . ' | rustling envelopes, proferring them, withdrawing, | and 'Master' I repeated to myself."

matalóg /ˈmɑt̪əloːg/ *n.* (*colloq.*), a vaguely defined disparaging term for a foolish, stupid person (SOM, Kerry, who adds: 'found in other dialects as 'PATALÓG', which is also in the English of Slieve Luachra [Co. Kerry] but with a different meaning – a thriving, chubby child').

match-maker /ˈmæʧmeːkər/ *n.*, a person whose acknowledged role it is to bring about a marriage < OE *gemæcca, n.,* mate + *macian*, v., arrange, manage. 'By this time there was a match made for my grandmother with a young man of her own age' (KM, Kerry). Kickham, *Knocknagow*, 38: "Tom is goin' to match-make down to the county Limerick.'

mau-galore, *see* MAITH GO LEOR.

mauryah, *see* MARYEAH.

mavourneen /məˈvuːrniːn/ *n.*, a term of endearment: my dear one < Ir *mo mhuirnín*. *See* MO.

mavrone /məˈvroːn/ *int.*, alas (KM, Kerry) < Ir *mo bhrón*.

Maynooth Catechism, *see* CATECHISM.

meadar /ˈmæd̪ər/ also **maddor, medher** *n.*, a drinking-vessel < Ir. Swift, *A Dialogue in Hybernian Stile,* 165: "*B*: . . .

we had nothing but a maddor to drink out of"; Joyce, *Ulysses*, 323.34–5: "He said and then lifted he in his rude great brawny strengthy hands the medher of dark strong foamy ale and, uttering his tribal slogan . . . "

meadhrán /'mairɔːn/ *n.*, dizziness; vertigo < Ir. 'I was dancing a polka set until I got a dreadful meadhrán' (SOM, Kerry).

mealbhóg /mælə'voːg/ *n.*, a small bag, a satchel (for shopping) (SOM, Kerry) < Ir.

meallaire /'mælərə/ *n.*, a deceiver, a flatterer (SOM, Kerry) < Ir. 'That meallaire is a melted old rogue, if ever there was one' (KG, Kerry).

méar /meːr/ *n.*, a finger; a toe < Ir. 'Méar fhada', the middle finger (SOM, Kerry) < Ir (lit. the long finger). 'On the méar fhada,' postponed indefinitely.

méaracán /'meːrəkɔːn/ *n.*, a finger; a thimble (KM, Kerry) < Ir. 'Hand me the méaracán till I darn these socks; I'm fed up looking at them.'

mearbhall /mæ'ruːl/ *n.*, bewilderment; confusion; dizziness < Ir. 'I don't know what mearbhal came over me; I just can't remember' (SOM, Kerry).

mearing /'meːrən/ *n.*, the boundary DITCH or fence between two farms < ME *mere*, boundary. Percy French, 'Slattery's Mounted Foot': "'Tis merely throwin' life away to face that mearin' dhrain"; Stoker, *The Snake's Pass*, 30: "But prisintly he seen the two min up on the side of the hill at the south, near Joyce's mearin'."

méaróg[1] /'meːroːg/ *n.*, a pebble (often used in a game of jackstones, played with the thumbnail and the loop of the forefinger) (SOM, Kerry) < Ir.

méaróg[2] /'meːroːg/ *n.*, a hay rope made with one finger or thumb < Ir. 'Better to be knotting a méaróg than to be idle' (saying).

mearúl /mæ'ruːl/ *n.*, bewilderment; confusion; dizziness < Ir MEARBHALL. 'I don't know what mearúl came over me – I just can't remember' (SOM, Kerry).

meas /mæs/ also **mass** *n.*, respect, esteem (SOM, Kerry); sense of worth, regard < Ir. 'Jim was in his early twenties and had little meas in Jack and Humphrey – both were only up to his shoulder and a lot older' (KM, Kerry); 'Everyone had great meas on him'; 'A MUSTRACH little man – he had terrible meas on himself' (SOM, Kerry); 'Some children have no mass on chocolate' (MH, Clare). Healy, *Nineteen Acres*, 100: "Jim had little meas on the apples." The formula 'mise le meas,' yours respectfully (lit. I am with respect) is used at the conclusion of formal letters in Irish and frequently also in English: Plunkett, *Farewell Companions*, 440: "Is mise le meas | L. Páircéir | Rúnaí . . . "; 'Meas madaidh', contempt (MOB, Mayo) < Ir (lit. dog's respect).

meat /miːt/, /meːt/, in expressions such as 'I've seen more meat on a Good Friday' or 'I've seen more meat on a butcher's knife,' commenting on a very thin person (HJ, Wexford). (The pronunciation of 'ea' as /eː/, a salient characteristic of Hiberno-English since about 1700, was common in England until the 18th century, as witnessed in this anecdote given by Samuel Johnson (entry in Boswell for 27 March 1772, cited by Bliss in *Spoken English in Ireland,* 209): 'When I published the Plan for my Dictionary, Lord Chesterfield told me that the word *great* should be pronounced so as to rhyme to *state*; and Sir William Yonge sent me word that it should be pronounced so as to rhyme to *seat*, and that none but an Irishman would pronounce it *grait*. Now here were two men of the highest rank, the one, the best speaker in the House of Lords, the other, the best speaker in the House of Commons, differing entirely.')

meathán /mæˈhɔːn/ *n.*, a delicate, weak, sickly person (KM, Kerry) < Ir. 'He was always a meathán when he was younger, but look at the buck he's grown into now!'

meathlóir /ˈmæhloːr/ *n.*, a weak or lazy person < Ir. 'Don't bring that meathlóir out to the bog with you; he's a waste of time' (Mayo).

mechil, *see* MEITHEAL.

medher, *see* MEADAR.

medical hall /ˈmɛdəklhɔːl/ *n.*, a pharmacy < F *médical*, mediaeval L *medicalis* + OE *heall*. 'There's only one medical hall in the town now' (TF, Cavan).

meela murder, *see* MÍLE MURDER.

meeaw, *see* MÍ-ÁDH.

meel, *see* MAOL.

meg /mɛg/ *n.*, a goatee or chin-whisker (LUB, Dublin, who adds: '*Meig*, the Irish imitative name of a goat'). *See* MEIGEALL.

meeleen, meely *see* MAOLAÍ.

meidhreach /ˈmairəx/ *adj.*, merry, joyful; beginning to become intoxicated < Ir. 'Magairlín meidhhreach', the early purple orchid, used for a love potion (LUB, Dublin, who gives this as the basis of 'mogolyeen-mire', a love potion: 'Oh! they'll catch him yet, even if they have to give him the mogolyeen-mire' (said of a young man frequently visiting a house where there are likely-looking daughters).

meigeall /ˈmɛgəl/ *n.*, a heavy beard; a goatee; goat's beard; fig. a person with a goatee (VQ, Kerry) < Ir. *See* MEG.

meigeallach /ˈmɛgələx/ *n.*, the bleating of a goat or sheep (SOM, Kerry) < Ir.

méigrim /ˈmeːgrəm/ *n.*, a headache, migraine (MK, Galway); a dizzy head (MOB, Mayo); noise in the head, a buzzing in the ears (mild tinnitus); vertigo (SOM, Kerry) < Ir < E *megrim* < MF *migraine*. 'POITÍN does give me a woeful méigrim of the head, so I don't take it no more' (TF, Cavan); 'Maura has a méigrim; she's lying down (TF, Cavan).

meila murder, *see* MÍLE MURDER.

méirín /meːˈriːn/ *n.*, a fairy thimble; a foxglove; a covering for a finger with a whitlow (SOM, Kerry) < Ir. 'Children picking méiríns from foxgloves to make a small explosion' (SOM, Kerry).

méirscre /ˈmeːrʃkrə/ *n.*, chapped skin; broken chilblains; scabs on hands < Ir. 'Méirscre can be very painful' (ML, Mayo).

meisce /ˈmɛʃkə/ *n.*, drunkenness (SOM, Kerry) < Ir.

meisceoir /ˈmɛʃkjoːr/ *n.*, a confirmed drunkard (SOM, Kerry) < Ir.

meitheal /ˈmɛhəl/ also **mihul, mechil** *n.*, a band of neighbouring farmers coming together to help each other for a day or two to thresh corn, pick potatoes, cut turf, make hay etc. (MOB, Mayo) < Ir. A party of voluntary farm workers (no payment was made, but the recipient of the help was expected to provide food and hospitality for the others when the job was done); 'for larger tasks like cutting turf, harvesting, and making a hay reek, eight to ten workers and upwards (for smaller jobs two farmers would exchange men and horses when COMHARING)' (SOM, Kerry) 'The days of the meithleacha [*plural*] are gone for ever, more's the pity – there was great CRAIC when they were stooking the oats' (MG, Cavan). Healy, *Nineteen Acres*, 14: "It was only when we had a meitheal you brought PORTER in a sweet can"; 120: "The tractor . . . cut out the meitheal of carts drawing turf from the bog . . . The first spring meitheal of turf-men would follow when, much later, the Sugar Company turf-cutting machine arrived"; 121: "We may cry about losing our language: we lost as much again when we lost the meitheal." *See* BOON.

melodeon /məˈloːʤən/ *n.*, a small type of accordion (possibly derived from E *melody* + *accordion* or *harmonium*). Kavanagh, 'A Christmas Childhood, II (*Collected Poems*, 71): "My father played the melodeon | Outside at our gate; | . . . Across the wild bogs his melodeon called | To Lennons and Callans"; Keane, *The Bodhrán Makers*, 68: "the Costigan brothers excelled themselves on the hard surface of the roadway accompanied this time by bones and melodeons only."

melt /mɛlt/ *n.* (pejor.), especially in the phr. 'hoor's melt' (origin uncertain, but cf. OE *milte, n.*, spleen, supposed seat of unpleasant moods; also E dial. *melt*, tongue). 'He's a melted old rogue' (KG, Kerry). Leonard, *Out After Dark*, 101: "'An' sure God is good, and the whoor's melt won't have a minute's luck."

merciful hour /mɛrsəfəl'aur/ *int.* expressing surprise. 'Merciful hour, you frightened the life out of me; I didn't know who was there!' (Dublin).

mess /mɛs/ *v.*, to confuse, to render untidy < OF *mes* + *-er* (ultimately derived from L suffix *-arius*, person connected with (*ODEE*, s.v. '-er²'). Doyle, *The Van*, 140: "No messin' now, Glenn"; Roche, *A Handful of Stars*, act II, iii, 63: "*Jimmy*: Alright Stapler, I was only messin'." *See* MESSER.

messages /'mɛsədʒəz/ *n.pl.*, errands; shopping (often means doing the shopping for someone else; the word is also used in this sense in Scotland). 'I must do the messages before I go to the Stations of the Cross'; 'Be a good GIRSHA and bring in the messages for me from the car, will you?' (KG, Kerry). Joyce, *Finnegans Wake*, 506, 34–5: "He is a man of around fifty . . . who does messuages"; Healy, *Nineteen Acres*, 8: "The child ran the messages."

messer /'mɛsər/ *n.*, a joker; a muddler < E dial. *mess*, a muddle, an insignificant something + *-er*. 'She should never have married a messer like that. He brought her nothing but trouble' (Dublin).

mhic ó /'vɪk'oː/ in the voc. phr. 'a mhic ó,' my son, my lad < Ir. 'Get up on the cross-bar, avick, and I'll give you a lift to Mass' (TF, Cavan). *See* AVICK.

mhuise /'wɪʃə/ *int.*, indeed; certainly < Ir *muise mhuise*. *See* MUSHA.

mí-ádh /miː'ɔː/ also **meeaw, miaw** *n.*, ill-luck, misfortune (MH, Clare; MOB, Mayo; KM, Kerry) < Ir. 'That family has an awful lot of mí-ádh, God help them' (MK, Galway); 'The deed was bad; no wonder the mí-ádh stuck to them!'

mian /miən/ *n.*, a desire, a longing, a passion (SOM, Kerry); ainmhian, an uncontrolled desire < Ir. 'She had an ainmhian for oranges (during pregnancy)' (SOM, Kerry).

mianach /'miənəx/ *n.*, strength of character; calibre (KM, Kerry) < Ir. 'A man of his mianach would never have done a thing like that.'

mias /miəs/ *n.*, a vessel, a dish, a basin < Ir. 'Give a mias of milk to the cat' (SOM, Kerry).

miaw, *see* MÍ-ÁDH.

mich, *see* MITCH.

mihul, *see* MEITHEAL.

midden /'mɪdən/ *n.*, a dung-heap < E dial. < ME *mydding*.

'There's a woeful smell off that midden on the day that's IN IT' (i.e. today's weather) (BC, Meath).

midlín /ˈmɪdliːn/ also **middhilin** *n.*, flail-joint (TF, Cavan) (traditionally made from eel skin) < Ir. 'The midlín is broken – you'll have to go and make a new one.' *See* BOOLTHAUN.

middling /ˈmɪdlən/ *adj.*, a reasonable state of health; moderate, fair; indifferent; just about all right; *adv.*, fairly, tolerably, not too bad < E dial. 'How's the patient today, then?' – 'Middlin' well, thanks be to God' (TF, Cavan).Griffin, *The Collegians*, 33: "'An' you have a good long pair of legs, I see.' 'Middlin, sir,' says I"; Synge, *The Playboy of the Western World*, act III (*FDA*, 2, 641): "*Pegeen*: . . . and he a middling kind of a scarecrow."

mighty /ˈmaiti/ *adj., adv.*, intensive; enjoyable, exciting; strong, hard < E dial. 'That was a mighty game'; 'We had a mighty night' (Mayo).

míle murder /ˈmiːləˈmʌrd̪ʌr/ also **meela murder; míle murdal** *n.phr.*, trouble, uproar, confusion; a violent outbreak; RUCTIONS (MOB, Mayo) < Ir *míle*, a thousand + E *murder*. 'There'll be míle murder when she comes home and finds the jug broken!' Joyce, *Ulysses*, 327.28–9: "he flogs the bloody backside off of the poor lad till he yells meila murder."

mill /mɪl/ *n., v.* (*colloq.*), a fight; to fight (cf. Ir *milleadh, n.*, injuring; destruction). 'There was a mill after the pub closed'; 'I'll mill ye if I get my hands on ye!' (Dublin).

milleán /mɪˈlɔːn/ *n.*, blame < Ir. 'There's no milleán on Paddy's part' (SOM, Kerry).

milseán /mɪlˈʃɔːn/ also (by metathesis) **misleán** (SOM, Kerry) *n.*, a sweet < Ir.

min /mɪn/ *n.*, meal; pinhead oatmeal (SOM, Kerry) < Ir. 'Min bhuí', Indian meal < Ir.

mín /miːn/ *n.*, a level green piece of land in the middle of rougher terrain (SOM, Kerry) < Ir. 'Check the sheep on the mínte [*plural*], will you?' (Galway).

minaun aerach, *see* MIONNÁN AERACH.

mind /maind/ *v.*, to remember < E dial. < ME *minden*. 'I mind when there were horses on every farm in this county' (BC, Meath). 'I don't mind,' I have no objection (Hayden and Hartog, 780).

minute /ˈmɪnət/, /ˈmɪnjɛt/ *n.*, in the phr. 'at the minute,' now, at the present time. 'I'm not so well at the minute, but, please God, I'll be better soon (JMF, Cavan).

miodailín /ˈmɪdəliːn/ also **middhilin** *n.*, a flail-joint (traditionally made from eel skin) (TF, Cavan) < Ir (dimin. of *miodal*). 'The miodailín is broken; you'll have to go and make a new one.' *See* BOOLTHAUN.

míog[1] /miːg/ *n.*, a noise, sound; a squeak < Ir. 'He hadn't a míog out of him' (SOM, Kerry).

míog[2] /miːg/ *n.*, a wink of sleep < Ir.

míogarnach /miːgərnəx/ *n.*, dozing to sleep in a sitting position; drowsiness that is almost beyond control (SOM, Kerry) < Ir.

míol /miːl/ *n.*, an insect; a louse (SOM, Kerry); fig. an unpleasant person < Ir.

míolach /ˈmiːləx/ *adj.*, louse-infested, LOUSY < Ir. 'The little BODACHÁN míolach' (SOM, Kerry).

mionnán /mɪˈnɔːn/ also **meannán** *n.*, a kid (KM, Kerry) < Ir.

mionnán aerach /ˈmɪnɔːnˈeːrəx/ *n.*, a kid; an alternative name for the GABHAIRÍN REO or jack-snipe (whose cry resembles the baying of a young goat) (SOM, Kerry; MOB, Mayo; JF, Cavan) < Ir. 'We heard a mionnán aerach near Hollygrove lake this morning' (Galway). Healy, *Nineteen Acres*, 8: "Over the bog, in the thin blue air, the minaun aerach climbed into the sky with the mating call."

miotóg /mɪˈt̪oːg/ *n.*, a piece (bitten off) (KM, Kerry) < Ir.

Miraculous Medal /mɪr ˈækjələsˈmɛdl/ *n.*, an oval medal with an image of the Blessed Virgin Mary on one side, with rays of light coming from her hands, surrounded by the words 'O Mary conceived without sin! Pray for us who have recourse to thee'; on the other side is a cross, the initial *M*, and a representation of the hearts of Jesus and His mother; it is worn on a blue ribbon as the badge of the Children of Mary (members of sodalities of the Blessed Virgin Mary); it is called 'Miraculous' seemingly because its design was revealed miraculously to Catherine Labouré, a sister of Charity of ST VINCENT DE PAUL, in 1830 < F *medaille*. 'The priest gave her a Miraculous Medal and she put it on her ROSARY' (JMF, Cavan). Joyce, *Finnegans Wake*, 410.16–17: "the miraculous meddle of this expending umniverse."

mí-rath /miːˈræh/ *n.*, misfortune (KG, Kerry) < Ir. 'She had nothing but mí-rath since she moved back in with the family after the husband died.'

miscaun /ˈmɪskɔːn/ also **mesgan, mescaun, miscin, maskin**, etc. *n.*, a lump of butter < Ir *mioscán*, variant of *meascán*. 'A miscaun of butter makes all the difference to the SPUDS' (TJ, Sligo).

mise /ˈmɪʃə/ *personal pron. (emphatic form),* I, me < Ir. 'Twenty people were summoned, including mise' (KG, Kerry).

mise le meas, *see* MEAS.

misfortunate /mɪs'fɔːrʧənət/ *adj*., unfortunate < E dial. < *mis-* + *fortunate*. 'That was a quare misfortunate thing to happen to that man' (BC, Meath).

misleán, *see* MILSEÁN.

mismín /mɪʃ'miːn/ *n*., water-mint (KM, Kerry) < Ir. 'Some of that mismín would be nice growing in the bottom of the garden.'

misneach /'mɪʃnəx/ *n*., courage; cheerfulness, good spirits; nourishment, state of health < Ir. 'How's the misneach today?' (SOM, Kerry).

mission /mɪʃən/ *n*., a visit to a parish by one or more missionary priests over a certain number of days (in the past, often one week for the women and one week for the men) with the object of providing a spiritual tonic for the congregation in a series of sermons and other spiritual exercises; such missions originated with the Franciscan and Dominican orders, but in more recent times other orders (*see* ORDER), such as the Redemptorists (Congregation of the Most Holy Redeemer, founded 1732 by St Alphonsus Liguori) and Jesuits (Society of Jesus, founded 1534 by St Ignatius Loyola), have distinguished themselves in the conducting of such popular visitations < L *mission*, F *mission*. Kavanagh, *Tarry Flynn*, 37: "And what did he decide to do but make arrangements for a big Mission to the parishioners by the Order of Redemptorists who were such specialists in sex sins"; Leonard, *Out After Dark*, 45: "My chance came some weeks later when the Redemptorists arrived for the yearly mission."

mitch /mɪʧ/ also **mich** *v*., to play truant from school < E dial. (origin obscure; *Chambers English Dictionary* comments: 'perhaps from OFr *muchier, mucier,* to hide, lurk'). Head, *Hic et Ubique*, 113: "I did creep in like a michear"; Joyce, 'An Encounter' (*Dubliners*, 20): "With Leo Dillon and a boy named Mahony I planned a day's miching."

mo /mʌ/ *possessive adj*. in interjections: my < Ir. 'Mo bhrón' /mʌ'vroːn/, alas. 'Mo léan' /mʌ'leːn/, 'mo léan géar' /mʌ'leːn'geːr/, alas (SOM, Kerry). 'Mo léir' /mʌ'leːr/, alas, woe is me < Ir.

mo chac ort /mə'xækʌrt̪/ insult: my excrement on you (MK, Galway) < Ir.

mogall /'mʌgəl/ *n*., a husk; a cluster of people (KM, Kerry) < Ir.

mogóir /'mʌgoːr/ *n*., hip (fruit of wild rose) < Ir. 'Let's go out picking the mogóir; I want to try my hand at making wine from it.'

mogolyeen-mire, *see* MEIDHREACH.

moiley /ˈmɔiliː/ also **mail, maileen, meeleen, moileen, mooley, moulleen** a hornless cow (SOM, Kerry) < Ir MAOLAÍ. 'They only ever have moiley cows up there, so they can eat the grass in between the rocks' (KM, Kerry); 'In Canada and in Ireland a hornless cow is called a mooley' (Hayden and Hartog, 783). Carleton, 'Shane Fadh's Wedding' (*Six Irish Tales*, 179): "Mary is to have her grandfather's sixty guineas, and the two *moulleens* that her uncle Jack left her four years ago has brought her a good stock for any farm"; Muldoon, 'Cherish the Ladies (*FDA*, 3, 1415): "There may be time enough | for him to fill their drinking-trough | and run his eye over | his three mooley heifers."

móinéar /moːˈneːr/ *n.*, a meadow (SOM, Kerry) < Ir.

moing /mʌŋ/ *n.*, an overgrown swamp, a fen; a wet field (Limerick); useless land < Ir.

móinteán /moːnˈʧɔːn/ *n.*, rough mountain land; land with rough, coarse grass (SOM, Kerry); cut-away bog; partly reclaimed land < Ir. 'FAITH, then, there'll be many a day's work picking stones if he wants to make anything out of that móinteán' (KG, Kerry).

mollafoosdar, *see* MALLAFOOSTHER.

monabhar /ˈmʌnəvər/ *n.*, murmuring; the sounds of a conversation that is almost out of hearing (SOM, Kerry); the sound of a stream < Ir.

moneen /ˈmoːniːn/ also **móinín** *n.*, a grassy patch in a bog (MK, Galway); a small field near a house for holding cows at milking-time < Ir. 'The cows are up at the moneen waiting to be milked; will you go up quick and do it before I have to go up myself!'

mónóg /ˈmoːnoːg/ *n.*, bogberry, cranberry < Ir. 'Don't eat those mónógs: they're very bitter' (BC, Meath).

monstrance /ˈmɑnstrəns/ *n.*, a vessel in which the Blessed Sacrament is exposed to view at BENEDICTION and EXPOSITION or carried in procession < mediaeval L *monstrantia*.

month's mind /mʌnt̪sˈmaind/ *n.phr.*, a Mass said for a deceased person one month or thereabouts after the death, attended by the family, friends and others who attended the funeral (and WAKE, if there was one) < *month* + *mind*, memory. 'His daughter's coming back from the States for the month's mind. She can't settle at all, poor thing: first the mother, and now the father gone' (KG, Kerry). Joyce, *Finnegans Wake*, 460. 29–30: "will smile on my fourinhanced twelvemonthsmind."

mooch (about) /muːʧ(əˈbaut)/ *n., v.,* to idle in a suspicious manner, to loaf about; to be on the look-out for picking up something for nothing < E dial. *mooch* < OF *mucher*. 'Stop mooching around the house and get out and do some work.'

mooley /ˈmuːliː/, *see* MOILEY.

mópán /moːˈpɔːn/ *n.* (*colloq.*), a person lacking in common sense or in drive (SOM, Kerry) < E *mope* + Ir suffix *-án*.

mopsy /ˈmɑpsi/ *n.*, a doll; a term of affection for a child < E dial.

mór /moːr/ *adj.*, big (SOM, Kerry) < Ir.

mórálach /moːrˈɔːləx/ *adj.*, boastful; haughty, conscious of one's own importance (SOM, Kerry) < Ir.

mórdháil /ˈmoːrɣɔːl/ *n.*, pomp; pride; boasting < Ir. 'Such mórdháil and airs there was at the Christening – you'd think they were really big people, instead of just like ourselves' (TJ, Sligo).

morode /məˈroːd/ *v.*, to travel about in search of plunder < E dial. *moroder* (marauder). 'There you go, moroding all over the COUNTRY, and your mother out of her mind with worry for you.'

mortaller /ˈmɔːrtlər/ *n.* (*colloq.*), a mortal sin (such as it would be obligatory to confess in CONFESSION). 'Mammy, she did a mortaller because she used a bad word' (Dublin).

mórtas /ˈmoːrt̪əs/ *n.*, pride; haughtiness, boastfulness (SOM, Kerry) < 'Mórtas cine', pride in one's people.

mórtasach /ˈmoːrt̪əsəx/ *adj.*, proud; given to bragging about one's possessions (MK, Galway) < Ir.

moryah, *see* MARYAH.

mot /mɑh/ *n.*, a girl, a female companion; 'the mot', the female in one's life, 'the little one'; 'fig. of a very small creature' (Poole, Forth and Bargy, s.v. 'mot, mothe') < E dial. mot (OE mot, ME mote) n., an atom; fig. (suggesting something precious, the object of great affection, etc.) a small creature (e.g. 'a mot of a lamb', a little lamb); the connection with Irish *maith*, *n.* and *adj.*, seems unlikely. 'She's my mot; what do you think of her?' (Dublin); 'Along we went, me, the mot, and the mot's mother' (Waterford); 'Tell me now: is Michael motting?' = Has Michael a regular girl-friend? (ML, Dublin) (colloquially invented forms such as 'motting' are a feature of HE); Beale gives 'mot, mott. The female pudend: Army mid-C.20. "Her big hairy mott", in a mock-Irish accent, was a pun on the insect *moth*.'

mothall /ˈmʌhəl/ *n.*, an unkempt mop of hair (SOM, Kerry) < Ir.

mothar /ˈmʌhər/ *n.*, an over-growth of briars and shrubs, a thicket (SOM, Kerry) < Ir.

mouldy /ˈmauldi/ *adj.* (*colloq.*), drunk (cf. E dial. *mould(y)*, ill-tempered, testy). 'John was mouldy drunk last night' (Dublin).

moulleen, *see* MOILEY.

mountainy /ˈmauntəni/ *adj.*, living in the mountains (EH, Wicklow) < E dial. (OF *montaigne*, + *-y*) (*ODEE*: 'denoting "having the character of" etc., OE *-ig*') 'He's the mountainy man saved the sheep' (note the omission of the relative pronoun 'that' before the verb, a common feature of HE); 'Marry a mountainy woman and you'll marry the whole mountain' (saying). Somerville and Ross, *Some Experiences of an Irish RM,* 311: "He's one of those mountainy men that live up in the hill behind Aussolas"; Leonard, *Out After Dark*, 89: "'That fellow's a SLEEVEEN,' he said. It was a pejorative word meaning a little mountainy fellow, as treacherous as he was unpredictable."

mouth-music /ˈmaut̪mjuːzɪk/ *n.phr.,* LILTING with the tongue, 'dowdelling' (vocal accompaniment for dancer) (DB, Cork).

moxie /mɑksi/ *adj.* (*colloq.*), large; plentiful, a lot (KMG, Dublin) (origin obscure). 'There was a moxie-load of them (KD, Dublin).

moya, *see* MARYAH.

muc /mʌk/ *n.*, a pig < Ir. 'Muc i mála,' a pig in a poke. 'Muc ar mala,' a scowl (lit. a pig on the brow). 'Ar mhuin na muice,' very well off, doing well (lit. on the pig's back). 'PUS muice', a permanent whiner (SOM, Kerry) (lit. pig-face); 'Is iad na muca ciúine a itheann an triosc' (proverb), It's the quiet pigs that eat the swill. Michelburne, *Ireland Preserved*, 145: "He does go and bring home de Seep and de Muck."

múchadh /ˈmuːxə/ *n.*, congestion of the bronchial passages; asthma (SOM, Kerry) < Ir. 'They say the poor child has got a touch of múchadh, but, please God, it's not too serious a dose' (KG, Kerry). *See* PLÚCHADH.

mugadán /ˈmʌgəd̪ɔːn/ *n.*, a pretentious youth; an 'OLD-FASHIONED' youth, trying to be a man before his time (MK, Galway) < Ir. 'That mugadán was telling me how to use a fishing rod; well, I can tell you, I told him where to get off!'

muic-iris /ˈmʌkɪrɪʃ/ *n.*, the fastener of a basket on the back; the handle of a basket (KM, Kerry) < Ir.

muin, in the phr. 'ar mhuin na muice,' *see* MUC.

muinéal /mɪˈneːl/ *n.*, the back (SOM, Kerry) < Ir.

muirnín, *see* AVOURNEEN, MAVOURNEEN.

muise, *see* MUSHA.

mullach /ˈmʌləx/ *n.*, the top (of a hill) (SOM, Kerry) < Ir.

mullán /mʌˈlɔːn/ *n.*, a heap (of large stones, turf, corn, etc.). SOM, Kerry) < Ir.

mullock /ˈmʌlək/ *n., v.,* slovenly work, a muddle; to idle about, to mess about < E dial. (OE *myl*, OE *-oc*) 'Stop your mullocking and do the MESSAGES!'

mulvather /mʌl'væd̪ər/ *v.*, to confuse, bamboozle; to act the fool < E dial. (origin obscure; the word seems to be restricted to HE usage). 'I knew the villian [*sic*] was mulvathered' (Dublin). Stoker, *The Snake's Pass*, 21: "an' he was so much mulvathered at the Shnake presumin' to shtay, afther he tould thim all to go, that for a while he didn't think it quare that he could sphake at all."

múnlach /'munləx/ *n.*, slurry (liquid manure); stinking mud; scum on stagnant water; the moist section of a dung-heap (SOM, Kerry) < Ir. 'Don't fall into the múnlach – the smell of it would knock you down!'

munya, munia /'mʌnjə/ *adj.* (*colloq.*), excellent; lovely, attractive (origin obscure). 'I saw a munia girl cusin' [walking] down the road yesterday' (HJ, Wexford); 'Seán is a munya hurler' (COL, Wexford).

Murcha /'mʌrəxə/ *n.*, severe treatment; a bad fright; great trouble < Murcha Ó Briain, 'Murcha na dTóiteán' (Murcha of the Burnings), Earl of Inchiquin, described by Dinneen as 'a terrorist of the Civil War'.

murdal /'mʌrd̪əl/, *n.*, murder < Ir (variant of *murdar*, murder). 'Míle murdal', uproar, confusion; violent outbreak < Ir *míle*, a thousand + *murdal*. 'There was míle murdal outside the dance hall last night' (SOM, Kerry). *See* MÍLE MURDAR.

muríneach /mʌ'riːnəx/ *n.*, marram (a type of grass, used in some parts of the country for thatching) < Ir. *See* CIB; SEISC.

murlach /'mʌrləx/ *n.*, a lagoon (MK, Galway); a lake near the sea < Ir.

musha /'mʌʃə/ also **maise, mhuise** /'wʌʃə/, /'wɪʃə/ *int.*, indeed; well, well; is that so?; let it be < Ir *muise* (< *más ea*, if so). Joyce, 'Ivy Day in the Committee Room' (*Dubliners*, 136): "Musha, God be with them times!"; *Finnegans Wake*, 427. 33–4: "Musha, beminded of us out there in Cockpit." *See* WISHA.

musicianer /mjuː'zɪʃənər/ *n.* (*colloq.*), a musician; a player on any musical instrument < E dial.

mustar /'mʌst̪ər/ *n.*, arrogance, pride, putting on airs (MK, Galway) < Ir. 'Look at him, the mustar of him, with his nose in the air.'

mustrach /'mʌst̪rəx/ *adj.*, pompous, haughty (SOM, Kerry) < Ir. 'A mustrach little man'; 'Mary was very mustrach at the son's wedding' (SOM, Kerry).

mútálaí /'muː't̪ɔːliː/ *n.*, a fumbler (KM, Kerry) < Ir.

mútóg /'muːt̪oːg/ *n.*, a finger-stall; a muzzle (KM, Kerry) < Ir. 'I lost the mútóg in the bog.'

N

naavo /ˈnævo/ *n.* (*colloq.*), a secret hiding-place, 'the sort of place you'd hide your BUTTS from your da' (KD, Dublin) (origin obscure).

ná bac leis /nɔːˈbɑklɛʃ/ also **nabocklesh** etc. *int.*, never mind; it's of no account; don't take any notice (MH, Clare) < Ir. 'Ná bac leis, a Sheáin, you'll get your chance another day.' Joyce, *Ulysses*, 314.32: "*Na bacleis*, says the citizen, letting on to be modest" (*see* LET ON).

nádúr /nɔːˈd̪uːr/ *n.*, affection (KG, Kerry) < Ir. 'I always had a great nádúr for him.'

nádúrach /nɔːˈd̪uːrəx/ *adj.*, kindly, helpful, good-natured < Ir. *See* NÁDÚR.

naggin /ˈnægən/ also **noggin** /ˈnɑgən/ *n.*, a small mug or drinking-vessel; 'a wooden vessel made of tiny staves, one of which is longer than the others and forms the handle' (Martin, 176); a measure of drink (equalling two glasses) < E (origin obscure). 'He had a lot more than a naggin of whiskey when I saw him' (BC, Meath); 'She has more than two noggins to wash' (proverbial saying, when an eighteenth or nineteenth child is born). Griffin, *The Collegians*, 187: "There isn't a noggin o' genteel blood in the veins o' your whole seed, breed, an' generation"; 'Finnegan's Wake' (song): "when a noggin of whiskey flew at him"; Healy, *Nineteen Acres*, 28: "I had my billy-can, my naggin of milk and my bacon and egg sandwiches." *See* PIGGIN.

naggy /ˈnægi/ *adj.*, peevish, irritable, prone to bouts of bad temper; always finding fault with someone or something < E dial. (origin uncertain, but there are parallels in Scandinavian languages). 'Don't mind her: that oul one is naggy with everybody. That's what keeps her going' (Meath).

naimhdeach /ˈnaudəx/ *adj.*, cross, peevish < Ir. 'That old naimhdeach one in the shop' (Kerry).

naíonán /ˈniːnɔːn/ *n.*, an infant (SOM, Kerry) < Ir. 'Look at the wee little naíonán in her arms' (KG, Kerry).

náire /ˈnɔːrə/ *n., int.*, shame; disgrace, scandal < Ir. 'Mo náire,' shame on you' (SOM, Kerry).

namplush /ˈnæmplʌʃ/ *n.*, the state of not being ready, at a disadvantage, nonplussed < E dial. < L *non plus*, not more, no further. 'Don't namplush me now – I'm trying to think what did I do with the key.' *See* AMPLUSH.

naomh /niːv/ *n.*, saint < Ir. 'Comaoine na Naomh', the Communion of Saints (SOM, Kerry) (i.e. the union of the Faithful on earth (the Church Militant), the souls in Purgatory (the Church Suffering), and the Blessed in Heaven (the Church Triumphant).

naomhóg /neːˈvoːg/ *n.*, a curach, coracle < Ir. Egan, 'Dooneen Pier' (*Peninsula*, 54): "returning in a naomhóg from the Blaskets."

naosc /niːsk/ *n.*, a snipe (SOM, Kerry) < Ir.

naprún /nɑpruːn/ *n.*, apron (SOM, Kerry) < Ir (the Ir form 'naprún' is a straight borrowing from E *apron*; the ModE form apron derives from ME *napron* (< OF *naperon*), which gave 'a napron', later through mis-division altered to 'an apron' (cf. 'an umpire' < ME *noumpere* < OF *noumpere* (*non, peer*)).

nasc /næsk/ *n.*, a noose; a collar; a fetter (SOM, Kerry); a chain around a cow's horns; a spancel for milking < Ir. 'Tie a nasc around the cow's neck' (SOM, Kerry).

national school /næʃnɜlskuːl/ *n.*, a system of primary education introduced in Ireland in 1831, which superseded the haphazard, informal but remarkably beneficial HEDGE-SCHOOLS; the polymath scholar P. W. Joyce (1827–1914), a product of the hedge-schools, was himself appointed a teacher by the Commissioners of National Education before he was twenty years of age < (O)F *nation* + *-al* (suffix representing L *-alis*), OE *scolu*. 'Thomas told me he went into the old national school before they knocked it down and collected all the old ink-pots from the desks – they were all made of delf, he said'; 'Mrs Reilly was a national school teacher – you'd know it by her lovely writing.' Kilroy, *The Big Chapel*, 14: "'The National Schools should be closed down altogether.' 'The National Schools is godless schools'"; McCourt, *Angela's Ashes*, 115: "there are boys in Leamy's National School who go to school barefoot on bitter days."

National University of Ireland /næʃnəljuːnəˈvɛrsətiːəv ˈairlənd/ *n.*, founded in 1908, with University College, Dublin, granted a charter as a constituent college < (O)F *nation* + *-al* (suffix representing L *-alis*), (O)F *université*, OE *Irland*, The name is sometimes abbreviated to 'the National', to distinguish it from 'Trinity' (TRINITY COLLEGE, Dublin). 'No, he went to National, but his wife went to Trinity' (Dublin).

nawbocklish, *see* NÁ BAC LEIS.

neamhní /ˈnævˈniː/ *n.*, nothing; very little (SOM, Kerry) < Ir.

neamhspleách /næːvˈsplɔːx/ *adj.*, independent (Carlow) < Ir. 'The money from her father made her neamhspleách at last; pity she's a bit too old to enjoy it.'

neantóg /njænˈt̪oːg/ *n.*, a nettle (SOM, Kerry); fig. a cranky person < Ir. 'I got stung by a neantóg and cured by a COPÓG'; 'She's a right neantóg, that one, since the brother came back from England.'

near /niːr/ *adj.* (*colloq.*), stingy, miserly < E dial. < OE *neah* (comparative of *neah*, nigh). 'He's very near' (PR, Mayo).

neb /nɛb/ *n.*, a bird's beak; the mouth; the face < E dial. < OE *nebb,* beak, face. 'Get that neb of yours out of my sight' (KG, Kerry).

Nelly /ˈnɛli/, /ˈnɪli/ *n.,* a woman's name (of a type that may suggest a maid-servant), in the expression 'up in Nelly's room behind the wallpaper' (or 'behind the wardrobe,' etc.), a sarcastic reply to an exasperating question. 'Where's my cap?' – 'Up in Nelly's room behind the wallpaper.'

newance /ˈnjuəns/ *n.*, a novelty < E dial.

níl focal bréige agam /niːlˈfʌkəl ˈbreːgɑgəm/ *phr.*, I've no news < Ir (lit. I haven't a false word) (KM, Kerry).

nimh /nɪv/ *n.*, poison < Ir. 'Nimh sa bhfeoil', 'bad blood'. 'They have the nimh sa bhfeoil for one another' (SOM, Kerry).

no /noː/ *adv*. Used more rarely in HE than in SE, because there is no separate Ir word for 'no'; in answer to a question, the verb used in the question is repeated: 'Ar léigh tú an leabhar?' (did you read the book?) – 'Níor léigh (mé)' ((I) did not read). Gerard Manley Hopkins noted (N. White, *Hopkins*, 370): "Everyone in the country parts and most markedly the smallest children, if asked a question, answer it without yes or no. 'Were you at school on Friday?' 'I was, sir.'"

nocht /nʌxt̪/ *adj.,* bare < Ir. 'Cosnochta', *adj.,* barefoot (SOM, Kerry).

noggin, *see* NAGGIN.

nóiméad /ˈnoːmeːd̪/ *n.*, a minute, in the phr. 'fan nóiméad,' wait a minute < Ir. 'Fan nóiméad, will you – can't you see I'm talking to somebody!' 'Nóimitín' /ˈnoːmətiːn/ *n.*, an instant; a minute < Ir. (dimin. of *nóiméad*). 'Just wait a nóimitín!'

nóiníní /noː'niːniː/ *n.pl.*, daisies (SOM, Kerry) < Ir.

Nollaig /'nʌlɪg/ *n.*, Christmas < Ir < L *natalis*. 'Nollaig na mBan', Little Christmas (6 January) (SOM, Kerry) < Ir (lit. Women's Christmas).

noodenaddy /'nudinædi/ *n.*, a dithering person; someone who is unable to make up their mind (KM, Kerry) < Ir *niúide neáide* (also *niúdar neádar*). 'What a noodenaddy she is!'; 'My mother always called him a noodenaddy, but he has his own business now, so it proves people can change.'

nor /nɔːr/ *conj.,* than < E dial. (cf. also Ir *ná*, nor, than: 'is airde mise ná Síle,' I am taller than Síle). 'He's bigger nor me'; 'She's worse nor she looks'; 'Better come at the end of a feast nor the beginning of a quarrel.' Stoker, *The Snake's Pass,* 18: "He was more nor tin [ten] times as big as any shnake"; O'Casey, *The Shadow of a Gunman*, act I, 96: "*Mrs Henderson*: Don't be put out, Mr Davoren, we won't keep you more nor a few minutes."

nough /nʌf/ *n.*, plenty (by apheresis from *enough, adj.*). As there is no indefinite article in Irish, there was sometimes confusion over the indefinite article in English when a word begins with an unstressed vowel /ə/. 'Enough' was regarded as 'a nough' (reinforced by the Ir construction 'tá mo dhóthain agam,' lit. I have my plenty). 'They've had their nough' (PR, Mayo). Healy, *Nineteen Acres*, 70: "It was Kitty who told me she had gone with her in the pony and trap to see my mother off and "she cried her 'nough" between the bottom of the BOREEN and the cottage at the top of the hill."

novena /nʌ'viːnə/ *n.*, nine consecutive days' public or private devotion < mediaeval L. 'If you come to the novena you'll get a plenary INDULGENCE – I think that's what the priest said' (JMF, Cavan); O'Brien, *A Pagan Place*, 34: "If you made a novena to St Theresa and were given a rose during the nine days of it, it meant your intention would be granted."

nuaíocht /'nuːiːəxt̪/ *n.*, newness, novelty < Ir. 'Go maire tú do nuaíocht' (saying), may you enjoy your new acquisition (SOM, Kerry).

O

-o, *familiarising suffix*, especially common in Dublin colloquial speech. 'Defo' (definitely); 'morto' (mortified, very embarrassed); 'mono' (monastery, house of the religious order attached to a boys' school); 'peno' (penalty kick in soccer); 'seco' (secondary school); 'Confo' (one's CONFIRMATION); 'CORPO'; also with place-names: 'Chapo' (Chapelizod); 'Phoeno' (Phoenix Park); and with personal names: 'Dekko' (Declan), 'Jacko'; 'Gaybo'; etc. (KD, Dublin).

ó /oː/ *n.*, grandson; descendant < Ir. In the first hereditary surnames (*c.* 10th century onwards), *Ó* (grandson) was prefixed to the name of a grandfather or remoter ancestor. 'Some families dropped the O from their names when times were bad, and now some people have put it back and others not, even in the same family; it's all very confusing' (KG, Kerry). Joyce, *Finnegans Wake,* 543. 19–20: "strutting oges and swaggering macks." *See* MAC.

oanshagh, *see* ÓINSEACH.

ócáid /oːˈkɔːʤ/ *n.*, a fool; an awkward person (KM, Kerry) < Ir. 'What an ócáid he is – he sold the cow too cheap.'

och /ɑx/, /ɑk/ *int.* expressing sorrow, woe (KG, Kerry) < Ir. 'Och, it's an awful thing to lose her daughter like that!'

ochón /əxˈoːn/ also **ochone** *int.*, cry of lamentation: alas (SOM, Kerry) < Ir. 'The woman used be ochóning at the WAKE.' See KEENING.

ockster, **see oxter**.

odious /ˈoːʤəs/ *adj., adv.,* terrible, dreadful; enormous; greatly (the HE pronunciation follows that of the combination 'di' in Irish; cf. EEJIT). 'That match was holy odious [very difficult] for us'(Cavan).

of /ɑv/ *prep.*, frequently used in place of SE 'on'. Griffin, *The Collegians*, 117: "Poll made a vow again' talkin' of a Tursday, bekeys it was of a Tursday her first child died"; Joyce, 'The Sisters' (*Dubliners*, 16): "If we could only get one of them new-fangled carriages . . . and drive out the three of us together of a Sunday evening"; *Finnegans Wake*, 399.21: "*It was of a wet good Friday*."

offerings /ˈɑfərɪŋz/ *n.pl.*, gifts made to the clergy of the Catholic Church for duties performed, e.g. saying Mass for a deceased relative. The term is particularly applied to the money given to the clergy for saying a funeral Mass. This is collected in various ways, according to local custom: in one area, after the Mass members of the congregation walk up the aisle to a table near the coffin, with male members of the deceased's family standing by, on which they place their monetary gifts; those who cannot be present send their offerings, and the names and the amounts are read out. 'The more popular the deceased, the greater the offerings paid' (POC, Cavan). 'That was a big funeral; there'll be a pile of offerings on the table, you can be sure of that!' (TF, Cavan). Binchy, *Firefly Summer*, 271: "'No need to give an offering, Papers,' Father Hogan had said gruffly. 'We'll be saying Mass for her anyway.'"

office men, *see* WAKE.

óg /oːg/ *adj.*, young < Ir. 'CAILÍN óg', a young girl. 'She's quite a cailín óg.' 'Brian óg', young Brian; Brian the bachelor. Joyce, *Finnegans Wake*, 543.20–1: "strutting oges and swaggering macks"; Kavanagh, 'The Christmas Mummers' (*Collected Poems*, 112: "*Sean Og O'Gum* | Here comes I Sean Og O'Gum." *See* MAC; Ó: ÓGÁNACH.

ógaí /ˈoːgiː/ *adj.*, junior < Ir (variant of ÓG). 'John ógaí', John, son of John (SOM, Kerry).

ógánach /oːˈgɔːnəx/ *n.*, a young person, a lad; a crafty rascal < Ir. 'He turned out to be a right ógánach; look what he did over that legacy!' (KG, Kerry).

ogham /oːm/ *n.*, an alphabet for Old Irish derived from the roman alphabet, employing twenty-five characters made of straight lines meeting or crossing; cf. *ODEE*: 'traditionally assoc. with the legendary name *Ogma* of the inventor of signs for a secret language (cf. *Ogmias*, name (acc. to Lucian) of a Gaulish deity who presided over language or eloquence) < ModIr ogham, OIr ogum.' Joyce, *Finnegans Wake*, 89.30–1: "Which was meant in a shirt of two shifts macoghamade."

oíche /iːhə/ *n.*, night < Ir. 'Oíche Nollag,' Christmas Eve (SOM, Kerry).

óige /ˈoːəgə/ *n.*, youth < Ir. 'An Óige', Irish youth hostels association. 'Mol an óige agus fiocfaidh sí' (proverb), youth reacts well to praise.

oigheann /ain/ *n.*, a pot-oven (a flat-bottomed vessel used on an open fire for baking and roasting) (SOM, Kerry) < Ir. *See* BASTABLE.

oighear /air/ *n.*, ice; wind-gall (chaffing behind knees from wind-chill and rain) (SOM, Kerry) < Ir. *See* OIGHREACH.

oighreach /'airəx/ *n.*, wind-gall (*see* OIGHEAR); chapped hands or feet (MOB, Mayo); cracked skin from being in bog; chapped hands or feet caused by alternate wet and dry conditions (or dirt) (JF, Cavan) < Ir. 'My hands are destroyed with the oighreach' (SL, Mayo).

óinseach /'oːnʃəx/ also **oanshagh, oonshugh, ownshook** *n.*, a fool (said of a woman, but can sometimes refer to a man: see Kallen, 1996, 120); a silly person; a girl who goes astray < Ir. 'She's a confirmed óinseach' (she is foolish beyond redemption) (SOM, Kerry); 'Look at that poor oanshagh – she'll never learn!' (KG, Kerry). Kickham, *Knocknagow*, 53: "'ARRA WHIST, Phil,' was her only reply. 'Don't be makin' an oonshugh uv yourself."

óinseachán /'oːnʃəxən/ n., 'a more intensive form of ÓINSEACH' (SOM, Kerry) < Ir.

óinsín /oːn'ʃiːn/ *n.*, a foolish, giddy woman (KM, Kerry) < Ir. 'Don't be such an óinsín and go back to him; you could do much worse!'

Oireachtas /'ɪrəxt̪əs/, /ə'rɑxt̪əs/ *n.*, the legislature of Ireland, comprising DÁIL ÉIREANN and SEANAD ÉIREANN < Ir.

ojus, *see* ODIOUS.

ól /oːl/ *n.,* drink < Ir. 'Ólta', *adj.*, drunk (SOM, Kerry) < Ir.

olagón /ʌlə'goːn/ *n.*, lament, wail, crying aloud < Ir. 'Did you ever hear such olagóning?' (SOM, Kerry).

old-fashioned /'oːldfæʃənd/ *adj.*, precocious; trying to act like an adult.

omadhawn, ommadhawn, *see* AMADÁN.

on /ɑn/ *prep*. 1. Indicating loss or injury: 'He lost my knife on me'; 'He broke the stick on me'. (i.e. he put me to the loss of my stick by breaking it); 'The cow died on me. All the hens are laying out on me. The cock was stolen on me' (LUB, Dublin). Hogan notes: 'Anglo-Irish [i.e. HE] has these constructions chiefly from Ir. ar'). Stephens, *The Crock of Gold*, 117: "Do tell me now – What did he do on you?"; 118: "the rest of the children died on me." Joyce, *Finnegans Wake*, 380.25–6: "he took to his pallyass with the weeping eczema for better and worse until he went under the grass quilt on us." 2. Following the use of prepositional pronouns, which are commonly used for a variety of connotations in Irish, HE tends to add a pronoun where it would be used in Irish, e.g. to indicate possession: 'Put your coat on you' (SE 'Put your coat on'). Joyce, *Ulysses*, 329.27–8: "and he quite excited with his DUNDUCKETY MUD-COLOURED mug on him"; Healy, *Nineteen Acres*, 127: "sure I remember when my own man went on me"; Johnston, *Shadows on Our Skin*, 115: "She's even lifted the shoes on me."

one and one /ˈwʌnənˈwʌn/, /ˈwɑnənˈwɑn/ *n.phr.*, fish and chips (from the order 'one and one' in a chip shop, i.e. one portion of fish and one portion of chips) (Dublin).

only /ˈoːnli/ *adv*. 1. Used loosely as an intensive. 'The music was only famous' (was really good); 'You're only gorgeous' (Dublin). Delaney, *The Sins of the Mothers*, 508: "'Her face,' they said afterwards, 'it was only fierce.'" 2. Used in the sense of 'but' in question formations. 'What did he want only to get his own money back?'; 'Who should walk in only her long-lost daughter'; 'He never gives me peace, only nagging at me night, noon and morning' (LUB, Dublin). Griffin, *The Collegians*, 50: "Who should he see only Dan Dawley"; Kavanagh, *Tarry Flynn*, 78: ". . . who should appear coming slowly around the bed only Mary"; Joyce, *Ulysses*, 297.7–9: "who was sitting up there in the corner that I hadn't seen snoring drunk, blind to the world, only Bob Doran."

on the pig's back, *see* MUC.

ór /oːr/ n., gold < Ir. 'Ór na cruinne', all the wealth in the world (SOM, Kerry).

orange[1] /ˈɑrənʤ/ *n*., in the phr. 'He'd peel an orange in his pocket,' said of a person who is very mean.

Orange[2] /ˈɑrənʤ/ *adj*., from the party colour of the house of Oranje-Nassau, now that of the Orange Order, whose members wear an orange sash to commemorate King William of Orange (1650–1702). McGuinness, *Observe the Sons of Ulster Marching towards the Somme*, part IV (*FDA*, 3, 1272): "*Pyper*: What's missing? *Anderson*: Your badge of honour. (*Anderson hands out an Orange sash to Pyper*)."

orlach /ˈʌrləx/ *n*., an inch (SOM, Kerry) < Ir.

ould /auld/ also oul /aul/ *adj*., HE pronunciations of 'old' (preserving the influence of 17th-century English). 'You oul EEJIT, will you shut up and sit down!' (JB, Kildare). Banim, *The Boyne Water*, 215: "An ould follower o' yours had the impudence to break faith with us"; Trollope, *The Kellys and the O'Kellys*, 514: "I'm sick of the nasty ould place."

ouns /aunz/ *n.pl*., in the phr. 'tare and ouns,' a contraction of '(Christ's) tears and wounds,' a mild expletive. The vowel sound in 'tare' retains the older pronunciation represented by the spelling 'ea' (cf. tea /te:/ etc.). *See* TARE AND 'OUNS.

out /aut/ *adv.*, used in various non-standard verbal formations. 'I slept it out,' I overslept; 'Give out the money!' – 'Divil an out you'll get given from me!' (you won't be given a penny by me).

oven /'ʌvən/ *n.*, a pot for cooking bread or cakes, covered with a lid, with red coals placed on top < OE *ofen*. The pot was hung from a crane or hook over the open fire; alternatively, 'the oven was set in a "greesh" and the lid was covered with more of the same' (SOC, Cavan). *See* BASTABLE.

over-right /oːvər'rait/ *adj.*, opposite, in front of (perhaps from Ir compound prep. *os comhair*, which sounds like *cóir*, right). 'Over-right the house there was the hen-house'; 'He did it over-right me' (in full view of me).

ownshook, *see* ÓINSEACH.

owze /auz/ *v.*, "to take water out of a pool, etc., with a bowl shaped shovel, as 'to owze the horsepond' if the bottom wanted cleaning up. Boys 'owze' pools to catch eels" (Browne, 135). The *EDD* s.v 'ouse' gives 'to empty out liquid; to bale out a boat' but does not cite an Irish occurrence; for 'owze' the *OED* gives 'obs. form of ooze' < OE *wesan*, *v.*, to steep, soak; to ooze, suppurate.

oxter /'ɑkst̪ər/, /'ɑkʃt̪ər/ also **oxther, ockster** *n.*, armpit (LUB, Dublin) < E dial. < OE *ohsta* (Hogan notes: 'a Scottish and Northern word'). 'Why don't you carry it under your oxter THE WAY you'll be able to bring the bucket as well' (TF, Cavan). Shaw, *John Bull's Other Island*, act II (*FDA*, 2, 441): "*Cornelius:* You can take the sammin [salmon] under your oxther."

P

pad /pæd/ *n.,* a path, pathway < E dial. < Du. 'Keep away off the pad, or the adders will get ye.' Heaney, 'Midnight (*Wintering Out*, 45: "The pads are lost or | Retrieved by small vermin."

Paddhereen /ˈpædʒriːn/ *n.*, the Rosary, which is a string of beads consisting of five DECADES, each of ten small beads and one larger bead, with the addition of crucifix and three small beads (also **padhren**, **padareen, paddhereen**) < Ir *paidrín.* The tradition that the Rosary was revealed to St Dominic (1170–1221), who encouraged its use, is unproved, but special devotion to the Rosary has always been associated with the Dominican order. Montague, 'The Living and the Dead' (*Collected Poems*, 17): "instead of a worn rosary | I tell these metal keys."

Paddhereeen Partaugh, Family Rosary < Ir. The practice of saying the Rosary in a family group was encouraged by Fr Patrick Peyton, 'the Rosary priest', born in Carracastle, Co. Mayo, in 1909, and, it is claimed, descended from a French soldier who survived the surrender of the French force at Ballinamuck, Co. Longford, in 1798.

Paddy's Day /ˈpædiːzdeː/ *n.* (*colloq.*), St Patrick's Day (17 March). 'What are you doing for Paddy's Day?' (MF, Washington).

padhsán /paiˈsɔːn/ *n.*, a delicate-looking person; a sickly, non-thriving child (or chicken) < Ir. 'The poor little padhsán is getting a hard run for his money' (SOM, Kerry).

páideog /ˈpɔːdʒoːg/ *n.*, a light made from a taper; a rushlight (KM, Kerry); fig. a person with careless table manners < Ir. 'What a páideog you are! Look at the mess you've made – just like a baby!'

páinteach /ˈpɔːntʃəx/ *n.*, a sleek, well-fed person or animal (KM, Kerry); a fat, heavy child; a large rabbit, rat, etc. < Ir. 'What a páinteach of a child she is; look at the condition [plumpness] on her!'

páirc /pɔirk/ *n.,* a field; grazing-land (SOM, Kerry) < Ir *páirc*, field of grass (as distinct from *gort*, a tilled field).

pairceen /ˈpɔirkiːn/ *n.*, a small field < Ir. *páircín* (dimin. of PÁIRC). 'I hear he's looking to sell the pairceen' (SL, Mayo).

páiste /ˈpɔːʃʧə/ *n.*, a child (SOM, Kerry) < Ir. 'She has only the one páiste and she has him spoilt rotten' (KG, Kerry).

páistín /pɔːʃʧiːn/ *n.* (*dimin.*), a small child (SOM, Kerry) < Ir.

pait /pæt/ *n.*, a leather bottle; fig. a chubby child (MK, Galway) < Ir. 'You'll have to do something with that pait of a child; he can hardly run, he's so fat'; 'She had the port poured into a pait, so I was a little worried about drinking it, but it tasted fine.'

páit /pɔːʧ/ *n.*, a fool, a simpleton < Ir. 'The poor páit never could hold down a job, no matter how hard he tried' (ML, Mayo).

Pale, the /peːl/ *n.*, that part of Ireland that was (figuratively) paled off as being under the jurisdiction of the English crown < ME *pal*, a stake (cf. 'paling', a fence of stakes). 'They think everyone is a CULCHIE who wasn't born inside the Pale' (KG, Kerry). Joyce, *Finnegans Wake*, 42.34: "a brace of palesmen."

paltóg /ˈpɑlt̪oːg/ also **pollthogue** *n.*, a blow; a blow with a stick; 'a big word' (MOB, Mayo) < Ir. 'He struck him a few paltógs and that quietened him' (SOM, Kerry).

pampooties /pɑmˈpuːtiːz/ *n.*, shoes of undressed cow-skin sewn together and tied across the instep, formerly worn in the Aran Islands (the term is not used locally, where they are called *bróga úrleathair*, rawhide shoes) (origin uncertain; the *OED* notes: 'possibly a corruption of *papoose, papauche*, or Sp. *babucha* . . . ' and refers to a suggestion in the *Folklore Journal*, vol. 2 (1884), 261, that they were introduced to the islands by an East Indies ship-captain who settled there).

panada /pəˈnæːdə/ *n.*, a dish made from boiling bread in milk and water, with seasoning added (EL, Dublin) < Spanish *panada*. 'Do you ever make panada any more? I remember you used give it to me as a child' (Dublin).

panaí /ˈpɑniː/ *n.*, a tin mug; a metal cup often coated with enamel < Ir. 'Give the child a panaí of buttermilk' (SOM, Kerry, who writes: 'used by Éamonn Kelly in his "seanchái" programmes, probably the same derivation as PANNIKIN').

pandy[1] /ˈpændi/ *n., v.*, a blow on the hand as a punishment; to strike, chastise < E dial. < L *pande (palmam)*, hold out (your hand). 'I got pandied for cogging (Dublin) (*see* COG). Synge, *The Playboy of the Western World*, act III (*FDA*, 2, 643): "*Pegeen*: That's it, now the world will see him pandied";

Joyce, *Portrait of the Artist as a Young Man*, 61: "Yes, sir, but Father Dolan said he will come in again tomorrow to pandy me for it."

pandy[2] /ˈpændi/ *n.*, a dish of potatoes mashed with milk, butter, salt, and pepper (SOM, Kerry) < Ir *peaindí*. 'Give some pandy to the child, will you, to shut him up. O'Brien, *A Pagan Place*, 123: " . . . you started to scoop the potatoes out of their skins and mash them. You made pandy for the dogs."

pannacar /ˈpɑnəkər/ *n.*, a porringer (JB, Kildare) < Ir. 'I love a pannacar of milk with my dinner; it settles the stomach.'

pannikin /ˈpænəkɪn/ *n.*, a small metal drinking-vessel < ME *panne*, pan + dimin. suffix *-kin*. 'She used to bring water back from the well in a pannikin' (BC, Meath).

pata, patta, *see* PEATA.

pardóg /ˈpɑrd̪oːg/ *n.*, a pannier (on a donkey); a CREEL used for bringing turf out of the bog; a basket with a detachable base (MOB, Mayo) < Ir. 'Open the bottom of the pardóg and let out the turf.' *See* BARDÓG.

parliament (whiskey) /ˈpærlə mənt (ʍɪskiː)/ *n.*, duty-paid whiskey (as distinct from POITÍN) (Omurethi, Kildare).

parlour /ˈpærlər/ *n.*, sitting-room; the downstairs front room in a house (KD, Dublin); a room set aside for special functions or visitors < AN *parlur* < F *parler*, *v.*, to speak. 'She kept her DELPH and Waterford glass in the parlour' (JF, Cavan).

parochial house /pæˈroːkjəl haus/ *n.*, a priest's house, a presbytery < AN *parochiel* + OE *hus*. 'I do go up to the parochial house every Wednesday for my dinner, and then we play a bit of bingo in the hall. It makes a change, and it's good to meet the old ones up there for a chat and a smoke' (TF, Cavan); 'I must pop into the parochial house after Mass and get Father to say a Mass for Packy; it's his anniversary coming up' (AF, Cavan). Kavanagh, *Tarry Flynn*, 42: "The people that's going in this place are only waiting for the chance to carry stories to the Parochial House"; Deane, *Reading in the Dark*, 109: "For God's sake, go to the door of the parochial house, ring the bell and ask the house keeper if you could see His Lordship."

paróiste /pɑrˈoːʃʧə/ *n.*, parish (SOM, Kerry) < Ir.

pasáil /ˈpɑsɔːl/ *n.*, the act of treading down, trampling the cut hay (in a barn etc.); pounding blankets in a KEELER of hot water and suds in one's bare feet < Ir. 'Willy only gave me a pound a day for pasáiling the hay' (Cavan).

patachán /ˈpɑt̪əxɔːn/ *n.*, a leveret; a weak young boy (KM, Kerry) < Ir. 'They'll need more than bread and margarine, they will, if those patacháns are going to grow any more.'

pataire /'pɑt̪ərə/ *n.*, a healthy, plump child; a short, thick-set adult (ML, Mayo) < Ir. 'Eating again! You're a real pataire.' Pearse, 'The Deargadaol' (*FDA*, 3, 823): "and she with the little, soft *pataire* of a child in her arms."

patalóg /pɑt̪ə'loːg/ *n.*, an extra-strong, well-nourished child (JOM, Kerry); a chubby child (SOM, Kerry) < Ir. 'Patalóigín', dimin. < Ir.

patron, *see* PATTERN.

pattern /pæt̪rən/ *n.*, a gathering around a holy well or place consecrated to a saint for prayer and other devotional practices < E *patron* (the spelling 'pattern' represents the way the word is pronounced in HE, which places an epenthetic (inserted) vowel (ə) between the consonants *r* and *n*). 'We went up to the pattern to say a few prayers for John's father, and the walk did us good as well.' Joyce, *Finnegans Wake*, 519.3: "And this pattern pootsch punnermine of concoon."

peaca /'pækə/ *n.*, a sin (SOM, Kerry) < Ir.

péacach /'peːkəx/ *n.*, a proud, neat, pert person (SOM, Kerry) < Ir.

peallóg /'pæloːg/ also **pealltóg** /'pælt̪oːg/ *n.*, a coarse cloth; a ragged garment; tattered old clothes; a cloth tied around the head (KM, Kerry); fig. an ill-dressed woman < Ir. 'Look at her in her peallógs; that's a fine way to come to Mass!'

peandaí, *see* PANDY[2].

peann /pæn/ *n.*, a pen < Ir < L *pinnus*, feather. 'Peann luaidhe', a pencil (SOM, Kerry) < Ir.

peannaid /'pænɪd/ *n.*, punishment, penalty (SOM, Kerry) < Ir.

péas /peːs/ *n. (sing. and pl.)*, police (man) < Ir < *Peace Preservation Force* (*see* PEELER).

peata /'pæt̪ə/ also **pata, pattha** *n.*, a pet, favourite child, etc.; a child who is inclined to cry without cause (MH, Clare) < Ir. 'Come over to me, peata!'; 'You're MAM'S peata, and don't say you're not.' Murphy, *Bailegangaire*, act I (*FDA*, 3, 1243): "*Mommo*: . . . Oh, mo pheata. Why didn't you send word?" 'Peata bán', term of endearment < Ir (lit. fair pet).

peatachán /pæt̪ə'xɔːn/ *n.*, one given to petting, hanging on to mother's apron strings (SOM, Kerry) < Ir.

pechaun, *see* PRÉACHÁN.

ped /pɛd/, *v. (past tense)*, paid (*see* HOT). Stoker, *The Snake's Pass*, 72: 'if there's no harrum [harm] done to his land – or, if there's harrum done, it's ped for."

peeler /'piːlər/ also **paler** /'peːlər/ *n.*, a policeman (< Robert *Peel*, Chief Secretary for Ireland, who established Peace

Preservation Force in 1814). 'I think the death of her son, Humphrey the peeler, upset her a lot' (KM, Kerry); 'Watch out for the peelers down by the quays' (KD, Dublin). Synge, *The Playboy of the Western World*, act III (*FDA*, 2, 644): "*Shawn*: Come on to the peelers, till they stretch you now."

peenge /piːnʤ/ *v.*, to whinge, complain; to make the POOR MOUTH < E dial. (possibly connected with *whinge*). 'That's a peenging-looking child you have there; she looks frozen with the cold. Bring her inside to the fire.'

peg /pɛg/ *v.*, to aim at, to throw (origin obscure). 'Don't be pegging stones at the cattle' (BC, Meath).

Peggy's leg /pɛgiːz'lɛg/ *n.*, a sweet in the form of a longish stalk; a stick of 'rock' (origin obscure, but cf. E dial. *peggy*, the stick used for turning the clothes around in a wash-tub; *peggy-legs*, the supports on the end of the peggy). 'May Stevens' was the only shop to sell Peggy's legs in the village, but now she's dead' (Mayo).

pegh /pɛg/ *n., v.,* a sigh; a cough; to pant, breathe heavily, sigh < E dial.

peil /pɛl/ *n.,* football (SOM, Kerry, who writes: 'also known as "caid" /kæʤ/, which earlier in the twentieth century was a separate game, more like rugby and free-for-all') < Ir.

péist, *see* PIAST.

péisteog /peːʃt'oːg/ *n.,* a small worm; fig. (pejor.) an unprepossessing person (KM, Kerry) < Ir (dimin. of *piast, péist,* worm). 'He's a bit of a péisteog, that fella; I didn't like the look of him at all.'

penance /pɛnəns/ *n.*, a punishment imposed by the priest on a person after CONFESSION, which usually takes the form of the devout recitation of certain prayers (e.g. Our Father, Hail Mary, and Glory Be (to the Father)) < OF *penance*. 'The sacrament of Penance' is the technical term for the sacrament instituted by Christ in which the priest absolves a person who confesses his or her sins with contrition and a firm purpose of amendment, as well as the intention to make reparation or satisfaction for the wrongs committed (e.g. by returning stolen goods). O'Brien, *A Pagan Place*, 41: "When the priest inquired into the bad thoughts you didn't divulge, but when he gave you a stiff penance like a whole rosary you thought he must know something"; McCourt, *Angela's Ashes*, 341: "so I go to COMMUNION the next day without penance or absolution."

penitent /'pɛnɪtənt/ *n.,* a term formerly used for a woman in unfortunate circumstances taken into a convent to work. 'She was a penitent, the poor thing –

and she was never the better for it' (Dublin).

pervert /ˈpɛrvərt/ *n.* (*colloq.*), a person who converted from Catholicism to Protestantism. 'He became a pervert after he left the home place, although not too many people ever knew about it' (Waterford). *See* TURN.

pet day /ˈpɛtdeː/ *n.,* a fine, dry day in the middle of a period of bad weather (GF, Galway) (origin obscure, but cf. Ir *peata*, pet). 'If we get a pet day I think we should cycle down to the lake; it's lovely when the weather is fine' (Galway).

philip-a-week, *see* PILLIBEEN.

phoney, *adj.,* fraudulent, counterfeit. It is often suggested that the Irish word *fáinne*, ring, is the origin of the term 'phoney' (originally American slang), based on the practice of selling fake gilt rings to gullible purchasers (cf. E dial. 'fawney', a ring, for which *EDD* gives Ir *fáinne* as the origin), but the connection is not certain. Less probable suggestions include 'whites who dyed their skin black' < F *faux noirs*, false blacks (Thomas Disch, *On Wings of Song*, 1979, reprint 1988, 215) and 'the notion that one's feelings could be readily falsified on the tele*phone*' < *phone* (*New Dictionary of American Slang*, ed. Chapman).

piachán /ˈpiəxɔːn/ also **píochán** hoarseness; wheeziness; loss of voice during or after a cold (MOB, Mayo) < Ir. 'There's such a piachán on me I can hardly speak' (KM, Kerry); 'Had you the flu? You have a fierce píochán' (SOM, Kerry). *See* CEOCHÁN.

piarda /ˈpiərd̪ə/ *n.,* a sturdy person; sometimes a nickname for members of a well-built family – the 'Piardas' (SOM, Kerry) < Ir. 'You've grown into a fine piarda of a man.'

piast /piəʃt/ also **péist** /peːʃt/ *n.,* a tape-worm; a serpent; a monster < Ir. *See* CLEAS NA PÉISTE; SNAIDHM NA PÉISTE.

piatees /ˈpjɔːtiːz/, /ˈpjætiːz/ also **piaties** etc. *n.pl.,* potatoes (representing an intermediate stage in the transformation of the original Irish word, *potáta* (< E *potato*), to PRÁTA). Griffin, *The Collegians*, 36: "'I only wanted to ask you what sort of a fair it was at Garryowen yesterday.' 'MIDDLING, sir, like the small *piatees*, they tell me.'" *See* PRÁTA.

pickey /ˈpɪki/ *n.,* a game formerly played by children, where a flat stone was kicked from square to square using one foot (DB, Cork) < E dial. (*EDD* s.v. 'pickie': 'the game of hopscotch or beds'; s.v. 'pick': 'a small flat stone used in the game of pickie'). 'We'll have a game of pickey' (SB, Cork).

pieceen /ˈpiːʃiːn/ *n.,* a little piece < E *piece* + dimin. suffix -EEN.

'Give us a pieceen of BRACK as it's Hallowe'en' (Mayo).

pig, *see* MUC.

pigeon /'pidʒən/ *n.* (*colloq.*), a urinary bottle used in hospital (presumably because of its shape). 'Nurse, a pigeon, please' (FD, Cork).

piggin /'pɪgən/ *n.*, a small pail or tub; a wooden dish or basin; a wooden drinking-vessel < E dial. (origin obscure; *piggin* is apparently the source of Ir *pigín*). 'A Piggin of larger dimensions is called a *noggin*' (Omurethi, Kildare, 535).

pilip /'pɪləp/ also **pilibín** /'pɪləbiːn/ *n.*, a crane-fly (daddy long-legs) (SOM, Kerry) < Ir.

piliúr /pɪ'luːr/ *n.*, a bolster; a pillow (SOM, Kerry).

pillibeen /'pɪləbiːn/ also **pilibín** *n.*, a plover; a crane-fly (daddy long-legs) (Cavan) < Ir *pilibín*. 'Did you see the pillibeen flying overhead?' (Dublin). 'Pilibín meek', also 'philip-a-week' (LUB, Dublin), a plover or lapwing. 'The pilibín-meeks are down off the mountain – a sign of bad weather' (RB, Waterford).

pillín /'pɪliːn/ also **pilliún** /'pɪljuːn/ *n.*, a pack-saddle (old style); a pillion; a small cushion < Ir.

pincín /'pɪŋkiːn/ also **pinkeen** *n.*, a minnow (SOM, Kerry); a very small fish < Ir. 'That's a terror [that's annoying] – all we caught were pinkeens' (TF, Cavan).

pingin /'pɪŋən/ *n.*, a penny < Ir < ON *penningr*. 'That's all we used get as pocket-money: a pingin for sweets, if that – and that was it!' (BC, Meath).

píobán /'piːbɔːn/ *n.*, a small pipe or tube; the windpipe (MH, Clare); an instrument made from straw < Ir. 'I'll wring your píobán for you if you do that again' (Meath).

píochán, *see* PIACHÁN.

piollárdaí /pɪl'ɔːrd̪iː/ *n.*, someone messing about; a person who makes a mess of what they undertake (KM, Kerry) < Ir. 'Look at the state of the HAGGARD! What a piollárdaí you are – just like your father.'

Pioneer /paiə'niːr/ *n.*, a member of the Pioneer Total Abstinence Association, a Catholic temperance association; members wear a white badge bearing the red heart symbol of the crucified Christ < E. 'My aunt's been a Pioneer for as long as I can remember – never takes a drink, even when she's sick' (Cavan).

píopa /'piːpə/ *n.*, a pipe (for smoking); the windpipe (SOM, Kerry) < Ir. 'Where did I put my píopa?' *See* DUDEEN.

piscín /'pɪ'ʃkiːn/ *n.*, a kitten < Ir. 'How many piscíní [*plural*] did the cat have?' (KG, Kerry). 'Piscín garsúin', a sickly child; an underdeveloped boy < Ir (lit. a kitten of a lad).

piseog, *see* PISHOGUE.

piseogaí /pɪʃ'oːgiː/ *n.,* one who practises piseogs (SOM, Kerry) < Ir. *See* PISHOGUE.

pishabed, *see* PISS-A-BED.

pishogue /'pɪʃoːg/ also **piseog, pishrogue** /'pɪʃroːg/ etc. *n.,* a charm, spell; superstitious practice; a tall tale < Ir. *piseog, pisreog*. 'She was full of piseogs, like hanging a St Brigid's cross near where she was doing the churning to ward off anyone stealing the butter' (KM, Kerry); 'He told me not to carry anything into the house over my left shoulder in case of bad luck, but that's only an old piseog' (TF, Cavan). Griffin, *The Collegians*, 104: "Mr. Enright's dairyman, Bill Noonan made a *pishog*, and took away our butter" (a footnote explains: "A mystic rite, by which one person is enabled to make a supernatural transfer of his neighbour's butter into his own churns. The failure and diminution of butter at different times, from the poverty of the cream, appears so unaccountable that the country people can only attribute it to witchcraft)"; Keane, *The Bodhrán Makers*, 313: "The Canon cited instances of pishoguery in Upper Dirrabeg"; Joyce, *Ulysses*, 319.25–6: "A pishogue, if you know what that is."

pishoguery /pɪ'ʃoːgəri/ *n.,* belief in *pishogues*.

pislín /pɪ'ʃliːn/ also **prislín** /prɪ'ʃliːn/ n., dribbling, saliva; a dribble, a slobber < Ir. 'There was always pislín running down his chin – disgusting!' (KG, Kerry).

pis mhionnáin /pɪs'vɪnɔːn/ *n.,* wild vetch (KM, Kerry) < Ir. 'The whole ditch is covered with pis mhionnáin.'

pismire /'pɪsmair/ *n.,* an ant (LUB, Dublin; Omurethi, Kildare) < E dial. < *piss* (because anthills have a urine-like smell) + *mire*, ant. 'Watch out for the pismires with that child' (TF, Cavan).

piss-a-bed /'pɪsəbɛd/ also **pishabed** /'pɪʃəbɛd/ (Omurethi, Kildare) *n.,* dandelion (because dandelions are diuretic) < E dial. 'Let's go and pick piss-a-beds and make a necklace for Mary.' O'Brien, *A Pagan Place,* 15 " . . . called you diddums and spoilsport and clown and piss-abed."

pitaties, *see* PRATIES.

piteog /'pɪtoːg/, /'pɪʧoːg/ *n.,* an effeminate man or boy, a sissy (MK, Galway); a weedy, insignificant man < Ir. 'That piteog's always using after-shave or perfume or something.'

plab[1] /plɑb/ *n.,* a bang, a sudden noise < Ir. 'There was a loud plab on the door' (SOM, Kerry).

plab[2] /plɑb/ *n.* (*colloq.*), a person who is easily taken in (SOM, Kerry) < Ir.

placa /plækə/ *n.,* a bundle < Ir. 'A placa of villians [*sic*], that's what you are!' (KG, Kerry).

plaic /plæk/ *n.,* a mouthful; fig. a flabby person < Ir. 'Look at that plaic – always eating; I don't know where he puts it' (BC, Meath).

plait /plɑʧ/, /plɑt/ *n.,* a bald head; a bald patch < Ir.

plaiting /ˈplɑtən/ in the phr. 'plaiting the CALLOPS' (walking drunkenly).

plámás /ˈplɔːmɔːs/ also **plaumause** (LUB, Dublin, 178) *n.,* flattery, empty praise; cajolery (SOM, Kerry) < Ir. 'You're all plámás'; 'Stop your plámásing and tell me what you really think about my new coat' (JMF, Cavan).

plámásaí /plɔːˈmɔːsiː/ *n.,* a flatterer; one who uses flattering, coaxing words, a 'soft-soap merchant' (SOM, Kerry) < Ir. *See* PLÁSAÍ.

plantation /plænˈteːʃən/ *n.,* the policy adopted by the English from the later 16th century onwards of 'planting' or colonising Ireland, in particular the provinces of Munster and Ulster (the areas furthest from the PALE), disinheriting the native landowners and abolishing Irish customs regarding property, family conduct, and agriculture. 'There was never much sign of the plantations down this part of the country'; 'She's from planter stock.' Swift, *A Dialogue in Hybernian Stile*, 164: "*A*: . . . You have a country house, are you planter?"

planter, *see* PLANTATION.

planxty /ˈplæŋsti/ *n.,* a type of lively dance-tune originally for the harp, slower than a jig < Ir *plancstaí* (onomatopoeic, from the sound of the harp; cf. E *plink* etc.).

plásaí /ˈplɔːsiː/ also **plausey, plausy** /ˈplɔːsiː/, /ˈplɔːziː/ *n.,* flattery; a flatterer (LUB, Dublin, 178); a plausible talker (KM, Kerry) < Ir (but cf. E *plausible, plausive*). 'You're a real plásaí, but I like you for it, though I don't believe a word you say!'; 'He's good at the plausy when he thinks he can make anything out of it. He's the greatest plausy you'd meet in a day's walk' (LUB, Dublin). *See* PLÁMÁS.

plaumause, *see* PLÁMÁS.

plausey, plausy, *see* PLÁSAÍ.

pléaráca /pleːˈrɔːkə/ *n.,* the noisy playing of children (KM, Kerry) < Ir *pléaráca*, revelry, boisterous entertainment. 'No more pléaráca from the national school now that it's had to be closed!'

pleibiste /plɛˈbɪʃtə/ *n.,* a soft, trusting, guileless person (ENM, Kerry) < Ir. 'She trusted him, the pleibiste, and look what happened to her legacy when the will was read out.'

pléicín /ˈpleːkiːn/ *n.,* a headscarf; a small shawl (MK, Galway) < Ir. 'Put a pléicín on your head when you go out, for fear of getting a cold.'

pleidhce /ˈplaikə/ *n.,* a fool, a simpleton < Ir. 'The poor wee pleidhce, he never harmed a fly'; 'He's a pleidhce amadáin [*see* AMADÁN],' he's a complete fool (SOM, Kerry).

plibín, *see* PILLIBEEN.

plispín /plɪʃˈpiːn/ *n.,* any small thing or animal (KM, Kerry) < Ir. 'She really loves that little plispín of a dog.'

plobaire /ˈplʌbərə/ *n.,* a chubby child; a child given to crying (SOM, Kerry) < Ir.

plodán /plʌˈd̪ɔːn/ *n.,* a puddle after rain; a pool of standing water (KM, Kerry) < Ir. 'The children love to play in the plodán, but it makes an awful mess of their good clothes.'

plodar /ˈplʌd̪ər/ *n.,* a muddy puddle; mire < Ir. 'You'll sink to your knees in that pludar!' (SOM, Kerry).

ploid, *see* PLUDA.

pluc /plʌk/ also **ploc, ploic** *n.,* swelling; the cheek; a fat cheek (LUB, Dublin) < Ir. Joyce, *Finnegans Wake*, 53.23: "pluk to pluk." 'Pluic' /plɪk/ *n.pl.,* the cheeks; prominent cheeks (KM, Kerry) < Ir. 'She has fine rosy pluics.'

plucamas /ˈplʌkəməs/ *n.,* mumps (SOM, Kerry); a swollen face < Ir.

plúch /pluːx/ *n.,* a draw or pull from a pipe (SL, Mayo) < Ir. 'He'd take a couple of plúchs from his DUDEEN and tell the best stories you've ever heard.'

plúchadh /ˈpluːxə/ *n.,* a feeling of suffocation; an asthmatic attack (SOM, Kerry) < Ir. *See* MÚCHADH.

pluda /ˈplʌd̪ə/ also **ploid** /plɪd/ *n.,* a muddy place; mud, mire (MK, Galway) < Ir. 'The STREET's all of a pluda after the rain.'

pludach /ˈplʌd̪əx/ *n.,* mud, mire; a muddy puddle; thin mud (LUB, Dublin, 179) < Ir. 'Look at the STREET after the rain – GUTTERS and pludach all over the place!'

pludar, *see* PLODAR.

pluic, *see* PLUC.

plúirín /ˈpluːˈriːn/ *n.,* violet (flower) < Ir. 'Plúirín sneachta', snowdrop (SOM, Kerry) < Ir.

plúr /pluːr/ *n.,* flour (for bread, or in potatoes) < Ir. 'Look at the plúr on those potatoes: they're laughing out at you!' (SOM, Kerry).

poage, *see* PÓG.

poc[1] /pʌk/ *n.,* a male goat < Ir. 'He still leaves the poc in the field with the cows for good luck' (Mayo). *See* PUCK.

poc[2] /pʌk/ *n.,* a puck (a stroke of the stick in hurling) (KG, Kerry) < Ir. 'He can poc the ball over the bar from fifty yards.'

pocáil /ˈpʌkɔːl/ *v.n.,* searching, poking (VQ, Kerry; TF, Cavan).

pocán /ˈpʌkɔːn/ *n.,* a he-goat (TF, Cavan) < Ir. 'Put the pocán out on the hill'; 'A pocán may be the spitting image of a goat but he'll not give milk' (proverb); 'Avoid a man with a narrow face, and never kiss a man that could kiss a pocán between the horns' (proverb).

póg /poːg/ *n.*, a kiss < Ir (*EDD* s.v. 'poage' notes: 'OIr. *póc*, fr. Church Lat. (acc.) *pacem*, 'the kiss of peace'). 'Give us a póg, and be off with you!' (KG, Kerry). Joyce, *Finnegans Wake*, 600.32: "Paudheen Steel-the-Poghue"; Binchy, *Firefly Summer*, 544–5: "'It's the poor French children I worry about,' Kate laughed. 'I got a letter from her this morning and she said that she has taught them all to say *pogue mahone* [*póg mo thóin*, kiss my backside]. They think it's Irish for good morning." 'Póigín', dimin.

póicín /poːˈkiːn/ *n.*, a small bag (KM, Kerry) < Ir. 'Hand me that little póicín to put the nails in.'

point /point/ *v. as n.*, in describing the dish called 'potatoes and point'. Griffin, *The Collegians*, 289: "When there's dry PIATEZ on the table, and enough of hungry people about it, and the family would have, may be, only one bit o' bacon hanging up above their heads, they'd peel a piatie first, and then they'd *point* it up at the bacon, and they'd fancy that it would have the taste o' the mait when they'd be aitin' it after"; Stoker, *The Snake's Pass*, 16: "'Yer 'an'r [your honour], we're in the hoight iv good luck! Herrins, it is, and it might have been only pitaties an' point.' 'What is that?' I asked. 'Oh, that is whin there is only wan [one] herrin' amongst a crowd – too little to give aich a taste, and so they put it in the middle and point the pitaties at it to give them a flaviour."

póirín /ˈpoːriːn/ *n.*, a small potato; a small seed-potato; a jackstone (SOM, Kerry) < Ir. 'What are you boiling them for? They're only PÓIRÍNS!' (BC, Meath).

póirseáil /ˈpoːrʃɔːl/, /ˈpoːrsɔːl/ *n.*, rummaging, searching anxiously in vain (MK, Galway); peering about < Ir. 'She's always póirseáiling about in my sewing-box.'

poitín /ˈpʌtiːn/, /ˈpʌtʃiːn/, also **poteen, potheen** etc. *n.*, home-made (illicit) spirits, once distilled from potatoes in a little pot (hence the name), as distinct from 'parliament whiskey', on which duty had been paid; 'whiskey with a very peat-smoky flavour, illicitly made in a private still; its colour is nearly white' (Omurethi, Kildare, 536) < Ir *poitín* (dimin. of *pota*, pot). 'The poteen I got last Christmas was the best I ever did taste' (TJ, Sligo). Joyce, *Finnegans Wake*, 451.1: "in vestments of subdominal poteen at prime cost"; Friel, *Translations*, act II, i (*FDA*, 3, 1222): "*Yolland*: Poteen – poteen – poteen. Even if I did speak Irish I'd always be an outsider here, wouldn't I?" *See* CREATURE; PARLIAMENT.

poke /ˈpoːk/ *n.,* a wallet; a bag; a sack (BC, Meath) < ONF *poque* < OF *poche.*

poll /pʌl̇/ *n.,* a hole (SOM, Kerry; MG, Cavan) < Ir. 'She fell into a poll in the bog, and that was the end of her' (KG, Kerry). 'Poll an tí' /pʌləˈʧiː/, a hole in the roof in place of a chimney (Mayo) < Ir (lit. hole of the house).

pollán /ˈpʌlɔːn/ *n.,* pollan < Ir. 'What's the best way to cook that pollán?'

pollóg /pʌˈloːg/ *n.,* a hole; an alcove, a recess (KM, Kerry) < Ir. 'Get the tea down from the pollóg and we'll have a cup before you go.'

ponc /pʌŋk/ *n.,* a decimal point, full point (MK, Galway); a delicate moment, a spot of bother < Ir. 'I'm in a ponc,' I'm in a fix, in a predicament < Ir (*táim i bponc*) (MK, Galway).

poncán /ˈpʌŋkɔːn/ also **poncánach** /pʌŋˈkɔːnəx/ *n.* (*colloq.*), an American, a 'Yank' (MK, Galway); a returned emigrant from America; a person born in America of Irish parents; fig. a lively, talkative person (origin obscure; cf. American slang *punk*, an inferior person, a petty criminal). 'Go and ask the poncán; she's a wonderful talker' (Kerry).

ponger /ˈpɑnʤər/ also **ponny** /ˈpɑniː/ *n.,* an earthenware or metal pot or mug (contraction of *porringer* < EModE *porridge* + intrusive *n* (cf. *message – messenger*) + *-er*). 'SHOW me that ponger, please' (AF, Cavan). Sheehan, *Glenanaar*, 212: "She took up a porringer of milk (into which she poured a little hot water)"; Healy, *Nineteen Acres*, 15: "He'd make him two ponnies – tin mugs – and bring them the next time he came the way."

ponny, *see* PONGER.

pooka, *see* PÚCA.

pookaun /ˈpuːkɔːn/ also **púcán** *n.,* a small sailing-boat < Ir *púcán*. 'There's too many in that pookaun; it's not safe!' (Mayo).

pookey bonnet, *see* TALLY-IRON.

pooly /ˈpuːli/ also **pooley** *n.* (*colloq.*), urine (BP, Meath) < E dial. < OE *pol*, pool (cf. Ir *poll*). Joyce, *Finnegans Wake,* 206, 27–8: "Flow now. Ower more. And pooleypooley."

poor-house /ˈpuːrhaus/ *n.,* one of the houses for the reception of the 'helpless poor' established from 1838 under the Poor Law < ME *poure*, OE *hus*. 'They took bodies out of the poorhouse and buried them in a long pit, like SPUDS' (Galway).

poor mouth /ˈpuːrmaut̪/ *n.phr.,* the habit of pretending poverty < Ir *béal bocht*. 'She always has the poor mouth, that one: if it's not one thing it's another' (KG, Kerry). *See* BÉAL BOCHT.

pór /poːr/ *n.,* a seed; a dock-seed (KM, Kerry) < Ir. 'What did you do with the bag I put the pórs in? I can't find it anywhere.'

porringer, *see* PONGER.

port[1] /pʌrt̪/ *n.,* the bank of a river (SOM, Kerry) < Ir.

port[2] /pʌrt̪/ *n.,* a tune; a jig < Ir.

porter /ˈpoːrt̪ər/ *n.,* heavy dark-brown beer (no longer brewed); *colloq.* stout < E *porter's beer*. 'You can't beat a pint of porter to kill the thirst.' Yeats, *The Unicorn from the Stars,* act II (*Collected Plays*, 361): "*Thomas*: . . . the smell of the spirits and the porter, and the shouting and the cheering within, made the hair to rise up on my scalp"; Joyce, *Ulysses*, 340.17–18: "GOB[2], it's turn the porter sour in your guts, so it would"; Kavanagh, 'Jungle' (*Collected Poems*, 96): "On Baggot Street they screeched, | Then dived out of my sight | Into the pools of blackest porter . . . "; McCourt, *Angela's Ashes*, 3: "After a night of drinking porter in the pubs of Limerick he staggers down the lane singing his favorite song." 'Porter-meal', oatmeal mixed with porter.

pósadh /ˈpoːsə/ *n.,* a marriage; a wedding feast (SOM, Kerry) < Ir *pósadh*, marriage.

poss /pɑs/ *v.,* to wash (BP, Meath) < E dial. (*EDD* s.v. 'poss, v. and sb.[3]': 'to dash or shake violently in water, especially to beat clothes in water for the purpose of washing them; to rinse them with water'); (origin uncertain, but Hogan, s.v. 'poss' (LUB, Dublin, 179), notes: 'A Scottish and Northern word; perhaps from Fr. *pousser*).' 'Possing-wet', saturated, wringing wet (LUB, Dublin).

Post, an /ɑnˈpʌst̪/ *n.phr.,* the postal service < Ir < E *post*. 'You can pay that bill through An Post if you want' (JF, Cavan).

pótaire /ˈpoːt̪ərə/ *n.,* a toper, a habitual drinker (SOM, Kerry) < Ir. 'Pótaires all in that family!'

poteen, potheen, etc., *see* POITÍN.

potheens /ˈpʌt̪iːnz/ *n.pl.,* small potatoes < Ir. Healy, *Nineteen Acres*, 12: "On top of every pot Grandma would have the potheens, the small SPUDS she'd pick from the eating potatoes above in the dairy."

pounder /ˈpaundər/, /ˈpaund̪ər/ *n., v.,* a wooden cudgel for beating potatoes etc. < E *pound* (< OE *punian*), *v.,* to beat. 'SHOW me the pounder, will you?' Healy, *Nineteen Acres*, 13: "Grandma made CALLY. You scraped the light skins off the new potatoes, pot-boiled them and then, with a pounder, pounded them into mash, mixing in salt and chopped SCALLIONS and some fresh milk."

power /paur/ *n.,* a large number, large quantity < E dial. (cf. Ir 'neart', which has a number of meanings, including 'force', 'power', 'strength', and also 'plenty'). 'More power (to you)!' well done (Omurethi, Kildare);

'He's won a power of money on the lottery' (TF, Cavan); 'It's AFTER raining a power' (Omurethi, Kildare). Banim, *The Boyne Water*, 221: "An' now cum the SASSENACHS . . . what a power of 'em is IN IT!"; Synge, *In the Shadow of the Glen* (*FDA*, 2, 633): "*Michael*: I'm thinking it's a power of men you're AFTER knowing if it's in a lonesome place you live ITSELF." *See* SIGHT.

PP abbreviation for 'parish priest', the priest in charge of a Catholic parish (from the initials usually written after the name). 'The PP always likes to say FIRST MASS, and then bring Communion to the sick in the hospital' (JMF, Cavan).

prácás /prɔːˈkɔːs/ *n.,* a mess, confused mixture; a mixed dish like stew, hotchpotch (KM, Kerry) < Ir. 'What prácás have you cooking there? It doesn't smell too bad at all'; 'You better clean that prácás quick before she comes back and sees it on the floor.'

práibín /prɔːˈbiːn/ *n.,* raw oatmeal and cream; soft mush (KM, Kerry); mud < Ir. 'You didn't leave the cake in long enough; it's a práibín in the middle.'

praiseach /ˈpræʃəx/ also **prashagh** *n.* 1. Porridge; gruel, STIRABOUT; a boiled dish of mixed ingredients; fig. a mess < Ir. 'He made praiseach of the car when he crashed it' (SOM, Kerry); Healy, *Nineteen Acres*, 86: "The torrential rain soaked the paper bag and the bottom burst: the strawberries fell out in a praiseach on the road." 2. Wild cabbage, kale; charlock (LUB, Dublin) < Ir.

praiseach bhuí /præʃəxˈwiː/ *n.,* charlock < Ir. 'Is that the praiseach bhuí I see growing in the wheat field? (Mayo).

práta /ˈprɔːt̪ə/ also **pitatie, piatee, pratie, phatie**, etc. *n.,* potato < Ir < E *potato*. 'I love a plate of praties, with LASHINGS of butter and a PONGER of milk to wash it down' (TF, Cavan). Carleton, 'The Hedge School' (*Six Irish Tales*, 162): "We tried the praties this mornin, Sir, an' we'll have new praties, and bread and butther, Sir"; Kickham, *Knocknagow*, 142–3: "'Praties' would be laughed at as a vulgarism only worthy of a SPALPEEN from Kerry, while 'potatoes' was considered too genteel except for ladies and gentlemen and school masters. The nearest approach we can make to the word we were about writing is 'puetas' or 'p'yehtes'" (see PIATEES); Joyce, *Finnegans Wake*, 56. 26: "POTEEN and tea and praties"; Kavanagh, *Tarry Flynn*, 39: "'You ought to hurry with the praties before the ground gets too dry." *See* POINT.

prawshkeen /ˈprɔːʃkiːn/ also **prauskeen, praushkeen** (LUB,

Dublin), **práiscín** *n.,* 'an apron of rough material, worn when sowing potatoes, picking new potatoes, gathering scutch, etc.; these are carried in the prauskeen' (LUB, Dublin) < Ir *práiscín*. 'She always had CHILDER streeling out of her prawshkeen' (*see* STREEL) (BC, Meath).

preab /præb/ *n.,* a start, a sudden motion; a bounce < Ir. 'He took a preab out of me; I wasn't expecting him' (cf. Ir *bhain sé geit asam*) (SOM, Kerry).

préachán /preː'xɔːn/ *n.,* a crow; a scaldcrow (SOM, Kerry) < Ir. Banim, *The Boyne Water*, 536: "Mind the *pechauns* that'ill come getherin' in the shky, afther a while."

prepositions with place-names are commonly used according to geographical position relative to the speaker, and sometimes also (as a reflection of Irish practice) according to local tradition. 'Up to Cork, in to Fermoy, over to Mallow, back to Shanballymore, down to Farrahy, in to Mitchellstown' (SOC, Cork).

press /prɛs/ *n.,* a cupboard < ME *presse*. Johnston, *Shadows on Our Skin*, 167: "His bed and Brendan's neatly made and the clothes back in the press"; Healy, *Nineteen Acres*, 118: "She found some old linen in the bottom of a press, mildewed"; Deane, *Reading in the Dark*, 146: "She took a jug from the press and emptied them all in." 'Hot-press' (SE airing-cupboard). 'Put your clothes in the hot-press' (BC, Meath).

priest /priːst/ *n.* In Ireland, until recently, priests were invested with magical powers in the popular mind, e.g. for the curing of ailments; a newly ordained priest was supposed to have especially effective powers, as also had SILENCED priests. Kilroy, *The Big Chapel*, 178–9: "They say that on certain nights a figure of a half-man, half-woman, dressed in the priest's alb and chasuble, is to be seen in the CHAPEL yard, dancing and shaking . . . A PARISH PRIEST of some years ago had a Mass said on the spot because he said it was a tormented soul.' *See* SPOILED PRIEST.

priesteen /priː'ʃtiːn/, /priː'stiːn/ *n.,* a little priest (term of affection or contempt) (KG, Kerry) < E *priest* + dim. suffix *-een*. 'You should have heard the priesteen shouting at the match!'

prioc /prɪk/ *n.*, a pinch, nudge, poke (KM, Kerry) < Ir. 'Give him a prioc to wake him up; it's time to go home.'

priocaire /'prɪkərə/ *n.,* a worn spade; a worn poker (ENM, Kerry) < Ir.

prislín /prɪ'ʃliːn/ *n.,* dribble, saliva; a dribbler (KM, Kerry) < Ir. 'Clean the prislín off the child, and don't let her go around looking like that.'

Pro /proː/ prefix, as in 'the Pro' (*colloq.*), with reference to the Pro-Cathedral (St Mary's Pro-Cathedral, now properly called the Cathedral), built between 1815 and 1825 in Marlborough Street, a street running parallel to the more conspicuous O'Connell Street, where it was originally intended to be built, but for opposition from the Protestant community. See MASS².

prochóg /'prʌxoːg/ *n.,* a wretched hovel (Mayo) < Ir. 'I don't know how he ever lived in that prochóg so long. He should have moved into a home long ago.'

prog¹ /prɑg/ *n., v.,* provisions; to look for food, to forage (origin obscure). 'We went progging for apples behind the house' (Meath)

prog² in the *phr.* 'Prog! prog!' /prʌgprʌg/, call to a cow (Meath). 'Progaí' /'prʌgiː/, call to a calf < Ir. 'If you call out "progaí" he'll come to you, don't worry' (MG, Cavan).

proimpín /prɪm'piːn/ *n.,* the fleshy tail end of fowl (KM, Kerry) < Ir.

protestant /'prɑdəstənt/ *n.*, a Christian whose faith and practice is based on the principles of the Reformation; the name 'Protestant' was first applied to reformers opposed to the decree of the second Diet of Speyer (1529), concerned with affirming the inviolability of Catholic belief and practices; the reformers made a formal 'Protestatio' addressed to the Archduke Ferdinand on 19 April; in recent times the word is often replaced by 'non-Catholic' < L *protestans*, present participle of *protestare, v.*, to bear witness, declare, assert in public. 'Half that family is Catholic and the other half Protestant; half go to the CHAPEL and half go to the church at the foot of the town' (TJ, Sligo). Kickham, *Knocknagow*, 74: "Is it a fact . . . that Protestants are less hard to be pleased in the choice of wives and husbands than Catholics in Ireland?"; Stoker, *The Snake's Pass*, 23: "MUSHA! how could Misther McGlown believe anythin', an' him a Protestan'." See TURN.

púca /'puːkə/ also **pooka** *n.* 1. A sprite; a mischievous and sometimes harmful spirit who can appear in various animal guises (especially as a horse) and entice unsuspecting people onto its back for a precipitous ride over rough country; a ghost; a bogey-man (SOM, Kerry, who adds: 'púcaís pl., the good people') < Ir (cf. E PUCK). 'The pooka's influence made blackberries uneatable after the first of November' (LUB, Dublin). 'If you're not asleep in ten minutes I'll tell the púca to come around and take you away' (BC, Meath). 2. A shy, introverted child; an uncommunicative person.

pucán /pʌ'kɔːn/ also **puckawn** *n.,* a male goat < Ir (*see* PUCK). Swift, *A Dialogue in Hybernian Stile*: "B: . . . But our cows will never keep a drop of milk without a puckawn." 'Pucán gabhair', a puck-goat (SOM, Kerry);

púcán, *see* POOKAUN.

púca na sméara /puːkənə 'smeːrə/ a mildew in blackberries (KM, Kerry) < Ir (lit. the blackberry sprite). 'Don't eat the blackberries: the púca na sméara was here last night.'

púca pile /'puːkə'pɪlə/ *n.phr.,* a toadstool or other inedible fungus (SOM, Kerry) < Ir *púca peill*. 'Don't let the CHILDER near the púca pile!'

puck /pʌk/ *n.,* a male goat; the white goat installed over the market square in Killorglin, Co. Kerry, for the duration of Puck Fair (held annually, 10–12 August) < Ir. *poc*. 'Are they getting ready for the Puck already?' (KG, Kerry). *See* PÚCA.

puckawn, *see* PUCÁN.

pucker /'pʌkər/ *n.,* bad humour < E dial. < *poke*, pocket ('the notion being that of forming small bag-like or purse-like gatherings' in the face – *OED*). 'He is in such a pucker that nothing will please him' (LUB, Dublin); 'He gave up his job in a pucker, and he is supping sorrow for it as he didn't get a tap to do ever since' (LUB, Dublin). Plunkett, *Farewell Companions*, 390: "'I'm in a pucker,' Cornelius confessed."

púcóg /puː'koːg/ *n.,* a mask for cows, often made of boards (KM, Kerry); a face-covering in blind man's buff < Ir (dimin. of *púic*, mask). 'It's safe to take the púcóg off of the cow now.' *See* PÚICÍN.

púdar /'puːd̪ər/ *n.,* powder; dust < Ir < AN *poudre*. 'Púdar gunna', gunpowder (SOM, Kerry) < Ir.

pueta, potato, *see* PRÁTA.

púic[1] /puːk/ *n.,* a covering over the good eye to encourage a lazy eye in a child (SOM, Kerry) < Ir.

púic[2] /puːk/ *n.,* a sour face, a scowl < Ir. 'Take that púic off you and make yourself useful' (BC, Meath).

púicín /puː'kiːn/ *n.,* a muzzle put on a calf to stop it drinking the urine from another calf; a covering put over the eyes of a thieving cow (KM, Kerry); blinkers to cover the eyes of a fidgety horse (SOM, Kerry); a hood worn when cleaning out the fireplace, a blind over the eyes; a little hut, with no opening except for the door < Ir (dimin. of *púic*, mask). 'Put a púicín on that red calf. ' *See* PÚCÓG.

puililiú /'pɪlɪluː/ *int.,* a shout in hunting (SOM, Kerry) < Ir < E *hullabaloo*.

puisín /pʌ'ʃiːn/ also **puseen, pusheen** *n.,* a kitten (VQ, Kerry) < Ir (cf. E *puss, pussy*).

'She put the puisín in her lap because she was so lonely' (KG, Kerry). Healy, *Nineteen Acres*, 8: "Now the puseens, mewling at the door of the cowhouse, could be heard in the calm of the evening." 'Puisín miáú', a cry-baby. 'Catch a hold /hoːlt/ of yourself and don't be a little puisín miáú!' (SOM, Kerry).

puiteach /ˈpɪʧəx/ *n.,* boggy ground (ENM, Kerry) < Ir. 'Indeed, then, he'll never make anything out of that puiteach.'

puithín /ˈpɪhiːn/ *n.,* a puff, a gust of wind < Ir (dimin. of PUTH). 'She's so frail a puithín of wind would knock her down' (JF, Cavan).

punch /pʌnʧ/ *n.*, beverage from wine, spirits, mixed with hot water or milk, etc.; 'in Scotland called toddy' (Omurethi, Kildare, 536) (*ODEE*: 'the etymology is complicated, but the word may be derived from Marathi and Hindi panch (Skr. pañchan five), so named from the five ingredients of the drink').

punt /pʌnt̪/ *n.,* the pound (currency) < Ir < E *pound.* 'The punt is very strong against the dollar these days; we probably won't get so many of the American tourists' (KG, Kerry).

purchase-house /ˈpʌrʧəshaus/ *n.*, 'a privately built house (as distinct from a Corporation-built house)' (KD, Dublin) < AN *purchacer*, OF *pourchacier* + OE *hus*. See SCHEME.

pus /pʌs/ also **puss** *n., v.,* the mouth; shaping the lips so as to make a pout (MK, Galway); sulking < Ir. Take that ugly sour puss off your face and get on with the MESSAGES' (KG, Kerry); 'He went off with himself [by himself] and a puss on him' (LUB, Dublin); 'Don't be always pussing' (Meath). O'Casey, *The Plough and the Stars*, act II, 175: "*Rosie*: If I was a man, or you were a woman, I'd bate th' puss o' you!" 'Pus muice', *see* MUC.

pusach /ˈpʌsəx/ *adj.,* sour-faced (MK, Galway) < Ir. 'You can take that pusach off; you're saying the ROSARY, and that's it.'

pusachán /ˈpʌsəkɔːn/ *n.,* a whiner, a complainer, a pouter (KM, Kerry) < Ir. 'What a pusachán she is; she never stops pusacháning.'

pusáiling /pʌˈsɔːlən/ *v.n.* (*colloq.*), whining; disproportionate, continuous sobbing (SOM, Kerry); whimpering; blubbering < Ir < PUS. 'Will you quit that pusáiling; I can't think with the noise!'

pusaíocht /pʌˈsiːəxt̪/ *n.,* complaining, whining < Ir. 'Stop pusaíochting and get on with the job' (KG, Kerry).

pusaire /ˈpʌsərə/ *n.,* a sulky person; a cranky, whinging child < Ir. 'What a pusaire you are!' (BC, Meath).

puseen, pusheen, *see* PUISÍN.

puss, *see* PUS.

put /pʌt/ *v.*, following the usage of 'cuir' in Irish, is often used in periphrastic constructions (cf. Bliss, *Spoken English in Ireland*, 304: 'Many English verbs can be rendered in Irish by variations on an idiom in which the verb *cuirim* "I put" is followed by some noun and the preposition *ar* "on". Thus "I frighten" can be rendered by *cuirim eagla ar* "I put fear on", "I delay" by *cuirim moill ar* "I put delay on", "I lock" by *cuirim glas ar* "I put a fastening on," and so on').

puth /pʌh/ *n.*, a puff (KM, Kerry) < Ir. 'There isn't a puth of smoke coming out of that fire.' *See* PUITHÍN.

putóg /pʌ'to̪ːg/ *n.* (plural 'putóga'), black and white puddings (SOM, Kerry), home-made pudding made after a pig was killed, shared with the neighbours < Ir.

Q

Quarant' Ore /kwɑrənt'oːr/ *n.*, the FORTY HOURS' exposition of the Blessed Sacrament < It *quarant' ore,* forty hours. 'Daddy wants the whole family to do the Quarant' Ore in turn at the CHAPEL; so who's to go first?' (Meath).

queer /kweːr/ also **quare** *adj.*, *adv.* (intensive), great < E dial. (origin obscure). 'He's a queer YOKE, that fella: I can't figure him out at all.' Stoker, *The Snake's Pass*, 199: "'That's a queer thing for him to say!' said Norah to her father. Murdock turned on her at once. 'Quare thing – no more quare than the things they'll be sayin' about you before long'"; Kavanagh, 'If Ever You Go to Dublin Town (*Collected Poems*, 143): "O he was a queer one"; Roche, *A Handful of Stars*, act I, i, 14: "*Tony*: I'll tell yeh one thing Conway he's trainin' queer hard for it." 'Queer and', extremely. 'He's queer and mean,' he's extremely mean.'Roche, *Poor Beast in the Rain,* act I, i, 76: "*Joe*: . . . We were queer and lucky not to be sent up the river that time boy."

quench /kwɛnʧ/, /kwɪnʧ/ also **quinch** *v.,* extinguish (candle, light, etc.) < OE *cwencan*. 'Quinch the lamp, will you?' (AF, Cavan). Healy, *Nineteen Acres*, 11: "They would build a slated house and quench the old hearth but the quenching would not be done before the new fire built of the coals from the old hearth across the street, was safely glowing."

quicken /kwɪkən/ *n.,* rowan (mountain ash) < E dial. (origin obscure). 'I love the colour of the berries on the quicken.'

quilt /kwɪlt/ *n. (pejor.),* a fat person; a silly person < ME *quilte*. 'He's an awful old quilt, that fella' (TF, Cavan).

quit /kwɪt/ *v.,* cease (speaking, making noise, etc.) frequently in the phr. 'Och, will you quit!' (BC, Meath) < OF *quitter*.

R

rábaire /ˈrɔːbərə/ *n.*, a strong, active, athletic person; a big strong man < Ir. 'A rábaire he was till the end of his days; and you've never seen the like of the funeral he had – all the local GAA turned out' (Mayo).

rabhán /ˈrauɔːn/ *n.*, thrift (herb) < Ir.

rabhcán /ˈraukɔːn/, /roːˈkɔːn/ also **rócán** *n.*, a simple song, a ditty; a ballad; a song with a personal or local story (MK, Galway); part of a song < Ir. 'Paddy, give us a rócán of a song' (SOM, Kerry).

rabhchán /ˈruːxɔːn/ *n.*, a noisy gathering; a tumult (MK, Galway) < Ir.

ráca /ˈrɔːkə/ *n.*, a rake; a comb (Waterford) < Ir. 'Show that ráca to your hair; it's a woeful mess.' *See* RACK.

racaid /ˈrɑkəd/ *n.*, a child's frock < Ir < ME or AN *rochet*, (bishop's) robe. 'Didn't she look a treat in her little white racaid when she got first Holy Communion?'

rachmas /ˈrɑxməs/ *n.*, wealth < Ir. 'There's great rachmas there,' there's likely to be fertile grounds for a fortune, in a made match (SOM, Kerry).

rack /ræk/ *n.*, *v.*, a comb; to comb < E dial < OE *reccan*, to rake. 'I seen a BANSHEE wonst [once] and she racking her hair' (Omurethi, Kildare, 536). *See* RÁCA.

racker, *see* WRACKER.

ragaire /ˈrɑgərə/ *n.*, someone who rambles late at night (MK, Galway) < Ir. 'There goes the bailiff, the old ragaire that he is!'

ragairne /ˈrɑgərnjə/ *n.*, wantonness; late-night drinking, carousing (often used in conjunction with AIRNEÁNING) (SOM, Kerry) < Ir.

ragairneálaí /rɑgərˈnɔːliː/ *n.*, a noisy playboy; a wastrel (KM, Kerry) < Ir. 'She always went for the ragairneálaí in the group, whoever he was, the ROSSEY!'

ráib /rɔːb/ *n.*, an estimable person; a heroic figure (ENM, Kerry) < Ir (cf. RÁBAIRE).

raic /ræk/ *n.*, a quarrel; an uproar, a racket, a disturbance, a violent quarrel; fun, sport < Ir. 'There was pure raic at the fair when the politicians started' (SOM, Kerry).

raideog /ˈrɪʤoːg/ *n.,* bog myrtle (KM, Kerry) < Ir. 'Don't walk over the raideog – it'll bring you bad luck!'

raidhse /ˈraiʃə/ *n.,* abundance, plenty (MK, Galway) < Ir. 'They think there's a raidhse of money in London; I hope they're right, for the sake of the family'; 'There was a raidhse of everything you could think of at the wedding' (SOM, Kerry).

ráig /rɔːg/ *n.,* a sudden outburst of temper (MK, Galway); fig. an outbreak of rain < Ir. 'She was wicked [= sharp-tongued], and you'd never know when she'd be taken with a ráig'; 'Quick, get under that bush over there before the ráig has us drownded.'

ráiméis /rɔːˈmeːʃ/ also **rawmaish** etc. *n.,* foolish, nonsensical talk (SOM, Kerry); raving talk; a senseless rhyme < Ir (variant of *raiméis* /ˈræmeːʃ/; cf. F *romance*). 'Don't be talking raumaish; I know exactly what happened' (KG, Kerry); 'Don't be rawmaishing; get away out of that!' Sheehan, *Glenanaar*, 141: "You were talking all the *raimeis* in the world"; Joyce, *Ulysses*, 324.26: "*Raimeis*, says the citizen"; Binchy, *Firefly Summer*, 542: ". . . She doesn't have any awful things to put up with like you do, not being able to walk, and getting stuck behind the counter listening to old bores drinking and rawmaishing on for hours."

raispín /ˈræʃpiːn/ *n.,* a miserly, niggardly person; an emaciated person < Ir. 'You'd know what sort of a raispín he is from the look of him, all skin and bones' (Galway).

ráithe /ˈrɔːhə/ *n.,* a quarter (period of three months) (SOM, Kerry) < Ir.

ráithín /ˈrɔːhiːn/ *n.,* a swampy place; a swath of new-mown hay (MH, Clare); sods of turf built up to dry < Ir.

raithneach /ræhnəx/ *n.*, bracken (sometimes called 'Mary's fern', because of the legend that St Joseph used it for bedding for his wife and the Christ-child; it is therefore regarded as blessed, and if people or cattle sleep on it they do not, it is claimed, catch a cold) < Ir. 'Spread the raithneach for the cattle.'

rake /reːk/ *n.,* an amount of something; a large quantity < E dial. (*EDD*: 'a load, as much as can be carried on one journey; a large quantity'). 'A rake of books' (MCR, Waterford).

raker /ˈreːkər/ *n.,* a vagabond < E dial. *rake, v.,* to roam about. *See* WRACKER.

rambling /ˈræmblən/ *pres.part.,* visiting from house to house for gossip and entertainment < E *ramble* < ME *ramblen*, *v.,* to ramble, roam about < MDu *rammelen* (of cats, rabbits, etc.), to frequent; to be sexually excited < *rammen*, to copulate with. 'He does be rambling in the winter nights' (TF, Cavan). 'Rambling-house' /ˈræmblən haus/, a house where men gather for conversation and hospitality (DOH, Limerick). 'I love to see him at a rambling-house.' *See* BOTHÁNTAÍOCHT; CÉILÍ; COORJEEKING.

rámhaille /ˈrɔːvəljə/ *n.*, delirium or raving, especially at death or during a fever (SOM, Kerry) < Ir.

rámhainn /rɔːn/ *n.*, a spade (SOM, Kerry) < Ir.

ramhar /raur/ *adj.*, stout, corpulent; thick < Ir. 'Bainne ramhar', *see* BAINNE.

ránaí /ˈrɔːniː/ *n.*, a thin, lanky person; a troublesome child; a delicate child; a thin animal (MK, Galway) < Ir. 'I have an ODIOUS time with that ránaí.'

rann /rɑn/, /rɔːn/ *n.*, a verse; a song < Ir. 'Give us an old rann of a song, Pat, and cheer us up!' Joyce, *Finnegans Wake*, 580. 33–4: "to rhyme the rann that flooded the routes in Eryan's isles."

rapid /ˈræpə/ *adj.* (*colloq.*), excellent (Dublin). 'That film was bleedin' rapid!' 'Caught rapid', caught red-handed (KD, Dublin).

rapparee /ˈræpəriː/ *n.*, a robber, a cut-purse; an outlaw < Ir *rapaire* (influenced by *rapairí*, plural), variant of *ropaire*. In the late 17th century rapparees acted as a mobile force on behalf of the Jacobites within territories controlled by the Williamites; hence their reputation, in some quarters, for what would now be called terrorist activities. Brewer, for instance, in *Dictionary of Phrase and Fable*, describes a rapparee as 'a wild Irish plunderer; so called from his being armed with a rapary or half-pike.' Michelburne, *Ireland Preserved*, 147: "Enter five Rapparees"; Banim, *The Boyne Water*, 214: "And the Rapparee general seized Evelyn's hand in his, with a grasp that almost crushed it."

rasher /ˈræʃər/ *n.*, a thin slice of bacon or ham for frying or grilling (origin obscure). 'She gave us a big feed of rashers and eggs and black puddin' when we got in from the fair, and home-made soda bread' (TF, Cavan). 'A ride and a rasher' *phr.* (*colloq.*), sexual intercourse followed by breakfast. 'I'd say she'd give you a ride and a rasher if you played your cards right' (Wexford).

rasp /rasp/ *n.*, an old tin can for grating potatoes (ML, Mayo); a cake like BOXTY < E dial. < OF *raspe (EDD)*. 'Grated potatoes are strained through a cloth, and then, with some flour added, baked into a cake . . . also called "rasp" in Longford' (Martin, Breifny, 176).

rath /ræh/ *n.*, luck, bounty; blessing < Ir. 'Rath Dé ort,' God bless you. 'Drochrath ort,' BAD CESS to you (SOM, Kerry).

ráth /rɔː/ also **ráith** *n.*, an earthen ring-fort, a circular fort < Ir. The word 'rath' occurs frequently in place-names, e.g. Rathmore, on which SOM (Kerry) writes with reference to the poem 'Tionól na Ráithe Móire': 'This poem, written by a local poet who died in 1932, shows that, unlike the Placenames Commission, the local version was Ráith Mhór'). Heaney, 'A New Song' (*Wintering Out*, 33: "A vocable, as rath . . . "

rawmaish, raumaish, etc., *see* RÁIMÉIS.

RDS abbreviation for Royal Dublin Society (founded 1731) and especially its showgrounds and halls in Merrion Road, Ballsbridge. 'There's a concert in the RDS on Saturday night. Would you like to come?' (MK, Dublin); 'Do me a favour, will you, and bring those books back for me to the RDS Library; they're long overdue' (Dublin).

Reading Made Easy /'riːdnmɛd 'iːziː/, /'reːdnmɛd'eːziː/ *n.phr.*, an elementary school reading-book widely used in the 19th century. Griffin, *The Collegians*, 132: "'There's a time for all things, as they say in the Readin'-made-asy.' 'Surely, surely,' returned Danny, with a yawn. 'DEAR knows, den, de Readin'-made-asy time is come now, for 'tis a'most mornin'."

reathaí /'ræhiː/ *n.*, a runner; a stroller; a wild person (KM, Kerry) < Ir. 'That fella was always a bit of a reathaí – you know what I mean?'

redd /rɛd/ *v.*, to tidy up, clean up; to clear < E dial. *red(d)* < ME *radden*, to prepare, make ready. 'Reddy up is to tidy up' (Omurethi, Kildare). 'Redd up your bedroom, Moira, or you're not going out tonight' (Meath).

Redemptorists, *see* MISSION.

reek /riːk/ *n.*, a heap, stack (of hay, turf, etc.) < E dial. < ME *hreac,* rick. 'We'll have to make a reek of turf up by the road' (Louth).

reel /riːl/ *n.*, a lively, whirling dance; the music for such a dance < Ir *ríl* (origin obscure; cf. E *reel*). 'I have a reel in my head from all that dancing.' Kavanagh, 'The Gambler: A Ballet' (*Collected Poems*, 176): "Here we go round the mystic wheel | Dancing a wild Gaelic reel."

reel-footed /'riːlfʌtəd/ *adj.*, club-footed (Omurethi, Kildare); 'bandiness supposed to be induced in pregnancy by walking on graves' (Dinneen) < Ir CAM REILIGE. 'Stephen has it hard to walk with that reel-foot of his, poor man, but he's put a bit of wood on the pedal, so he's fine on the bike' (TF, Cavan).

réidh /reː/ *adj., n.,* level; a level field; level land near a river; flat reclaimed bogland; coarse bog-land; a moor; a row of heaps of manure on a field < Ir. 'Take the cattle back to the réidh'; 'There are grouse back in the réidh' (SOM, Kerry).

reilig /'rɛlɪg/ *n.,* a graveyard (SOM, Kerry) < Ir < L *reliquiae. See* REEL-FOOTED.

réiteoir /reː'ʧoːr/ *n.,* a pipe-cleaner (often fashioned out of a knitting-needle) (KM, Kerry) < Ir. 'Where's my réiteoir? I can't find it anywhere.'

réleaba /'reːlæbə/ *n.,* a bed made up at short notice (MK, Galway) < Ir. 'She made a réleaba for me near the fire and I slept a bit there.'

relic /rɛlək/ *n.*, the body of a saint, or any part thereof; any part of the saint's attire; any object or thing closely associated with him or her; the Church has permitted and encouraged the veneration of relics for many centuries; regulations for the veneration of relics were made and promulgated at the Council of Trent (1545–1563); the feast of all Holy Relics is held on 5 November < OE *relicgang*, *n.*, veneration of relics < ME *relike*. 'Relics of old decency, memorials of better family circumstances. *The relics of old decency was the hat my father wore* – old song' (LUB, Dublin, 180). *See* RUB.

relict /'rɛlɪkt/ *n.,* widow; survivor (used in official documents and legal notices) < L *relictus*. 'Mrs O'Connor, relict of Mr John O'Connor, died on 6 April.'

removal /rə'muːvəl/ *n.,* the bringing of a body from the home or mortuary to a church on the evening before the funeral. The relatives and friends of the deceased customarily wait outside for the arrival of the hearse and then follow the remains into the church; after a short service they form a queue up the centre aisle to shake hands and offer sympathy to the family, who sit in the front row on the right (in earlier times the sympathy was expressed in the formula 'I'm sorry for your trouble' < Ir *Ní maith liom do thrioblóid,* but nowadays the words are usually more personal). 'The removal's at HALF FIVE, so we can just get there after work.'

renegue /rə'neːg/ *v.,* to go back on one's word (not restricted to games of cards) < E dial. < OF *renier* < L *renegare*. 'She renegued on me AND I only trying to help her.'

resetter /riː'sɛtər/ *n. (historical)*, a harbourer of thieves or criminals (MB, Tipperary) < ME *ressettour* < OF *recetour*.

residenter /rɛzɪ'dɛnt̪ər/ also **residenther** *n.,* an old inhabitant

< E dial. 'Residents – families of old standing in the countryside – are old *residenters*; others are *runners*' (LUB, Dublin, 180); 'Larry O'Byrne is one of the oldest residenthers about the place, so he is' (Omurethi, Kildare, 537).

retreat /rətriːt/ *n.*, a period, short or long, spent in silence in which a person withdraws from his or her ordinary life and is occupied with meditation or other religious exercises, including spiritual guidance from a priest; the forty days that Christ spent in the wilderness is the ultimate authority and model for this practice; the clergy of every diocese meet in retreat once a year; retreats may be given in religious houses, 'retreat houses', churches, and schools < Late ME *retret*, OF *retret*. 'I used hate retreats at school – all that no talking, and yon teachers looking out to see who's breaking the rule' (Mayo).

rí /riː/ *n.*, king < Ir. 'A Rí na bhFlaitheas,' *int.* to indicate surprise (SOM, Kerry) < Ir (lit. King of Heaven, *voc.*).

RIA abbreviation for Royal Irish Academy, the leading learned society in Ireland, founded in 1783, now housed at 19 Dawson Street, Dublin; also known as 'the Academy'.

riabhach /riəvəx/ *v.*, brindled, speckled, striped; bó riabhach, cú riabhach, a brindled cow (SOM, Kerry); 'riabhach days', the last days of March, or the first few days of April < Ir. (March is called the Month of the Brindled Cow because of the legend 'that the brindled cow complained at the dawn of April of the harshness of March, whereupon March borrowed a few days from April, and these were so wet and stormy that the bó riabhach (brindled cow) was drowned; hence March has a day more than April, and the borrowed days are called laetheanta na riaibhche (the days of the brindled cow) (*see* Dinneen s.v. 'riabhach').

riabhóg /riə'voːg/ *n.*, a hedge-sparrow, wren, etc. (KM, Kerry) < Ir. 'I could hear the riabhógs chattering from my room in the evening; and every time I hear them I'm always reminded of my room.'

riasc /riəsk/ *n.*, low-lying marsh; very wet ground (SOM, Kerry); a moist, rushy field; a STRAND < Ir. 'That riasc is dangerous for the children'; 'You should go down to the riasc at dusk if you want to catch the duck coming in' (KG, Kerry).

ribe /'rɪbə/ *n.*, a single hair; a whisker; long, fine grass < Ir. 'Not a ribe of his head did I harm' (Mayo); 'He hadn't a ribe' (he was completely bald) (LUB, Dublin).

ricil /'rɪkəl/ *n.*, a pile of turf set out to dry (KM, Kerry) < Ir (cf.

E dial. *rickle*, loose heap or pile).

rife /raif/ also **riff** /rɪf/ *n., v.,* an instrument for sharpening a scythe; to sharpen a scythe < E dial. Heaney, *The Midnight Verdict,* 32: "you cold-rifed blirt."

righneálaí /riːˈnɔːliː/ *n.,* a slow person; an idler, loiterer, dawdler < Ir.

rightify /ˈraitəfai/ *v.*, to rectify, correct < E dial. (EDD s.v. 'rightify' cites only Ireland, with the meaning 'to put to rights, rectify; to correct,' and provides a quotation from Lover, *Legends and Stories of Ireland*, II, 357: "I wondher any one would throw away their time sthrivin' to rightify you"); cf. rectify < F *rectifier* < LL *rectificare*.

rince /ˈrɪŋkə/ *n.,* dancing ('as of the sun') (SOM, Kerry) < Ir < E *rink*.

rince fada /rɪŋkəˈfɑd̪ə/ *n.,* a kind of country dance (KM, Kerry) < Ir *rince fada*, long dance. 'There was great sport with the rince fada at the crossroads.'

ríobal /ˈriːbəl/ *n.,* mud, mire; wet < Ir. 'Where on earth have you been? Look at the ríobal on your clothes!'

rioball /ˈrɪbəl/ *n.,* a tail (SOM, Kerry) < Ir.

rip /rɪp/ *n. (pejor.)*, general term of abuse for a woman < E dial. (origin obscure). 'Get that old rip out of here!' (Louth).

rírá /ˈriːrɔː/ *n.,* a hubbub, an uproar (MK, Galway); confusion; revelry < Ir. 'Such a rírá there was after the quiz!'; 'There was total rírá when the teacher left the room' (SOM, Kerry). *See* RUAILLE BUAILLE.

rócán, *see* RABHCÁN.

rod, *see* SCALLOPS.

rógaire /ˈroːgərə/ *n.,* a rogue (said with a hint of approval) (SOM, Kerry) < Ir.

roilleach /ˈrʌləx/ *n.,* an oyster-catcher (MK, Galway); fig. a brindled animal (i.e. like an oyster-catcher's coat) < Ir. 'Bring in that roilleach cow and milk her.'

roolyeh, *see* RUAILLE.

room /ruːm/ *n.,* frequently refers to a room other than the kitchen, especially a bedroom (cf. Ir *seomra*, room, bedroom < AN *chambre*). 'Where's the cat?' – 'She's DOWN in the room.'

Rosary /ˈroːzəri/ *n.*, a string of beads (sometimes referred to as 'a beads': *see* BEAD) used as a guide in devotions to the Blessed Virgin Mary < L *rosarium*, *n.*, rose-garden. 'We always used to kneel down, the whole family of us, when we were children and say the rosary before we went to bed of an evening' (*see* PADDHEREEN) (Mayo). At sea there was a custom that fishermen recited the Rosary at midnight, while the men waited to cast or haul in their nets, to ensure a good catch. Kickham, *Knocknagow*, 27: "Instead of summoning the servants to prayers in the parlour it is the general custom, among Irish Catholics of the middle class, for the master and mistress of the house with their children and guests – unless the latter should happen not to be Catholics – to 'say the Rosary' in the kitchen"; Kavanagh, *Tarry Flynn*, 156: "And now in the name of God . . . let us all kneel down and say the Rosary for my special intention"; Heaney, 'The Other Side', III (*New Selected Poems, 1966–1987*, 29): "Then sometimes when the rosary was dragging I mournfully on in the kitchen I we would hear his step round the gable"; Doyle, *The Van*, 154: "He's very religious, yeh know. He always has rosary beads in his kit bag."

Rosary beads /ˈroːzəribiːdz/ also **(a) beads** *n.phr.*, a string of beads consisting of five groups (DECADES) of ten small beads separated by a larger bead, used as a guide in saying the ROSARY. Montague, 'The Living and the Dead' (*Collected Poems*, 17): "Instead of a worn rosary I I tell these metal keys"; Doyle, *The Van*, 154: "He's very religious, yeh know. He always has rosary beads in his kit bag."

Rosary Crusade /ˈroːzəriː kruːˈseːd/ *n.phr.*, a movement to encourage families to say the ROSARY together. Kavanagh, 'Adventures in the Bohemian Jungle' (*Collected Poems*, 107): "*Interviewers:* . . . Did the Cleaner Films and Rosary Crusade I Bring further customers to the Cinema?"

rose /roːz/ *n.*, erysipelas, usually affecting the face, turning it a red colour < E dial. 'He must have a touch of the rose – what else could it be?' (BC, Meath).

rossey /ˈrɑsi/ also **rossie** *n.*, a strumpet; a woman on the look-out for fun (Dublin) < Ir *rásaí.* 'Rossie maggot' (Dublin). Joyce, *Finnegans Wake*, 95.4: "and the O'Briny rossies chaffing him bluchface."

rothail /ˈrʌhəl/ *n.*, a hurry, a rush; a hurried visit (KM, Kerry) < Ir. What's the rothail on you?'

rothán /ˈrʌhɔːn/ *n.*, a fit of anger; angry words (ML, Mayo); a huff < Ir. 'With him it's peace one minute and rothán the next.'

rounds /raundz/ *n.pl.*, religious ceremony carried out at a blessed well (Omurethi, Kildare, 539, who notes: 'turrases [Ir *turais*] are "rounds" at a blessed well.' *See* TURAS.

RTE /ɔːrtiːˈiː/ for Radio Telefís Éireann, the public radio and television service, a name adopted under the Broadcasting (Amendment) Act (1966) and derived from the amalgamation of Radio Éireann and Telefís Éireann. 'Do you MIND the time we used listen to the match on

RTE in London of a Sunday afternoon? We had to bring the set out onto the landing for the best reception' (SOC, Kerry).

rua /ruə/ *adj.,* red-headed < Ir. 'Madra rua', a fox (SOM, Kerry).

ruadog /ˈruədʌg/ *n.*, a cord of plaited flax; a waxed flaxen cord used by cobblers (KM, Kerry) < Ir.

ruaig /ruəg/ *n.,* a swoop; a chase, a pursuit (MK, Galway); putting to flight, banishment (SOM, Kerry) < Ir. 'The fox was in the HAGGARD. I put a ruaig on him when I called the dogs'; 'The scare-crow put the ruaig on them for a TAMALL, but they were back in the evening as bad as ever' (SOM, Kerry).

ruaille /ˈruːljə/ also **roolyeh** (LUB, Dublin) *n.,* a slovenly, untidy woman < Ir. 'When you think what a ruaille she was before she married, and look at her now in her fine feathers!'

ruaille buaille /ruːljəˈbuːljə/ *n.,* a row; uproar, confusion; a free-for-all (SOM, Kerry) < Ir. 'There was such ruaille buaille looking for the pincers; the whole house was TRÍNA CHÉILE' (KM, Kerry).

rua piast /ˈruəˈpiːst̪/ also **rua péiste** /ˈruəˈpeːʃtə/ *n.,* 'red-water' (a disease in cattle) (KM, Kerry) < Ir.

ruathaire /ˈruːhərə/ *n.,* a vagrant cow or goat that would forage in a neighbour's garden (SOM, Kerry) < Ir. 'Ruathaire práta' /ˈruːhərəˈprɔːt̪ə/, a stray potato or stone missed in the original picking; a small potato; fig. a runt < Ir.

ruathar /ˈruːhər/ *n.,* a headlong attack, a foray, a charge < Ir. 'The gadfly came out and the heifers took off in a fierce ruathar' (SOM, Kerry).

rub /rʌb/ *v.,* in the *phr.* (*colloq.*) 'a rub of the relic,' sexual intercourse – 'a rude allusion to an exemplary Catholic practice' (KD, Dublin).

rúcach /ˈruːkək/ *n.,* a rough, boorish person; a very rough animal (KM, Kerry) < Ir. 'Don't let that rúcach in to me'; 'Keep that rúcach away from me. I hate that look he gives me.'

ruction /ˈrʌkʃən/ *n.,* a disturbance, agitation; disorderly behaviour (origin obscure; J.J. Hogan, quoted by LUB, Dublin, 180, notes: 'Now in general dialect and colloquial use in Britain and America, but originally Irish; alteration of *insurrection*, and referring at first to that of 1798'; Griffith, 35: 'Ruction, a disturbance, is not uncommon in the speech of Irish Americans . . . a corruption of *insurrection'*; another suggestion (*ODEE*) is that it is a humorous formation based on L *ructus*, belch). 'If you don't bring back that bike there'll be ructions! How do think am I to get into town? The bus has gone down early' (Meath). 'Finnegan's Wake' (song): "And a row and a ruction soon began."

rúisc /ruːʃk/ *n.,* a shot, a volley; a large, lumpish person (ML, Mayo) < Ir.

rúitín /'ruːʧiːn/ *n.,* the ankle (SOM, Kerry); a knuckle; the fetlock or pastern of a horse; the hoof of a cow or a pig < Ir.

rún /ruːn/ *n.,* a secret; an intention; a loved one < Ir. 'A rún (*voc.,* darling) < Ir.

runner, *see* RESIDENTER.

runt /rʌnt/ *n.,* the smallest pig in a litter; a small pig; a small animal < E dial. (origin unknown). 'She took the runt into the house and fed it with a bottle, poor little thing.'

rúóg /'ruːoːg/ *n.,* a cord of plaited flax; a waxed cord used by cobblers (KM, Kerry) < Ir.

rut /rʌt/ *n.,* the smallest of a litter of pigs (Omurethi, Kildare); the smallest child of a family (LUB, Dublin). Hogan notes: 'Apparently Anglo-Irish [i.e. HE] only' < E dial. (cited for Ireland only). *See* RUNT.

rútáil /ruː't̪ɔːl/ *v.n.,* rooting about, searching (KM, Kerry); rooting about (as of a pig) < Ir. 'Stop rútáiling in the press.'

ruth ruth /rʌhrʌh/ also **rith rith** /rɪhrɪh/, words used to encourage a bull to service a cow (Mayo) < Ir *ruth* (variant of *rith*). 'All the ruth ruth in the world isn't going to calm her down.'

S

sagart /ˈsɑgərt̪/ also **saggarth, soggart** *n.*, a priest; sometimes used as a nickname for someone who left the seminary, e.g. 'the Sagart', 'Jack the Sagart' (SOM, Kerry) < Ir. Joyce, *Finnegans Wake*, 98.16: "he saw the family saggarth"; O'Casey, *Juno and the Paycock*, act II, 33: "*Joxer*: Who was it led the van, Soggart AROON? | Since the fight first began, Soggart Aroon?"

saileog /ˈsæloːg/ *n.*, willow (SOM, Kerry) < Ir. 'I'll go and cut a saileog from the garden, and then I'll put manners on you [chastise you]' (Cavan). *See* SALLY.

sáimhín só /ˈsɔːviːnˈsoː/ *n.*, contentment, ease (SOM, Kerry) < Ir.

St Vincent de Paul, Society of /seːntˈvɪnsəndəˈpɔːl/ *n.phr.*, a Catholic lay association for helping people in difficult financial circumstances, founded in 1833 by the French scholar Antoine-Frédéric Ozanam and named after St Vincent de Paul (*c.* 1580–1660), founder of the Lazarists (also known as the Vincentians) and the Sisters of Charity. 'He does a lot of work for the V de P' (MCR, Waterford). O'Casey, *Juno and the Paycock*, act I, 28: "I hereby order and wish my property to be sold and divided as follows: – £20 to the St Vincent de Paul Society . . ."; McCourt, *Angela's Ashes*, 65: "an' if there's one word out of the St Vincent de Paul Society I'll take the face of 'em, so I will."

sáiteán /sɔːˈʧɔːn/ *n.*, a perpendicular stake used in the making of baskets or CREELS (KM, Kerry) < Ir. 'The sáiteáns were crooked, and the creel fell apart.'

sáith /sɔː/ *n.*, a sufficient quantity, enough < Ir. 'I had my sáith of trouble' (SOM, Kerry).

salach /sɑˈləx/ *adj.*, dirty (SOM, Kerry) < Ir. 'Salach by nature and in dress!'; 'Páidín salach!', dirty Páidín.

salachar /ˈsɑləxər/ *n.*, dirt, filth (SOM, Kerry) < Ir.

sally /ˈsæli/ *n.*, willow < Ir *saileach*. 'Sally (rod)', a stick for discipline (MOB, Mayo). 'The teacher had the sally out that day, because everyone was talking in the class' (KG, Kerry).

sambo /'sæmbo/ *n.* (*colloq.*). 1. A sandwich < E *sandwich* (*see* -o). 'Give us two cheese sambos' (KM, Dublin). 2. Stale bread < Ir *sambó.*

sámh /sɔːv/ *adj.,* comfortable, peaceful, untroubled (as of sleep) (SOM, Kerry) < Ir.

samhadh /'sɑuə/ *n.,* wood sorrel < Ir.

Samhain /saun/ *n.,* an ancient Celtic festival (1 November) marking the beginning of winter < Ir. *See* SOWENS.

samhaircín /'saurkiːn/ *n.,* primrose < Ir. 'The samhaircín flowers again in autumn, and even winter if we're lucky.'

sámhán /'sɔːvɔːn/ *n.,* a nap, a short sleep; fig. a sleepy, dozy person (ENM, Kerry); 'a quiet reflective mood or day-dream; a state of repose or tranquility' (Moylan, 223) < Ir. 'I do always like to take a sámhán after my dinner; they reckon nowadays it's a healthy thing to do' (TJ, Sligo).

samlach /sɑmləx/ *n.,* 'insipid putrid drink, tea brewed to the point of being almost black and then allowed to stand for an inordinate time' (SOM, Kerry) < Ir. 'That tea is pure samlach' (SOM, Kerry, who writes: 'I discussed this term at length with T. de Bhaldraithe and he thought it might have the same origin as sambó, stale hard brown bread').

sanatorium /sænə'toːriəm/ *n.,* a hospital, especially one for the care of convalescents and of people suffering from tuberculosis (coined from L *sanatorius,* curative). '. . . Others spent long terms in sanatoria, of which Newcastle, Co. Wicklow, was the most convenient to Dundrum' (Nolan, 69).

saoiste /'siːʃtʃə/ *n.,* a seat of plaited straw or rushes; a small seat in a corner; a footstool (KM, Kerry) < Ir. 'Draw up the saoiste and take your ease!'

Saorstát Éireann /'siːrst̪ɔːt̪ 'eːrən/ *n.,* Ir name of the Irish Free State (1922–1937) < Ir *saorstát*, free state (originally republic) + *Éireann* (genitive), Ireland. Joyce, *Finnegans Wake*, 69.14–15: "In the drema of Sorestost Areas." *See* FREE STATE.

saothar /'siːhər/ *n.* 1. Hard work; a great effort; working in a busy fashion, in a hurry (SOM, Kerry) < Ir. 2. Breathlessness (DB, Cork); shortness of breath from running, cycling, or working hard < Ir.

saothrach /'siːhrəx/ *adj.,* busy, industrious (SOM, Kerry) < Ir.

sásamh /'sɔːsəv/ *n.,* pleasure, satisfaction < Ir. 'Have you your sásamh yet, gutsy?' (Mayo).

Sassenach /'sɑsənəx/ also **Sassanagh, Sassenagh**, etc. *n.,* an English person < Ir *Sasanach* < E *Saxon*. 'Well, I never seen as many Sasanachs as there are here this year – the place is overrun with them' (KG, Kerry). Sheehan, *Glenanaar*, 154: "And think of your father swung by the throat by thim Sassanachs in Cork"; Joyce, *Finnegans Wake*, 552.29: "'and she sass her nach."

sass her nach, *see* SASANAGH.

sásta /ˈsɔːst̪ə/ *adj.,* contented, comfortable < Ir. 'Are you sásta over there in the SETTLE-BED?' (AF, Cavan).

sauvaun, *see* SÁMHÁN.

says /sɛz/ *v.,* in such expressions as 'says he,' 'says she,' etc. < Ir *ar* (defective verb), says, said + personal pronoun (used only with third person singular and plural). '"Get out of the car," says she to me' (KG, Kerry). Stoker, *The Snake's Pass*, 21: "'Because,' sez he, 'this is my own houldin',' sez he, 'be perscriptive right,' sez he.'"

sbrogue *see* BROGUE.

SC abbreviation for senior counsel. 'He's an SC now and is doing very well on the Munster circuit' (KG, Kerry).

scadán /ˈskɑd̪ɔːn/ *n.,* a herring; a small fish (SL, Mayo) < Ir. 'I'm not going all the way up to that lake again; there's nothing in it only scadáns.'

scafaire /ˈskɑfərə/ *n.,* a healthy, strapping young man; 'scafaire mná', a fine healthy girl (KM, Kerry) < Ir. 'Come on, me scafaire, and lift the bucket!'; 'I'd have hardly recognised her now, she's turned into such a fine scafaire of a girl.'

scailp /skælp/ also **scalp, scalpeen, scolp** *n.,* a crude shelter made of sods etc. erected for travellers in need of protection from the elements; a rude cabin < Ir. The Poor Relief (Ireland) Act (1838) permitted landlords to throw out unwanted tenants, who often resorted to digging a hole in the ground and roofing it over with sticks (see O'Connor, *The Workhouses of Ireland*, 156).

scailtín /ˈskælʧiːn/ also **scawlteen, scaultheen** *n.,* hot whiskey (sometimes flavoured with butter, caraway seed, etc.); whiskey punch; 'a hot drink, consisting of burnt whiskey [i.e. that has been heated and set alight], hot milk, ginger, butter, and sugar . . . Another form of scaultheen was composed of burnt whiskey, hot buttermilk, and thin oatenmeal, forming a gruel-like mixture' (Omurethi, Kildare, 537) < Ir. 'You're wet through; that scáiltín will do you good' (KG, Kerry); 'Every time I have a scailtín it always reminds me of Christmas: we used to drink loads of them on Christmas Eve' (Mayo).

scaird /skærʤ/ *n.,* a jet, a squirt, a splash < Ir. 'I'll just take a scaird of tea' (TJ, Sligo).

scairt[1] /skærʧ/ *n.,* the midriff, the innards < Ir. 'I had a pain in my scairt' (SOM, Kerry) < Ir. 'Greadadh trí lár do scairt!' (curse), a scorching through your stomach (SOM, Kerry) < Ir.

scairt[2] /skærtʃ/ *n.,* a thicket; a bush < Ir. 'Put a scairt in the gap to stop the sheep getting out' (Mayo).

scairt[3] /skærtʃ/ *n.,* a shout; a fit of laughing < Ir.

scalded /'skɔːldəd/ *p.part.,* tormented < E dial. *scald, v.,* to vex; disgust. 'That impudent-face has me scalded with his bad manners' (LUB, Dublin).

scalder /'skɔːl̪dər/ n., an ill-tempered person (HJ, Wexford) < E dial. (*see* SCALDED). 'Here come the scalders (Wexford).'

scaldered / 'skɔːl̪dərd/ *p.part.,* (a piece of wood) with the surface peeled off to reveal the bare knots (Wexford) < E dial. (*see* SCALDED).

scald, scaldy /'skɔːld/, /'skɔːldi/ *n.,* an unfledged bird; an unfledged crow; the bare top of the head (LUB, Dublin); a rabbit without fur < E dial. (cf. ON *skalli*, a baldhead). *See* SCALLTÁN; SCAULS.

scalladh croí /skɑlə'kriː/ *n.,* heart-burn; fig. ill-treatment < Ir. 'She gave her scalladh croí from the day she was born – but she still loves her all the same' (KG, Kerry).

scallan, *see* SCÁTHLÁN.

scallion /'skæljən/ *n.,* a spring onion; an onion with a small or undeveloped bulb < E dial. < OF *escalogne*. 'Go out to the garden and pick some scallions for the tea' (BC, Meath).

scallop, *see* SCOLLOP.

scalltán /'skɑl̪tɔːn/ *n.,* a fledgling; fig. a frail little creature < Ir. 'Ah, the poor wee scalltán, give it some water!' (BC, Meath). *See* SCALD.

scalp, *see* SCAILP.

scanradh /'skɑnrə/ *n.,* fear, fright < Ir. 'She put the scanradh on them' (KG, Kerry).

scaothaire /'skiːhərə/ *n.,* a bombastic talker, a windbag < Ir. 'One of my grand-uncles was known within the family as Dan the Scaothaire' (SOM, Kerry).

scapular /'skæpjuːlər/ *n.,* a garment of varying sizes, ranging from the two ankle-length strips of cloth (put over the head and falling front and back of the body), worn originally as part of the working attire of Benedictine monks (prescribed in chapter 55 of the Rule of St Benedict, drawn up *c.* AD 540), to two pieces of cloth, about 3 inches by 2 inches, joined by strings and worn back and front under the clothes by members of the faithful, clerical and lay; in shape the scapular symbolises the yoke of Christ, as referred to in Matthew 11:29: 'Tollite iugum meum super vos,' Take up my yoke upon you'; many Irish people, especially members of the THIRD ORDER, wear the scapular < L *scapula*, shoulder. 'I wouldn't feel right without my scapular' (KG, Kerry).

scarting /'skærtən/ *v. (pres. part.),* trimming hedges and clearing ditches at the side of the road, normally done by county council workmen (RB, Waterford) < E dial. *scart* (metathesis of SCRAT, *v.*, to scratch, scrape; cf. also SCAIRT[2]).

scáth /skɔː/ *n.*, a shadow < Ir.

scáthán /'skɔːhɔːn/ *n.*, a mirror (BC, Meath) < Ir.

scáthlán /'skɔːlɔːn/ also **scallan** *n.*, a makeshift hut or shed in which Mass was said in Penal Law times < Ir. PWJ, 145: 'In Donegal and elsewhere they had a movable little wooden shed that just sheltered the priest and the sacred appliances while he celebrated Mass, and which was wheeled about from place to place in the parish wherever required.'

scauls /skɔːlz/ *n.pl.*, unfledged birds or young rabbits without fur (Omurethi, Kildare). *See* SCALD.

scaultheen, *see* SCÁILTÍN.

sceabha /ʃkau/ *n.*, a slant; a wall on the tilt, out of plumb (SOC, Kerry) < Ir. 'Sceabha-ways', tilted (*see* SKEW-WAYS).

sceabhach /ʃkaux/ *adj.*, slanting, sloping < Ir. 'I think your chimney's sceabhach' (BC, Meath).

sceach /ʃkæx/ also **skeoch** (Omurethi, Kildare) *n.*, a whitethorn bush; a bush; fig. a prickly, tetchy person < Ir. 'Put a few sceachs in the DITCH to keep out those conniving thieves of cows!' (SOM, Kerry). 'Sceach gheal', whitethorn (SOM, Kerry).

sceachóir /ʃkæ'xoːr/ also **sceachóid** /ʃkæ'xoːʤ/ *n.*, rosehip; a haw (KM, Kerry) < Ir. Kickham, *Knocknagow*, 46: "'What have you under the crib to tempt the birds to go into it?' 'A bit of biled PUETA, sir,' Tommy answered readily. 'An' a SHILLIG-A-BOOKA, and a few skhehoshies [*sceachóidí*].' Richard explained that the . . . skhehoshies [meant] the scarlet hips of the wild briar."

sceadóg /ʃkæ'd̪oːg/ *n.*, an animal with a white mark on its face; an animal with a spotted coat < Ir. 'Sceadógach' *adj.* 'Milk the sceadógach cow first' (KM, Kerry).

scéal /ʃkeːl/, /ʃkiːl/ *n.*, a story; news < Ir. 'Well, once he started with this scéal about this woman he met in America there was no stopping him – we listened to him all night'; 'Have you any scéal from town?'; 'Ní fiú dada scéal gan údar' (proverb), A story without authority is worthless; 'Scéal bacach é,' that's a lame story (SOM, Kerry). 'Sin scéal eile,' that's another story.

scealbóg /'ʃkæləboːg/ *n.*, a splinter (ML, Mayo) < Ir. 'There's a scealbóg in my finger'; 'You'd better wear these gloves or your nails will be full of scealbógs.'

sceall /skæl/ *n.*, the outer roof on a hay-stack (JOM, Kerry) < Ir.

sceallán /ʃkæl'ɔːn/ also **sciollán, skillaun** /'ʃkɪl'ɔːn/ *n.*, a seed-potato with an 'eye' (ENM, Kerry); a cut portion of a potato containing an eye used as a seed for the next crop (KM, Kerry) < Ir. 'Make sure there's an eye in each of those scealláns before you cut them up' (BC, Meath); 'Have you sciolláns made of the potatoes yet?' 'Sceallán knife', a knife used for cutting seed-potatoes.

scealp /ʃkælp/ *n.,* a bit cut off; bits of fat meat fried crisp < Ir. 'Give me the scealps any day – that's the bit I like best' (BC, Meath).

sceartán /'ʃkært̪ɔːn/ also **sciortán** /ʃkɪr't̪ɔːn/, **sceortán, schirtaun** *n.,* a tick; a cow's vermin; a leech; a louse; sticky green seeds that stick to clothes (MK, Galway) < Ir. 'That's a sceartán on your finger, isn't it?'; 'Don't go near those ones; they're full of sceartáns, and I don't want you to catch any'; 'You're clinging to me like a schirtaun' (MC, Kildare).

Sceilg's List /'ʃkɛləgz'lɪst/ *n.phr.,* a lampoon formerly circulated at Shrovetide (just before Lent) about couples who had not yet married (SOM, Kerry). The reference is to the inhospitable island of Sceilg Mhichíl, regarded as being outside church jurisdiction, where couples who had not married within the customary period between Christmas and Lent would supposedly have to go to marry.

sceilmis /'ʃkɛləmɪʃ/ *n.,* fright; shame, disgrace; mischievous gossip (SOM, Kerry) < Ir. 'Sceilmis ort!' (shame on you); 'What's the latest sceilimis from town?'

sceilp, *see* SKELP.

sceon /ʃkjoːn/ *n.,* terror; a frightened look (VQ, Kerry) < Ir. 'There was a sceon to her' (she had a look of terror in her eyes) (KM, Kerry).

sceortán, *see* SCEARTÁN.

scheme /skiːm/ *n.,* a housing estate, especially a council one (KD, Dublin) < *housing scheme*. *See* PURCHASE-HOUSE.

schlooderer, *see* SLUTHER.

scholard /'skɑlərd/ *n.,* one who can read and write < E dial. (variant of *scholar*). Doyle, *Irish Cottagers*, 73: "Aren't you a scollard?"; Joyce, *Finnegans Wake*, 215.26: "Latin me that, my trinity scholard."

scian /ʃkiən/ *n.,* a knife (SOM, Kerry) < Ir. 'Mind that scian – it's very sharp' (Cavan). 'Scian na coise duibhe', a black-handled knife (regarded as protection against the spirit world) < Ir.

sciathán /'ʃkiəhɔːn/ a wing; an arm (SOM, Kerry) < Ir. 'His sciathán is in a sling.'

sciathán leathair /'ʃkiəhɔːn 'læhər/ *n.,* a bat (SOM, Kerry) < Ir (lit. leather-wing).

sciathóg /'ʃkiəhoːg/ *n.,* a wicker basket for potatoes; a basket for holding cooked potatoes on the dinner-table; the detachable base of a pannier < Ir. *See* BARDÓG; PARDÓG.

scib /ʃkɪb/ *n.*, a basket; a potato-basket (Moylan, 227); a turf-basket; a small load < Ir. 'Get me a scib of turf for the fire.'

scileach /'ʃkɪləx/ *n.*, shelled corn < Ir. 'What's to be done with them scileachs?'

scilléad /'ʃkɪleːd̪/ *n.*, a small pot; a skillet < Ir < E *skillet* (perhaps an aphetic form of OF *escuelete*, a small platter). 'When you've picked the mushrooms, put them in the scilléad and boil them in salt water – delicious!' (BC, Meath).

sciob /ʃkɪb/ also **skib** *v.*, to snatch < Ir. 'Will you stop skibbing the spuds off the table!'

sciodar /'ʃkɪd̪ər/ *n.*, sour milk; watery STIRABOUT (SOM, Kerry); diarrhoea; the dregs; fig. a useless person < Ir. 'The fool gets the sciodar' (i.e. the dregs) (SOM, Kerry).

sciollán, *see* SCEALLÁN.

sciollóg /ʃkɪ'loːg/ *n.*, the discarded portion of the potato after the SCEALLÁN is cut off (SOM, Kerry, who adds: 'the sciollógs were boiled and used as animal feed') < Ir.

sciortán, *see* SCEARTÁN.

sciotaire /'ʃkjʌt̪ərə/ *n.*, a giggler; a hale and hearty person (SOM, Kerry) < Ir. 'Sciotaire mná', a hearty woman < Ir.

scíth /ʃkiː/ *n.*, rest; a pause, a break < Ir. 'Lig do scíth' /lɪgd̪ʌ'ʃkiː/, have a rest (MC, Kildare) < Ir. 'Tóg do scíth' /t̪oːgd̪ʌ'ʃkiː/, take a break; take it nice and easy (SOM, Kerry) < Ir. 'Lig do scíth there for a few minutes TILL we have a smoke.'

sciuird /ʃkuːrd/ *n.*, a rush; a quick visit < Ir. 'I'm making a sciuird into town – will you bring in the cows?' (SOM, Kerry).

scléip /ʃkleːp/ *n.*, fun, a good time (especially as applied to children) (SOM, Kerry) < Ir.

scobe /skoːb/ *v.*, to scoop out roughly, to make hollow < E dial. (cf. E *scobe, v.*, to gag).

scobs, scobbing, *see* BOLD; SCOBE.

scodalach /'skʌd̪ələx/ *n.*, a big lanky person (KG, Kerry) < Ir. 'Watch where that scodalach's going with the ball!'

scoil /skʌl/ *n.*, a school < Ir. 'All the girls went to Scoil Mhuire – I don't know where the boys went' (Dublin).

scoilt /skʌltʃ/ *n.*, a split, a crack (SOM, Kerry); a fissure; the mouth of an underground passage; a furrow < Ir.

scoilteán /'skʌltʃɔːn/ *n.*, a small stick < Ir. 'He'll have the scoilteán out to you if he sees you anywhere near the orchard!' (TF, Cavan).

scóipéalach /skoːp'eːləx/ *adj.*, roomy; wide-reaching and energetic; having a good reach (SOM, Kerry) < Ir. 'She's a fine scóipéalach woman' (i.e. she can achieve a fine rate of work) (SOM, Kerry).

scoláire /skʌ'lɔːrə/ *n.,* a scholar; a student; often used as a term of affection for a well-behaved, hard-working child (PR, Mayo). 'He was always a bit of a scoláire; it's a pity he never made more use of it.' 'Scoláire bocht', a 'poor scholar', a wandering student such as attended HEDGE-SCHOOLS.

scolb, *see* SCOLLOP.

scollard, *see* SCHOLARD.

scollop /'skɑləp/ also **scallop** /'skæləp/, **scolb** /skʌləb/ *n.,* a SALLY ROD or hazel twig used in thatching and other work involving straw, e.g. CREELS (Mayo); a splinter of wood; fig. a thin, wiry man < Ir *scoilb*. 'These were also known as rods or spars, and the slightly longer ones as sways' (Sharkey, 16). 'Ní hé lá na gaoithe lá na scolb' (proverb), The windy day is not the day of the scollops (i.e. of preparing for thatching) (SOM, Kerry). Heaney, 'Land' (*Wintering Out*, 21): "a woman of old wet leaves, rush-bands and thatcher's scollops." 'Scolb giúise', a splinter of bog-wood < Ir.

scológ /skʌ'loːg/ *n.,* a small farmer; a hard-working young man < Ir. 'He'd always be saying "scológs are the backbone of this country," Lord have mercy on him' (KG, Kerry),

sconsa /'skʌnsə/ *n.,* a fence; a drain; fig. a corner-boy (Galway) < Ir.

scoraíocht /'skʌriːʌxt̪/, /skʌ'riːəxt̪/ *n.,* a social evening; a party in the house; a visit at night to a neighbour's house to make merry or exchange gossip; roving about < Ir. 'Scoraíochting', *v.n.,* making such a visit (SOM, Kerry) < Ir.

scorán /'skʌrɔːn/ *n.,* a pin, a toggle (MK, Galway) < Ir. 'Hand me that scorán over there, will you?'

scornach /'skʌrnəx/, /'skɔːrnəx/ *n.,* the throat (KM, Kerry) < Ir.

scourer /'skaurər/ *n.,* a grabbing, greedy person, e.g. a farmer wanting to gain more land and using any means to do so < E dial. (origin obscure). 'Watch out for that old scourer at the auction; he'll make you pay a good price for that land if he doesn't get it himself' (BC, Meath).

scráib /'skrɔːb/ also **scráb, scrawb, scraub** (LUB, Dublin) *n., v.* 1. A scrape; to wound or scratch, as with briars, fingernails, etc. (LUB, Dublin) < Ir. 2. A shower < Ir. 'Scráib shneachta', a shower of snow (Galway).

scráideog /'skrɔːʤoːg/ *n.,* a scrawny thing; a small person; a useless, insignificant person or thing < Ir. 'Such a scráideog she turned out to be, and all the talk there was of her when she was a child!' (Kerry).

scráidín /'skrɔːʤiːn/ also **scrawdeen** *n.,* scrap of food; a small apple; a little potato; fig. a small, puny person < Ir. 'What are you boiling those scráidíns for? They're hardly worth peeling' (TJ, Sligo); 'She married a small little scráidín, but the match turned out very well, thanks be to God' (BC, Meath).

scraiste /ˈskræʃtʃə/ *n.*, a loafer, a lazy man < Ir.

scraith /skræh/ *n.*, the rough sods grubbed off a turf bank before cutting turf (SOM, Kerry); SCRAW < Ir.

scraith bhogáin /skræhˈvʌgɔːn/ *n.*, a quagmire (KM, Kerry) < Ir. 'Be careful of the scraith bhogáin when you're coming home – it's turning foggy!' (Kerry).

scraitheog /ˈskræhoːg/ *n.*, a grassy sod < Ir. 'Lie the child down on that scraitheog' (BC, Meath).

scran /skrɑn/ *n.*, provisions; a labourer's food; poor food unfit for human consumption < E dial. (origin obscure). 'Bad scran to you,' bad luck to you. Sheehan, *Glenanaar*, 167: "Sure, they say her father and mother, bad scran to them, are safe and sound in America"; Leonard, *Out After Dark*, 134: "I suppose me curse-o'-God horse is down the field again, bad scran to it?"

scrat /skræt/ *v.*, to scratch potatoes out of the soil after the land has been ploughed < E dial. < ME *scratten, v.*, to scratch. 'Scrattin' spuds is hard on the back' (JL, Mayo). SEE SCARTING.

scraw /skrɔː/ *n.*, a strip of sod cut out of grassy or boggy land for making a fire or for protecting a thatched roof; 'a shaking scraw is what looks like firm walking on a bog; but when one's weight is on it, it begins to heave all around one, owing to its almost floating condition' (Omurethi, Kildare) < Ir SCRAITH. 'I'll have to put a few scraws on the roof' (TF, Cavan).

screab /ʃkræb/ *n.*, scum, crust; fig. a detestable person < Ir. 'Pay up, ye screab ye!' (JL, Mayo).

scréach /ʃkreːx/ *n.*, a screech; a yell < Ir. 'Such a scréach the pig let out when we put the ring in its nose!' (TF, Sligo).

scread /ʃkræd̪/ *n.*, a scream, a shout, a yell < Ir. 'He gave an almighty scread out of him' (SOM, Kerry) < Ir. May be used as a nickname: 'Cronin Scread'; 'the Screads' (SOM, Kerry).

screadal /ˈʃkræd̪əl/ *n.*, crying, screaming, yelling (KM, Kerry) (cf. Ir *screadaíl*). 'He ran out of the house screadaling.'

screamh /ʃkræv/ *n.*, scum; fig. an unpleasant, unprepossessing person (KM, Kerry) < Ir. 'I hate it when that screamh comes to the house; I don't know what to say to him.'

screan /skræn/ *n.*, in the phrase 'Screan ort!' (= bad luck to you) < Ir. *See* SCRAN.

screatall /ˈskrætəl/ *n.*, a fragment, a bit; (with negative) nothing (MK, Galway) < Ir. 'Not a screatall done!'

screed /skriːd/ *n.*, a rag; a shred, a fragment; a stitch of clothing < E dial. 'They were so badly off there wasn't a screed of clothes by them [on them]' (KG, Kerry).

scríob /ʃkriːb/ *n.*, a scratch; a scraping, a scoring; a mark in a field to guide the ploughman (TF, Cavan) < Ir. 'FOLLY the scríob.'

scrios /skrɪs/ *n.*, destruction, ruin (JOM, Kerry) < Ir. 'There was terrible scrios at the fight' (SOM, Kerry); 'She tore the book and made a scrios of it' (TJ, Sligo). 'Scrios MÍLE MURDER', great damage, destruction (VQ, Kerry).

scroblach /ˈskrʌbləx/ *n.*, a morsel, a remnant; refuse; fig. rabble < Ir. 'Not a scroblach did she leave for the CHILDER; it all went on the drink.'

scrogall /skrʌgəl/ *n.*, the throat; a narrow passage-way in the body; a scraggy neck; the spout of a kettle, teapot, or bottle < Ir. 'Get that drink down your scrogall – there's plenty more where that came from'; 'The opening of a pig's bladder. After a pig was killed and butchered, the kids would ask for the ball, and I remember my grandfather telling me to get a goose quill. He cut it and "freed" it out and used it like a drinking straw and blew up the bladder to make a drinking straw' (KM, Kerry).

scroodge /skruːʤ/ also **scrouge** *v.*, squeeze, press together (LUB, Dublin) < E dial. (*Chambers* s.v. 'scrouge', refers to *scruze, v.,* to squeeze (dialect); 'perh. screw combined with squeeze'; Hogan: 'a general dialect word'). 'There was terrible scroodging in to the pictures' (LUB, Dublin).

scruta /ˈskrʌtə/ also **scrut** /skrʌt/ *n.*, a stunted person; a good-for-nothing, mean person (sometimes used as a nickname) < Ir (cf. *EDD* s.v. 'SCUT'). 'Nothing good will ever come to that scruta; he hasn't a friend in the world' (KG, Kerry).

scuaibín /ˈskuːbiːn/ also **skoobeen** *n.*, sweepstake; a game at cards; the final game at a card party when the pool as well as the stakes are played for (Martin, 183–4) < Ir (dimin. of *scuab*, brush). 'You couldn't beat the pair of them at scuaibín; they're always tricking!'

scunner /ˈskʌnər/ also **scunder** /ˈskʌndər/ *n., v.,* a feeling of disgust or loathing; to disgust (origin obscure, but cf. ME *scunneren*, to loathe, avoid). 'She took a scunner to me as soon as ever she set eyes on me' (JMF, Cavan).

scut[1] /skʌt/ *n. (pejor.),* a contemptible person; a person of bad character (sometimes found as a nickname, e.g. 'Paddy the Scut') < E dial. *scut*, tail of hare or rabbit. 'Come in here, you little scut, and eat your dinner' (BC, Meath). Kavanagh, *Tarry Flynn*, 34: "'Go lang, ye scut, ye,' said the mother"; Heaney, 'Midnight' (*Wintering Out*, 45–6): "The PADS are lost or | Retrieved by small vermin | That glisten and scut."

scut^2 /skʌt/ *n., v.* (*colloq.*), to hang onto the back of a bus or lorry (KD, Dublin) (cf. SCUT^1).

scuttered /ˈskʌt̪ərd/ *p.part.* (*colloq.*), drunk (*see* SCUT^1).

sea /ʃæ/ *adv.phr.* of affirmation: yes; that is so < Ir *sea* < *is ea*, it is. 'Sea, too,' you don't say! (usually sarcastically) (SOM, Kerry).

seach /ʃɑx/, /ʃʌx/ also **shaugh, shough** etc. *n.*, (to take) a pull at a pipe < Ir *seach*, a turn or spell at something. 'There's nothing to beat the first seach of the pipe in the evening'; 'Well, he took a seach at the pipe and died – that's the truth of it' (TF, Cavan). Kickham, *Knocknagow*, 38: "Mat produced his flint and steel, and, lighting a bit of touch-paper, laid it with his own hand on Phil Lahy's pipe, while Phil commenced to 'draw' with such vigour that his first 'shough' frightened the sparrows;" Swift, *A Dialogue in Hybernian Stile,* 164: "*B*: . . . and once a month I take a pipe with him, and we shoh it about for an hour together"; Sheehan, *Glenanaar*, 162: "'Take another *seach*,' said Thade. 'N-no!' said Jim. 'But I'll take the lind [lend] of a loan of your 'baccy-box till tomorrow."

seachain /ˈʃɑxən/ *v. (imper.),* beware; watch out (SOM, Kerry) < Ir.

seachrán /ˈʃɑkrɔːn/, /ˈʃɑxrɔːn/ also **seacharán, shaughraun, shockrawn** *v.n.*, in the phr. 'on the seachrán', wandering, going astray; looking for work; overtaken by misfortune (JOM, Kerry); living a life on the roads; down and out (SOM, Kerry); wandering mentally; much the worse for drink (DB, Cork) < Ir. 'He lost his job a month ago and is still on the shaughraun for another' (LUB, Dublin); 'The poor AINNISEOIR is still in the seachrán' (SOM, Kerry); 'I remember a time when he used to be going the roads like a shaughraun, but look at him now!' (TF, Cavan); 'What a seachrán she's become since her mind went!'

Seachtain na Cásca /ʃɑxt̪ənə ˈkɔːskə/ *n.phr.*, Holy Week (the week preceding Easter, when Christians manifest their devotion to the Passion of Christ) (SOM, Kerry) < Ir.

seafóid /ˈʃæfoːʤ/ *n.*, fooling, folly; a person of unbalanced mind (MK, Galway) < Ir. 'Take no notice of him: he's a bit seabhóideach' (KM, Kerry). Murphy, *Bailegangaire*, act I (*FDA*, 3, 1242): "*Mary*: Tell her about the children. *Dolly*: Seafóid, nonsense talk about forty years ago . . .” ‘Seafóideach’ *adj.*, foolish, silly; not making much sense; (mentally) wandering < Ir.

sea-grass, *see* DILLISK.

seal /ʃæl/ *n.*, a turn, a spell < Ir. ‘Wait your seal and I’ll serve you then; be patient!’ (Galway).

seamaide /ˈʃæmədʒə/ *n.*, a blade of grass; fig. an apathetic person < Ir. ‘What’s the point of that seamaide being at the meeting at all?’

seamair /ˈʃæmər/ *n.*, clover < Ir. ‘Luck comes with the seamair!’ (BC, Meath). *See* SHAMROCK.

seamhnán /ˈʃaunɔːn/ *n.*, a seed-basket; a clothes-basket < Ir. ‘Bring out the seamhnán to the washing-line’ (TJ, Sligo).

sean /ʃæn/ *adj. (prefixed),* old; mature < Ir. *See* SEANBHEAN; SEANDUINE.

Seanad Éireann /ˈʃænəd̪ˈeːrən/ *n.phr.,* the second chamber of the national parliament < Ir (lit. Senate of Ireland). *See* DÁIL ÉIREANN.

séanas /ˈʃeːnəs/ *n.,* a gap between the front teeth; a hare-lip < Ir.

seanbhean /ˈʃæn(ə)væn/ *n.,* an old woman; fig. a precocious girl < Ir.

Seanbhean Bhocht /ˈʃæn(ə) vænˈvʌxt̪/ *n.,* an 18th-century literary name for Ireland < Ir (lit. poor old woman). It is the name of a popular ballad commemorating the rising of 1798; *Shan Van Vocht* was also the name of a literary periodical published in Belfast, 1896–99. Joyce, *Finnegans Wake*, 48.3: “Bigamy Bob and his old Shanvocht!”; O’Casey, *The Plough and the Stars*, act II, 174: “*Fluther*: . . . bein’ taught at his mother’s knee to be faithful to th’ Shan Van Vok!”

Seán Buí /ʃɔːnˈbwiː/ *n.,* ‘John Bull’, England < Ir *Seán* (representing John) + *buí* (disparaging epithet). ‘That Seán Buí would want a kick up the behind’ (KG, Kerry). *See* JACKEEN; SEOINÍN.

seanchaí /ˈʃænəxiː/, /ˈʃænəkiː/ also **shanachee** *n.,* a traditional story-teller < Ir. ‘He’s a great oul shanachee if you can get him started.’

seanchas /ˈʃænəxəs/ *n.,* chatting (about old times); fireside talk; story-telling, especially about local happenings in the past (SOM, Kerry) < Ir *seanchas*, folk knowledge. Sheehan, *Glenanaar*, 288: “ . . . He would . . . welcome every one who stopped for a little *seanchus*.”

sean-cheirteach /ʃænˈkeːrtʃəx/ *n.,* an old rag (KM, Kerry) < Ir.

seandraoi /ˈʃænd̪riː/ *n.,* an ‘OLD-FASHIONED’ child; a delicate young man < Ir. ‘That little seandraoi is old before his time’ (KG, Kerry).

seanduine /ˈʃænd̪ɪnə/ *n.,* an old man; fig. ‘a child with an old man’s head on its shoulders’ (KM, Kerry) < Ir. ‘He’s a seanduine before his time!’

seangán /ˈʃæŋgɔːn/ *n.*, an ant; a flying ant; fig. a thin, puny person (MK, Galway) < Ir. 'Keep your mouth closed when you're cycling down the hill or the seangáns will choke you' (Mayo).

sean-nós /ˈʃænoːs/ *n.*, lit. 'old style', i.e. traditional manner; the term used to refer to the traditional native song tradition in Ireland; it is an oral tradition; the songs, which address a wide range of subjects and moods, are usually unaccompanied; originally all the songs were in Irish, but now many of them are sung in English. *See* Breandán Ó Madagáin, 'Functions of Irish Song', *Béaloideas*, 53 (1985).

seanpholl /ʃænˈfʌl/ *n.*, the hole left after turf has been cut (MK, Galway) < Ir. 'The seanpholl is full of water since the rains last week; we'll have to wait another few weeks before we'll be able to get the tractor in there.'

searbh /ˈʃærəv/ *adj.*, bitter, sour; caustic (KM, Kerry) < Ir. 'Searbh Jane is what they used call her – and she was, too!'

searbhán /ˈʃærəvɔːn/ *n.*, a bitter person < Ir. 'He's a searbhán,' he's a 'bitter pill'.

searbhas /ˈʃærəvəs/ *n., v.*, bitterness; vexation; sarcasm < Ir. 'Quit your searbhasing!' (BC, Meath).

searbhasach /ˈʃærəvəsəx/ *adj.*, bitter, sarcastic < Ir.

searbhóg /ˈʃærəvoːg/ *n.*, a sulky expression; a sour puss < Ir. 'She'll never get a man with that searbhóg on her' (KG, Kerry) 'What CALL have you to go around with that searbhóg on your face? You're the luckiest girl I know' (BC, Meath).

searc /ʃærk/ *n.*, love (SOM, Kerry) < Ir. *See* BALL SEARC.

seas /ʃæs/ *n.*, a heap of straw < Ir. 'SHOW me that seas TILL I put some bedding under the calves before I finish for the night' (Cavan).

seasc /ʃæsk/ *adj.*, dried-out (as of a cow at the end of the lactic cycle or one beyond calf-bearing age); barren; also used pejoratively of people, as in 'The seasc hageen [little hag] – fat business she has getting married!' (SOM, Kerry) < Ir.

seascair /ˈʃæskər/ *adj.*, cosy, comfortable < Ir. 'The old pair will never go into the new house: they're fine and seascair with the thatched roof where they are' (SOM, Kerry).

secondary top /ˈsɛkəndriˈtɑp/, *n.*, a primary school with a secondary section (ENM, Kerry).

seem, *see* SUIM.

segocia /səˈgɔːʃə/ also **segotia**, **skeowsha** *n.* (*colloq.*), old friend; term of endearment (VQ, Kerry) (origin obscure; it has been suggested that it derives from a corruption of Ir 'seo duitse!' (= here it is you are!); Joyce, *Finnegans Wake*, 215.12–13: "Ah, but she was the queer old skeowsha anyhow, Anna Livia, trinkettoes!"; 'Irishman's Diary', *Irish Times*, 23 June 1965, 7: "Segocias and Segotias. Where did John Molloy get the title for his new show, opening at the Gate on Monday next? Well, it's a logical progression. Molloy's last show was called 'There Y'are', and whenever a Dublinman says 'There y'are,' he inevitably follows it up with 'Me oul' Segotia.' So 'Me oul' Segotia' the show becomes." As for the derivation: "One story has it that members of a club called 'The Oul' Segotias' never tipped less than half a sovereign and that when less well-heeled passengers tipped tuppence, the JARVEY would say with that delicate irony that typified the breed: 'T'ank you, me oul' segotia.'" The same column on 1 October 1965, p. 9, cites Donn S. Piatt as suggesting that "Segotia has been Gaelicised as 'sagoiste' and may be connected with French 'sacoche' – wallet, money-bag, saddle-bag."

seibineach /'ʃɛbənəx/ *n.*, a large, fat person or animal < Ir. 'Well, she let out a yell when she saw this big seibineach of a rat running across the curtain-rail; as big as a cat it was' (Cavan),

seileog /'ʃɛloːg/ *n.*, spit, saliva < Ir. 'It's not worth a seileog' (worthless), Mayo.

seilide búrc /'ʃɛlədʒə'buːrk/ also **shellika pooka, shillig-a-booka** *n.*, a snail in its shell (IF, Waterford) < Ir. Kickham, *Knocknagow*, 46: an' a shillig-a-booka."

seilmide /'ʃɛlmədʒə/ *n.*, a snail; a slug < Ir. 'He walks and looks like a seilmide, so he does' (TJ, Sligo).

seisreach /'ʃɛʃrəx/ *n.*, a pair of horses harnessed for ploughing (SOM, Kerry) < Ir.

self /sɛlf/ *pron.*, frequently used in an intensive role in such expressions as 'Is it yourself that's IN IT? (is it you?); 'Is herself [the woman of the house] in?' Doyle, *The Van*, 205: "'Good girl yourself,' said Jimmy Sr." *See* ITSELF.

senator /'sɛnətər/ *n.*, a member of SEANAD ÉIREANN.

seoch, *see* SHEUGH.

seoithín seothó /ʃʌ'hiːnʃʌ'hoː/, refrain of a lullaby < Ir.

seoinín, *see* SHONEEN.

seordán /'ʃoːrd̪ɔːn/ *n.*, a wheeze in the chest; a whistling sound in the chimney < Ir. 'With that seordán I'm thinking he'll be lucky if he lasts through the winter' (BC, Meath).

serve /sɛrv/ *v.*, to assist at Mass. 'The only time I used to like serving was at weddings, because we used always get money afterwards' (JL, Mayo). Kickham, *Knocknagow*, 67: "He was not a little surprised to see Hugh Kearney, officiously assisted by Phil Lahy, 'serving Mass'." *See* SERVER.

server /ˈsɛrvər/ *n.*, a lay person who helps the priest with the execution of the Mass etc. *See* SERVE.

set /sɛt/ *p.part.*, rented to a tenant < ME *setten*. 'She has the house set at last'; 'I think he should set the land; he's getting too old, and there's no-one interested in coming back to take it up anyway' (TJ, Sligo).

settle(-bed) /ˈsɛtəl(bɛd)/ *n.*, an oblong box-shaped bench or seat in the kitchen that serves as a seat by day and, when opened, as a bed at night, or a place for storing things < E dial. (ME *setel*). 'Let Tommy sleep in the settle-bed and Bridgie have the ROOM' (JMF, Cavan). Kickham, *Knocknagow*, 40: "She was in the act of climbing over a high-backed settle behind the priest."

sevendable /səˈvɛndəbəl/ also **savendible**, **sevendible** *adj.*, serious; very great, outstanding < EModE *seven-double* (with a shift of stress), seven-fold. 'Jack gave him a sevendable thrashing' (PWJ); 'It is a sevendible fine day' (Martin, 189).

shaffoige /ʃæˈfoiəgə/ *adj.*, confused; senile < Ir *seafóideach*. 'MUSHA, I'm getting shaffoige in my old age – where did I leave my glasses?' (KG, Kerry).

shag /ʃæg/ *v.* (*colloq.*), to have intercourse with < OE *sceagga*, *n.*, hair of the head.

shagging /ʃægən/ *adj.* (*pejor.*), intensive < SHAG. 'Get your shagging bike out of here' (Monaghan). Leonard, *Out After Dark*, 61: "'Oh, the shaggin' cur, my lovely ice-cream,' Mary groaned."

shall, *see* WILL.

shamrock /ˈʃæmrɑk/ *n.*, clover < Ir *seamróg* (dimin. of SEAMAIR). The shamrock (i.e. a leaf of clover) is used as a symbol of Ireland; a legend (dating from the 17th century) has it that St Patrick used the leaf to explain the doctrine of the Trinity to the Irish people.

shanachee, *see* SEANCHAÍ.

shanty /ˈʃænti/ *n.*, a makeshift cabin; a ramshackle house; a shabby liquor-house < Ir *seantigh*, old house. 'He's up there living in an old shanty at the BUTT of the mountain, waiting for them to build him a council house' (TF, Cavan).

Shan Van Vok, *see* SEANBHEAN BHOCHT.

shaping /ˈʃeːpən/ *pres.part.*, making a display; showing off. 'He's only shaping, = acting the great fellow' (LUB, Dublin). Hogan notes: 'Apparently Anglo-Irish [i.e. HE] only.'

shaugh, *see* SEACH.

shaughraun, *see* SEACHRÁN.

shaver /ˈʃeːvər/ *n.*, a cunning person, a trickster; a miserly person < E dial. Hogan notes: 'An obsolete Standard sense.' 'You could never be up to that old shaver!' (LUB, Dublin); 'He's a funny old shaver – pots of money, and no-one to leave it to' (KG, Kerry).

shawlie /ˈʃɔːli/ *n.*, a woman who wears a shawl, sometimes (but not always) with associations of dissolute behaviour.

shebeen /ˈʃiːbiːn/ *n.*, an unlicensed liquor-house < Ir *síbín*. 'It's a bit of a shebeen that place: it stays open all hours.' Kickham, *Knocknagow*, 69: "Peg Naughton, that keeps the shebeen house at the church"; Stoker, *The Snake's Pass*, 71: "At the foot of the mountain . . . there was a small, clean-looking sheebeen."

sheean, sheeaun, *see* SÍÁN.

shee-geeha, *see* SÍ GAOITHE.

Shelta /ˈʃɛltə/ *n.*, a dialect of Hiberno-English formerly spoken by members of the travelling community (origin obscure; possibly a corruption of 'Celt'). It drew on some vocabulary from Irish, with many words deliberately disguised for the sake of secrecy, e.g. 'gop', kiss < Ir *póg*, 'nuspog', spoon < Ir *spúnóg*. See Macalister, *The Secret Languages of Ireland*. Joyce, *Finnegans Wake,* 421. 21–2: "Celebrated! Shaun replied under the sheltar of his broguish." *See* CANT.

shenanigans /ʃəˈnænəgənz/ also **shinannickin'** *n.* (*colloq.*), mischievous behaviour, trickery (origin unknown; McCrum et al., 189, note: '*Shenanigan*, meaning "trickery, mischief" is first recorded in America in 1855, and comes from the Irish Gaelic [i.e. Irish] *sionnach-uighim* [i.e. *sionnachaím*] meaning "I play the fox, I play tricks". Or does it? One authority believes the word to be American Indian. Another folk etymology gives a contraction of the Irish names, Sean [i.e. Seán] Hannigan'). 'Will you stop the shenanigans and get down to work?' O'Casey, *The Plough and the Stars*, act II, 166: "*Covey*: . . . I've something else to do besides shinannickin' afther Judies!"

sheogue, *see* SÍÓG.

sheugh /ʃʌx/ also **seoch**, **shugh** *n.*, embankment, ditch; drain, open gutter; small stream; a ditch filled with slow or stagnant water (RMM, Antrim) < E dial. (variant of *sough*, boggy or swampy place; *OED* s.v. 'sough sb.²' compares 'Antwerp dial. *zoeg*, a small ditch in a meadow'). 'A man slow at his trade can be referred to as "slow as shugh water"' (RMM, Antrim). 'To be in the sheugh', to be ruined (Braidwood, 1969). Paulin, 'Father of History' (*FDA*, 3, 1409): ". . . these rebel minds | endure posterity without a monument, | their names a covered sheugh, remnants, some brackish signs."

shift /ʃɪft/ *n.*, a chemise < E dial. 'She used put out my shift on the hedge; it'd soon dry in the sunshine' (BC, Meath).

shillelagh /ʃɪl'eːlə/ *n.*, a cudgel < Ir *sail*, willow + *éille*, genitive singular of *iall*, thong, strap. 'Give me my old shillelagh and we will go and take a walk.' (There seems to be no connection with the place name Shillelagh (*Síol Éalaigh*, Descendants of Éalach), a village in County Wicklow, which used to have very extensive oak woods in its neighbourhood); 'a carefully seasoned oak or blackthorn stick, about two and a half feet in length, with a good butt, used in the days of the faction fights. After being cut it was buried in a dung-heap, tied to a rake handle to get it straight; it was then put up the old-fashioned "chimbly" to season, and finally given a natural polish by rubbing on it a mixture of grease and turf-soot' (Omurethi, Kildare, 537). 'Finnegan's Wake' (song): "Shillelagh law did all engage"; Kavanagh, 'Adventures in the Bohemian Jungle' (*Collected Poems*, 102): "*American*: if there's no Sex, what good is my shillelagh?"; Griffith, 'Irish Usage in American English', 34: 'the foremost authority on the American language, H. L. Mencken, once said that the Irish between 1812 and the Civil War contributed only three words: *speakeasy*, *shillelagh*, and *smithereens*. Mencken erred in two of his three examples, for *speakeasy* is not of Irish origin and *shillelagh* has never been naturalized and is used humorously as an Irishism.'

shillig-a-booka, *see* SEILIDE BÚRC.

shinannickin, *see* SHENANIGAN.

shindig /'ʃɪndɪg/ *n.* (*colloq.*), a lively (dinner) party; a row, a commotion (origin obscure, but cf. *shindy, shinty,* a spree; *ODEE*: 'shinty' appears to be derived from cries used in the game shinty (a game resembling hockey), *shin ye, shin you, shin t'ye,* shin to you; *Chambers*: 'shindy, perh. shinty, a game like hockey, of Scottish origin . . . Perh. from Gael. *sinteag*, a bound, pace'). MT, Donegal, cites the phrase 'shinny your own side' from the game of common (*camán*). 'Such a shindig there was after the match; you've never heard the like' (Cavan).

Shinners, *see* SINN FÉIN.

shite /ʃait/ *n., v.,* the usual HE pronunciation of E 'shit' < OE *scitan, v.,* to defecate. 'Shut up or I'll kick the shite out of you'; 'That fella talks more shite – I wouldn't believe a word he says' (Mayo). Montague, 'Time in Armagh 3' (*Collected Poems,* 337): A system | Without love is a crock of shite'; Doyle, *The Van,* 101: "'I couldn't give a shite wha' her da looks like,' said Jimmy Sr." *See* GOBSHITE; BLATHER(COME)SKITE; SKITE.

shoneen /ˈʃoːniːn/ also **seoinín** *n. (pejor.),* a person more interested in English language and customs than Irish ones; a 'West Briton' (ENM, Kerry); a pretentious person affecting airs and graces, with a preference for things English; an upstart; a hanger-on < Ir *Seon* (variant of *Seán*), John (as a typical English name: cf. John Bull) + dimin. suffix *-ín*. 'That seoinín hasn't one word of Irish' (KG, Kerry); 'What's that seoinín doing down here? He has no business down this part of the country' (TF, Cavan). Jordan, *The Past*, 27: "Would Una have talked to him incessantly about the Hungarian policy and Arthur Griffith, about SINN FÉIN and shoneenism . . . ?" *See* JACKEEN; SEÁN BUÍ.

shook /ʃʌk/ *p.part.,* showing signs of having been through a stressful experience < E dial. (OE *scacan, v.*, to shake) (irregular p.part. of *shake*). Deane, *Reading in the Dark*, 147: "'He's far shook, that man, far shook,' he said."

shore /ʃoːr/ *n.,* (open) drain < E dial. (variant of 'sewer'). 'There's a woeful smell coming off that shore!' (TF, Cavan).

shough, *see* SEACH.

show /ʃoː/ *v.,* to give, to hand over < ME *scheawen*. 'Show me that screwdriver' (i.e. hand it to me). Birmingham, *The Lighter Side of Irish Life*, 175: "'Show' used in the sense of 'give me for a moment,' is a word which is exceedingly useful, but which once got me into trouble. I was an Irish boy making the acquaintance of my companions in an English school. Wanting to point a pencil, I said to the boy next me, 'Show me your knife, please.' He gaped at me at first and then, wondering, I suppose at my curious request, showed me his knife"; Joyce, *Dubliners*, 149: "O, I forgot there's no corkscrew! Here, show me one here and I'll put it at the fire."

Shraft /ʃræft/ *n.*, Shrovetide (the period comprising Quinquagesima Sunday (= the fiftieth day before Easter) and the two following days, just before the beginning of Lent, when the faithful enjoyed themselves with dancing, feasting, and general merry-making (cf. Carnival, in other countries) < E dial. (cf. OE *scrifan, v.*, to shrive).

siamsa /ˈʃiəmsə/ *n.,* sport; musical entertainment; a friendly evening; a house dance, a celebratory gathering (SOM, Kerry) < Ir.

síán /ˈʃiːɔːn/ also **sheean, sheeaun** *n.,* a fairy hill < Ir.

síbín, *see* SHEBEEN.

sidelong /ˈsaidlɑŋ/ *v.,* to fasten together the front and back foot (usually of a sheep) to stop it straying < E dial.

sí gaoithe /ʃiːˈgiːhə/ *n.,* a sudden blast of wind; a small whirlwind (regarded as a 'fairy wind' through mistaken association with *sí*, spirit world, an unrelated word); a flurry of dust on the road (considered bad luck) < Ir *sí gaoithe,* gust of wind. 'People were conscious of sí gaoithe during hay-making, turf-saving, and fine weather in general, when hay or turf-dust was blown about for no obvious reason' (SOM, Kerry); 'A man can lose his hat in a sí gaoithe' (proverb); 'Did you hear the sí gaoithe at Mac's funeral?' (Mayo).

sight /sait/ *n., adv.,* an amount, a quantity; a great deal; very (intensive) < E dial. (OE *sihþ*). 'There was a sight of wild ducks on the lough' (Omurethi, Kildare); 'What a sight of people went to see the Pope in the Phoenix Park!' (JMF, Cavan); 'The journey to New York is a sight dangerous for me now' (Mayo).

signs /sainz/, *n.pl.,* in the remark 'signs on it,' he looks it, he shows the effects of it, etc. < Ir *dá chomhartha sin* (LUB, Dublin, 181) or *tá a rian air* (Dinneen, Ó Dónaill). 'Tom Kelly never sends his children to school, and sign's on they are growing up like savages' (PWJ). 'He did all the wiring himself.' – 'Signs on it!'

Síle /'ʃiːlə/ *n.,* an effeminate man < Ir *Síle*, regarded as a typical woman's name. 'Fan go fóill go bpósfaidh Síle' (proverb), Wait your turn (lit. Wait for a while until Síle gets married – i.e. the oldest daughter had to get married first when marriages were arranged). 'He's a right Síle when it comes to killing a pig – his wife has to do it, every time' (BC, Meath). Sheridan, 'To the Dean, when in England, in 1726' (*Verse in English from Eighteenth-Century Ireland,* 187: "I'm charmed at home, with our Sheelina." *See* TADHG; TEAGUE.

Síle an phortaigh /'ʃiːlən'fʌrt̪ɪg/ *n.,* a heron < Ir. 'There's a síle an phortaigh down at the river' (TF, Cavan).

silenced priest /'sailənst'priːst/ *n.phr.,* a priest forbidden to carry out the functions of the ministry. 'I think he was silenced, but I don't know why' (JMF, Cavan).

silteach /'ʃɪltəx/ *adj.,* weak; feeling off colour (MK, Galway) < Ir. 'Let you go on ahead; I'm feeling a bit silteach.'

sin[1] /sɪn/ *n., v.,* blame < E dial. 'There'll be no sin for you in that' (Mayo).

sin[2] /ʃɪn/ *pron.,* in Ir phrases. 'Sin é an saol' /ʃɪneːən'siːl/, 'that's the life' (MC, Kildare). 'Sin scéal eile' /'ʃɪnʃkeːl'ɛlə/, that's another story. 'I could go on – but sin scéal eile.' 'Sin sin' /ʃɪnʃɪn/, that's that. 'That's the last I want to hear about it – it's over, sin sin.'

Sinn Féin /ʃɪn'feːn/ *n.,* a political party dedicated to the nationalist cause, founded in 1905, reconstructed in 1917 < Ir (lit. ourselves). 'Sinn Féin have been in the news a lot lately.' Joyce, *Finnegans Wake*, 552.6: "arked for covennanters and shinners' rifuge."

sioc /ʃʌk/ *n.,* frost (KM, Kerry) < Ir. 'Mind the sioc doesn't get to the flowers.'

siocán /ʃʌ'kɔːn/ *n.,* frosty weather; a light frost; fig. a cold person (KM, Kerry) < Ir. 'She was a bit of a siocán at the best of times; I could never make her out'; 'I reckon we're in for a spell of siocán. It'll be a good time to go out shooting.'

síofra /'ʃiːfrə/ *n.,* a talkative little fellow who 'was there before' (i.e. had come in contact with the spirit world); a precocious little know-all (with the hint that he was a changeling who had been left behind by the spirit world in place of a human child) < Ir *síofra*, changeling. 'You little síofra' (an insult) (SOM, Kerry); 'The little síofra – keep well away from him!'

síofrach /'ʃiːfrəx/ *n.,* an elf; fig. a weakling; (*pejor.*) a mean, deceitful, churlish person (MK, Galway) < Ir. 'I won't have that síofrach working for me!'; 'The síofrach would steal the eyes out of your head and come back for the lashes.'

síóg /'ʃiːoːg/ also **sheogue** *n.,* a fairy (MK, Galway) < Ir. 'The síógs do come at night'; 'If you see any síógs, don't talk to them or they'll trick you' (Mayo).

síógach /ʃiː'oːgəx/ *adj.,* fairy-like; effeminate (man); stunted or delicate (person or animal) < Ir. 'He's a bit of a síógach, but I'm sure there's no harm in him' (KM, Kerry).

siogairlín /'ʃɪgərliːn/ *n.,* tassels, hanging ornaments < Ir. 'She has a little stall in the market every week selling siogairlíns, wherever she gets them from.'

síogán /'ʃiːgɔːn/ *n.,* a hand-piled stack of oats; a thin pile of turf < Ir. 'He spends most of his time these days out in the bog making síogáns.'

síol /ʃiːl/ *n., v.,* a seed (KM, Kerry) < Ir. 'He's out síoling the upper field.'

síomáinín /ʃiː'mɔːniːn/ a useless, dead-and-alive person; a dawdler (KM, Kerry) < Ir. 'They said he was always a síomáinín, but I wonder, when you think what he did.'

síománach /ʃiː'mɔːnəx/ *n.,* a child who fails to thrive (sometimes, it is said, because he or she has been marked out by the 'good people' for themselves); a delicate chicken < Ir. 'The poor little síománach – he went [died] last year' (Meath).

síománaíocht /ʃiː'mɔːniːəxt̪/ *v.n.,* idling about < Ir.

sionnach /'ʃʌnəx/ *n.,* a fox (SOM, Kerry, who adds: 'MADRA RUA' is more common') < Ir.

siopa /ˈʃʌpə/ *n.*, a shop < Ir < E *shop*. 'Go up to the siopa for a few MESSAGES for me, will you?' (BC, Meath).

siota /ˈʃʌt̪ə/ *n.*, child; a brat, an urchin, a good-for-nothing; a pet, a gutless spoilt child (SOM, Kerry) < Ir.

siúlóir /ˈʃuːloːr/ a wanderer, walker, itinerant; 'the word was used to denote a certain type of lady' (POC, Cavan) < Ir.

skean, *see* SCIAN.

skelly /ˈskɪli/ also **skilly** *n., v., adj.*, to squint; to aim askew; squint-eyed < E dial. < OE *sceolh, adj.*, oblique, wry. 'She was skellied in one eye, and never had it fixed' (BC, Meath).

skelp[1] /ʃkɛlp/ *n.*, a slap, blow < Ir *sceilp*. 'She clattered him a skelp on the back'; 'I nearly got a nice skelp in the lug with that hurley ball' (JL, Mayo); 'One gets a *skelp* in the PUS, but a *slap* on the jaw' (LUB, Dublin, 182). Hogan notes: 'A Scottish and Northern word'.

skelp[2] /ʃkɛlp/ *n.*, a bite, a nip; a bit of something (e.g. bread) < Ir *scealp*.

skene, *see* SCIAN.

skeoch, *see* SCEACH.

skeowsha, *see* SEGOCIA.

sketch /skɛʧ/ *v. (imp.)*, look out; run for it (KD, Dublin) < E *sketch*? < Du *schets*.

skewbald /ˈskjuːbɔːld/ *n.*, a particoloured (brown-and-white) horse (as distinct from 'piebald', black-and-white) < E dial. < ONF *eskiu(w)ere, eskuer* (variant of OF *eschuer, v.*, to eschew) + bald (*ODEE*).

skew-ways also skow-ways /ˈskjuːweːz/ *adj.*, crooked, oblique (MMB, Meath) < E dial. (*see* SKEWBALD; cf. Ir SCEABHA).

skhehoshies, *see* SCEACHÓIR.

skillaun, *see* SCIOLLÁN.

skinnymalink /ˈskɪniməlɪnk/ *n.* (*colloq.*), a tall bony person (LUB, Dublin). (Origin uncertain; Beale s.v. 'skinny malink' gives it as a Canadian variant of *skinamalink*, which is itself a variant of *skilamalink* (19th-century London slang), secret, 'shady'; a correspondent quoted s.v. 'skilamalink' writes: 'In my early youth (*c.* 1910–1925) I occasionally met "skinamalink", a derisory noun or nickname for unusually skinny and undersized individuals . . . its form is, apparently, based on *skilamalink,* but its meaning is that of "skilligareen",' which is glossed as 'an extremely thin person' and as possibly being derived from a slurring of 'skin-and-bones'; cf. Ó Dónaill s.v. 'scilligeoir': '1. sheller (of grain, etc.), 2. incessant talker, prater, prattler.') 'Skinnymalink melodeon-legs, big banana feet' (child's rhyme) (JF, Dublin).

skite[1] /skait/ *n.*, an unpleasant person < E dial. (*EDD*: 'an opprobrious epithet for an unpleasant or conceited person; a meagre, starved-looking, ugly fellow').

skite[2] /skait/ *v.,* to splash < E dial. (*EDD*: 'to squirt; to eject any liquid forcibly; to spit; to have diarrhœa'). *See* BLATHER(COME)SKITE.

skiver /ˈskɪvər/ *n., v.,* a skewer; a skewer used in thatching (LUB, Dublin) < E dial. (probably the earlier form of *skewer*; cf. ME *schive*). 'I'll have to ask around for a skiver; I wonder who'd have one?' *See* Clark, 43.

slabrachán /slɑbrəˈkɔːn/ *n.,* an untidy person < Ir. 'The smell off that slabrachán! – does he ever wash himself at all?' (KG, Kerry).

slacht /slɑkt̪/ *n.,* tidiness, neatness; good organisation (MK, Galway) < Ir.

slachtmhar /ˈslɑkt̪vər/ also **slachtar** *adj.,* tidy, neat; having everything in its proper place; used as a nickname for one given to neatness, e.g. 'Dan Slachtar', 'the Slachtars' < Ir. 'You've every place shining and fine and slachtar' (SOM, Kerry).

slag /slæg/ *v.,* to cast uncomplimentary remarks at someone in a playful way (cf. E dial. *slagger*, to besmear with mud, to bespatter). 'We were only slagging each other' (Dublin); 'I'll be slagged [caught out, mocked]' (HJ, Wexford).

slaidín /ˈslɪd̪iːn/ also **sloidín, sluidín** *n.,* a bolt, rod or SÚGÁN to secure the movable bottom of a PARDÓG (JF, Cavan) < Ir. 'Make sure the slaidín is in before you load up the pardóg.'

sláimín /ˈslɔːmiːn/ also **slaimín** /ˈslæmiːn/ *n.,* an untidy person; a dirty, untidy woman (MK, Galway) < Ir. 'Don't let that sláimín anywhere near the house; if you see her coming, run her.' Healy, *Nineteen Acres*, 103: "You would never think my mother regarded her as a 'slawmeen Saturday', the woman who was washing all the week and still hadn't finished on Saturday what should have been completed on Monday."

sláinte /ˈslɔːntʃə/ *int.* used as a toast: health! < Ir. 'Seo do shláinte!', here's health to you.

slaitín tomhais, *see* SLAT.

slám /slɔːm/ *n.,* a handful (KM, Kerry) < Ir. 'Give me a slám of that wool to test it.'

slamaire /ˈslɑmərə/ *n.,* a glutton, a voracious eater (MK, Galway) < Ir. 'That slamaire doesn't know when he's had enough; he'd eat you out of house and home!'

slámóg /slɔːˈmoːg/ *n.,* a slatternly, untidy woman < Ir. 'What's to be done with that slámóg? I just don't know what will become of her' (KG, Kerry).

slán /slɔːn/ *n.* (greeting, toast): health < Ir. 'Slán agat' /slɔːn ˈɑgət̪/, /slɔːnəˈgʌt̪/, goodbye (said by one going away from the listener). 'Slán leat' /slɔːn ˈlæt̪/, goodbye (said to the person departing). 'Slán abhaile' /slɔːnəˈwɑljə/, safe home, safe journey. Joyce, *Ulysses*, 313. 2: "'*Slan leat*', says he"; *Finnegans*

Wake, 72.29: "after he had so slaunga vollayed [*slán abhaile* + -d]"; O'Brien, *The Best of Myles*, 67: "Slawn lat arish [*slán leat arís*]!' (goodbye again). *See* SO LONG.

slane /ʃlɔːn/, /ʃleːn/ also **sleán** *n.*, a sharp-bladed spade for cutting turf; a winged spade (SOM, Kerry) < Ir *sleán*. 'He was a great man with the *slane*' (a good turf-cutter) (TF, Cavan).

slang /ʃlæŋ/ also **sling** /ʃlɪŋ/ *n.*, a narrow strip of land beside a river (PMD, Mayo; LUB, Dublin); a long, narrow piece of fenced-in grazing-land on a farm (Omurethi, Kildare); an awkward or irregularly shaped field (MMB, Meath) < E dial. (*EDD*: 'a narrow piece of land running up between other and larger divisions of ground; a long and narrow strip of ground'; Hogan notes: 'a West of England word').

slapaire /ˈslæpərə/ *n.*, an untidy person; a quick but untidy worker (KM, Kerry) < Ir. 'I told him it's better to take his time than be a slapaire at the job.'

slat /slæt/ *n.*, a stick, a rod < Ir. 'Slaitín' (dimin.), a little stick. 'Slaitín tomhais' /slætiːnˈt̪ɔːʃ/ *n.phr.*, a yardstick; a criterion (SOM, Kerry) < Ir.

sleá /ʃlɔː/ *n.*, a spear; a large splinter < Ir. 'I have a sleá under my nail and it's causing me great pain.'

sléacht /ʃleːxt̪/ *n.*, slaughter, havoc < Ir. 'In other dialects also means adoration, genuflection, submission (bending the knee: derivation L *flecto*, (I) bend (the knee)' (SOM, Kerry).

sleamhain /ʃlaun/ *adj.*, slippery, smooth; dishonest < Ir. 'Mind yourself – the stepping-stones are very sleamhain' (SOM, Kerry).

sleamhnán /ˈʃlaunɔːn/ *n.*, a slippery patch; fig. a smooth-spoken person (MK, Galway) < Ir.

sleamhnánach /ʃlauˈnɔːnəx/ *adj.*, slippery, sly; full of BLARNEY < Ir. (KM, Kerry).

sleán, *see* SLANE.

sleveen /ˈʃliːviːn/ also **sleeveen** (JP, Forth and Bargy), **slíbhín** *n.*, a sly person; a trickster; a smooth-tongued rogue; a toady; a crooked person (LUB, Dublin) < Ir *slíbhín*. 'Look at that sleveen creeping around the priest – I wonder what he's after now?'; 'Keep away from that sleveen!' (KG, Kerry).

slew /sluː/ *n.*, a large number or amount of something < Ir *slua*, a crowd, a host, a multitude. Griffith, 35: 'A slew of reasons . . . slew, meaning a large number, is a common Americanism and there can be no doubt of its Irish character.' *See* SLUA.

slewsthering /ˈsluːʃt̪ərən/ *v.n.*, coaxing, flattering (origin uncertain, but cf. Ir *slúisteoireacht*, lounging, idling). Carleton, 'Shane Fadh's Wedding' (*Six Irish Tales*, 190): "When we arrived, there was nothing but shaking hands and kissing, and all kinds of *slewsthering* – men kissing men – women kissing women – and after that men and women all THROUGH OTHER."

slíbhín, *see* SLEVEEN.

slibire /ˈʃlɪbərə/ *n.,* a tall, gaunt, loosely built man (JOM, Kerry) < Ir. 'Would that slibire be any good for a day's work?' (BC, Meath).

slinge /slɪnʤ/ also **slindge**, **slendge** *v.,* to dawdle; to idle, loaf around; to MITCH from school < E dial. (*EDD*: 'to slink off, or about (origin obscure)'; cf. Ir *sleamhnaigh*, to slide, slip). '"Where is he today?" "Oh, he's slinging, sir," the bold boy would reply' (MOC, Limerick, who draws attention to a similar usage in Irish: 'Ó Dónaill has "sleamhnaigh" = slide, slip, and gives an example of use, i.e. "shleamhnaigh sé amach as an teach").

sliodarnach /ˈʃlɪd̪ərnəx/ *n.*, slithering, slipping, sliding (ENM, Kerry) < Ir.

slíomadóir /ˈʃliːməd̪oːr/ *n.*, a deceitful flatterer (SOM, Kerry) < Ir. 'Look at her, slíomadóiring about the place' (KG, Kerry).

sliotar /ˈʃlɪt̪ər/ *n.*, a hurling-ball < Ir. 'If you get a shot of the sliotar in the head you could be killed stone dead.'

slip /slɪp/ *n.*, a girl; a young woman; a young pig, older than a BONNIVE, running almost independent of its mother (PWJ) (origin not entirely certain: *ODEE* gives 'Middle Low German, MDu *slippe* (Du *slip*), cut, slit, strip (but the earliest Eng. sense is not recorded in these langs.)'; *Chambers* concurs).

slipe /slaip/ *n.*, a sledge < E dial. 'A triangular framework of wood in which large boulder stones are drawn out of fields; a large trough like a cart without wheels, used for drawing earth or wet peat from one part of a field or bog to another' (Simmons, *Glossary*, 1890). Traynor, *Donegal*, s.v. 'slipe n. v.[2]' quotes from the collector H. C. Hart (d. 1908): 'about twenty years ago there were several about Glenalla, but I have not seen one for some time.'

sliseog /ʃlɪˈʃoːg/ *n.*, a slip of a girl; a lazy, useless person (KM, Kerry) < Ir. 'Don't send that sliseog over to me; I wouldn't tolerate her for a minute.'

slitther, *see* SLIOTAR.

slob /slɑb/ *n.*, mud, oozy mire; fig. a soft or ill-mannered or slovenly person < Ir *slaba*, *slab* (Griffith, 35: 'Slob, meaning a dull, slow, or untidy person, comes from *slab*, mud. Two Irish writers were the first to use it, Frank Clington in 1861 ("A heavy looking poor slob of a man") and Le Fanu in 1863 ("A fat slob of a person")'). 'If he looks like a slob, why shouldn't I call him one?' (Mayo).

slog, *see* SLUG.

slogaire[1] /ˈslʌgərə/ *n.*, a glutton < Ir. 'The slogaire would eat you out of house and home.'

slogaire[2] /ˈslʌgərə/ *n.*, a pool; a quagmire in the middle of a field (MK, Kerry) < Ir *slogaide*.

slogan /ˈsloːgən/ *n.*, a war-cry; a motto (KM, Kerry) < Ir *sluaghairm* (lit. army cry).

slogtha /ˈslʌghə/ *p.part.*, eaten up quickly (KM, Kerry) < Ir.

sloidín, *see* SLAIDÍN.

sloother, *see* SLUTHER.

slough, *see* CESH.

slua /sluə/ *n.*, a crowd, a multitude (KM, Kerry); a host of people; an army; a group (MK, Galway) < Ir. 'There was a slua of people at the concert last night.' *See* SLEW.

sluasaid /ˈsluːsədʒ/ *n.*, a shovel < Ir. 'SHOW me that sluasaid, will you?' (TF, Cavan).

slug /slʌg/ also **slog** *n.*, *v.*, a drink; drinking or gulping; a 'pull' of a drink (LUB, Dublin, 182); to swallow, to gulp < Ir *slog*. 'Here, take a slug and give it back to me' (TF, Cavan); 'Nothing cuts away the thirst like a slug of buttermilk. He slugged it off' (LUB, Dublin). O'Brien, *A Pagan Place*, 123: "He could drink a great slug without stopping."

slugabed /ˈslʌgəbɛd/ *n.* (*colloq.*), a sluggard (PWJ, who adds: 'general in Limerick') < *slug* (OED: 'perhaps of Scandinavian origin, cf. Sw. dial. *slogga*') + ME *abedde*.

sluther /ˈsluːt̪ər/ also **sloother** *v.*, *n.*, to flatter, cajole; to coax, wheedle; flattering talk < E dial. *sluther* (variant of *slither*, to slip, slide; cf. Ir *lústaire*, flatterer). 'He's been sluthering him all the morning looking for a loan' (BC, Meath); 'That fellow would coax the birds off the bushes with his sloother' (SL, Mayo). 'Slutherer', a coaxer (LUB, Dublin); a flatterer or toady (BP, Meath, heard in Mayo). *See* SLEWSTHERING.

smacht /smɑxt̪/ *n.*, control, discipline (in a positive sense), constraint < Ir. 'There's great smacht in that family' (SOM, Kerry).

smachtín /smɑxˈt̪iːn/ *n.*, a cudgel, a stick (KM, Kerry) < Ir. 'He was forever beating the poor ass with a smachtín.'

smahan /ˈsmæhən/ *n.*, a taste, a small amount, a nip < Ir *smeachán*. 'Give us a smahan of whiskey; I'm stiff with the cold' (JOC, Kerry). Joyce, 'Counterparts' (*Dubliners*, 107): "We'll just have one little smahan more and then we'll be off"; Plunkett, *Farewell Companions*, 397: "I'd WISH on me for a *smahan* of punch, if you wouldn't mind?" *See* SMEACHÁN.

smailc /smælk/ *n.*, *v.*, a gobble, a mouthful (MK, Galway); to gulp, gobble, chew with relish < Ir. 'I gave the dog a smailc of bread.'

small /smɔːl/ *adj.*, often combined with 'little' to intensify the sense of smallness. 'He saw Dinneen; he was a small little man with a pucey-blue priest's coat' (ENM, Kerry).

smaois /smiːʃ/ *n.*, a running nose (MK, Kerry) < Ir. 'Wipe that smaois off your face, you're a HOLY SHOW.'

smashing /'smæʃən/ *adj.* (*colloq.*), fine, excellent, possessed of great charm; large < E dial. < *smash*, *v.*, to strike (it is often claimed, improbably, that 'smashing' derives from Ir *is maith sin*, that's good). 'We had a smashing time last night – the best in a long time'; 'It was a smashing game: we were on our toes right up to the last minute' (Mayo). 'Smasher', *n.*, a fine-looking person, a 'swell'. *See* MASHER.

smathers /'smæd̪ərz/, in the phr. 'to make smathers of', to defeat utterly < Ir *smeadar*. 'He made smathers of him,' he beat him in a fight (SB, Cork). *See* SMEADAR.

smeach /smæx/ *n.*, a kick; a blow, a smack; a breath of life; a kiss; a taste (SOM, Kerry) < Ir. 'He could get the smeach of jam still from his lips' (SOM, Kerry).

smeachán /'smæxɔːn/ *n.*, a taste, a drop; a small quantity of food or liquid < Ir (cf. E *smack* < OE *smæc*, taste, enough to taste). 'I'll only have a smeachán of whiskey; any more and I'll be legless' (TF, Cavan). *See* SMAHAN.

smeadar /'smæd̪ər/ *n.*, a mess; a daub; a smattering (MK, Galway); a beating, a pasting < Ir. *See* SMATHERS.

sméara dubha /'smeːrə'd̪ʌvə/ *n.pl.*, blackberries (KM, Kerry) < Ir. 'Let's go and pick sméara dubha for Mother's jam.'

smeg /smɛg/ *n.*, a chin-whisker, a goatee (LUB, Dublin). *See* SMIG.

smidgeon /'smɪʤən/ *n.*, a small amount; a taste (origin obscure; but cf. Ir SMEACHÁN). 'I'll have just a smidgeon of sugar in my tea, thanks' (TJ, Sligo).

smidiríní, *see* SMITHEREENS.

smig /smɪg/ *n.*, the chin < Ir. 'He has his father's smig about him' (KG, Kerry). 'Lán go smig', full to the lip of the cup (SOM, Kerry) < Ir. *See* SMEG.

smior /smɪr/ *n.*, marrow < Ir. 'I was frozen right into the smior' (SOM, Kerry).

smitheán /smɪ'hɔːn/ *n.*, a small quantity of spirits, 'a half one' (SOM, Kerry). *See* TAOSCÁN.

smithereens /smɪd̪ər'iːnz/ *n.pl.*, small broken fragments; little pieces (KM, Kerry) < Ir *smidiríní* (plural of *smidirín*, dimin. of *smiodar*, fragment); but cf. E dial. *smaddereen*, a small quantity (a dialectal form of *smattering*); Hogan, 182, notes: 'The origin of this word is doubtful. Ir. *smidirín* is probably borrowed from the Anglo-Irish [HE] word. *OED* thinks that the latter is English dialectal *smithers* = fragments + Anglo-Irish suffix *-een*. But *smithereens* is recorded (1825) much earlier than *smithers*; and there is an Anglo-Irish *smither* = to break in bits'). 'The horse has the car kicked to smithereens' (Omurethi, Kildare); 'The plate broke into smithereens on the floor' (Dublin). Heaney, 'May' (*Wintering Out*, 75): "When I looked down from the bridge | Trout were flipping the sky | Into smithereens . . ."

smólach /'smoːləx/ *n.*, a thrush < Ir. 'Look at yon smólach!' (TF, Cavan). *See* CÉIRSEACH.

smoor /smuːr/ *v.*, to suffocate; to suppress, hide < E dial. < OE *smorian*, to choke, suffocate. Paulin, *Seize the Fire*, 37: "Promethus: 'Desire punishes | because it hates itself | for wanting . . . | smoored in the dirtiest places | desire gets satisfied." *See* SMÚR.

smuga /'smʌgə/ *n.*, mucus, snot (MK, Galway) < Ir.

smugachán /smʌgə'hɔːn/ *n.*, a snotty-nosed person; fig. a person full of self-importance (KG, Kerry) < Ir. 'She's become an awful smugachán ever since she got the call to go for that job in the civil service.'

smugarlach /'smʌgərləx/ *n.*, a running nose and consequent unkempt face (SOM, Kerry) < Ir.

smuilceachán /'smɪlkəxɔːn/ *n.*, a snooty person; a sulky person (KG, Kerry) < Ir. 'That smuilceachán will rue the day she crossed me – I'll make sure of that!'

smúr /smuːr/ *n.* 1. Dust, rust, soot, grime; the black deposit on a kettle; the embers of a fire. 'Will you just look at the smúr on that kettle hanging on the crane over the fire!' < Ir. 2. A fine shower of rain < Ir. *See* SMOOR.

smúrabhán /'smuːrəvɔːn/ *n.*, soot; a coating of black dust on a kettle or pot (KM, Kerry) < Ir. 'The gas is great: no more smúrabhán on the kettle from when it was hung from the crane over the open fire in the old house.'

smush /smʌʃ/ *n.*, *v.*, *adj.*, rubbish; refuse; scraps < E dial. (origin uncertain). 'The vase fell and was broken into smush' (SB, Cork).

smut[1] /smʌt/ *n.* 1. The remains of a nearly burnt-out candle; a small cocked nose (LUB, Dublin, 182) < Ir. 2. A sulky expression < Ir. 'Take that smut off of your face; it doesn't become you!' (KG, Kerry).

smut[2] /smʌt/ *n.*, a bit of dust < E smut. 'A smut of dust'; 'Smuts on the glass' (SOM, Kerry).

smután /smʌ't̪ɔːn/ *n.*, a piece of bog-deal; a piece of wood (KM, Kerry) < Ir. 'If you see any smutáns in the bog take them in with you; there's great heat out of them.'

snab /snɑb/ *n.*, the end or stub of a candle (KM, Kerry) < Ir. 'He's so mean he uses the snabs of the candles to make new ones.'

snabóg /ˈsnɑboːg/ *n.*, the wick of a dip candle; straw soaked in wax; a rag or string in resin or fat (ML, Mayo) < Ir (dimin. of SNAB). 'There's no more heat out of that fire than you'd get out of a snabóg.'

snag /snæg/ *v.*, to cut the heads off turnips; to thin out turnips to give them space to grow (EH, Wicklow) < E dial. (*OED*: 'probably of Scandinavian origin . . . The stem is also found in Old Icelandic *snag-hyrndyr*, said of an axe having a sharp point'). 'You'll never find me snagging turnips!' (MCR, Waterford). *See* SNIG; SNIOGADH.

snag-man /ˈsnægmæn/ *n.* (*colloq.*), a man (e.g. a builder) who comes to the house to identify and deal with faults < E *snag*, a piece of wood projecting from a tree, a piece of wood in a river obstructing navigation, hence an obstacle). 'Do you know, I'll have to find a snag-man somewhere; I have a SIGHT of things need fixing in this house' (Dublin). 'Snag list', a list of faults in a new house handed over to the builder.

snaidhm /snaim/ *n.*, a knot; marriage (SOM, Kerry) < Ir. *See* SNAIDHM NA PÉISTE.

snaidhm na péiste /snaimnə ˈpeːʃtʃə/ *n.*, an intricately knotted cord formerly used as a charm to cure colic in cattle (KM, Kerry) < Ir (lit. knot of the worm).

snáithín /snɔːˈhiːn/ *n.*, a little thread; fig. train of thought < Ir. 'Your eyes are better than mine – will you put the snáithín in the needle for me, please?'; 'Don't make me laugh, or I'll lose the snáithín of what I'm telling you!' 'Snáithín tathaig', cohesion; a common thread (SOM, Kerry).

snaois /sniːʃ/ *n.*, snuff (SOM, Kerry) < Ir (probably < E *sneeze*)

snap-apple /ˈsnæpæpəl/ *n.*, 'a play with apples on Hallow-eve, where big apples are placed in difficult positions and are to be caught by the teeth of the persons playing. Hence Hallow-eve is often called "Snap-apple night"' (PWJ, 329).

snas /snɑs/ also **snoss** *n.* 1. A shine; refined manners < Ir. 'There's always a snoss on the house when that girl has cleaned it' (LUB, Dublin, 182). 2. Scum on water or stones < Ir.

snasta /ˈsnɑst̪ə/ *adj.*, well or tidily completed < Ir. 'Well, you have the garden looking very snasta now' (TJ, Sligo).

snáth /snɔː/ *n.*, a thread < Ir. *See* SNÁITHÍN.

sneachta /ˈʃnɑxt̪ə/ *n.*, wind-blown snow (KM, Kerry) < Ir. 'We had sneachta for Christmas all right, but sure it was all melted the next day.'

sned /snɛd/ also **snead** 1. *n.*, a scythe-shaft < E dial. < OE *snæd*. 'You won't get anyone to make a sned any more; if it breaks, that's it – finished' (BC, Meath). 2. *v.*, to cut, prune < E dial. < OE *snædan*. 'We'd better sned that tree to let the light get through to the house' (TJ, Sligo).

snig[1] /snig/ *n.*, an eel, especially a young or small eel < E dial. (origin obscure).

snig[2] /snɪg/ *v.*, to cut, chop off; to lop off the branches of a tree; to cut heads off turnips; to pull a cock of hay with a rope (JF, Cavan) < E dial. (origin obscure). 'He's been down the field snigging turnips for the last couple of hours' (TF, Cavan); 'The shoots of that apple tree are growing out too long; I must snig off the tops of them' (PWJ). *See* SNAG.

sniog /ʃnɪg/ *v.*, to strip a cow (abstracting the final few drops of milk) (KM, Kerry) < Ir. 'I used always have to sniog the cows when I was a child. My father used to say that you'd get the best of milk by doing that.'

sniogadh /ˈʃnɪgə/ *v.n.*, stripping a cow (abstracting the final few drops, which were supposed to be very creamy, after the main milking) (SOM, Kerry) < Ir.

sniving /ˈsnaivən/ *pres.part.*, overwhelmed < E dial. *snive* (variant of *sny*, to swarm). 'Sniving with bees.'

snoss, *see* SNAS.

snug /snʌg/ *n.*, a small private room or alcove in a pub, in the past often used for informal discussions with solicitors, or arranging dowries and MATCH-MAKING, or preparing funerals (MOB, Mayo) < E dial. (origin obscure). 'Come into the snug for a Baby Power (brand of whiskey)' (AF, Cavan); 'We had our lunch in the snug' (TJ, Sligo). O'Casey, *The Plough and the Stars*, act II, 177: "*Fluther*: Come on into th' snug, me little darlin', an' we'll have a few dhrinks before I see you home"; Brown, *Down All the Days*, 79: "she could from now on come home from those furtive visits to the women's snug down the street without having to suck liquorice allsorts to kill the whiskey smell"; Leonard, *Out After Dark*, 139: "an old friend would . . . steer her into a snug for just a thimbleful of sherry."

so /soː/ *adv*. 1. Frequently used for emphasis, in the sense of 'in that case' < ME *swa*. 'Did you do your ECCERS?' – 'I did so' (BC, Meath); 'He's unwell today.' – 'He won't be at work so.' Doyle, *The Van*, 4: "'You're not even inhalin' properly,' said Linda. – 'I am so, Linda'"; Kearney, *Sam's Fall*, 43: "'There's another painter in the family so,' said Aunt Madeleine"; McCourt, *Angela's Ashes*, 347: "He can read numbers so he can." 2. If, provided that. 'I will pay you well so you do the work to my liking' (PWJ) (cf. Bosworth and Toller, s.v. 'swa' V.5: 'with a conditional force, *provided that*, *if so be that*.'

sobal /'sʌbəl/ *n.*, lather; foam; the soap on a man's face from shaving (KM, Kerry) < Ir. 'Wipe that sobal off your face before you answer the door.'

socair /'sʌkər/ *adj.*, quiet, still < Ir. Birmingham, *The Lighter Side of Irish Life*, 174: "'There I was,' said a woman to me once, 'sitting socar and easy.' She believed that 'socar' was an English word and assured me that she knew no Gaelic."

soccer /'sɑkər/ *n.* (*colloq.*), a popular name for association football (from the second syllable of which (*-soc*) the word 'soccer' is derived). 'We'd always play soccer in the field below the house after school' (Mayo). *See* FOOTBALL.

sodality /sə'dæləti/ *n.*, an alternative name for a confraternity (a formally established Catholic association or guild devoted to good work or service of some kind or to prayer, e.g. the CHILDREN OF MARY. 'Wednesday night is sodality night; don't forget to bring your medal and ribbon.' McGahern, *The Leave-Taking*, 13: "Mrs. Maloney is at CONFESSIONS, it's the women's Sodality"; Jordan, *The Past*, 162: "And the mothers of the sodality claimed the old man had got himself another model."

sodar /'sʌd̪ər/ *n.*, trotting; a quick trot; a hurry (DB, Cork) < Ir. 'Look at the sodar of him' (said of a horse running).

soft /sɔːft/, /sɑft/ *adj.*, misty and rainy (usage influenced by Ir *bog*, soft and wet); over-generous, lenient, gullible; slightly retarded or 'simple' (GF, Galway). 'It's a fine soft morning'; 'Soft day!' (a common greeting). Joyce, *Finnegans Wake*, 619.20: "Soft morning, city!"

soggart, *see* SAGART.

soirée, *see* SWARRA.

solas /'sʌləs/ *n.*, light < Ir. 'Shed some solas on this, will you?' (TJ, Sligo).

so long /sə'lɑŋ/ *phr.* It has been claimed that the American farewell 'so long' may be derived from Ir SLÁN (e.g. Griffith, 34: 'When Americans heard Irish laborers saying *Slán* . . . instead of *Goodbye*, they thought they were hearing *So long*), but the connection is improbable – as are the suggestions that it may originate with Hebrew *sholom* or Arabic *salām*, peace. *See* SLÁN.

something like /'sʌmt̪ən'laik/ *phr.*, fine, excellent. 'That's something like a horse,' that's a fine horse and no mistake (PWJ).

sonas /'sʌnəs/ *n.*, contentment, happiness (SOM, Kerry) < Ir.

'She came home and gave her parents great sonas.' *See* SONSE.

sonasach /'sʌnəsəx/ *adj.*, happy, contented, placid (SOM, Kerry) < Ir.

sonohur, *see* SONUACHAR.

sonse /sʌns/ *n.*, plenty, abundance (KG, Kerry) < Ir *sonas*, happiness. 'There hasn't been any sonse in that family for a long time.'

sonsy /'sʌnsi/ *adj.*, healthy; good-looking; lucky; thriving and jolly (generally said of a girl) (LUB, Dublin, 182; Hogan notes: 'A Scottish and Northern word, from Sc. Gaelic; compare Ir. sonasach') < Ir *sonasach*.

sonuachar /sʌ'nuəxər/ also **sunoohar** *n.*, a good spouse < Ir *sonuachar*, spouse. 'Sonuachar chugat!', may you get a good spouse. 'Good sunoohar to you' (MH, Clare). Griffin, *The Collegians*, 148: "'Nelly AROO,' he added, changing his tone – '*Sonohur* to you.'"

soogan, soogaun, *see* SÚGÁN.

sooleens /'suːliːnz/ also SÚILÍNÍ /suː'liːniː/ *n.pl.*, the rings of fat floating on top of broth (KM, Kerry) < Ir *súilíní* (lit. little eyes). 'When I saw the sooleens floating on top of the stew I knew there was no way I could eat it.'

sop /sɑp/ *n.*, a wisp of hay or straw used for feeding cattle (JQ, Kerry) < Ir. 'Give the MOILEY cow a sop of hay'; 'He hadn't a sop of hay left after the long winter.'

soretost, *see* SAORSTÁT ÉIREANN.

sorra /'sɑrə/ also **sorrow** *n.*, used to express absence or emphatic negative < E dial. (Hogan notes: '*sorrow* as a mild imprecation and emphatic negative is mediaeval English, and survives in Scotland and Ireland'; see Odlin, 1996). 'Sorra the one came to his funeral'; 'You'd think he'd be flabbergasted, but sorra bit of him' (LUB, Dublin). 'The sorra one,' not one; 'the sorra one of me knows,' I don't know; 'the sorra a bit of me cares,' I don't care (LUB, Dublin). Trollope, *The Kellys and the O'Kellys*, 331: "Sorrow a lie I'm telling you"; Joyce, *Finnegans Wake*, 80.3: "sorrel a wood knows"; 381. 32–3: "whatever surplus rotgut, sorra much, was left by the lazy lousers of maltknights"; O'Casey, *The Plough and The Stars*, act III, 184: "*Bessie*: . . . Sorra mend th' lasses that have been kissin' an' cuddlin' their boys."

sorrel, sorrow, *see* SORRA.

sot /sɑt/ *v.*, sit or set (cf. *hot*, past tense of hit). Stoker, *The Snake's Pass*, 31: "an' the two min sot down the chist [chest] an' they turned."

souper /'suːpər/ *n. (pejor.)*, a Catholic who adopted the Protestant faith in return for food during the Great Famine < *soup* + *-er*. 'I know of one family in Baltinglass, Co. Wicklow, the last of whom died only a few years ago [1992–93]; that family was always known as the 'Soup —s' (GF, Galway) Sheehan, *Glenanaar*, 156: "'He offered to take the child, and do for her, and rare [rear] her up a lady – ' 'An' make a souper of her?"; Joyce, *Finnegans Wake*, 289.4–5: "allsods of esoupcans."

sowans /saunz/ also **sowens, sowins** *n.*, a dish resembling porridge, in which oat husks are broken up, mixed with meal, and then soaked in water till fermented, after which the water is drained off (perhaps from Gaelic *sùghan*, water in which oatmeal has been steeped; cf. Ir *suán*; cf. also Ir SAMHAIN, on the eve of which (Hallowe'en) the dish was traditionally served). 'It's funny that I used to eat sowans all the time when I was young, and I don't think I could look at a bowl of it now.' Swift, *A Dialogue in Hybernian Stile*, 164: "A. And what breakfast do you take in the country? B. Why, sometimes, sowins, and sometimes STIRABOUT."

spadach /ˈspɑd̪əx/ *adj., n.*, soft, heavy, wet (of turf); soft white turf (JF, Cavan) < Ir. 'Spread those spadachs out to dry.'

spág /spɔːg/ *n.*, a large, clumsy foot (JF, Cavan) < Ir. 'Get those spágs out of my way'; 'Did you ever see such a pair of spágs?' (SOM, Kerry).

spagh, *see* SPEACH.

spailpín, *see* SPALPEEN.

spairt /spærʧ/ *n.*, wet turf (ML, Mayo) < Ir. 'I can't get that spairt to light.'

spalpeen /ˈspælpiːn/ also **spailpín** *n. (now pejor.)*, an agricultural labourer who travelled about the country at certain seasons seeking work and who sometimes got into scraps, for whatever reason; hence fig. a rascal, scamp < Ir *spailpín*. PWJ, 331: 'They travelled about each with his spade, or his scythe, or his reaping-hook. They congregated in the towns on market and fair days where the farmers of the surrounding districts came to hire them. They were fed and given places to sleep in barns – as one of them said to me, "a bed fit for a lord, let alone a spalpeen."' 'If I catch you, you spalpeen, I'll clatter you' (Mayo). Swift, *A Dialogue in Hybernian Stile*, 165: "B. . . . In short, he is no better than a spawlpeen."

spancel /ˈspænsəl/ *n.*, a hobble (e.g. a tie put on animals' legs) often made of hay-rope or old clothing < Du *spansel*. 'Put a spancel on that dródánaí (a cow that won't stand still to be milked)' (KM, Kerry). Kiely, *A Ball of Malt and Madame Butterfly*, 183: "The wife has him tethered and spancelled in the HAGGARD."

spar, *see* SCOLLOP.

sparán /spərˈɔːn/ *n.*, a purse, a

wallet (ENM, Kerry) < Ir. 'Put that in your sparán and don't lose it.'

spawg, *see* SPÁG.

spawlpeen, *see* SPALPEEN.

speach /spæx/ also **spagh** *n.*, the kick of a horse or cow (LUB, Dublin) < Ir. 'He got a speach from the horse' (SOM, Kerry).

speailín /'spæliːn/ *n.*, a little scythe; a knife fashioned out of a scythe (MK, Galway) < Ir (dimin. of *speal*, scythe). 'You'll have to use the speailín along by the wall' (Galway).

spideog /spɪ'd̪oːg/ also **spidogue** (LUB, Dublin) *n.*, a robin; fig. a delicate child, small for its age; a small and weakly grown-up < Ir. 'Is it that little bit of a spidogue?' (LUB, Dublin).

spin /spɪn/ *n.*, the teat of an animal (LUB, Dublin, 183) (Hogan notes: '*spean* is an old English word, and survives in some English and Irish dialects; spin, with short vowel, has not been recorded since 1525; but E.D.D. gives *spen* for Pembrokeshire') (cf. OE *spana, spona*).

spíon /spiːn/ *n.*, a thorn; a thorn bush < Ir (cf. E *spine*). 'She used spread out the clothes on the spíons to dry.'

spíonán /spiː'nɔːn/ *n.*, a gooseberry < Ir. 'She gave me a spíonán pie to sell at the bazaar' (KG, Kerry).

spit /spɪt/ *n.*, a trench; the depth of a spade-blade brought to the surface (Omurethi, Kildare, 538) < ME *spittan*, *v.*, to dig with a spittle (a kind of spade with a curved edge) < OE *spittan*. 'Yez might deepen the dhrain be another spit, boys' (Omurethi, Kildare).

splanc /splæŋk/ *n.*, a flash, a spark; fig. a spark of sense (SOM, Kerry) < Ir. 'There wasn't a splanc of light down there' (TF, Cavan); 'I saw a splanc of light through the trees but I couldn't be sure how many of them were IN IT' (BC, Meath); 'That boy hasn't a splink of sense' (MH, Clare).

spoiled priest /'spɔild'priːst/ *n.phr.*, a postulant for the priesthood who left the seminary before ordination; up to the 1950s and indeed into the 1960s it was regarded almost as a badge of shame for the whole family (GF, Galway). 'They say he was a spoiled priest; and you know, he has the look of one.'

sponc[1] /spʌŋk/ also **spunk** *n.*, a spark of life; spirit or courage < Ir. 'There wasn't a sponc in him; he's quite dead, poor soul' (KG, Kerry).

sponc[2], *see* SPUNK[1].

spondulicks /spɑn'ʤuːlɪks/ also **spondulix, spondulics** *n.*, money (origin obscure; probably of American origin). 'Come on, hand over the spondulicks' (Dublin). Joyce, 'Ivy Day in the Committee Room' (*Dubliners*, 136): "Anyway, I wish he'd turn up with the spondulics."

spré /spreː/ *n.*, dowry (MC, Kildare) < Ir. 'She took a big spré with her into the convent.'

spreasán /ˈspræsɔːn/ also **sprizaun** *n.*, a small twig; fig. a weakling (Hayden and Hartog); a good-for-nothing (VQ, Kerry) < Ir. 'If ye don't behave yourselves, me little sprizauns, we'll soon find yez a lodging for the night' (Hayden and Hartog).

sprizaun, *see* SPREASÁN.

spuds /spʌdz/ *n.pl.* (*colloq.*), potatoes < E (origin obscure; dated to the 19th century). 'Are the spuds done yet?'; 'He has to have spuds every day for his dinner' (BC, Meath). Heaney, 'A Constable Calls' (*North*, 66): "Heating in sunlight, the 'spud' of the dynamo gleaming and cocked back."

spunk[1] /spʌŋk/ *n.*, colt's-foot (LUB, Dublin, 183) (Hogan notes: 'the word is English, and one of its meanings is "tinder". This herb gets its name, in Anglo-Irish [i.e. HE] and in Irish [*sponc*] from its use as tinder; it is not apparently so named in England').

spunk[2], *see* SPONC[1].

spútrach /ˈspuːt̪rəx/ *n.*, rain-soaked, mucky ground (KM, Kerry) < Ir. 'It's all spútrach after that rain'; 'They shouldn't play on the pitch – it's too spútrach.'

Spy Wednesday /spaiˈwɛnzdeː/ *n.*, the Wednesday before Easter (because of Judas spying to see how best he could betray Jesus).

squireen /ˈskwairiːn/ *n.* (*pejor.*), a petty squire with pretentions < E *squire* + dimin. suffix -EEN.

sram /srɑm/ *n.*, gum; matter running from the eyes; bleariness of the eyes (MK, Galway); collection in the eyes of dirt after night (JF, Cavan) < Ir. 'Wash your face – you've got sram in your eyes.'

sramach /ˈsrɑməx/ *adj.*, blear-eyed (MK, Galway) < Ir. 'The dancers were sramach after the night that was IN IT.'

srán /srɔːn/ *n.*, a rush at something (KM, Kerry) < Ir. 'He made a srán for the ewe, but she got away.'

sraoill /sriːl/ *n.*, a slovenly woman < Ir. 'Bíonn snáth fada ag sraoill' (proverb), A slattern has a long thread (i.e. sews untidily).

srathair /ˈsrɑhər/ *n.*, a straddle or horse-pad (MK, Galway) < Ir. 'Make sure you put the srathair on the horse before you ride him!'

srathair fhada /srɑhərˈɑd̪ə/ *n.phr.*, a pannier-straddle: two baskets attached across a donkey's back to transport turf from the bog (SOM, Kerry) < Ir. 'Put the srathair fhada on the donkey; it's the only way we'll get this turf in.' *See* CREEL.

srón /sroːn/ *n.*, nose < Ir. 'She gave him a biff on the srón' (Galway).

stag[1] /stæg/ *n.* (*colloq.*), an obstinate, hard-hearted woman (cf. PWJ, 334) < Ir *staga*.

stag[2] /stæg/ *n.* (*colloq.*), an

informer (LUB, Dublin, 184) < E dial. (*EDD* s.v. 'stag sb.[3], 13': 'an informer, a betrayer').

stagger /ˈstæɡər/ *v.*, to mispronounce; to make an attempt at pronouncing. 'I think that's what his name was, but sure I staggered it anyway' (JOC, Kerry).

staic /st̪æk/ *n.*, a stockily built man < Ir. 'He was a staic of a man in his day, but he was too fond of the drink, and it ruined him' (KM, Kerry).

stail /st̪æl/ *n.*, a stallion; (humorous) a male, a husband, as when Ansty remarked of Tailor Buckley, 'Look at my old stail' (SOM, Kerry) < Ir.

stailc /st̪ælk/ *n.*, a fit of sulkiness or bad temper (in people or animals), a tantrum (DB, Cork) < Ir. 'He went off in a stailc – as if I cared.'

stailín /ˈst̪æliːn/ *n.*, a diminutive stallion (MK, Galway); fig. a little man < Ir (dimin. of STAIL). 'He's a wee little stailín, but what a goer he is!'

stalctha /ˈst̪ɑlkə/ *adj.*, stiff and stodgy (MK, Galway) < Ir. 'What kind of bread did you make? It's very stalctha.'

standard /ˈstænd̪ərd/ *n.*, an old inhabitant < E dial. (aphetic of AN *estaundart*). 'I'm one of the rale [real] ould standards, your honour; me and mine has been here for nine generations' (Omurethi, Kildare). *See* RESIDENTER; RUNNER.

standing /ˈstændən/ *vn.*, used in such phrases as 'He fell out of his standing', = He fell from an upright position < Ir *thit sé as a sheasamh*, lit. fell he from his standing; cf. 'táim i mo sheasamh,' lit. I am in my standing (= I am standing up). 'I had like to fall out of my standing with fright' (LUB, Dublin, 183) (Hogan notes: 'Ir. *tuitim as mo sheasamh*; in 18th century English *standing* had this sense'). '"You know what this song ('Begat') is about, don't you?" asked the ex-priest, who was directing this part of the show. "Er, no," answered the schoolgirl. "Sex!" he answered, and she nearly fell out of her standing' (Limerick speaker, female, 21–23 years of age, reported by S. McGibben).

stare /steːr/ *n.*, a starling (Omurethi, Kildare) < E dial. < OE *stær*. 'The stares have a nest built in the gutter, and they're making an awful racket' (TJ, Sligo).

staróg /ˈst̪ɑroːɡ/ *n.*, an anecdote; a wild story, a ridiculous statement < Ir. 'He's full of the old starógs, and I love listening to them, even if they're not true' (BC, Meath).

starrfhiacail /st̪ɑːˈriəkəl/ *n.*, a prominent tooth (KG, Kerry) < Ir.

starving /ˈstærvən/ *pres.part.*, very cold, freezing < OE *steorfan*, *v.*, to die. 'I'm starvin'' (RMM, Antrim).

station /ˈsteːʃən/ *n.*, the custom

of a priest saying Mass in a private house for the family and neighbours, followed by hospitality; the practice works by rotation < L *statio*. 'We're having the stations at the house on Wednesday.' Kickham, *Knocknagow*, 26: "You will be put to some inconvenience tomorrow, as we are to have the Station . . . Catholics go to Confession and Communion at Christmas and Easter. And, in country districts instead of requiring the people to go to the CHAPEL, the priests come to certain houses in each locality to hear confessions and say Mass."

Stations (of the Cross) /'steːʃənz (ɑvd̪ə'krɔːs)/ *n.phr.*, fourteen crosses, and the corresponding images, associated with the incidents of Christ's passion and death; 'doing the Stations' is the practice of saying prayers before each of them in turn, a custom that originated with the Franciscans in the 15th century. 'I lost count of the number of Stations she did before the funeral.' McCourt, *Angela's Ashes*, 381: "I do the Stations of the Cross three times."

status /'stæːtəs/ *n.*, like a number of other words of Latin origin, such as 'data' /'dæːtə/, has a pronunciation in Ireland that retains what is perhaps thought of as the Classical sounds of the original, instead of the Anglicisations of SE /'deːtɑ/, /'steːtəs/, etc. It has been suggested (on no firm grounds) that the retention of this pronunciation may ultimately be due to the influence of the pronunciation used and taught by the hedge-school masters, many of whom would have been imbued with Latin learning (cf. Kickham's reference in *Knocknagow*, 71–72, to differences between the Latin pronunciaton taught at Trinity College, Dublin, and that taught in 'Larry O'Rourke's mud-wall seminary in Glounamuckadhee').

steall /ʃʧæl/ *n.*, a quantity of liquid (especially tea); a splash < Ir. 'Pour yourself a steall from the pot' (SOM, Kerry). *See* STREALL.

steeler /'stilər/ also **steely** /'stiliː/ *n.*, a child's marble made of steel (KD, Dublin).

steven /'stɛvən/ *n.*, a time, a turn; vicissitude; occasion < OE *niwan stefne*, afresh, anew (*OED*). 'To change (by) stevens, to take turns.

sthreeling, *see* STREEL.

stim /ʃtɪm/ *n.*, a gleam of light, a glimmer; a small quantity or a small amount < E dial. (origin obscure). 'I can't see anything; there's not a stim of light here' (TF, Cavan); 'He hasn't a stim of sense, that fella' (Monaghan); 'There wasn't a stim of light in the house' (LUB, Dublin) (Hogan notes:

'A Scottish and Northern word. The vowel is long except in some Scottish dialects and Anglo-Irish.').

stirabout /ˈstʌrəbaut/ *n.*, porridge; fig. a fussy person < E *stir + about*. 'Never scald your lips on another man's stirabout'; 'She's a right stirabout that one – she must have the children driven up the wall.' Behan, *The Quare Fellow*, act I (*FDA*, 3, 202): "Real bog-man act. Nearly as bad as a shotgun, or getting the weedkiller mixed up in the stirabout"; Joyce, 'The Sisters' (*Dubliners*, 7: "While my aunt was ladling out my stirabout he said . . ."

stiver /ˈstɪvər/ *n.*, *v.*, bristling of the hair; (of the hair) to stand up; fig. to anger, to become angry; to tremble < E dial. < ME *stive*, *adj.*, stiff + *-er*. 'Don't you be always stivering; let's have some peace'; 'You can tell when there's going to be a dog fight: you can see the stiver on the dog's back.'

stocious /ˈstoːʃəs/ *adj.* (*colloq.*), very drunk (origin obscure; Braidwood, 34, refers to 'down-to-earth Ulsterisms like stocious or putrid drunk'). 'He fell down stocious' (TF, Cavan); Roche, *A Handful of Stars*, act I, iii, 36: "*Linda*: . . . He'd have come in stocious drunk and gave me poor Ma a couple of belts."

stóilín /ˈstoːliːn/ *n.*, a small stool, often three-legged, as used for milking < Ir (dimin. of *stól*, stool). 'You can stand on that stóilín; it's safe.'

stompa, *see* STUMP.

stook /stuːk/ *n.*, a stack of sheaves of corn or barley, usually twelve (MOB, Mayo), about four couples of sheaves leaning against one another in a row (Omurethi, Kildare, 539) < E dial. < late ME *stouk*. 'They made stooks and all in the same day' (MG, Cavan). Yeats, *The Unicorn from the Stars*, act III (*Collected Plays*, 377: "*Paudeen*: . . . It is you yourself will have freed all Ireland before the stooks will be in stacks!" *See* STÚICÍN.

stookaun, *see* STUACÁN.

stooleen /ˈstuːliːn/ *n.*, a small stool < E *stool* + dimin. suffix -EEN. 'Mind that stooleen; it's not very steady since John jumped on it' (Meath). *See* STÓILÍN.

stoor /stuːr/ *n.*, dust < OF *estour*. 'The ribbonmen'll be raisin' the stoor th'morra' (RMM, Antrim).

stór /st̪oːr/ *n.*, term of endearment: beloved one < Ir (lit. treasure). Usually found in vocative in this sense, e.g. 'Jackie, a stór,' Jackie, my beloved. 'Stór mo chroí,' my heart's beloved (SOM, Kerry).

strácáil /st̪rɔːˈkɔːl/ *v.n.*, an effort of doubtful efficiency, 'pulling the Devil by the tail' < Ir. 'Strácáiling' /st̪rɔːˈkɔːlən/ *pres.*

part., struggling against the odds (SOM, Kerry); just about coping with life; dawdling; tearing, pulling, tugging (ENM, Kerry). 'Sure I'm only strá-cáiling' (SOM, Kerry).

strácálaí /st̪rɔːˈkɔːliː/ *n.*, a struggler; a hard worker with little to show for his or her efforts (SOM, Kerry) < Ir. 'That poor strácálaí's always got his head in his books, but he never passes anything' (KG, Kerry).

straddy /ˈst̪rædiː/ *n.*, a street-walker; an idle person always sauntering the streets < Ir *stráid* (variant of *sráid*), STREET.

strand /strænd/ *n.*, a beach < E dial. (origin obscure); 'We went for a nice walk down by the strand.'

strange, *see* MAKE STRANGE.

straoill, *see* STREEL.

strap /st̪ræp/ *n.*, an impudent girl; a slut < E dial. 'She's a forward strap' (LUB, Dublin, who adds: 'also applied to a goat or cow which gives trouble when being milked'); 'You little strap, wait till your mother hears about this!' (BC, Meath).

strate, *see* STREET.

stravague /st̪rɑˈveːɡ/ also **stravaig, stravage** *n.*, *v.*, to wander about aimlessly; to saunter, to stroll (LUB, Dublin, 184) < E dial. < OF *estraier*, to wander; Hogan comments: '*Stravage* is the normal dialect form; this, not recorded elsewhere, is very interesting as the back-stop g [i.e. /ɡ/] confirms the derivation from O.Fr. *extravaguer*).' Hayden and Hartog, 781, comment that 'stravague' is one of the words that 'may have been introduced by the hedge-schoolmaster of the seventeenth century, with his pedantic and ultra-classic vocabulary.' 'He's always stravaging the streets' (PWJ); 'Stop your stravaiging and make yourself useful!' (Cavan). Joyce, *Ulysses*, 301.11: "Mother kept a kip in Hardwicke street that used to be stravaging about the landings." *See* HEDGE-SCHOOL; STATUS.

straw boys /ˈst̪rɔːbaiz/ *n.pl.*, young men who act the fool in fancy dress. Dunphy, 191: 'Strawboys who attend wedding festivities are called "fools" in New Ross District. They do not deck themselves out in straw, but disguise themselves with horse-hair beards, variegated gartments, etc. . . . If they are well treated, they are pleased, but if not, they do damage to the gates and fences of the farm or otherwise show their displeasure.'

streall /ʃtræl/ *n.*, a quantity of liquid (variant of STEALL, often used by the same person on the next occasion of using the word (SOM, Kerry)) < Ir. 'A steall of tea for you, and a streall for myself.'

streancán /ˈʃtræŋkɔːn/ *n.*, a gush; a quantity of liquid (much the same as STEALL, STREALL); a verse of a song, a tune (SOM, Kerry) < Ir.

streel /s̪triːl/ *n.*, *v.*, anything untidy; a slovenly, untidy person, usually female (LUB, Dublin); to saunter aimlessly < Ir. *straoill* (variant of *sraoill*). '"You're not going out dressed like that, you streel!" she said. "Go back upstairs and change your clothes"' (KG, Kerry). 'Walking through wet grass is called "sthreeling" by women who have had the lower portion of their skirts saturated in the grass' (PA, Fingall). 'Her clothes are all streeling after her'; 'There she goes and her childer streeling after her.' Heaney, *The Midnight Verdict*, 24: "With a swatch of her shawl all japs [jaups, splashes of mud] and glar [GLÁR] | Streeling behind in the muck and mire."

streelish /'s̪triːlɪʃ/ *adj.*, untidy (of a house or a woman) (LUB, Dublin). 'She's a bit streelish, in spite of her grand ways.'

street /s̪triːt/ *n.*, a (paved) space in front of a house; a farmyard; a back yard < ME *strete*. 'She HUNTED the cattle out of the street'; 'We never left the cattle in the street after milking – they'd have an awful mess made of the place if we did' (AF, Cavan). Joyce, *Finnegans Wake*, 110.33–4: "on a strate that was called strete"; Healy, *Nineteen Acres*, 70: "her eyes would be dry by the time she reached 'the street' in front of the cottage"; 109: "Now the 'street', more properly, the yard at the back of the house, began to look a little unkempt."

stretch /s̪trɛʧ/ *n.*, in the idiomatic phr. 'there's a stretch in the evening' (MCR, Waterford), the days are getting longer (in the spring). Delaney, *The Sins of the Mothers*, 225: "Hallo, Doctor, there's a great stretch in the evenings, isn't there?"

striapach /'s̪triəpəx/ *n.*, prostitute < Ir. Joyce, *Finnegans Wake*, 90.31–3: "Bladyughfoulmoecklenburgwhurawhorascortastrumpapornanennykock sapastippatappatupperstrippuck puttanach, eh?"

strig, *see* STRIPPINGS.

strip /s̪trɪp/ *v.*, to drain the last drop of milk from the cow after milking < E dial. < ME *stripe*. 'Be sure to drain all the milk from the udder; it prevents mastitis' (GF, Galway).

stripper /'s̪trɪpər/ *n.*, a cow giving little milk, fit to be sold (GF, Galway) < E dial. < ME *stripe* + *-er*. 'That stripper will have to go the next fair-day'; 'He has nothing but strippers and calveens [little calves]'; 'Few cows were bulled this year, and I've only a field of strippers – no calves in them' (KM, Kerry).

strippings /'s̪trɪpənz/ *n.pl.* also **strig** /'s̪trɪg/ (PWJ), the last milk taken from a cow at each milking (KM, Kerry) < E dial. (*OED* compares West Flemish 'strip', stream of milk from a teat). *See* BEESTINGS.

stronesha /'st̪roːnʃə/ *n.*, an unreliable, clumsy girl or woman; sometimes said playfully of a little girl (LUB, Dublin) < Ir *stróinse*, vagrant.

stuacán /st̪uə'kɔːn/ *n.*, a STOOK, a pile (KM, Kerry); fig. (also stookaun) a stubborn person; an obstinate and silent person (KM, Kerry) < Ir. 'The turf will stay dry in the stuacáns in the bog'; 'You won't get the better of him: he's a terrible stuacán.'

stuaic /stuək/ also **stook** *n.*, a sullen appearance; also used as an affectionate term of abuse for a fairly harmless type of fool (MK, Galway) < Ir. 'He's only a poor old stook.'

stuicín /'ʃtʌkiːn/ *n.*, a small stook of hay or barley < Ir. (dimin. of *stuc*, *stuca*). 'Make a stuicín with any hay that's left over.'

stump /ʃtʌmp/ *n.*, an animal that's hard to move; a cow that refuses to stir for the milker' (MH, Clare) < Ir *stumpa*, *stompa*.

sturk /stʌrk/ also **stirk** *n.*, a young heifer or bull; fig. a short, stout thick-set boy or girl < ME *stirke*, heifer. 'He bought a sturk of a calf' (Dublin); 'He's a fine sturk of a child; how old is he?' (BC, Meath).

suachmán /'suːkmɔːn/ *n.*, a relaxed, easy-going adult or child < Ir. 'That suachmán will never get anywhere the way he's going on.'

suáilceach /suː'ɔːlkəx/ *adj.*, pleasant, happy < Ir. 'Those children are very suáilceach, God bless them!'

suaimhneasach /'suəvnəsəx/ *adj.*, at ease; tranquil < Ir. 'Ye're fine and suaimhneasach for yourselves!' (SOM, Kerry).

suan /suən/ *n.*, sleep < Ir. 'Stop your suaning and just do some work, will you!' (KG, Kerry).

suantraí /'suənt̪riː/ *n.*, a lullaby; a LILTING song, such as 'She didn't dance and dance and dance, | She didn't dance all day' (SOM, Kerry) < Ir.

suarach /'suərəx/ *adj.*, small and mean; of no significance < Ir. 'Johnny Suarach they used call him.'

suarachán /'suərəxɔːn/ *n.*, a wretched, miserable fellow; a mean, miserly person < Ir. 'He's a miserable suarachán' (SOM, Kerry).

subh /sʌv/ *n.*, jam < Ir. 'A touch of red subh on the toast, please!' (JF, Cavan).

suck suck /sʌksʌk/ an onomatopoeic call to calves < E. 'All you have to do is say "suck suck" and the calves will run up to you.'

súdaire /'suːd̪ərə/ *n.*, a rogue; a sponger < Ir. 'Don't listen to that súdaire; he's filling your head with RÁIMÉIS.'

súgach /ˈsuːgəx/ *adj.*, mildly drunk, merry < Ir. 'They're fine and súgach' (SOM, Kerry).

súgán /ˈsuːgɔːn/ also **soogawn, sougawn, suggan** /sʌgən/ (CS, Mayo) *n.*, a rope made by twisting straw or hay (used to tie hay-cocks) (LUB, Dublin, 184); a saddle made of straw < Ir. 'A single pig when driven to a fair has a rope or a soogaun tied to one of its hind legs. A soogaun was also the name of the straw collars put on to plough-oxen' (Omurethi, Kildare). 'Better to be knotting a súgán than to be idle' (saying). Swift, *A Dialogue in Hybernian Stile*, 165: "B. . . . and I have seen him often riding on a sougawn"; Carleton, 'The Hedge School' (*Six Irish Tales*, 170): "'Bah! Come back TILL we put the *soogaun* about your neck" (in a footnote Carleton explains that "the *soogaun* was a collar of straw which was put round the necks of the dunces, who were then placed at the door, that their disgrace might be as public as possible"); Sheehan, *Glenanaar*, 100: ". . . removing his hat and placing it on the *sugan* chair where he had been sitting." 'Súgán chair', a chair with the seat made from twisted straw (SOM, Kerry).

súil /suːl/ *n.*, an eye < Ir. 'One of her súils was a funny colour.' Joyce, *Finnegans Wake*, 512.25–6: "Suilful eyes and sallowfoul hairweed and the sickly sigh from her gingering mouth like a Dublin bar in the moarning."

súilíní /ˈsuːliːni/ *n.pl.*, little eyes (MK, Galway); fig. bubbles of fat floating on top of a stew or clear soup (SOM, Kerry) < Ir. 'He likes the súilíní; he says they're good for him' (KG, Kerry). *See* SOOLEENS.

suim /sɪm/, /siːm/ also **seem** *n.*, account, value; attention (KM, Kerry) < Ir. 'He took great suim in the conversation when he heard about the amount of money involved'; 'He always put seem on [paid attention to] his students; they'll look back in years to come and be thankful for it' (Mayo).

súiste /suːʃtʃə/ *n.*, a flail (SL, Mayo) < Ir. 'My father told /tauld/ me how to use the súiste.'

súlach /ˈsuːləx/ *n.*, juice; gravy (MK, Galway) < Ir. 'The súlach of the oranges is running down your chin'; 'My mother would always mop up the súlach from the pan with bits of bread.'

sult /sʌlt̪/ *n.*, fun < Ir. 'They're having great sult; they're getting great SÁSAMH from the ball'; 'I got great sult from the singing' (SOM, Kerry).

sultmhar /ˈsʌlt̪vər/ *adj.*, enjoyable, pleasant (SOM, Kerry) < Ir.

súmaire /ˈsuːmərə/ *n.*, a sponger; a blood-sucker; a vampire (MK, Galway) < Ir. 'Keep away from that súmaire!'

sunoohar, *see* SONUACHAR.

sup /sʌp/ *n.*, *v.*, a small quantity (of liquid); to sip < Ir *sup* < ME *supen*. 'Will you give me a sup of the hard stuff [whiskey] before I fall over?' (Cork); 'a sup and a TILLY' (EOC, Tipperary). Joyce, 'Ivy Day in the Committee Room' (*Dubliners*, 134): "He takes th'upper hand of me whenever he sees I've a sup taken"; Behan, *The Quare Fellow*, act I (*FDA*, 3, 203): "*Dunlavin*: And the two screws nod to each other across the fire to make a sup of tea"; Keane, *The Bodhrán Makers*, 283: "WET us a sup of tea."

sure /ʃʌr/ a common emphatic opening to sentences (cf. SE 'but'). 'Sure that's what you asked me to do'; 'Sure I'm just after telling you he's gone to the States this last three months' (JB, Kildare).

Swaddler /ˈswɑdlər/ *n.*, a Protestant (LUB, Dublin); nickname for a Methodist (1747), subsequently generalised (Hogan). Southey, *Wesley* (1820), 2, 109: 'said to have originated with an ignorant Romanist . . . who, hearing one of . . . Wesley's preachers mention the swaddling clothes of the Holy Infant . . . shouted out in derision "A swaddler! a swaddler!" as if the whole story were the preacher's invention.'

swarra /ˈswɑːrə/ *n.* (*colloq.*), an evening of conversational entertainment, with the drinking of tea and a song or two (DOH, who adds that this is 'Clare usage') < F *soirée*. *See* CÉILÍ.

sway, *see* SCOLLOP.

swithers /ˈswɪd̪ərz/ *n.*, a state of confusion or hesitation < E dial. (origin obscure). Traynor, Donegal, includes 'swithering, *p.part.*, *a.*, hesitating, irresolute' and cites 'in (the) swithers'. 'Ye may be sure I was in the swithers what to do with myself'; 'He's in swithers what to do.' Todd exemplifies with 'I swithered one way an another for years.'

T

tá /t̪ɔː/ *v.* 'is', 'are'. This verb and all other verbs in Irish retain the same form for singular and plural: tá mé (I), tú (you singular), sé (he), sí (she), muid (we), sibh (you plural), siad (they), with the first person singular and plural normally connected: táim, táimid. This may account for the common solecism in HE of using a singular verb with a plural subject, e.g. 'Your hands is cold' (Irish tá do lámha fuar). Joyce, 'Ivy Day in the Committee Room' (*Dubliners*, 141): "No, but the stairs is so dark"; Roche, *Poor Beast in the Rain*, act I, i, 73: "tá sé mahogany gaspipe. Tá sé bore the hole in the bucket."

tabhairt amach /t̪uːrtə'mɑx/ *v.n.,* the act of giving out (food etc.); hospitality (especially at wakes) (DB, Cork).

taca /'t̪ɑkə/ *n.*, support, a prop; a helping hand < Ir. 'He gets great taca from the wife's people.' 'I dtaca le holc', a Johnny-come-lately (SOM, Kerry) < Ir. 'Lán-taca', full-back (in football games) < Ir.

tacar /'t̪ɑkər/ *v.*, gleaning, harvest (KM, Kerry) < Ir.

tack[1] /tæk/ *n.*, a job < E dial. 'He has good tack now, if he only minds it' (LUB, Dublin, 184). Hogan comments: 'This is no doubt *tack* = food, but the idiom seems to be local.'

tack[2] /tæk/ *n.*, a stitch (of clothes); a shred (LUB, Dublin, 184) < E dial. Hogan notes: 'This use of *tack* = stitch is peculiar to Anglo-Irish [i.e. HE].' 'The poor woman had hardly /'hɑːrliː/ a tack on her and it the middle of winter' (BC, Meath); 'He hadn't a tack on his back. He hadn't a tack on his feet = his boots were worn out' (LUB, Dublin).

tad /tæd/ *n.* (*colloq.*), a small amount < E *tad(pole)* (*ODEE* s.v. tadpole: EarlyModE taddepol, from *tadde* toad (OE tade) + *pol* poll (cf. obsolete Low German, Du polle, head), as if a toad that is all head); 'He didn't do a tad of work for me'; 'I'll just put a tad more sugar in that if you don't mind', Dublin.

Tadhg /t̪aig/ *n.*, used in phrases as a typical man's name. 'Gruth do Thadhg agus meadhg do na cailíní' (proverb), The best of everything for the menfolk (lit. Curds for Tadhg and whey for the girls). *See* TEAGUE.

Tadhg an dá thaobh /t̪aigə'd̪ɔː 'heːv/ *n.phr.*, someone who takes both sides, who 'runs with the hare and hunts with the hounds' (MK, Galway); a double-dealer < Ir (lit. Tadhg of the two sides). 'You couldn't trust him as far as you'd throw him: he's only a Tadhg an dá thaobh' (SOM, Kerry).

tadhlach /'t̪ailəx/ *n.*, soreness; swelling; cramp in wrist or fingers (KM, Kerry) < Ir. 'I have an awful tadhlach in my fingers from milking them cows.'

táilleog /'tɔːloːg/ *n.*, a small loft; a wall press (ENM, Kerry) < Ir. 'The children used always sleep in the táilleog, because it was warmer up there'; 'They say he has all his money hidden in the táilleog in the house.'

táithín /t̪ɔː'hiːn/ *n.*, a wisp, a tuft, a tiny fistful (of rough grass, bog cotton, etc.) (SOM, Kerry); a lock of hair < Ir. 'He used take a táithín of grass and wipe his boots before going into the house.'

taitneamh /'t̪ænəv/ *n.*, satisfaction (SOM, Kerry) < Ir. 'He got great taitneamh out of that pint' (SOM, Kerry).

táláid /t̪ɔː'lɔːʤ/ *n.*, a deep shelf on both sides of the chimney; a half-loft over the kitchen fire < Ir. 'Leave the tea up in the táláid; it'll get damp in the press' (BC, Meath).

tally-iron /'tæliːaiərn/ *n.*, a crimping-iron for ironing linen into a fluted shape, crimping cap-frills, etc.; formerly used on the white borders of caps worn under POOKEY-BONNETS < E dial. < *Italian iron*. 'She used to iron his cotta [surplice] with a tally-iron, so he always looked really smart when he was serving the priest at Mass' (AJF, Cavan).

tally-stick /'tæliʃtɪk/ also **bata scóir** *n.*, a stick hung around children's necks in national schools in the 19th century, marked with a 'score' or notch every time a child spoke Irish, used for determining the amount of punishment for doing so; in some instances they were punished by the teacher each day according to the number of marks put on the stick by their parents the evening before (Seán Ó Súilleabháin). In some districts each pupil had a tally; elsewhere there would be one tally for the whole class, and the offending pupil would have to wear it during school hours. In Mayo a piece of string, with knots as markers, was used as an alternative to the stick. Montague, 'A Grafted Tongue' (*Collected Poems*, 37): "An Irish | child weeps at school | repeating its English. | After each mistake ||

the master | gouges another mark | on the tally stick | hung about its neck || like a bell | on a cow, a hobble | on a straying goat."

támáilte /ṱɔː'mɔːlʧə/ *adj.*, mawkish, sluggish (KM, Kerry) < Ir. 'Finish that quick and don't be so támáilte, I'm fed up looking at you!'

tamall /'ṱɑməl/ *n.*, a period, a while < Ir. 'He spent a tamall in America'; 'I haven't seen him for a tamall' (SOM, Kerry).

Tánaiste /'ṱɔːnəʃtə/ *n.*, deputy head of the Government < Ir (lit. heir, deputy chief).

t'anam 'on Diabhal *see* D'ANAM 'ON DIABHAL.

tanna bugger, *see* BOGADH.

Tans /tænz/ *n.pl.*, abbreviation for BLACK AND TANS.

taobhán /ṱiːv'ɔːn/ *n.*, a cross-rafter; a beam crossing from wall to wall to support a roof (JOM, Kerry) < Ir. 'You can hang the rope from the taobhán.'

taobhfhód /'ṱiːvoːḓ/ *n.*, a side-sod in a potato ridge during planting < Ir. 'Don't break the taobhfhód if you can help it' (KM, Kerry).

taoibhín /'ṱiːviːn/ also **theeveen** (LUB, Dublin, 185) *n.*, a patch on the upper of a shoe (SOM, Kerry) < Ir. 'Look at the taoibhíns on those old boots; they owe you nothing' (you've had great wear out of them); 'Nellie, girleen, isn't it a wonder you wouldn't get a taoibhín for your shoe?' (SOM, Kerry).

Taoiseach /'ṱiːʃəx/ *n.*, head of the Government < Ir (lit. chief).

taom[1] /ṱeːm/ also **teem** *n.*, a bout of sickness; a fit; an outburst of rage. 'Some taom came on him last year, and he made no headway since' (SOM, Kerry).

taom[2], *see* TEEM[1].

taoscán /'ṱeːskɔːn/ *n.*, a small helping; a small measure (of liquid or drink) (SOM, Kerry, who adds: 'in the case of spirits it would indicate a more generous quantity than a SMITHEÁN'; a drink of tea, milk, or stout; a small drop of water in a bucket (Mayo) < Ir. 'Just a taoscán for me, please.'

tap /tæp/ *n.*, in negative constructions, 'a stroke of work' (LUB, Dublin, 184) (Hogan notes: 'Apparently Anglo-Irish only, though very common'). 'He gave up his job in a PUCKER, and he is supping sorrow for it, as he didn't get a tap to do ever since' (LUB, Dublin).

tarbh /ṱɑrəv/ *n.*, a bull (SOM, Kerry) < Ir.

tarbh bán /ṱɑrəv'bɔːn/ *n.phr.*, artificial inseminator (KM, Kerry) < Ir (lit. white bull, from the use of white cars by staff of the cattle breeding station).

tare and ages /teːrən'eːgz/ *int.*, (Christ's) tears (shedding) or tears (torn flesh) and agues. Joyce, *Finnegans Wake*, 582.2–3: "Let us wherefore, tearing ages, presently preposterose a snatchvote of thanksalot."

tare and ’ouns /teːrən'ɑunz/ *int.*, (Christ’s) tears (shedding) or tears (torn flesh) and wounds. Trollope, *The Kellys and the O’Kellys*, 9: "‘Tear and ’ouns Misther Lord Chief Justice!’ exclaimed Martin"; Kickham, *Knocknagow*, 26: "Tare-an-’ouns, I’ll be KILT"; Sheehan, *Glenanaar*, 182: "‘But tare an’ ’ouns, man,’ said Donal, highly delighted, ‘what about Nodlag herself?"

targe /tɑːrʤ/ *v.*, to scold < E dial. (origin obscure, but cf. L *tergere*, *v.*, to scour, to wipe, to cleanse). ‘He’ll get a right targing from the mother when she sees him going home in that state!’ Heaney, *The Midnight Verdict*, 31: "And then the awful targe who’d brought me, | The plank-armed bailiff, reached and caught me."

targer /'tɑːrʤər/ also **targe** *n.*, a bad-tempered, domineering woman < E dial. (*see* TARGE). ‘That targer was on the phone again this morning; she won’t let the priest alone: she’s always giving out about something.’

tart /tart/ *n.*, thirst (SOM, Kerry) < Ir. ‘Well, there’s such a tart on me!’ (KG, Kerry).

tá sé /'t̪ɔːʃeː/ it is < Ir. ‘Is it true he gave all the money to the son and left none for the daughter?’ ‘Tá sé.’

taspey, taspy, *see* TEASPACH.

tasty /'teːsti/ *adj.* (*colloq.*), in the phr. ‘he’s very tasty,’ he’s a very competent, polished worker (NL, Mayo) < OF *taster*.

táthaire /'t̪ɔːhərə/ *n.*, an impertinent, precocious, ill-mannered or cheeky person (SOM, Kerry) < Ir. ‘If you aren’t the MANLY little táthaire, you little BOICÍN you!’ (SOM, Kerry, who adds: ‘nuance of cheeky and good-for-nothing, ? < táthán, cement, adhesive’).

táthfhéithleann /t̪ɔː'heːhlən/ *n.*, a heavy honeysuckle branch (KM, Kerry) < Ir. ‘He’ll be all right; he’s as tough as táthfhéithleann.’

tatie-howker /'teːtiːhaukər/ *n.*, a (migrant) potato-digger, especially those from Co. Donegal working in Scotland < E dial. < *tatie* (corruption of *potato*) + *howker* (variant of *holker* < ME *holk, v.*, to hollow out by digging, to dig up or dig out). ‘A bus leaves Letterkenny for Scotland with the tatie-howkers’ (FD, Cork).

tatoo /ta'tuː/ *v.*, to scold, beat, BALLYRAG < E dial. < *tap-too* (17th century), drum-beat (the *EDD* s.v. ‘tatoo’ cites Ireland only and exemplifies with Barrington, *Sketches* (1827–32), 1, xxxv: ‘I should not only have got my full portion of the tatooing (as they termed it)’).

tawse /tɔːz/ *n.*, a strap made of strips of leather < E dial. *EDD*: ‘a few strips of leather tied to a shaft, used by boys in spinning tops,’ citing *Ballymena Observer*

(1892); MT, Donegal: 'a leather strap used by a schoolmaster as an instrument for punishment . . . lashes for dogs . . . dog-whip lashes loaded with lead.'

tay, *see* TEA.

TD /tiː'diː/ for teachta Dála, member of DÁIL ÉIREANN < Ir (lit. Dáil deputy).

tea /teː/ also **tay** *n.*, HE pronunciation of ModE 'tea' < Chinese *te*, represents the older fashion of pronouncing 'ea' as /eː/. 'The tea' /tiː/, /teː/, the evening meal in Ireland. 'Wet the tea, will you?' (boil the water and make the tea). 'You have your tea!' /teː/ *int.* expressing genial exasperation or disbelief. 'Have a cup of tea in your hand' (without sitting down formally at the table). O'Brien, 'The Brother' (*The Best of Myles*, 59): "You should see the face of her nibs [HERSELF] the landlady, her good black market tay at fifteen bob [shillings] a knock."

teach /ʧæx/ also **tigh** /tɪg/ *n.*, a house, a building < Ir. 'That's a fine teach he married into' (TJ, Sligo). 'This is a saying folks had: "Dá mbeinnse id' thigse | Mar atá tú im' thigse | Raghad abhaile | Agus fan tusa anso go lá" (If I were in your house | As you are in my house | You can stay here | And I'd go home' (KM, Kerry). 'Tá na leacracha sleamhain ag teach an rí' (proverb), The floors are slippery in the king's house. Joyce, *Finnegans Wake*, 56.22–3: "lift wearywilly his slowcut snobsic eyes to the semisigns of his zooteac."

Teague /tiːg/ also **Teigue, Taig** *n. (pejor.)*, nickname for the typical Irishman, especially a Catholic < Ir TADHG (cf. *A Dialogue between Teigue and Dermot*, 149–50; cf. also Yeats's character Teigue the Fool in *The Hour-Glass*). Banim, *The Boyne Water*, 465: "These men, an English and an Irish soldier . . . were also in conversation. 'Good night, goodman Teague,' began the Englishman, heartily. 'MUSHA, good night to hur, kindly, a-vich [A MHIC],' answered the other, jeeringly." *See* SÍLE.

teallach, *see* COIS TEALLAIGH.

teanam /'ʧænəm/ *v.*, come along! (Cork) < Ir *téanam* /'ʧeːnəm/, let's go. 'Teanam, you're going to Mass, and that's it!' (Kerry).

tear and 'ouns, *see* TARE AND 'OUNS.

tearing ages, *see* TARE AND 'OUNS.

teaspach /'ʧæspəx/ also **taspey, taspy** /'tæspiː/ (SB, Cork) *n.*, liveliness, high spirits (JOM, Kerry); playfulness; exuberance < Ir. 'He has great taspy on him,' he's in high spirits (SB, Cork). 'The new MASTER won't be long taking the teaspach off them!' 'The colt is still full of teaspach' (i.e. unbroken) (SOM, Kerry).

teem[1] /tiːm/ also **taom** /t̪iːm/ *v.*, to pour (out), to empty, drain off, strain < ME *temen* (cf. also Ir *taom*, *v.*, to empty of water, pour off). 'It's teeming rain' (Omurethi, Kildare, 539); 'Teem the water out of the barrel, will you? There's worms in the bottom' (AF, Cavan); 'Taom the spuds quick before they go into a mush' (Mayo). Kavanagh, *Tarry Flynn*, 28–9: "'Come down and give us a hand to teem the pot' . . . Teeming the pot into a bucket . . . holding one of the legs of the pot with his right hand and the pot lid with his left he drained off the water."

teem[2], *see* TAOM[1].

Teigue, *see* TEAGUE.

teil, *see* AIL.

tent, *see* TINT.

terrible /ˈtɛribəl/ *adj., adv.* (*colloq.*), intensive < OF *terrible*. 'That's terrible nice of you' (JB, Kildare); Roche, *Poor Beast in the Rain*, act I, i, 71: "*Georgie*: . . . She's a terrible nice girl Joe ain't she?"

terror /ˈtɛrər/ *n.*, intensive, in such phrases as 'that's a terror,' referring in a general way to something very bad, or very good. 'He's a little terror – he never does what I tell him' (BC, Meath). Kavanagh, *Tarry Flynn*, 67: "It's a terror the trade he's getting for that young stallion"; Bolger, *Emily's Shoes*, 53–4: "'Your mother was a terror for having everything right and in its place,' she says."

'th', representing HE /t̪/, is sometimes substituted for **'t'** /t/, and vice versa, a phenomenon that is due to the similar, though not identical, sounds represented by 't' in Irish (on neutral /t/ and dental stop /t̪/ see Bliss, 1979, 232), e.g. "Dere be none, dat [that] be after coming in de Nort [North]" (Michelburne, *Ireland Preserved*, 147). In the marriage service the bride often used to promise what sounded like 'And thereto I plight thee my throat [troth]' (JMF, Cavan). 'I thought him everything I knew' (TJ, Sligo). Joyce, *Finnegans Wake*, 511.12: "she's a lamp in her throth."

thall /hɑl/ *adv.*, yonder, beyond, over there. 'Thall in Crowley's' (SOM, Kerry) < Ir.

thanum-on-dioul, *see* D'ANAM 'ON DIABHAL.

that, who /d̪æt/, /huː/ *relative prons.*, are often omitted in sentences that begin with the formula 'It is' or 'It was' (HE equivalents of the Irish copula verb 'is'). 'It was Mary bought the new car, not Catherine,' rather than 'It was Mary who (*or* that) bought the new car' as in SE. 'It's me was frightened of her'; 'It's Jack Hanlon painted *The Masher*'; etc. (On the use of the copula in Irish and its rendering in HE see van Hamel, 275–8; on clefting and topicalisation in HE see Filppula, 1988, 87–265.) The omission of the relative pronoun in so-called 'non-introduced subordinate clauses' was a common feature of both Old and Middle English as well as Early Modern English (see Mustanoja, 203–6). Joyce, *Ulysses*, 320.16–17: "One of the bottlenosed fraternity it was went by the name of James Wought"; *Finnegans Wake*, 381.26–7: "he finalised by lowering his woolly throat with the wonderful midnight thirst was on him"; McDonagh, *The Cripple of Inishmaan*, scene ix, 68: "*Doctor*: Your daddy was an oul drunken tough, would rarely take a break from his fighting."

thaulach, *see* TRÁLACH.

the /d̪ə/ *definite article*. As there is no indefinite article in Irish, the definite article in HE – following and sometimes extending the usage of the definite article 'an' in Irish – has some distinctive functions that mark it out from SE. 'She came home for the Christmas'; 'My mother has the arthritis'; 'The grandfather (i.e. my grandfather) will be expecting me for my tea.' Kickham, *Knocknagow*, 38: "the county Limerick"; McCourt, *Angela's Ashes*, 61: "'Of course,' he said, 'you're bound to have the cough when you live in Limerick because this is the capital city of the weak chest and the weak chest leads to the consumption"; Doyle, *The Van*, 221: "Better give her the both o' them"; Joyce, *Ulysses*, 320. 20–1: "skivvies and badhachs [BODACHS] from the county Meath." Yeats, 'The O'Rahilly' (*Collected Poems*, 322): "Sing of the O'Rahilly, | Do not deny his right; | Sing a 'the' before his name" (see P. W. Joyce, *English As We Speak It in Ireland*, 82–3). 'Even with the definite article . . . the Irish county-names exclude of: "the County Kildare", "the County Cork", and so on, are idiomatic in Ireland' (MB, 1988, 43).

theeveen, *see* TAOIBHÍN.

them /d̪ɛm/ *pron.* (*colloq.*), frequently used as the demonstrative pronoun instead of 'those', e.g. 'Them's the boyos did it' (those are the rogues who did it) < E dial. Wright, *English Dialect Grammar*, 279: '*Those* is seldom or never heard in genuine dialect speech. Its place is suppled by (1) *them* in all dialects of Sc. Irel. and Eng.'

thick /t̪ɪk/, in the expression 'thick alive', to indicate great numbers of something. 'It's thick alive' (it's full of people) (PMD, Mayo); cf. 'black with' (Ir. *dubh le*), indicating huge numbers (PMD, Mayo).

Third Order /'t̪ʌrd'ɔːrd̪ər/ *n.phr.*, a branch of a religious order whose members are lay men and women; they wear a SCAPULAR under the clothing, and they have a habit (not normally worn in public). Members are affiliated to one of the mendicant orders: Franciscan (principally), Dominican, Augustinian, Carmelite, and Servite. 'Mick was buried in a brown habit; he was a member of the Third Order of Franciscans, I think' (KG, Kerry).

thivish /ˈt̪ɪvɪʃ/ *n.*, a ghost, an apparition (KM, Kerry) < Ir. *taibhse*. 'I don't know what kind of a thivish I saw, but it put the fear of God into me anyways.'

thole /θoːl/ *v.*, suffer, endure, put up with < E dial. < ME *þolien*, suffer, endure, bear. 'She tholed that terrible pain' (Louth). Joyce, *Finnegans Wake*, 541.23–4: "Under law's marshall and warshouw did I thole till lead's plumbate"; Heaney, *The Midnight Verdict*, 28: "O head of all hosted sisters, | Thomond can thole no more!"

thrawneen, *see* TRÁITHNÍN.

threena-chela, threenahayla, *see* TRÍNA CHÉILE.

through-other /ˈt̪ruːʌd̪ər/, also /ˈtruːʌd̪ər/ *n., adj., adv.*, a state of confusion; unplanned, formless, chaotic < Ir (direct translation of TRÍNA CHÉILE). 'There was a right through-other when he let the cards fall and they caught him cheating at last' (BC, Meath). 'Through-otherness', *n.*, a comfortable state of untidiness. 'Seán was telling Séamas about the through-otherness of the loft-room where he writes his poetry' (Dublin).

tiachóg /ˈʧiəxoːg/ *n.*, a little bag; a wallet; a bag for hens to lay in; a basket of pleated rushes for bringing in eggs (KM, Kerry) < Ir. 'His oul tiachóg is falling apart, but he won't let me buy him a new wallet'; 'Get the tiachóg and collect the eggs.'

tiarcas *n.*, in the phr. 'a thiarcais' /əˈhiːrkəʃ/ (*voc.*), a common expression to denote amazement (real or feigned) or delight (SOM, Kerry) < Ir (origin unknown). 'Oh, a thiarcais, will you listen to that!'

tiarna /ˈʧiərnə/ *n.*, a lord < Ir. 'A Thiarna' *int.*, Lord (*voc.*) (SOM, Kerry). 'Tiarna talún', landlord (SOM, Kerry) < Ir.

tick /tɪk/ *n.*, a feather mattress (Mayo); a home-made mattress filled with feathers or straw (SOM, Kerry) (origin obscure; cf. Ir *tocht*).

tigín /ˈʧɪgiːn/ *n.*, a small house or hut (SOM, Kerry) < Ir (dimin. of *tig*, house; *see* TEACH). 'She moved to a lovely little tigín when her husband died' (KG, Kerry).

till /tɪl/ *conj.*, can carry more than the temporal sense it has in SE, reflecting the wider meaning of the corresponding conjunction in Irish, *go*. 'Stand still, Mary, till I comb your hair' means 'Stand still, Mary, so that I may comb your hair,' as if it were an adverbial clause of purpose. Joyce, *Ulysses*, 341:

"Where is he till I [so that I may] murder him?"; Beckett, *Waiting for Godot*, 58: "*Vladimir*: Come here till I embrace you"; Roche, *A Handful of Stars*, act II, iii, 60: "*Jimmy*: Tell me who's to blame will yeh til I tear his FRIGGIN' head off"; McCourt, *Angela's Ashes*, 142: "Come here till I comb your hair."

tilly /ˈtɪli/ also **tuilleadh** *n.*, a small amount added to anything as a token gift or for good measure, especially by milkmen (LUB, Dublin) < Ir *tuilleadh*, extra. 'Han "Bán" always gave a tuille with a pint of milk' (SOC, Cork); 'A sup and a tilly' (EOC, Tipperary). *See* HANDSEL.

timpeall /ˈʧimpəl/ *n.*, a circuitous way, a roundabout way (SOM, Kerry) < Ir.

tinckler, *see* TINKER.

tinker /ˈtɪŋkər/ *n.*, a member of the travelling community – a mildly pejorative term < ME *tynekere*, a mender of pots and kettles. Yeats, *The Unicorn from the Stars*, act II (Collected Plays, 356): "*Martin*: . . . We will get no help from the settled men – we will call to the lawbreakers, the tinkers, the sievemakers, the sheepstealers"; Joyce, *Finnegans Wake*, 405.6–7: "but I, poor ass, am but as their fourpart tinckler's dunkey"; McCourt, *Angela's Ashes*, 162: "that bunch of tinkers and KNACKERS and BEGRUDGERS that hang around the pubs."

tint /tɪnt/ also **tent** *n.*, taste; a small quantity < E dial. (origin obscure). 'I didn't get a tint since morning' (LUB, Dublin, 185); Hogan adds: a Scottish word; app. from Latin *tentare* = to try.' 'I'll just have a wee tint, thanks very much, because I have to drive home afterwards' (Dublin).

tinteán /ˈʧɪnt̪ɔːn/ *n.*, fireplace, hearth < Ir. 'Níl aon tinteán mar do thinteán féin' (proverb), There's no place like home (lit. There's no fireside like your own fireside).

tionól /tɪˈnoːl/ *n.*, a gathering; a crowd; 'a group convening outside the church gate to discuss affairs of state' (SOM, Kerry).

tirim /ʧrɪm/ *adj.*, dry (SOM, Kerry) < Ir.

Tír na nÓg /ˈʧiːrnəˈnoːg/ *n.phr.*, 'land of youth', a legendary land of eternal youth < Ir. 'You must have been spending a lot of time in Tír na nÓg: you haven't aged a bit!' (Kerry). Joyce, *Finnegans Wake*, 91. 24–6: "he skuld never ask to see sight or light of this world or the other world or any either world, of Tyre-nan-Og."

'tis /tɪz/ a contraction of 'it is,' commonly used in HE as the equivalent of the copula construction in Irish (see Harris, 1993, 175–6). ''Tis Maura goes line-dancing, not Jennette'; Griffin, *The Collegians*, 71: "I thought, at first, 'tis to be shaved he was coming"; Joyce, *Finnegans Wake*, 380.30: "'tis good cause we have to remember it."

to /tə/ *prep.*, often omitted where it would appear in SE, e.g. 'I wasn't allowed play'; 'They weren't allowed walk across his land.' The infinitive is sometimes used in place of a clause in HE: 'I'd rather him not to come to the party' (I'd prefer that he didn't come to the party). Yeats, *The Unicorn from the Stars*, act III (*Collected Plays*, 367–8: "*Biddy*: It's a pity you not to have left him where he was lying . . . It's on ourselves the vengeance of the red soldiers will fall, they to find us sitting here the same as hares in a tuft." *See* FOR TO.

tobar /'tʌbər/ *n.*, spring well; 'Holy Well, going to the Tobar at 'the City' (i.e. Shrone, southwest of Rathmore) (SOM, Kerry).

tober /'t̪ʌbər/ *n.*, an impermanent site used for a fair < Shelta *tobar*, road < Ir *bóthar* (by reversal). 'There's a nice tober for the Fair of Muff near Kingscourt' (Cavan).

tóchar /'t̪oːxər/ *n.*, a bog road; a raised road through a bog; a causeway, an improvised crossing over a damp patch in a bog (SOM, Kerry) < Ir.

tochas /'t̪ʌxəs/ *n.*, an itch; the mange < Ir. 'The BLACKGUARD has it coming to him, but he'll get the tochas yet and have no nail to itch it' (SOM, Kerry).

tocht[1] /t̪ʌxt̪/ *n.*, a fit of crying; the appearance after crying; a catch in the throat, an emotional lump in the throat < Ir. 'He was speechless with a tocht' (SOM, Kerry).

tocht[2], *see* TICK.

toice /'t̪ʌkə/ *n.*, a cheeky little girl; a hussy < Ir. 'Toicín' (dim.), also 'troicín' (Moylan, Kilkenny, 278–9). 'She's a right little toice, that one. Did you hear the language out of her? I know what she'd want!' (KG, Kerry).

tóin /t̪oːn/ *n.*, rump, bottom < Ir. 'I'll redden your tóin if I see you doing that again' (Galway).

tóin creiche /t̪oːn'krɛhə/ *n.* 1. Plunder, prey; ruin, loss < Ir (lit. the bottom of loss). 2. A deep swamp. 'Mind the cattle don't get into the tóin creiche!'

tóir /t̪oːr/ *n.*, pursuit; crowd, gang; row, trouble < Ir. 'He put the tóir on me' (he put me astray, he got me into trouble), Sligo.

toirtín /'t̪ʌrʧiːn/ *n.*, a small bannock of bread; a thick pancake (KM, Kerry) < Ir. 'That's a nice smell coming from the kitchen – is it a toirtín you're baking?

tollaire /'t̪ʌlərə/ *n., adj.*, headstrong, stubborn (person); stocky (person) (KM, Kerry) < Ir *tollaire* (variant of *stollaire*). 'She's a right tollaire; there's no doubt about it, she'd argue black was white.'

tomhaisín /ˈt̪oːʃiːn/ also **tosheen** (MC, Kildare) *n.*, a small measure or quantity; a cone made of twisted paper to hold sweets etc. (SOM, Kerry) < Ir. 'When I lived in Limerick as a child we would go to the shop and buy a tosheen of brown sugar, which we spread on bread – delicious to us then' (MC, Kildare).

tónóg /ˈt̪oːnoːg/ *n.*, a bottom; a wooden cover for a pot < Ir (dimin. of TÓIN). 'Tónóg pardóige', the bottom of a PARDÓG.

took weak /tʌkˈweːk/ *v.phr.* (*colloq.*), became weak < E. 'I took weak when I finished the painting' (TF, Cavan).

topney /ˈtɑpniː/ *n.*, a knot of feathers on a hen's head (a hen having one is called a topney hen) (LC, Dublin) (form and origin obscure; not in *EDD* or *OED*; Hogan tentatively suggests 'top-knot').

topper /ˈtɑpər/ *n.* (*colloq.*), a fine person < *top* + *-er*. 'You're a real topper' (TF, Cavan).

toppin /ˈtɑpɪn/ also **topping, tapping** *n.*, a tuft of feathers, especially on a hen < E dial. Traynor, Donegal, s.v. 'toppin(g)' includes 'topping-hen' and 'the top of the head.'

toradh /ˈt̪ʌrə/ *n.*, heed, regard, esteem < Ir. 'There was always a great toradh for him in the community – God bless him, may he rest in peace' (KG, Kerry).

tormas /ˈt̪ʌrəməs/ *n.*, carping at food; grumbling; being bad-tempered; sulking < Ir. 'He has a fierce tormas – oh, he has the sulks all right' (SOM, Kerry).

tortóg /t̪ʌrˈt̪oːg/ also **turtóg** *n.*, a tuft, a clump; a raised knot of earth; a hummock (KM, Kerry). 'I jumped from tortóg to tortóg to get across the bog'; 'Mind! You could sprain your ankle very easy running across them tortógs.'

tosac /ˈt̪ʌsəc/ *n.* (The etymology and provenance of this word are obscure.) 1. A drink, especially of spirits. 'They're gone for a few tosacs' (SOM, Kerry). 2. A pull or a puff on a pipe or cigarette. 'He gives the grandson a few tosacs on the pipe every time – you'd think he'd have more sense!' (SOM, Kerry).

tosheen, *see* TOMHAISÍN.

tóstalach /ˈt̪oːst̪ələx/ *adj.*, conceited; arrogant (KM, Kerry) < Ir. 'She was always tóstalach, despite her circumstances.'

tradesman /ˈtreːdzmæn/ *n.*, a skilled worker; a craftsman. Hayden and Hartog, 779: 'an artisan belonging to a trades union, which in many parts of Ireland, notably Cork, is a closed hereditary caste – the son of a tradesman having the right to be apprenticed to his father's trade and to none other.' 'That carpenter's a real tradesman: look at the finish on that door!' (SOC, Kerry).

tráithnín /'t̪rɔːniːn/ also **thrawneen, thraneen, traneen** etc. *n.*, a blade of grass, a straw, a rush, a sop of hay, etc.; blades of grass that grow to a greater height than surrounding grass; grass tossed in the air to get the direction of the wind; a rush used as a pipe-cleaner (SOM, Kerry); something of little or no value; fig. long spindly legs; 'thrawneens' *n.pl.*, long stems of dog's-tail grass < Ir. 'Get me a thrauneen to ready my pipe' (LUB, Dublin); 'I don't give a tráithnín for his opinion' (KG, Kerry); 'A little of anything is not worth a tráithnín, but a little sense is worth a lot' (Mayo). Sheehan, *Glenanaar*, 181: "I don't care a *thraneen* for all that the gossips can say agin her."

trálach /'t̪rɔːləx/ also **tálach** /'t̪ɔːləx/, **thaulach** (LUB, Dublin) *n.*, stiffness of the wrist; soreness of the wrist from overwork (LUB, Dublin) < Ir. *tálach, trálach*. 'He was complaining about being a BITEEN trálach after spending a day cutting turf' (Mayo).

tram /træm/ *n.*, hay made into large cocks by forking it to a man standing on the cock (Omurethi, Kildare) (origin obscure). *See* TRAMP.

tramp /tramp/ *n., v.*, a large rick of hay compressed by tramping; to stamp on < E dial. < ME *trampin, v.*, to stamp heavily on). 'They used to call them tramps, but it's all done away with now' (MG, Cavan). Gregory, *Spreading the News* (*FDA*, 2, 618): "*Jack Smith*: It isn't to the fair I came myself, but up to the Five Acre Meadow I'm going, where I have a contract for the hay. We'll get a share of it into tramps today." *See* TRAM.

tranglam /'træŋləm/ *n.*, a row, confusion (MK, Galway) < Ir. 'I'm never playing cards with that crowd again – such a tranglam over the scores! I got fed up in the end.'

trasnán /'t̪ræsnɔːn/ *n.*, a beam to support a roof from wall to wall (MK, Galway) < Ir.

tráthnóna, *see* EVENING.

traveller /t̪rævələr/ *n.*, a member of the travelling (nomadic) community, with semi-fixed or no fixed abode; the community formerly had a distinctive dialect of English known variously as CANT, Gammon, and SHELTA (see Binchy, 'Travellers' language'; Ó Baoill, 'Travellers' cant'). *See* KNACKER; TINKER.

trick /t̪rik/ *v.*, to play about mischievously < OF *trique*. 'Stop that tricking!' (JL, Carlow).

triduum /'t̪rɪʤuəm/ *n.*, a series of special prayers or private devotions, or a RETREAT, over a period of three days, usually in preparation for a feast-day, e.g. the three concluding days of Holy Week (before Easter) < L *triduum*, a space of three days.

'There'll be a triduum before the feast of St Joseph: the nineteenth of March is a Friday this year' (JMF, Cavan).

trig /trɪg/ 1. *n.*, the line marking the start of a race or long jump < E dial. 2. *adj.*, reliable, neat < E dial.

trína chéile /t̪riːnəˈkeːlə/ also **threena-chela, threenahayla** *adj.phr.*, mixed up, in disorder; upset, worried < Ir *trína chéile*, disordered (lit. through each other). 'Your sheep and mine are all threenahayla' (LUB, Dublin); 'Everything in the house is threenahayla' (LUB, Dublin); 'She was trína chéile with worry, the poor thing' (JF, Cavan). Banim, *The Boyne Water*, 221: "While the two throops is at their work, *threena-chela*, look how he lays round him." 'Trína chéile cake' (i.e. of mixed bread), a loaf of bread made of white flour and maize-meal baked in a BASTABLE oven (ENM, Kerry). *See* THROUGH-OTHER.

Trinity /ˈtrɪnəti/ *n.*, for Trinity College, Dublin, founded in 1592 as 'Queen Elizabeth's College of the Holy and Undivided Trinity near Dublin,' sole college of the University of Dublin. Leonard, *Out After Dark*, 57: "I could hardly afford to take a tram into Dublin, never mind the cost of transporting myself into Trinity." *See* NATIONAL.

trinket /ˈtrɪŋkət/ *n.*, a watercourse; an artificial channel for water < E dial. (*EDD* cites Ireland only – 'a small channel or artificial watercourse; an open sewer; a little stream or watercourse by the roadside' – and exemplifies with "you'll get it lying in the trinket," *Ballymena Observer*, 1892). PWJ gives a reference to east Ulster; MT, Donegal, has a citation for Ulster and Dublin.

triopall /ˈt̪rɪpəl/ *n.*, a cluster; a small bunch of turf or grass (MK, Galway) < Ir. 'Bring in a triopall; I need it to light the fire.'

triopallach /t̪rɪpələx/ *n.*, gay; nimble; tidy (KM, Kerry) < Ir.

triuch /t̪rʌx/ *n.*, whooping-cough (ML, Mayo) < Ir. 'The child got the triuch last week; the poor thing is still weak after it.'

trom crithe /trʌmˈkrɪhə/ 'land that shakes under your feet as you walk on it; the water is under the sod, but can't penetrate the mud' (KM, Kerry) < Ir. (the lexical form of 'crithe' is unclear).

tromluí /ˈt̪rʌmliː/ *n.*, a nightmare (ENM, Kerry) < Ir. 'I had an awful tromluí last night – I woke up in the middle of it.'

troth /t̪roːt̪/ also **throth** *int.* indeed, truly < E dial. < ME *trouthte, trowthe*. 'Did he ever get married?' – 'Troth and he did' (TF, Cavan). Stoker, *The Snake's Pass*, 14: "Throth, it's a bit iv a gap in the rocks *beyant* that they call Shleenanaher";

Shaw, *John Bull's Other Island*, act I (*FDA*, 2, 437): "*Keegan*: . . . I'm not a saint. *Patsy*: Oh in throth yar, sir"; Healy, *Nineteen Acres*, 133: 'A wonder you wouldn't go up on the train now that you have free travel.' 'Throt'n I won't."

trousers /'t̪rauzərz/ *n.pl.*, though considered a plural in SE, is often regarded as singular by HE speakers, possibly because the Irish word for trousers, 'bríste', is a singular noun (and has a plural form also: bristí). (ModE 'trousers' is from Ir *triús*, also a singular noun.) 'I went down the town to buy a trousers.' Joyce, 'Ivy Day in the Committee Room' (*Dubliners*, 138): "And the men used to go in on Sunday morning before the houses were open to buy a waistcoat or a trousers – MOYA!"

true /t̪ruː/ *adj.*, in the expression 'true for you,' you're right < *Ir is fíor duit* (lit. it is true for you). 'True for you, that's the way it is in politics.' Banim, *The Boyne Water*, 508: "'Supporting Sheldon's horse?' 'Thrue for you, I'm thinking"; Griffin, *The Collegians*, 52: "'True for you,' says Mr. Chute"; 339: "'It's thrue for me!' he repeated gruffly"; Stoker, *The Snake's Pass*, 18: "Thrue for ye, ACUSHLA"; Joyce, *Ulysses*, 316.25–7: "'The traitor's son. We know what put English gold in his pocket.' 'True for you,' says Joe."

trup /t̪rʌp/ *n.*, noise (MK, Galway) < Ir. 'There was a trup outside the door.'

truslóg /t̪rʌ'sloːg/ *n.*, a long, heavy step (KM, Kerry) < Ir. 'It must be Paddy: I'd know that truslóg anywhere.'

tuaiplis /'tuːpləʃ/ also **túplais** *n.*, a mistake; a bad outcome < Ir. 'You made a bad túplais!' (SOM, Kerry).

tuathalach /'t̪uəhələx/ *adj.*, left-handed; tactless, rude; blundering; awkward (SOM, Kerry) < Ir. 'She's very tuathalach, just like her mother!' (KG, Kerry).

tuathalán /'t̪uəhəlɔːn/ *n.*, a good-for-nothing (MK, Galway) < Ir. 'What a tuathalán she is! No-one will marry her.'

tubaiste /'t̪ʌbəʃtə/ *n.*, a calamity, a disaster < Ir. 'The poor fella met one tubaiste after another' (SOM, Kerry).

tufaire /'tʌfərə/ *n.*, an ill-tempered, uncouth person (SOM, Kerry) < Ir.

tug, *see* BOOLTHAUN.

tuigeann tú? /'t̪ɪgənt̪uː/ *phr.*, do you understand? do you TWIG? < Ir. 'But that's in Poland, dtuigeann tú?' (POC, Cavan) (from a popular First World War ballad). Leonard, *Out After Dark*, 166: "He asked: 'Tuigin tu Gaelig?' ('Do you understand Irish?') My friend proudly answered: *'Tuigim.'* ('I understand'). Whereupon Behan unleashed the deafening roar of '*Tuigim* me BOLLIX!' and went on his way."

tuirne /ˈt̪ɪrnə/ *n.*, a spinning-wheel < Ir. 'The tuirne mór was the big spinning wheel, or wool-spinner. It consisted of a large wheel on a simple platform with the spindle works positioned at one end, directly opposite the wheel' (Sharkey, 66). 'Tuirnín', a (basic) spinning-wheel (SOM, Kerry) < Ir (dimin. of *tuirne*).

tuirse /ˈt̪ɪrʃə/ *n.*, tiredness < Ir. 'Tuirseach', *adj.*, tired, weary, worn out (SOM, Kerry).

tuisle /ˈt̪ɪʃlə/ *n.*, a stumble, a trip (SOM, Kerry) < Ir.

tuitimeas /ˈt̪ɪʧəməs/ *n.*, epilepsy < Ir. 'He fell off a gate when he was young, and he's had a touch of tuitimeas ever since' (TF, Cavan).

tulach /ˈt̪ʌləx/ *n.*, a mound; a low hill (KM, Kerry) < Ir. 'The sheep rolled off the tulach onto her back and she smothered.'

tulcais /ˈt̪ʌlkəʃ/ *adj.*, fat < Ir. 'That's a very tulcais child you have there; what have you been feeding him?' (BC, Meath).

tumbling-jack /ˈtʌmbləndʒæk/ *n.*, a horse-drawn machine formerly used in meadows at hay-making (SMC, Limerick).

tundish /ˈtʌndɪʃ/ *n.*, a funnel; a kind of funnel originally used in brewing < ME *tundys* < *tun*, a vessel + *dish*. Joyce, *Portrait of the Artist as a Young Man*, 165: "'What is a tundish?' – 'That. The . . . the funnel' – 'Is that called a tundish in Ireland?' asked the dean. 'I never heard the word in my life.' – 'It is called a tundish in Lower Drumcondra,' said Stephen laughing, 'where they speak the best English"; 217: "*13 April*: That tundish has been on my mind for a long time. I looked it up and find it is English"; Heaney, *Station Island*, 93: "the Feast of the Holy Tundish."

túplais, *see* TUAIPLIS.

turas /ˈt̪rʌs/ *n.*, a visit; a pilgrimage to a holy place; going around and stopping to pray at designated points in a sacred place (KG, Kerry) < Ir. 'I did the turas at that shrine when I was a child, but I wouldn't be able for it now.'

turn /tʌrn/ *v.* (*colloq.*), to convert to another faith. 'That family must have turned' (Kerry).

turtóg /t̪ʌrˈt̪oːg/ also **tortóg** *n.*, a tuft, a clump; a raised knot of earth; a hummock; turtógs *n.pl.*, knobs of ground (KM, Kerry). 'I jumped from turtóg to turtóg to get across the bog'; 'Mind! You could sprain your ankle very easy running across them turtógs.'

tuth /t̪ʌh/ *n.*, a bad odour, a stench; filth (MK, Galway) < Ir. 'There's a tuth coming off that ditch: there must be a dead animal there, a badger or something.'

Twenty-Six Counties /twəntiː sɪksˈkauntiːz/ *n.*, term given to the part of Ireland that constitutes the Republic of Ireland, since the Government of Ireland Act (1920), i.e. twenty-six of the thirty-two counties of which the whole country is composed < OE *twentig*, OE *siex*, AN *counté*. 'They always come over and take their holidays in the Twenty-Six Counties, but maybe they'll venture to the North this year' (JB, Kildare).

twig /twɪg/ *v.*, to comprehend, understand (origin uncertain but possibly < Ir *tuig*, understand). 'I never twigged what was happening till it was too late'; 'Do you twig what I'm saying, or do I have to spell it out?' Joyce, 'Ivy Day in the Committee Room' (*Dubliners*, 139): "*They won't suspect you.* Do you twig?"; Roche, *Poor Beast in the Rain*, act I, i, 76: "*Joe*: . . . And do you want to know how she twigged it?"

U

uachtar /'uəxt̪ər/ *n.*, cream (KM, Kerry) < Ir. 'I'll take a touch of uachtar in the coffee, please.'

uafásach /uə'fɔːsəx/ *adj.*, terrible; also used as an intensive: very, enormous, etc. (KM, Kerry) < Ir. 'You never heard such uafásach carry-on!'

uaigh /uːɪɣ/ *n.*, the grave < Ir. 'Is iomaí lá ag an uaigh orainn' (proverb), It's many a day we'll be in the grave.

uaigneach /'uəgnəx/ *adj.*, lonely, sad (ENM, Kerry) < Ir. 'It does be uaigneach round here in the winter, so it does.'

uaigneas /'uəgnəs/ *n.*, loneliness, sadness (especially at the departure or death of a friend) (KM, Kerry) < Ir. 'Such uaigneas came on me when Kathleen died so sudden!'

uaill /uəl/ *n.*, howling; a wail; a sharp shout (BC, Meath) < Ir. 'The dogs were uailling away, and I didn't know what was at them.'

ualach /'uələx/ *n.*, a load < Ir. 'He went with an ualach of turf to Mrs Kelly.'

uallóg /'uəloːg/ *adj.*, a light-headed, giddy girl < Ir. 'She's a bit of an uallóg at the minute, but she'll settle down as she grows older – she'd want to!'

uamhan Dé /uəvən'ʤeː/ *n.phr.*, the fear of God < Ir. 'That sister always used put the uamhan Dé into me.'

uan /uən/ *n.*, a lamb < Ir. 'Luigh leis an uan agus éirigh leis an éan' (proverb), Early to bed, early to rise (lit. Lie down with the lamb and rise with the bird) < Ir. 'Uan Dé' /uən'ʤeː/, the Lamb of God < Ir.

uililiú /'ɪləluː/, /'ʌləluː/ *int.*, a cry of sorrow (origin uncertain; cf. E *ululation*, *n.*, < L *ululare* (imitative)). 'She let out an uililiú that would wake a dead man.'

uilleann pipes /'ɪlənpaips/ *n.phr.*, bagpipes played by squeezing a bellows under the elbow < Ir *píb uilleann* (lit. elbow pipe). 'There's not too many people can play the uilleann pipes any more.'

úirín /'uːriːn/ *n.*, a 'cabby' or 'cubby' house; a house built by children, often used for the storing of their toys and treasures < Ir. 'Go out and play in the úirín, as it's such a fine day.'

uisce faoi thalamh /ˈɪʃkəfwiː ˈhɑləv/ *n.phr.*, intrigue, conspiracy < Ir (lit. water under the ground). 'There's some uisce faoi thalamh going on – they're up to no good, for sure.'

ulchabhán /ˈʌləxəvɔːn/ *n.*, an owl < Ir. 'She drew an ulchabhán in her copy-book.'

ullagone, *see* OLAGÓN.

ullamh /ˈʌləv/ *adj.*, ready, prepared, on alert < Ir. 'I'm as ullamh as I'm ever like to be!'

umar /ˈʌmər/ *n.*, a trough; a vat < Ir. 'Umar na haimléise', *n.phr.*, a woeful situation, dire straits < Ir (also *corrach na haimléise*; cf. E 'slough of despond'). 'The poor man is in umar na haimléise.'

unbeknownst /ʌnbəˈnoːnst/ *adj., adv.*, unknown; lying outside one's knowledge or acquaintance (the *OED* cites a first occurrence from 1854; the reason for the addition of 'st' to 'unbeknown' is unclear). 'Av [if] he was at the wake, it was unbeknownst to me' (Omurethi, Kildare); 'Unbeknownst to me, she was going out with him all along' (BC, Meath). Gregory, *Spreading the News* (*FDA*, 2, 617): "*Bartley*: . . . and I myself that will be dying unbeknownst some night, and no one a-near me."

unionist /ˈjuːnjənɪst/ *n.*, one who wishes to retain the union of Ireland and Britain; an opponent of independence for Ireland. 'I think we've got quite a lot of unionists down here in these parts: look how many go up North on the Twelfth [of July]' (JMF, Cavan).

útamáil /ˈuːt̪əmɔːl/ *n.*, fumbling; aimless activity; 'much ado about nothing'; 'MESSING' (KM, Kerry) < Ir. 'Stop your útamáiling and do an honest day's work.'

útamálaí /uːt̪əˈmɔːliː/ *n.*, a fumbler, a clumsy person; a MESSER < Ir. 'You can't thread a needle, you útamálaí!' (KM, Kerry); 'Here, give it me, you útamálaí; I can't be waiting all day for you to finish it' (Mayo).

V

VDP /ˈviːdəˈpiː/ *(colloq.)* for Society of ST VINCENT DE PAUL.

veins /veːnz/ *n.*, in the phr. 'the veins of nicety', the height of style. 'He is a dandy, always dressed up to the veins of nicety' (LUB, Dublin, 185). Hogan notes: 'No doubt based on some sense of Ir. *cuisle* [vein]' (*see* ACUSHLA; MACUSHLA).

venters /ˈvɛntərz/ *n.pl.*, pieces of wood blown in on the beach (origin obscure).

vex /vɛks/ *v.*, to annoy, harass < (O)F *vexer*. 'Don't vex me while I'm counting!' Carleton, 'Shan Fadh's Wedding' (*Six Irish Tales*, 177): "I was vexed not to take all I could out of him."

vocation /voˈkeːʃən/ *n.*, a call given by God to become a priest or nun; Holy Orders are conferred on a man by a bishop in the Rite of Ordination (which was much simplified in the Roman Catholic faith in 1968); in the Anglican faith the Sacrament of Orders is conferred by a bishop; a nun is a member of a religious order or congregation of women who take vows of poverty, chastity, and obedience; in earlier times a nun who took solemn vows ('monialis') was called 'mother' or some other title, to distinguish her from those women who took only simple vows ('sorores') who were normally called 'sister' < L *vocare*, *v.*, to call. 'There was a priest used to come round to our school every year looking for vocations to his order – and several joined up later, and they're still all priests, all but one' (*see* SPOILED PRIEST); 'She had a vocation but had to leave the convent when her mother took sick – she was an only child, and there was no-one else to look after her. She found it very hard to leave the convent – she'd been very happy there' (CS, Cork). Bolger, *Emily's Shoes*, 217: "'He claims I have a vocation. Me?' She laughed incredulously."

voteen /ˈvʌʧiːn/ also **votcheen, vokeen** *n. (pejor.)*, zealously pious person; 'vokeens, that is, bad Christians' (Omurethi, Kildare) < Ir. *móidín* (cf. CRAWTHUMPER). 'I suppose you'd call him a bit of a voteen – what do you think of him?'

W

wain /weːn/ also **wean** *n.*, child < WEE, small + *ane*, one (MT, Donegal; RMM, Antrim).

wake /weːk/ *n., v.,* a vigil beside a dead body, often accompanied by drinking; to watch over a dead body < ME *waken, v.*, < OE *wacan, n., wacian, v.*, to awake, keep watch. 'She said she was going to have a wake for him when he died, and she did.' 'Finnegan's Wake' (song): "Wasn't it the truth I told you, | Lots of fun at Finnegan's Wake | . . . So they carried him home his corpse to wake"; Deane, *Reading in the Dark*, 220: "Joe was invited to nothing and he came to everything – weddings, wakes, birthday parties, anniversaries, dances." 'American wake', a meeting of friends with one of their number who was about to emigrate to America and, in the days of uncertain travel, might never be able to return. 'Times have changed from when there would be an American wake: people are flying over for the weekend now' (KM, Kerry). Healy, *Nineteen Acres*, 94: "I spent the last day on Long Island . . . I suppose we had an Irish wake that night"; McCourt, *Angela's Ashes*, 418: "Mam says we'll have a bit of a party the night before I go. They used to have parties in the old days when anyone would go to America, which was so far away the parties were called American wakes because the family never expected to see the departing one again in this life." *See* OFFICE MEN.

wall-wagger /'wɔːlwægər/ *n.* (*colloq.*), 'a clock without case for its weights and pendulum, hung high on the wall' (LUB, Dublin, 185).

wan /wɑn/, representing a HE pronunciation of 'one'. Dunton, *Report of a Sermon*, 133: "Ecclesiasticus de won-and-fortiet shapter"; Kickham, *Knocknagow*, 78: "Let me at him, an', be the livin', I'll put his two eyes into wan!"; Stoker, *The Snake's Pass*, 24: "bought by wan side or the other." *See* WANST.

wan and wan, *see* ONE AND ONE.

wanst /wɑnst/, representing a HE pronunciation of 'once'. Stoker, *The Snake's Pass*, 43: "Me grandfather wanst tould me . . ."

wax /wæks/ *v.*, to climb, shin up a pipe or pole' (SB, Cork) (origin obscure).

way /weː/ in *adv. phr.* 'the way', often used in place of the conjunction 'so that', introducing a subordinate adverbial clause (in imitation of Ir 'sa chaoi go' or 'sa dóigh go', lit. the way that). 'I left home early the way I'd miss the traffic'; 'He used always jump in behind the ditch the way no-one would see him if there was anyone coming along the road.' Synge, *The Playboy of the Western World*, act III (*FDA*, 2, 642): "*Christy*: . . . for I'm mounted on the spring-tide of the stars of luck, the way it'll be good for any to have me in the house"; Stephens, *The Crock of Gold*, 120: "'I wish,' said the sergeant bitterly, 'that all them beasts were stuffed down your throttle the way you'd have to hold your prate.'"

wean, *see* WAIN.

wear, wearing /weːr/, /ˈweːrən/ *n.* (*colloq.*), extended kiss (KD, Dublin); sexual intercourse (TG, Dublin) < OE *werian, v.*, to weary. 'Did you get your wear off her?' (KD, Dublin).

wee /wiː/ *adj.*, small; young (TF, Cavan) < E dial. (cf. OE *wegan, v.*, to weigh; *ODEE*: 'the use appears to have originated in such a phr. as *a little wee thing*, "a small amount of a thing," similar to *a bit thing*, "a bit of a thing," hence "a little thing"). 'Sure a wee drop will do him no harm!'

weeny /ˈwiːni/ *adj.* (*colloq.*), tiny, minute < E dial. < WEE + *-ny*. 'Just a weeny drop of whiskey in that, if you don't mind' (TJ, Sligo).

weeshy /ˈwiːʃi/ also **weeshie** *adj.*, very small < E dial. (cited as restricted to Ireland in *EDD*; cf. WEENY). Sheehan, *Glenanaar*, 86: "Any wan [anyone] would be glad to take from ye that purty, weeshy little crachure in yer arms"; O'Casey, *The Shadow of a Gunman*, act I, 89–90: "*Minnie*: . . . a weeshy, DAWNY bit of a man that was never sober."

well /wɛl/ *adv.* (*colloq.*), in the phr. 'well (to) wear,' a wish expressed to someone who is displaying something newly purchased (usually a new piece of clothing): may you have the health to wear your new clothes. 'Look at my new dress, Mary.' – 'Oh, Katty, it's lovely. Well to wear!' Kickham, *Knocknagow*, 137: "'Well wear!' ''Tis a grand fit,' exclaimed Honor, moving the candle all round Mat to the imminent danger of the new coat."

welshtbreton, *see* WEST BRITTON.

west /wɛst/ *adj*. In Irish 'siar' means both 'west' and 'BACK', which can give rise to some odd-sounding expressions. 'Let's move west before the tide comes in.'

West Briton /wɛst'brɪtən/ also **West Brit** *n. (pejor.)*, an Irish person with extreme pro-British attitudes and prejudices (coined by analogy with *North Briton*, a Scot). 'That lot does be full of West Britons; they make me very uneasy, so they do.' Joyce, *Finnegans Wake*, 491.31–3: "He was resting between horrockses' sheets, wailing for white warfare, prooboor welshtbreton." *See* JACKEEN; SHONEEN.

wet (tea) /wɛt/ *v.*, to make tea (i.e. to pour boiling water into the teapot). 'Wet the TAY, will you?' (JL, Mayo). Keane, *The Bodhrán Makers*, 283: "Wet us a sup of tea."

whateen, **whauteen**, *see.*

wheen /ʍiːn/ *n.*, a number; a few, a good few (RMM, Antrim) < E dial. < OE *hwene*. Stoker, *The Snake's Pass*, 17: "MUSHA! but there's a wheen o' both laygends and shtories"; Murphy, 'Return of the Boy' (*FDA*, 3, 961): "But the little man in the seat before us half-turned and said over his shoulder knowingly that it was a 'wheen o' years since there was a forge there.'"

when /ʍɛn/ *conj.*, sometimes replaced by the phrase 'the time' (in imitation of Ir 'nuair', when < *an uair*, the time). 'That night, the time he was getting ready to leave, there was a knock at the door with the bad news' (BC, Meath).

whether /'ʍɛd̪ər/ *interrogative.* The use of 'whether' to introduce indirect questions (e.g. 'She asked whether I was all right') is much rarer in HE than in SE, because HE-speakers (following the way that indirect questions in Irish simply repeat the inverted order of the original direct question) retain the inversion: the question 'Are you all right?' is therefore reported as 'She asked was I all right.' (Similarly, the interrogative 'if' is also much rarer in HE, because of the retained inversion, a common feature with all indirect questions in HE.) 'They don't know where is he'; 'Do you think will it work this time?' Joyce, 'Eveline' (*Dubliners*, 39): "In the end he would give her the money and ask her had she any intention of buying Sunday's dinner"; Joyce, 'A Mother' (*Dubliners*, 161): "Mr Holohan limped into the dressing-room at that moment and the two young ladies asked him who was the unknown woman"; Doyle, *The Van*, 283: "'You'll ask me can yeh wipe your arse next,' said Bimbo once." See Harris, 1993, 167–8.

whileen /'ʍailiːn/ *n.*, a short period < E *while* + dimin. suffix -EEN. 'I'll see you in a whileen; I have to go and see a man about a dog [I have some business to do].'

whin /ʍɪn/ *n.*, furze, gorse (origin uncertain; probably Scandinavian). 'Granny sent us out to get whin bushes to light the fire, but she didn't want the neighbours to see us.' Stoker, *The Snake's Pass*, 30: "Me father hid behind a whin bush, an' lay as close as a hare in his forrum [form]"; Montague, 'Home Again, 3' (*Collected Poems*, 10): "Between small, whin-tough hills, | the first slated house in the district."

whinge /ʍɪnʤ/ *v.*, to cry in a peevish manner, to whine < E dial. < ME *hwinsianne, v.*, to whine. Roche, *A Handful of Stars*, act I, i, 4: "*Jimmy*: Look stop whingein' and fire." 'Whinger' /ˈʍɪnʤər/ *n.* 'Stay quiet, you whinger – I'm tired listening to you' (BC, Meath).

whipster /ˈʍɪpst̪ər/ *n.*, a playful girl < E dial. < *whip, v.*, + *-ster* (*ODEE* s.v. 'whipper-snapper': 'prob. based on whipster [16th century] "cracker of whips", lively, violent or mischievous person, also insignificant fellow'; cf. *whipstock* (< *whipping-stock*), a person who is frequently whipped). 'You're a little whipster, aren't you?' Kavanagh, *Tarry Flynn*, 34: "The divil thank ye and thump ye, Bridie, ye whipster, ye."

whiskey /ˈʍɪski/ *n.* < Ir *uisce*, water + *beatha*, life; 'usquebaugh', whiskey (Poole, Forth and Bargy). 'What butter or whiskey'll not cure there's no cure for' (saying).

whist, whisht /ʍɪʃt/ *v. (imp.)*, stop; listen; please be quiet (may be derived from an obsolete E verb *whister*, to whisper, but more likely to be an aspirated form of the sound represented by the spelling 'st!', enjoining silence or attention, with the 'sh' spelling perhaps indicating the HE pronunciation of 's' as /ʃ/; cf. also Ir *éist*, please be silent (lit. listen) (PMD, Mayo)). 'Hold your whist' *phr.*, be silent. 'Haul [hold] your whisht' (RMM, Antrim). Stephens, *The Crock of Gold*, 126: "'Hold your whist,' said Shawn fiercely to them."

Whiteboys /ˈʍaitbɔiz/ *n.phr.*, a widespread secret society that developed in the 1760s in Co. Tipperary and north Co. Waterford to ventilate a range of local grievances, especially rents, whose members wore white shirts at night (Foster, 1988, 223–5). Yeats, *The Unicorn from the Stars*, act II (*Collected Plays*, 356): "*Biddy*: . . . Ribbons I can understand, Whiteboys, Rightboys, Threshers, and Peep o' Days, but Unicorns I never heard of before"; act III: "*Biddy*: . . . Or maybe that fleet of Whiteboys had the place ransacked before we ourselves came in."

white scourge, the /ˈʍaitˈskʌrʤ/ *n.phr.* (*colloq.*), tuberculosis.

Nolan, 69: 'Tuberculosis was fairly widespread until recent years. It was called the "White Scourge".' *See* SANATORIUM.

whitteret /ˈʍɪtərət/ also **whitrack, whutrick** (RMM, Antrim) *n.*, a weasel (BF, Dublin) < E dial. < *white rat* (it has also been suggested that it is derived from *white throat*). 'There must have been a whitteret in at the hen-house last night: all the eggs are gone' (AF, Cavan).

who, *relative pron.*, often omitted by HE speakers. Kavanagh, *Tarry Flynn*, 195–6: "That's the man will make a spoon or spoil a horn." *See* THAT.

who-began-it /huːbiˈgænɪt/ *n.* (*colloq.*), 'a warning or threat, said quickly as one word, used in Cork, Kerry, and Limerick' (MC, Kildare, ex Limerick) (origin obscure). 'If you do that again I'll give you who-began-it!'

whoor, whore, *see* HOOR.

whutrick, *see* WHITTERET.

wicked /ˈwɪkəd/ *adj.*, angry, cross < E dial. *wick* < adjectival use of OE *wicca*, wizard. 'He's getting wicked' (DOH, Limerick).

widdy /ˈwɪdi/, **widdy woman** (Omurethi, Kildare) *n.*, widow (cf. 'folly', follow). Stoker, *The Snake's Pass*, 15: "Hurry up to Widdy Kelligan's."

widow-woman /ˈwɪdəwʌmən/ *n.*, a widow (cf. Ir *baintreach mná*, a widow < *baintreach*, widow + *mná* (genitive) woman). 'She's been a widow-woman for the past fifty years' (TJ, Sligo). Griffin, *The Collegians*, 136: "'Whose farm-house,' says he, 'is that I see over there?' 'It's belongin' to a widow woman, sir,' said the boy."

will /wɪl/ *v.* HE does not make the distinction that SE makes between 'will' and 'shall' in forming the future tense, i.e. 'shall' for first person (singular and plural), 'will' for second and third person, non-emphatic ('I shall go, you will go,' etc.), with 'shall' and 'will' reversed for the emphatic future ('I will go, you shall go,' etc.) – no doubt reflecting the single form for the future tense in Irish. Griffin, *The Collegians*, 362: "Will I get the priest? Will I get the priest ITSELF?" Leonard, *Out After Dark*, 172: "The man, somehow without giving the least suggestion of loudness, wore a jacket you could play draughts on. His bearing told you that he was the kind of person who would say 'shall' instead of 'will' all the time, as we did." See Harris (1993), 158.

wirra /ˈwɪrə/ also **wurra** /ˈwʌrə/ (KM, Kerry) *int.* expressing grief < Ir *a Mhuire*, Mary [i.e. the Virgin Mary] (*voc.*). 'Wirra, Margaret – it's the hard life I have – you can't deny it'; 'Oh wurra wurra, what am I going to do now?'

wirrasthru /wɪrəs'ṯruː/ also **wirrasthroo, wurrasthroo** *int.*, alas < Ir *a Mhuire, is trua*, Mary [i.e. the Virgin Mary] (*voc.*), it's true. 'Wirrasthru, why did I ever let him go out cutting silage!' Stoker, *The Snake's Pass*, 222: "Oh no! God help us! Wirrastru! wirrastru!"

wish /wɪʃ/ *n.*, liking; desire; something wished for (from usage of Ir *mian*). 'She used have a great wish for me'; 'He always had a great wish for the girls when he was a young fella, and the next thing he joined the priesthood – I'll never understand it' (BC, Meath). Plunkett, *Farewell Companions*, 397: "I'd wish on me for a SMAHAN of punch, if you wouldn't mind?"

wisha /'wɪʃə/ *int.*, indeed; well < Ir *muise mhuise* (duplication of *muise*). 'Wisha, is that what he did?' *See* MUSHA.

with /wɪṯ/ *prep.*, appears in a number of idiomatic usages in HE (cf. the many connotations, temporal and otherwise, of the Irish preposition 'le'): 'She hasn't been home with [for] years'; 'The children went off with [by] themselves.'

without /wɪ'ḏaut/, /ə'ḏaut/ 1. *conj.*, unless < E dial. (*EDD* s.v. 'athout 3': 'the use of *without* as a conjunction was originally standard, but by the eighteenth century it had become colloquial and even vulgar'). 'You can't ride that bike athout you fix the pumpture [puncture]' (TF, Cavan). Bliss (1979), 288: 'She'll not go into the room without you go in first'; Swift, *A Dialogue in Hybernian Stile*, 165: "B. . . . Will you go see him when you come into our parts? A. Not *without* you go with me"; Griffin, *The Collegians*, 48: "'Fat!' exclaimed Lowry, in a voice of surprise, 'you may say fat. There isn't that door on hinges that he'd pass in, walkin' with a fair front, widout he turned sideways." 2. *adv.* (in this context generally /əḏ'aut/), outside. 'He's without in the yard.'

woeful /'woːfəl/ *adj.*, intensive, as in 'He's a woeful BLACKGUARD' (DOH, Limerick).

wolfworm, *see* LUACHRA.

woodquest /'wʌdkwɛst/ *n.*, the wild wood-pigeon (Omurethi, Kildare) < ME *wode*, wood + *quisht*, ring-dove, wood-pigeon.

worrit /'wʌrət/ *n., v.,* pestering; to worry, harass, tease < E dial. (*OED*: 'app. a vulgar alteration of worry *v.*). 'Will yous CHILDER stop worriting your mother! Yous have her worn out' (Meath).

wracker /'rækər/ also **racker** *n.*, 'a kind of horse-boy possessed of speed, stamina, and knowledge of a district in which he operates, attends a hunt and follows the field on foot for the purpose of assisting (for due recompense) riders who may get into difficulty by being thrown from their horses' (PA, Fingall); 'a man that follows the hunt to assist in catching a riderless horse, or in dragging one out of a *gripe*, etc.' (Omurethi, Kildare) (origin obscure; cf. *wrack*, wreckage < MDu *wrak*).

wran, *see* WREN.

wren /rɛn/ also **wran** /ræn/ *n.*, as used in traditions associated with St Stephen's Day (26 December). 'Wren boys' or 'wran boys', young men, often wearing straw masks, who travel around their locality with a dead wren (nowadays an object made to look like a dead wren), asking for money or hospitality. St Stephen is believed to have been stoned to death by the Jews (*c.* AD 35); according to legend, his pursuers could not find him until they noticed a couple of wrens flying in and out of a furze-bush in an agitated fashion; inside the bush, hiding from his pursuers, was St Stephen, and the wren is therefore indictable for his discovery and subsequent martyrdom. The rhyme associated with the custom begins: 'The wran, the wran, the king of all birds | on Stephens's [*sic*] Day was caught in the furze,' which Joyce, *Finnegans Wake*, 504. 1–2, renders: "The cran, the cran the king of all crans." Kickham, *Knocknagow*, 19–20: "They are only called 'wren boys' who carry the wren in a holly bush decorated with ribbons from house to house on St Stephen's Day; and many who hunt the wren do not join in this part of the proceedings. We may remark also that though the 'king of all birds' is said and sung to be 'caught in the furze' on St Stephen's Day, he is invariably 'caught,' and often ruthlessly slain, too, on Christmas Day . . . "; Sheehan, *Glenanaar*, 88: "The boys who had been home early from Mass went out with their sticks to hunt the wren; and *Hy Droleen* [Ir *dreoilín*, wren]! *Hy, Droleen*! echoed from copse and thicket." See Mullen, *Béaloideas*, 64–5 (1996), 131–69.

wurra, *see* WIRRA.

wurrum /ˈwʌrəm/ *n.*, HE pronunciation of 'worm', representing the epenthetic (inserted) vowel sound that would occur with the same combination of letters in Irish (cf. 'elm' /ˈɛləm/, 'film' /ˈfɪləm/, etc.; on epenthesis in Irish see Ní Chiosáin). O'Casey, *The Plough and the Stars*, act I, 144: "*Fluther*: G'way, you wurum! *Covey*: 'Who's a worum?"

Y

yahoo /ˈjæhuː/ *n.* (*colloq.*), a boor (a name invented by Swift in *Gulliver's Travels* (1726) for an imaginary race of animals having the form of humans but the comprehension of brutes). 'Look at the way that old yahoo's behaving over there; he must be drunk or something, but you know, it sets a bad example for the young people.' O'Casey, *The Plough and the Stars*, act I, 144: "to look back in rememberin' shame of talkin' to a word-weavin' little ignorant yahoo of a red flag Socialist"; Leonard, *Out After Dark*, 190: "I had, he [Ernest Blythe] said, exposed him to the sneers of journalistic cornerboys and yahoos"; Kennelly, *Poetry My Arse*, 94: "Bearing bits of paper, bags and condoms | the hissing Liffey yahoos tonight | seawards with a cargo of our latest scandals."

yeer /jiːr/ *poss. adj.*, your (formed from YE by analogy with *your*). McCourt, *Angela's Ashes*, "What are ye having for yeer dinner?"

yeos[1] /joːz/ *n.pl.*, representing HE pronunciation of 'ewes' (Omurethi, Kildare, 539) < OE *eowu*.

Yeos[2] /joːz/ *n.pl.*, Yeomen, members of the Irish Yeomanry, a part-time force raised by Dublin Castle in 1796, later to become a by-word for brutality < E *yeomanry*, small landed proprietors in England, hence a part-time force recruited from yeomen. 'The Boys of Wexford' (ballad): "In comes the Captain's daughter | the Captain of the Yeos"; Lover, *Legends and Stories of Ireland*, 1, 174: "If the Husshians [Hessians] or the Yeos ketches you . . . "

yerra /ˈjɛrə/ also **erra** /ˈɛrə/, *int.* expressing mild disbelif or surprise, indifference, etc. < Ir *dhera* < *a Dhia*, God (*voc.*) + *ara* (*see* ARRAH). 'Yerra, don't be pulling my leg – he can't be back from the States already!' (KG, Kerry); 'Yerra, there's no good in talking to you' (MH, Clare). Joyce, *Finnegans Wake*, 477.4: "Yerra, why dat, my leader?"; Leonard, *Out After*

Dark, 33: "Erra, boy, sure all you need is a bed and a frying pan!"

yes /jɛs/ *adv.*, used more rarely in HE than in SE, because speakers follow the practice of Irish – in which there is no single word for 'yes' or 'no' – in repeating the verb or some form of it. 'Is this yours?' – 'It is.' 'Will you be going tomorrow?' – 'I will.' (The English adverb 'yes' itself ultimately derives from two words, *yea* and the subjunctive *sie*, let it be.) See Gerard Manley Hopkins's remarks on this phenomenon s.v. NO.

yoke /joːk/ *n.*, any contrivance or implement; something whose name does not spring immediately to mind; (*pejor.*) an indescribable person (a distinctive HE usage of an English word, deriving – like HAMES – from rural culture) < ME *yokke* < OE *geoc* 'Give me that yoke'; 'You're an odious /'oːʤəs/ yoke, you really are!'; 'Get out of my way, you big yoke you' (Cavan). Friel, *Translations*, act I (*FDA*, 3, 1211): "*Jimmy*: What shape's the yoke?"; Leonard, *Out After Dark*, 80: "I'm producing a French yoke called *Villa for Sale*"; Doyle, *The Van*, 114: "Tryin' to get poor Bimbo to throw his money away on tha' yoke"; Roche, *A Handful of Stars*, act I, 10: "*Conway*: But as for that other yoke. The world's worst is right"; *Poor Beast in the Rain*, act I, ii, 85: "*Molly*: What do yeh think of the locket she got Steven? It's a nice lookin' yoke ain't it?"; Durcan, *Christmas Day*, III, 26: "Will I put another log on the fire, Paul? | Great yokes – logs."

Yola /'joləl/ also **Yole, Yolaw** *n.*, the dialect of English formerly spoken in the baronies of Forth and Bargy, Co. Wexford < *old (yold) (English)*. 'Yola zong', an old song; 'Yole teoun', old town. Dolan and Ó Muirithe, *The Dialect of Forth and Bargy*, 76–7: "Fade teil thee zo lournagh, co Joane, zo knaggee? | Th'weithest all curcagh, wafur, an cornee" (What ails you so melancholy, quoth John, so cross? | You seem all snappish, uneasy, and fretful).

your man /jʌr'mæn/ *n.phr.* (*colloq.*), any specific individual < loose usage of second person possessive adjective (cf. Ir *mo dhuine*, lit. my man). 'Your man over there needs a drink'; 'Who is it?' – 'It's your man over there in the blue jacket.' Behan, *The Quare Fellow*, act I (*FDA*, 3, 203): ". . . Didn't he tell the wrong man he was reprieved? Your man was delighted for a few hours and then they had to go back and tell him. 'Sorry, my mistake, but you're to be topped after all"; Roche, *A Handful of Stars*, act I, i, 13: "*Jimmy*:

We're runnin' a bus down to see Stapler kickin' the shit out of your man tomorrow night"; Muldoon, 'Christo's' (*FDA*, 3, 1416): ". . . By the time we got to Belfast | the whole of Ireland would be under wraps | like, as I said, 'one of your man's landscapes.' | 'Your man's? You don't mean Christo's?"; Doyle, *The Van*, 241: "Behind the bar. Between Tom Cruise an' your man from Thornbirds."

yous /juːz/ also **yiz** /jɪz/, /jəz/ *personal pron.* (*colloq.*), plural of 'you' (cf. YE). In Irish there is both a singular and a plural second person pronoun, as there used to be in English, with 'thou' as the singular (< ME *þou* < OE *þu*) and 'ye' (< ME *ye* < OE *ge*) as the plural. The form 'you' was originally the accusative and dative plural of 'ye'. From the 14th century it became customary to use the plural form, 'you', in addressing superiors, in place of 'thee' and 'thou'; from the 15th century, 'you' began to be used in place of 'ye'. From the time large numbers of Irish people became exposed to English, in the late 16th century and onwards, the 'you' form was therefore the normal form of address to a single person. As regards the verbal forms, there is evidence that in the 17th and 18th centuries some people tried to distinguish between singular and plural by making changes in the verb: we thus find 'you is' and 'you are'; but this useful device was abandoned in the interests of so-called purity of language. Confronted with this bewildering volatility in the use and formation of the second-person pronoun, it would appear that Irish speakers of English decided to distinguish singular from plural by attaching the plural signal *s* to the singular 'you', on the analogy of regular pluralisations such as 'cow – cows'. 'Yous all better be back here on the dot of six o'clock or we're leaving without ye.' Joyce, 'A Mother' (*Dubliners*, 160): "He said *yous* so softly that it passed unnoticed"; Brown, *Down All the Days*, 125: "She has a heart of pure bloody gold, that woman, and none of yous appreciates it!"; Doyle, *The Van*, 20: "Did yis have your dinners at half-time or somethin?"

Z

zooteac, *see* TEACH.

Sources

LITERARY SOURCES

Banim, Michael, *The Boyne Water, by the O'Hara Family*, Dublin: James Duffy 1865.

Beckett, Samuel, *Waiting for Godot*, 1952 (reprint, London: Faber and Faber 1973).

Binchy, Maeve, *Firefly Summer*, London: Coronet 1988.

Birmingham, George, *The Lighter Side of Irish Life*, Edinburgh and London: Foulis 1912.

Bolger, Dermot, *Emily's Shoes*, Harmondsworth (Middx): Penguin 1992.

Breval, John Durant, *The Play is the Plot*, 1718 (ed. Alan Bliss, *Spoken English in Ireland*, 1979).

Brown, Christy, *Down All the Days*, 1970 (reprint, London: Pan 1972).

Captain Thomas Stukeley, 1596 (ed. Alan Bliss, *Spoken English in Ireland*, 1979).

Carleton, William, *Six Irish Tales, Newly Selected* (ed. Anthony Cronin, London: New English Library 1962).

Carpenter, Andrew (ed.), *Verse in English from Eighteenth-Century Ireland*, Cork: Cork University Press 1998.

Cowan, Cathal, and Sexton, Regina, *Ireland's Traditional Foods*, Dublin: Teagasc 1997.

Cuffe, Maurice, *The Siege of Ballyally Castle*, 1642 (ed. Alan Bliss, *Spoken English in Ireland*, 1979.

Deane, Seamus (ed.), *The Field Day Anthology of Irish Writing* (3 vols.), Derry: Field Day Publications 1991.

Deane, Seamus, *Reading in the Dark*, London: Jonathan Cape 1996.

Delaney, Frank, *The Sins of the Mothers*, London: Harper-Collins 1992.

A Dialogue between Teigue and Dermot, 1713 (ed. Alan Bliss, *Spoken English in Ireland*).

Dorgan, Theo, *The Ordinary House of Love*, Galway: Salmon Publishing 1990.

Doyle, Martin [Rev. William Hickey], *Irish Cottagers*, Dublin: Curry 1833.

Doyle, Roddy, *The Van*, London: Minerva 1991.

Dunton, John, *Report of a Sermon*, 1698 (ed. Alan Bliss, *Spoken English in Ireland,* 1979).
Durcan, Paul, *Christmas Day*, London: Harvill Press 1996.
Edgeworth, Maria, *Castle Rackrent* [1800] and *The Absentee* [1812] (reprint, London: Macmillan 1996).
Egan, Desmond, *Peninsula: Édition Bilingue* (translated by Jean-Paul Blot), 1992 (reprint, Église-Neuve d'Issac: Fédérop 1996).
Friel, Brian, *Translations*, 1980 (reprinted in *Field Day Anthology*, vol. 3, 1991).
Gogarty, Oliver St John, *As I Was Going Down Sackville Street*, London: Sphere 1968.
Griffin, Gerald, *The Collegians: A Tale of Garryowen*, Dublin: James Duffy 1904.
Head, Richard, *Hic et Ubique*, 1663 (ed. Alan Bliss, *Spoken English in Ireland,* 1979).
Healy, John, *Nineteen Acres*, 1978 (reprint, Achill: House of Healy 1987).
Heaney, Marie, *Over the Nine Waves: A Book of Irish Legends*, London: Faber and Faber 1994.
Heaney, Seamus, *Death of a Naturalist*, London: Faber and Faber 1966.
Heaney, Seamus, *Wintering Out*, London: Faber and Faber 1972.
Heaney, Seamus, *North*, 1975 (reprint, London: Faber and Faber 1979).
Heaney, Seamus, *New Selected Poems, 1966–1987*, London: Faber and Faber 1990.
Heaney, Seamus, *The Midnight Verdict*, Oldcastle: Gallery Press 1993.
The Irish Hudibras, 1689 (ed. Alan Bliss, *Spoken English in Ireland,* 1979).
Johnston, Jennifer, *Shadows on Our Skin*, 1977 (reprint, Harmondsworth (Middx): Penguin 1991).
Jordan, Neil, *Night in Tunisia*, London: Vintage 1976.
Jordan, Neil, *The Past*, London: Abacus 1982.
Joyce, James, *Dubliners*, 1914 (reprint, London: Paladin 1988).
Joyce, James, *Portrait of the Artist as a Young Man*, 1916 (reprint, Boston and New York: St Martin's Press 1993).
Joyce, James, *Exiles*, 1918 (reprint, London: New English Library 1962).
Joyce, James, *Ulysses*, 1922 (reprint, Harmondsworth (Middx): Penguin 1969).
Joyce, James, *Finnegans Wake*, 1939 (reprint, Harmondsworth (Middx): Penguin 1992).
Kavanagh, Patrick, *Tarry Flynn: A Novel*, 1948 (reprint, London: Martin Brian and O'Keeffe 1975).

Kavanagh, Patrick, *Collected Poems*, London: Martin Brian and O'Keeffe 1972.
Keane, John B., *The Bodhrán Makers*, Dingle: Brandon 1986.
Kearney, Richard, *Sam's Fall*, London: Sceptre 1995.
Keegan, John, *Songs of the Gael*, Dublin: Browne and Nolan 1915.
Kennelly, Brendan, *Poetry My Arse*, Newcastle-upon-Tyne: Bloodaxe Books 1995.
Kennelly, Brendan, *Federico García Lorca, 'Blood Wedding': A New Version*, Newcastle-upon-Tyne: Bloodaxe Books 1996.
Kickham, Charles, *Knocknagow, or The Homes of Tipperary*, 1879 (reprint, Dublin: Anna Livia 1988).
Kiely, Benedict, *A Ball of Malt and Madame Butterfly*, London: Gollancz 1973.
Killanin, Michael, and Duignan, Michael, *The Shell Guide to Ireland*, London: Ebury Press 1969.
Kilroy, Thomas, *The Big Chapel*, London: Faber and Faber 1971.
Leonard, Hugh, *Out After Dark*, 1989 (reprint, Harmondsworth (Middx): Penguin 1990).
McCall, P. J., 'The Fenian Nights' Entertainments', *Shamrock Magazine*, 1897.
McCourt, Frank, *Angela's Ashes: A Memoir of Childhood*, London: Flamingo 1997.
McDonagh, Martin, *The Cripple of Inishmaan*, London: Methuen 1997.
McGahern, John, *The Leave-Taking*, London: Faber and Faber 1974.
McGuinness, Frank, *Observe the Sons of Ulster Marching towards the Somme*, London: Faber and Faber 1986.
Michelburne, John, *Ireland Preserved*, 1705 (ed. Alan Bliss, *Spoken English in Ireland*, 1979).
Montague, John, *Collected Poems*, Oldcastle: Gallery Press 1995.
Myles na Gopaleen [Brian O'Nolan], *The Best of Myles* (ed. Kevin O'Nolan), London: MacGibbon and Kee 1975.
Nolan, J., *The Changing Face of Dundrum*, Dundrum: St Vincent Burial Society 1987.
O'Brien, Edna, *A Pagan Place*, 1970 (reprint, Harmondsworth (Middx): Penguin 1971).
O'Brien, Flann [Brian O'Nolan], *The Best of Myles*, London: MacGibbon and Kee 1968.
O'Brien, Flann [Brian O'Nolan], *At Swim-Two-Birds*, Harmondsworth (Mddx): Penguin 1977.
O'Brien, Flann [Brian O'Nolan], *The Third Policeman*, London: Hart-Davis 1967.

O'Brien, Kate, *The Ante-Room*, London: Heinemann 1934.
O'Casey, Seán, *Three Plays* (reprint, Basingstoke: Macmillan 1973).
Paulin, Tom, *Seize the Fire: A Version of Aeschylus's 'Prometheus Bound'*, London: Faber and Faber 1990.
Plunkett, James, *Farewell Companions*, London: Hutchinson 1977.
Purcell, Deirdre, *On Lough Derg*, Dublin: Veritas 1988.
Roche, Billy, *The Wexford Trilogy,* London: Nick Hern Books 1992.
Sheehan, Patrick Augustine, *Glenanaar*, Dublin: Educational Company of Ireland 1905.
Sheridan, Thomas, *The Brave Irishman*, 1754 (ed. Alan Bliss, *Spoken English in Ireland*).
Somerville, Edith Œnone, and Ross, Martin, *Some Experiences of an Irish RM*, 1899 (reprint, London: Everyman 1969).
Somerville, Edith Œnone, and Ross, Martin, 'Children of the Captivity' in *Some Irish Yesterdays*, London: Longmans Green 1906.
Spenser, Edmund, *The Faerie Queene*, 1596 (ed. A. C. Hamilton), London: Longman 1977.
Stephens, James, *The Crock of Gold*, 1912 (reprint, London: Pan Books 1965).
Stoker, Bram, *The Snake's Pass*, 1891 (reprint, Dingle: Brandon 1990).
Swift, Jonathan, *A Dialogue in Hybernian Stile by A and B, and Irish Eloquence*, Dublin: Cadenus Press 1977 (ed. Alan Bliss).
Trollope, Anthony, *The Kellys and the O'Kellys*, 1848 (reprint, London: Oxford University Press 1929).
Yeats, W. B., *Collected Plays*, London: Macmillan 1934.
Yeats, W. B., *Collected Poems* (ed. Augustine Martin), London: Arena 1990.

KEY TO PRINCIPAL NON-LITERARY SOURCES

AC, Down: Art Cosgrove
AF, Cavan: A. Fleming
AH, Donegal: Anne Hunt
AKB, Antrim: A. K. Barron, 'Our strange dialect' (1987)
AMW, Cork: Alice Moore West
BC, Meath: Brigid Clerkin
BD, Cavan: B. Dolan
BF, Cork: Breeda Fennessy
BP, Meath: Bridie Padian
BR, Dublin: Barry Raftery

Sources

BT, Dublin: Betsey Taylor
COL, Wexford: Colm O'Loughlin
CS, Cavan: Carmel Scott
CS, Cork: Catherine Stafford
CS, Dublin: Ciara Steven
CS, Mayo: Chris Slack
DB, Cork: Dorothy Bowman
DOH, Limerick: Dáithí Ó hÓgáin
DOS, Kerry: Denis B. O Sullivan
EH, Wicklow: Eddie Harmon
EMF, Westmeath: Éamonn Mac an Fhailigh, 'A Westmeath word-list' (1945–47)
ENM, Kerry: Eibhlín Ní Mhurchú
EOC, Tipperary: Éamonn Ó Carragáin
EOF, Dublin: Éamon O'Flaherty
FD, Cork: Frank Duggan
GF, Galway: Gerard Fahy
HC, Cork: Helen Clayton
HJ, Wexford: Hazel Jacob
IF, Waterford: Ignatius Fennessy
JF, Cavan: Jack Foley
JL, Carlow: John Lawlor
JL, Cavan: John Leonard
JL, Mayo: J. Loftus
JMC, Dublin: J. McCabe
JMF, Cavan: Jane Mary Flemming
JOC, Kerry: Jack O'Connor
JOD, Tipperary: John O'Doherty
JOM, Kerry: John O'Mahony
JP, Wexford: T. P. Dolan and Diarmaid Ó Muirithe, *The Dialect of Forth and Bargy, Co. Wexford* (1996) (revised edition of Jacob Poole, *A Glossary . . . of the Old Dialect . . . of Forth and Bargy*)
JQ, Kerry: Jacques Quilter
KD, Dublin: Kevin Denny
KG, Kerry: Kathleen Griffin
KM, Kerry: Kathleen Moynihan
KMG, Dublin: Kieran McGuire
LGS: Linda Gavin Steiner (New York)
LUB, Dublin: Liam Ua Broin, 'A south-west Dublin glossary' (notes by J. J. Hogan) (1944)
MB, Tipperary: Michael Benskin, 'Irish adoptions in the English of Tipperary, c. 1432' (1988)

MC, Kildare: Mary Cotter
MCR, Waterford: Mary Catherine Reilly
MG, Cavan: M. Gargan
MH, Clare: Michael Hewson, 'A word-list from south-west Clare' (1965)
MJ, Mayo: Mary Jordan
MK, Cork: Maria Kelleher
MK, Galway: Martin Kenny
ML, Dublin: Michael Laffan
ML, Mayo: Maureen Loftus
MMB, Meath: Micheál Mac an Bhaird
MOB, Mayo: Mary O'Brien
MOC, Limerick: Micheál Ó Conaill
MT, Donegal: Michael Traynor, *The English Dialect of Donegal* (1953)
ND, Limerick: Norah Davis
NH, Mayo: Nancy Hopkins
NL, Mayo: N. Loftus
OS: Olive Sharkey, *Old Days, Old Ways* (1985)
PA, Dublin: Patrick Archer, *Fair Fingall* (1975)
PC, Cork: Patrick Connolly
PG, Dublin: Patricia Gillen
PJG, Dublin: Patrick Joseph Gernon
PM: Peter Martin, 'Some Peculiarities of Speech Heard in Breifny' (1921)
PMD, Mayo: Patrick McDermott
POB, Dublin: Patrick O'Brien
POC, Cavan: Pádraig Ó Corbaigh, 'An Ghaeilge: Irish words used in the English of Co. Cavan' (1983)
PON, Dublin: Patrick C. O'Neill, 'A north County Dublin glossary' (introductory notes by J. J. Hogan) (1947)
PR, Mayo: Paddy Ruane
PWJ: P. W. Joyce, *English as We Speak It in Ireland* (1910)
RB, Waterford: Rita Byrne, 'Irish words still in use in the Fenor area' (1984)
RC, Cavan: R. Corbally
RMM, Antrim: Rod MacManus
SB, Cork: Seán Beecher, *A Dictionary of Cork Slang* (1983)
SL, Mayo: Seán Loftus
SMC, Limerick: Susan McCarthy
SOC, Cork: Seán Ó Coileáin, 'Irish and English in Kildorrery in the 1920s' (1986)

SOC, Kerry: Seán O'Connor
SOM, Kerry: Seán Ó Mathúna (Sliabh Luachra)
TD, Kerry: Tomás Dowling
TF, Cavan: Thomas Fleming
TG, Dublin: Tom Garvin
TH, Laois: Therèse Hunt
TJ, Sligo: T. Jones
TK, Dublin: Terence Killeen
VQ, Kerry: Vincent Quilter
WL, Cork: William Lawlor

Bibliography

Adams, G. B., 'An introduction to the study of Ulster dialects', *Proceedings of the Royal Irish Academy*, vol. 52C (1948), 5–23.

Adams, G. B. (ed.), *Ulster Dialects: An Introductory Symposium*, Holywood (Co. Down): Ulster Folk and Transport Museum 1964.

Adams, G. B. (Michael Barry and Philip Tilling, eds.), *The English Dialects of Ulster: An Anthology of Articles on Ulster Speech*, Cultra Manor: Ulster Folk and Transport Museum 1986.

Ahlqvist, Anders, and Capková, Vera (eds.), *Dán do Oide: Essays in Memory of Conn R. Ó Cléirigh*, Dublin: Institiúid Teangeolaíochta Éireann 1997.

Aldus, Judith Butler, 'Anglo-Irish dialects: a bibliography', *Regional Language Studies . . . Newfoundland*, vol. 7 (1976), 7–28.

Archer, Patrick, *Fair Fingall*, Dublin: An Taisce (reprint) 1975.

Barron, A. K., 'Our strange dialect', *The Corran*, vol. 44 (1987), 2.

Barry, M. V., 'The English language in Ireland' in R. Bailey and M. Görlach (eds.), *English as a World Language*, Ann Arbor 1982, 84–133.

Bartley, J. O., 'The development of a stock-character, I: the stage Irishman to 1800', *Modern Language Review*, vol. 37 (1942), 438–47.

Bartley, J. O., *Teague, Shenkin and Sawney: Being an Historical Study of the Earliest Irish, Welsh and Scottish Characters in English Plays*, Cork: Cork University Press 1954.

Beale, Paul (ed.), *A Concise Dictionary of Slang and Unconventional English: Edited from the Work of Eric Partridge*, London: Routledge 1989.

Benskin, Michael, 'Irish adoptions in the English of Tipperary, *c.* 1432' in E. G. Stanley and T. F. Hoad (eds.), *Words: For Robert Burchfield's Sixty-Fifth Birthday*, Cambridge: D. S. Brewer 1988, 37–67.

Bigger, Francis Joseph (ed.), *Montiaghisms: Ulster Dialect Words and Phrases Collected by the Late William Lutton, with Brief Biography*, Armagh: Armagh Guardian 1923.

Binchy, Alice, 'Travellers' language: a sociolinguistic perspective' in McCann et al., *Irish Travellers*.

Birmingham, George A., 'The Brogue' in *The Lighter Side of Irish Life*, London and Edinburgh: Foulis 1912, chap. 8.

Bliss, Alan, 'The language of Synge' in Maurice Harmon (ed.), *J. M. Synge Centenary Papers, 1971*, Dublin: Dolmen Press 1972, 35–62.

Bliss, Alan, 'A Synge glossary' in Suheil Sadi Bushrui (ed.), *Sunshine and the Moon's Delight: A Centenary Tribute to John Millington Synge*, Gerrards Cross (Bucks.): Colin Smythe 1972.

Bliss, Alan, 'Languages in contact: some problems of Hiberno-English', *Proceedings of the Royal Irish Academy*, vol. 72C (1972), 63–82.

Bliss, Alan, 'The development of the English language in early modern Ireland' in T. W. Moody, F. X. Martin and F. J. Byrne (eds.), *A New History of Ireland*, 3, 1976, 546–60.

Bliss, Alan, *Spoken English in Ireland, 1600–1740*, Dublin: Cadenus Press and Dolmen Press 1979.

Bliss, Alan, 'Irish proverbs in Swift's "Polite Conversation"', *Irish University Review*, vol. 9 (1979), 23–30.

Bliss, Alan, 'English in the south of Ireland' in Trudgill, *Language in the British Isles*, 135–51.

Bosworth, Joseph, and Toller, T. Northcote, *An Anglo-Saxon Dictionary*, London: Oxford University Press (reprint) 1973.

Bradley, Henry (ed.), *Stratmann's Middle English Dictionary* (reprint, Oxford: Oxford University Press 1974).

Braidwood, John, *The Ulster Dialect Lexicon: An Inaugural Lecture Delivered before the Queen's University of Belfast on 23 April 1969*, Belfast: Queen's University 1969.

Bramsbäck, Birgit, and Croghan, Martin (eds.), *Anglo-Irish Literature: Aspects of Language and Culture* (Studia Anglistica Upsaliensia, 64) (2 vols.), Uppsala: Almqvist och Wiksell 1988.

Brewer, E. C., *Dictionary of Phrase and Fable*, London: Cassell 1897 (reprint, London: Wordsworth 1996).

Browne, Kathleen, 'The ancient dialect of the baronies of Forth and Bargy, County Wexford', *Journal of the Royal Society of Antiquaries of Ireland*, vol. 57 (1927), 127–37.

Burchfield, R. W. (ed.), *The Cambridge History of the English Language, vol. 5: English in Britain and Overseas: Origins and Development*, Cambridge: Cambridge University Press 1994.

Burke, William, 'The Anglo-Irish dialect', *Irish Ecclesiastical Record*, vol. 17 (1896), 694–704, 777–89.

Byrne, Rita, 'Irish words still in use in the Fenor area', *Decies: Old Waterford Society Journal*, vol. 26 (1984), 13–15.

Cahill, E., 'Norman French and English languages in Ireland', *Irish Ecclesiastical Record*, vol. 51 (1938), 159–73.

Cassidy, Frederic (chief ed.), *Dictionary of American Regional English, vol. 1: A–C*, Cambridge (Mass.): Harvard University Press 1985.

Cassidy, Frederic, and Hall, J. (chief eds.), *Dictionary of American Regional English, vol. 2: D–*, Cambridge (Mass.): Harvard University Press 1991.

Chambers English Dictionary, Edinburgh: W. and R. Chambers and Cambridge: Cambridge University Press 1988.

Chapman, Robert, *New Dictionary of American Slang*, London: Macmillan 1987.

Cheshire, Jenny (ed.), *English Around the World: Sociolinguistic Perspectives*, Cambridge: Cambridge University Press 1991.

Clark, James Midgley, *The Vocabulary of Anglo-Irish*, Saint-Gallen: Handels-Hochschule 1917.

Committee for the Study of Anglo-Irish Language and Literature, *Handlist of Work in Progress and Work Completed on Anglo-Irish Dialect Studies*, Dublin: Royal Irish Academy 1972.

Connolly, S. (ed.), *The Oxford Companion to Irish History*, Oxford: Oxford University Press 1998.

Conway, Margaret, *A South-Meath Glossary*, Drogheda: Drogheda Independent n.d.

Corrigan, Karen, 'Gaelic and English influences on south Armagh English', *Ulster Folklife*, vol. 39 (1993), 1–14.

Corrigan, Karen, 'The Syntax of South Armagh English in its Socio-Historical Perspective', PhD dissertation, University College, Dublin, 1997.

Cowan, Cathal, and Sexton, Regina, *Ireland's Traditional Foods: An Exploration of Irish Local and Typical Foods and Drinks*, Dublin: Teagasc and the National Food Centre 1997.

Craigie, William, and Hulbert, James (eds.), *A Dictionary of American English on Historical Principles* (4 vols.), London: Oxford University Press 1938.

Croghan, Martin, 'A bibliography of English in Ireland: problems with names and boundaries' in Bramsbäck and Croghan, *Anglo-Irish Literature: Aspects of Language and Culture*, 103–15

Croghan, Martin, 'Swift, Thomas Sheridan, Maria Edgeworth and the evolution of Hiberno-English', *Irish University Review*, vol. 20 (1990), 19–34.

Crystal, David, *The Cambridge Encyclopedia of the English Language,* Cambridge, Cambridge University Press 1995.

Curtis, Edmund, 'The spoken languages of medieval Ireland', *Studies*, vol. 8 (1919), 234–54.

Daly, Mary, *The Famine in Ireland*, Dundalk: Dundalgan Press (for Dublin Historical Association) 1986.

de Bhaldraithe, Tomás (ed.), *English-Irish Dictionary*, Dublin: Stationery Office 1959.

de Bhaldraithe, Tomás, 'Notes on the diminutive suffix *-ín* in Modern Irish' in A. Matonis and Daniel Melia (eds.), *Celtic Languages – Celtic Culture: Festschrift for Eric P. Hamp*, Van Nuys (Calif.): Ford and Bailie 1990, 85–95.

Dinneen, Patrick (ed.), *Foclóir Gaedhilge agus Béarla: An Irish-English Dictionary*, Dublin: Educational Company of Ireland (for Irish Texts Society) 1927 (reprint, 1996).

Dobson, E. J., *English Pronunciation, 1500–1700* (2 vols.), Oxford: Clarendon Press 1968.

Dolan, T. P. (ed.), 'The English of the Irish: special issue [dedicated to Alan Bliss]', *Irish University Review*, vol. 20, no. 1 (1990).

Dolan, T. P., 'The language of *Dubliners*' in Augustine Martin (ed.), *James Joyce: The Artist and the Labyrinth*, London: Ryan Publishing 1990, 25–40.

Dolan, T. P., 'Language in *Ulysses*' in Jacqueline Genet and Elisabeth Hellegouarc'h (eds.), *Studies on Joyce's 'Ulysses'*, Caen: Centre d'Études Anglo-Irlandaises, Université de Caen, 1991, 131–42.

Dolan, T. P., 'The literature of Norman Ireland' in Deane, *The Field Day Anthology of Irish Writing*, vol. 1, 141–70.

Dolan, T. P., 'Samuel Beckett's dramatic use of Hiberno-English', *Irish University Review*, vol. 14 (1994), 45–56.

Dolan, T. P., 'Seán O'Casey's use of Hiberno-English' in D. Siegmund-Schultze (ed.), *Irland: Gesellschaft und Kultur, IV*, Halle-Wittenberg: Martin-Luther Universität 1985.

Dolan, T. P., and Ó Muirithe, Diarmaid (eds.), *The Dialect of Forth and Bargy, Co. Wexford* (revised edition of Poole, *A Glossary . . . of the Old Dialect . . . of Forth and Bargy*), Dublin: Four Courts Press 1996.

Duggan, G. C., *The Stage Irishman: A History of the Irish Play and Stage Characters from the Earliest Times*, Dublin: Talbot Press 1937.

Edwards, J., 'Irish and English in Ireland' in Trudgill, *Language in the British Isles*, 480–98.

Filppula, Markku, *Some Aspects of Hiberno-English in a Functional Sentence Perspective*, Joensuu: University of Joensuu Publications in the Humanities 1988.

Filppula, Markku, 'Subordinating "and" in Hiberno-English syntax: Irish or English origin?' in P. Sture Ureland and George Broderick (eds.), *Language Contact in the British Isles: Proceedings of the Eighth International Symposium on Language Contact in Europe, Douglas, 1988*, Tübingen: Max Niemeyer 1991, 617–31.

Filppula, Markku, 'Changing paradigms in the study of Hiberno-English', *Irish University Review*, vol. 23 (1993), 203–23.

Filppula, Markku, 'Investigating the origins of Hiberno-English perfects: the case of "PII"' in Klemola et al., *Speech Past and Present*, 33–55.

Foster, R. F., *Modern Ireland, 1600–1972*, London: Penguin Press 1988.

Gimson, A. C., *An Introduction to the Pronunciation of English*, London: Arnold 1962.

Görlach, Manfred, 'Language Death and the History of English' (photocopy) 1992.

Görlach, Manfred, 'Irish English and Irish Culture in Dictionaries of English' (photocopy) 1993.

Green, Jonathon, *Chasing the Sun: Dictionary-Makers and the Dictionaries They Made*, London: Jonathan Cape 1996.

Griffith, Francis, 'Irish usage in American English', *Irish America*, Nov. 1986, 34–5.

An Gúm, *Foclóir Póca: English-Irish, Irish-English Dictionary*, Dublin: Department of Education 1986 (reprint, 1995).

Harris, John, 'The Hiberno-English "I've it eaten" construction: what is it and where does it come from?', *Teanga*, no. 3 (1983), 30–43.

Harris, John, 'English in the north of Ireland' in Trudgill, *Language in the British Isles*, 115–34.

Harris, John, *Phonological Variation and Change: Studies in Hiberno-English*, Cambridge: Cambridge University Press 1985.

Harris, John, Little, David, and Singleton, David (eds.), *Perspectives on the English Language in Ireland*, Dublin: Centre for Language and Communication Studies 1986.

Hayden, Mary, and Hartog, Marcus, 'The Irish dialect of English: its origins and vocabulary', *Fortnightly Review*, vol. 85 (1909), 775–85, 933–47.

Henry, Alison, *Belfast English and Standard English: Dialect Variation and Parameter Setting*, New York and Oxford: Oxford University Press 1995.

Henry, P. L., *An Anglo-Irish Dialect of North Roscommon: Phonology, Accidence, Syntax*, Dublin: Department of English, University College, 1957.

Henry, P. L., 'A linguistic survey of Ireland: preliminary report', *Lochlann*, vol. 1 (1958), 49–208.

Henry, P. L., 'The land of Cokaygne: cultures in contact in medieval Ireland', *Studia Hibernica*, no. 12 (1972), 120–41.

Heuser, W., *Die Kildare Gedichte* (Bonner Beiträge zur Anglistik, 14), Bonn 1904 (reprint, Darmstadt: Wissenschaftliche Buchgesellschaft 1965).

Hewson, Michael, 'A word-list from south-west Clare', *North Munster Antiquarian Journal*, vol. 9 (1965), 182–6.

Hickey, R., 'Syntactic ambiguity in Hiberno-English', *Studia Anglica Posnaniensia*, vol. 15 (1983), 39–45.

Hogan, Jeremiah J., *The English Language in Ireland*, Dublin: Educational Company of Ireland 1927.

'Irish words in the spoken English of Leinster', *Irisleabhar na Gaedhilge* [1900–1902], vol. 11, 93–4, 108–10, 123–5, 140–2, 153–4, 174–5, 187–90, 205–6; vol. 12, 14–15, 25–9, 41–2, 61–3, 78–9, 96–112, 126–8, 141–3, 149–152.

Irwin, P. J., 'Ireland's contribution to the English language', *Studies*, vol. 22 (1933), 637–52.

Jones, Daniel, *The Phoneme: Its Nature and Use*, Cambridge: Cambridge University Press 1962.

Jones, Daniel, *The Pronunciation of English*, Cambridge: Cambridge University Press 1969.

Joyce, P. W., *English as We Speak It in Ireland*, 1910 (reprint, Dublin: Wolfhound Press 1997).

Kallen, Jeffrey, 'Tense and aspect categories in Hiberno-English', *English World Wide*, vol. 10 (1989), 1–39.

Kallen, Jeffrey, 'The Hiberno-English perfect: grammaticalisation revisited', *Irish University Review*, vol. 20 (1990), 120–36.

Kallen, Jeffery, 'English in Ireland' in Burchfield, *The Cambridge History of the English Language*, vol. 5, 148–96.

Kallen, Jeffrey, 'Entering lexical fields in Irish English' in Klemola et al., *Speech Past and Present*, 101–29.

Kiberd, Declan, *Synge and the Irish Language*, 1979 (reprint, London: Macmillan 1994).

Klemola, Juhani, Kytto, Merja, and Rissanen, Matti (eds.), *Speech Past and Present: Studies in English Dialectology in Memory of Ossi Ihalainen* (University of Bamberg Studies in English Linguistics, 38), Frankfurt-am-Main: Peter Lang 1996.

Kurath, Hans, et al. (eds.), *Middle English Dictionary, A–R*, Michigan: University of Michigan Press 1954.

Lass, Roger, '"Irish influence": reflections on "Standard English" and its opposites, and the identification of calques', *Studia Anglica Posnaniensia*, vol. 18 (1986), 81–7.

Leerssen, Joseph Theodor, *Mere Irish and Fíor-Ghael: Studies in the Idea of Irish Nationality, Its Development and Literary Expression Prior to the Nineteenth Century* (revised edition), Amsterdam: John Benjamins 1996.

Lewis, Charlton, and Short, Charles, *A Latin Dictionary*, 1879 (reprint, Oxford: Clarendon Press 1962).

Longman Dictionary of American English (second edition), New York: Addison-Wesley Longman 1997.

Macafee, C., *A Concise Ulster Dictionary*, Oxford: Oxford University Press 1996.

Macalister, R. A. S., *The Secret Languages of Ireland: With Special Reference to the Origins and Nature of the Shelta Language*, Cambridge: Cambridge University Press 1937.

Mac an Fhailigh, Éamonn, 'A Westmeath word-list', *Éigse*, vol. 5 (1945–47), 256–66.

McArthur, Tom (ed.), *The Oxford Companion to the English Language*, Oxford: Oxford University Press 1992.

McCann, May, Ó Síocháin, Séamas, and Ruane, Joseph (eds.), *Irish Travellers: Culture and Ethnicity*, Belfast: Institute of Irish Studies, Queen's University (for Anthropological Association of Ireland), 1994.

McCrum, Robert, Cran, William, and MacNeil, Robert, *The Story of English*, New York: Viking Penguin 1986.

Mac Gréine, Pádraig, 'A Longford miscellany', *Béaloideas*, vol. 4 (1934).

McIntosh, Angus, and Samuels, M., 'Prolegomena to a study of medieval Anglo-Irish', *Medium Aevum*, vol. 37 (1968), 1–11.

Martin, Peter, 'Some Peculiarities of Speech Heard in Breifny', *Breifny Antiquarian Society Journal*, vol. 1 (1921), 174–91, 360–1.

Moylan, Séamus, *The Language of Kilkenny: Lexicon, Semantics, Structures*, Dublin: Geography Publications 1996.

Mustanoja, T. F., *A Middle English Syntax, Part I: Parts of Speech*, Helsinki: Société Néophilologique 1960.

Ní Chiosáin, Máire, 'Patterns of epenthesis in Irish' in Ahlqvist and Capková, *Dán do Oide*, 367–77.

Ó Baoill, Dónall P., 'Travellers' cant: language or register?' in McCann et al., *Irish Travellers*, 155–69.

Ó Catháin, Séamas, *The Festival of Brigit, Celtic Goddesses and Holy Women*, Dublin: DBA Publications 1995.

Ó Coileáin, Seán, 'Irish and English in Kildorrery in the 1920s', *Mallow Field Club Journal*, vol. 4 (1986), 38–40.

Ó Conchubhair, Pádraig, 'An Offaly glossary', *Béaloideas*, vol. 20 (1952), 188–91.

O'Connor, J. D., *Phonetics*, 1973 (reprint, Harmondsworth (Middx): Penguin 1977).

O'Connor, John, *The Workhouses of Ireland: The Fate of Ireland's Poor*, Dublin: Anvil 1995.

Ó Corbaigh, Pádraig, 'An Ghaeilge: Irish words used in the English of Co. Cavan', *The Heart of Breifni*, vol. 2 (1983), 37–43.

Ó Cuív, Brian, *Irish Dialects and Irish-Speaking Districts*, Dublin: Dublin Institute for Advanced Studies 1951.

Ó Cuív, Brian (ed.), *A View of the Irish Language*, Dublin: Stationery Office 1969.

Odlin, Terence, *'Sorrow penny yee payed for my drink': Taboo, Euphemism and a Phantom Substrate* (CLCS Occasional Paper no. 43), Dublin: Centre for Language and Communication Studies, Trinity College, 1996.

Ó Dónaill, Niall (ed.), *Foclóir Gaeilge-Béarla*, Dublin: Stationery Office 1977 [1978].

O'Farrell, Pádraic, *How the Irish Speak English* (revised edition), Cork: Mercier 1991.

Ó hÉaluighthe, Diarmuid, 'Irish words in Cork speech', *Journal of the Cork Historical and Archaeological Society*, vol. 49 (1944), 33–48.

Ó hEithir, Breandán, *A Gaelic Lexicon for 'Finnegans Wake' and Glossary for Joyce's Other Works*, Berkeley and Los Angeles: University of California Press 1967.

O'Higgins, Elizabeth, 'Irish words in William Blake's mythology', *Dublin Magazine*, vol. 26 (1951), 25–39.

Oifig an tSoláthair, *Foclóir Béarla-Gaeilge de Théarmai Míleata agus de Théarmaí Gaolmhara*, Dublin: Stationery Office 1953.

O'Kane, William (ed.), *You Don't Say: The Tyrone Crystal Book of Ulster Dialect*, Dungannon: Tyrone Crystal 1991.

O'Leary, Pat, 'The unique Wexford dialect', *People* (Wexford), 21 June 1990, 5 July 1990.

Ó Muiris, Tomás, 'Oidhreacht Ghall-Ghaelach: Focail Ghaeilge ó Cheantar Chill Náile (1920–1940)', *Tipperary Historical Journal*, 1990, 190–5.

Ó Muirithe, Diarmaid (ed.), *The English Language in Ireland*, Dublin and Cork: Mercier Press 1977.

Ó Muirithe, Diarmaid, *A Dictionary of Anglo-Irish: Words and Phrases from Gaelic in the English of Ireland*, Dublin: Four Courts Press 1996.

Ó Muirithe, Diarmaid, *The Words We Use*, Dublin: Four Courts Press 1996.

Ó Muirithe, Diarmaid, *A Word in Your Ear*, Dublin: Four Courts Press 1997.

Ó Murchú, Máirtín, *The Irish Language*, Dublin: Department of Foreign Affairs and Bord na Gaeilge 1985.

'Omurethi', 'Irish and Anglo-Irish words in use in County Kildare', *Journal of the County Kildare Archaeological Society*, vol. 6 (1909–11), 528–39.

O'Neill, Patrick C., 'A north County Dublin glossary' (introductory notes by J. J. Hogan), *Béaloideas*, vol. 17 (1947), 262–83.

Onions, C. T., *The Oxford Dictionary of English Etymology*, Oxford: Clarendon Press 1966.

O'Rahilly, T. F., *Irish Dialects, Past and Present*, Dublin: Browne and Nolan 1932.

Ó Sé, Diarmuid, 'Word stress in Hiberno-English' in Harris et al., *Perspectives on the English Language in Ireland*, 97–110.

Ó Siadhail, Micheál, 'Agus (is)/and: a shared syntactic feature', *Celtica*, vol. 16 (1984), 125–37.

Ó Siadhail, Micheál, *Learning Irish*, New Haven: Yale University Press 1988.

Ó Siadhail, Micheál, *Modern Irish: Grammatical Structure and Dialect Variation*, Cambridge: Cambridge University Press 1989.

Patterson, W. H., *A Glossary of Words in Use in the Counties of Antrim and Down*, London: English Dialect Society 1880.

Paulin, Tom, *A New Look at the Language Question* (Field Day Pamphlet no. 1), Derry: Field Day Theatre Company 1983.

Piatt, Donn S., *Dialect in East Mid-Leinster Gaelic Survivals: Containing Numerous Place-Names as Spoken by the People, and Several Hundred Local Gaelic Words with Pronunciation*, Dublin: Browne and Nolan 1935.

Poole, Jacob (T. P. Dolan and Diarmaid Ó Muirithe, eds.), *A Glossary with Some Pieces of Verse of the Old Dialect of the English Colony in the Baronies of Forth and Bargy, Co. Wexford*, Wexford: Cumann Seanchais Uí Cinnsealaigh 1979.

Quinn, E. G., 'Irish and English', *Hermathena*, no. 93 (1959), 26–37.

Ryan, Mary T., 'Appendix 5: Some Irish words in common use in the parish of Cappamore up to the 1960s' in *Cappamore: A Parish History*, Cappamore (Co. Limerick) 1992, 426–32.

Sharkey, Olive, *Old Days, Old Ways*, Dublin: O'Brien Press 1985.

Simmons, D. A., *A List of Peculiar Words and Phrases Formerly in Common Use in the County Armagh, together with Expressions at One Time Current in South Donegal*, Dublin: Freeman's Journal 1890.

Simpson, J. A., and Weiner, E. S. C. (eds.), *The Oxford English Dictionary* (20 vols.), Oxford: Clarendon Press 1989.

Sinclair, Isabel, *The Thistle and Fleur de Lys: A Vocabulary of Franco-Scottish Words*, Edinburgh and London: Blackwood 1904.

Story, G., Kirwin, W., and Widdowson, J. (eds.), *Dictionary of Newfoundland English*, Toronto: University of Toronto Press 1982.

Strang, Barbara, *A History of English*, 1970 (reprint, London: Methuen 1976).

Sullivan, J., 'The validity of literary dialect: evidence from the theatrical portrayal of Hiberno-English', *Language in Society*, vol. 9 (1980), 195–219.

Sweeney, Peggy, 'So you think you can't speak Irish', *Doon Parish Journal*, 1992, 95–6; 1993, 74–5.

Taniguchi, Jiro, *A Grammatical Analysis of Artistic Representation of Irish English, with a Brief Discussion of Sounds and Spelling*, Tokyo: Shinozaki Shorin 1972.

Todd, Loreto, *The Language of Irish Literature*, Basingstoke: Macmillan 1989.

Todd, Loreto, *Words Apart: A Dictionary of Northern Irish English*, Gerrards Cross (Bucks): Colin Smythe 1990.

Toller, T. Northcote (ed.), *An Anglo-Saxon Dictionary: Based on the Manuscript Collections of Joseph Bosworth*, 1921 (reprint, London: Oxford University Press 1973).

Tomelty, Joseph, 'A note on Belfast slang', *The Bell*, vol. 2 (1941), no. 4, 70–1.

Traynor, Michael, *The English Dialect of Donegal: A Glossary, Incorporating the Collections of H. C. Hart MRIA*, Dublin: Royal Irish Academy 1953.

Tristram, Hildegard, *Draft Bibliography: The Celtic Englishes*, Potsdam: Institut für Anglistik und Amerikanistik, Universität Potsdam, 1996.

Tristram, Hildegard (ed.), *The Celtic Englishes*, Heidelberg: Universitätsverlag C. Winter 1997.

Trudgill, Peter (ed.), *Language in the British Isles*, Cambridge: Cambridge University Press 1984.

Ua Broin, Liam, 'A south-west Dublin glossary' (introductory note by J. J. Hogan), *Béaloideas*, vol. 14 (1944), 162–86.

Upton, Clive, and Widdowson, J., *An Atlas of English Dialects*, Oxford: Oxford University Press 1996.

van Hamel, A. G., 'On Anglo-Irish syntax', *Englische Studien*, vol. 45 (1912), 272–92.

Wagner, Heinrich, *Linguistic Atlas and Survey of Irish Dialects, vol. 1: Introduction*, Dublin: Dublin Institute for Advanced Studies 1958.

Wales, Katie, *The Language of James Joyce*, Basingstoke: Macmillan 1992.

Wall, Richard, *An Anglo-Irish Dialect Glossary for Joyce's Works*, Gerrards Cross (Bucks): Colin Smythe 1986.

Wall, Richard, *A Dictionary and Glossary for the Irish Literary Revival*, Gerrards Cross (Bucks): Colin Smythe 1995.

Ward, Ida, *The Phonetics of English*, 1929 (reprint, Cambridge: Heffer 1962).

Welch, Robert (ed.), *The Oxford Companion to Irish Literature*, Oxford: Clarendon Press 1996.

White, Norman, *Hopkins: A Literary Biography*, Oxford: Clarendon Press 1992.

Wright, Joseph (ed.), *The English Dialect Dictionary* (6. vols.), London: Henry Frowde 1898–1905.

Wright, Joseph, *The English Dialect Grammar: Comprising the Dialects of England, of the Shetland and Orkney Islands, and of those Parts of Scotland, Ireland and Wales where English is Habitually Spoken*, Oxford: Henry Frowde 1905.

Younge, K. E., 'Irish idioms in English speech', *Gaelic Churchman* [1923–26], vol. 5, 155, 167, 176, 203–4, 214–15, 225, 241, 266–7, 286–7; vol. 6, 310–11, 333–4, 347, 383, 391, 401, 413, 428.